Integrating Interdisciplinary Research for Societal Well-Being

Integrating Interdisciplinary Research for Societal Well-Being

Editors

Dr. Santosh Dhar

Dr. Upinder Dhar

Dr. Anjali Gupta

ALLIED PUBLISHERS PVT. LTD.

Noida • Mumbai • Kolkata • Chennai • Bangalore

ALLIED PUBLISHERS PRIVATE LIMITED

D-5, Sector-2, **Noida**–201 301
Ph. Nos.: 0120-4320295/2542557/4352866 • E-mail: delhi.books@alliedpublishers.com

17 Chittaranjan Avenue, **Kolkata**–700072
Ph.: 033-22129618 • E-mail: cal.books@alliedpublishers.com

15 J.N. Heredia Marg, Ballard Estate, **Mumbai**–400001
Ph.: 022-42126969 • E-mail: mumbai.books@alliedpublishers.com

No. 25/10, Commander-in-Chief Road, Ethiraj Lane (Next to Post Office)
Egmore, **Chennai**–600008
Ph.: 044-28223938 • E-mail: chennai.books@alliedpublishers.com

P.B. No. 9932, No. 15, 3rd Floor (Next to Vijaya Bank), 5th Cross, Gandhinagar,
Karnataka, **Bangalore**–560009, Ph.: 080-41530285 / 22386239
E-mail: bngl.books@alliedpublishers.com

Website: www.alliedpublishers.com

ISBN: 978-93-89934-56-4

Published by Sunil Sachdev and printed by Ravi Sachdev at Allied Publishers Pvt. Ltd.,
D-5, Sector-2, Noida–201 301

PROLOGUE

Interdisciplinary Research: Challenges for Integration

Integrating interdisciplinary research is vitally important for addressing complex social issues and promoting social well-being. By blending insights and methods from multiple disciplines, researchers can develop a more comprehensive understanding of social problems and create effective solutions. The benefits being:

Interdisciplinary research provides a more complete and nuanced understanding of social issues, considering multiple perspectives and factors. Holistic understanding refers to a comprehensive and integrated approach to understanding complex systems, phenomena, or concepts. It involves considering multiple perspectives, factors and relationships to gain a deeper and more refined understanding. It can help identify and address complex problems while fostering personal growth, self awareness, and empathy. Holistic understanding can lead to more effective and sustainable solutions.

Integrating varied disciplines can lead to innovative solutions, as researchers blend unique insights and approaches. These solutions often involve thinking outside the box, leveraging technology, and collaborating with diverse stakeholders. Creativity, risk-taking, collaboration, iteration and scalability are the characteristics of innovative solutions. Competitive advantage, improved efficiency, enhanced customer experience, social impact and economic growth are the benefits of innovative solutions.

Interdisciplinary research fosters collaboration among researchers from diverse backgrounds, promoting knowledge sharing and mutual understanding. Improved collaboration refers to the process of working together more effectively, efficiently and harmoniously to achieve common goals. It leads to increased productivity, enhanced creativity, improved communication, better decision making, and increased employee engagement. The strategies required for improving collaboration include establishing clear goals, fostering open communication, encouraging active listening, emphasizing mutual respect, and using collaboration tools. Communication platforms, video conferencing tools, file sharing tools, and collaboration platforms are necessary for improved collaboration.

Interdisciplinary research can inform policy decisions, providing a more comprehensive understanding of social issues and their potential solutions. Enhanced policy relevance refers to the process of making research and analysis more relevant, useful, and applicable to policy-making and decision-making processes. Research questions are framed to address specific policy concerns and needs, whereas data and analysis are tailored to inform policy decisions and address policy challenges. Insights and recommendations are provided in a timely manner to inform policy decisions, as researchers collaborate with policy makers to ensure that research is relevant and useful besides being communicated in a clear and concise manner.

Interdisciplinary research can lead to more effective and sustainable solutions, ultimately improving social well-being and quality of life. Increased impact refers to the process of amplifying the effects or consequences of an action, decision, or initiative. The ability to scale up an initiative or project to reach a wider audience or achieve greater impact is a key characteristic, besides sustainability, reach, influence, and effectiveness. Building partnerships and collaborations with other organizations or stakeholders are necessary to amplify impact. Continuously evaluating and learning from initiatives or projects facilitate to identify the areas for improvement and optimize impact in addition to raising awareness and advocating for issues or causes to increase impact and influence. Research and development can increase impact by identifying new and more effective ways to address complex challenges.

Challenges of Interdisciplinary Research

1. **Communication barriers:** Researchers from various disciplines may use distinct languages, methodologies, and paradigms, creating communication challenges. Differences in dialect can create barriers to communication. Cultural differences can affect communication styles, norms, and expectations. Technical issues, such as poor internet connectivity or equipment malfunctions, can disrupt communication. Differences in terminology, methods, or perspectives can create barriers to communication among researchers from different disciplines.

   Barriers can exist between researchers and stakeholders, such as policymakers, practitioners, or community members. Communication barriers can lead to misunderstandings, misinterpretations, or miscommunications. They can cause delays in the research process, affecting timelines and deadlines, resulting in inaccurate or incomplete data, affecting the reliability and validity of research findings. They can lead to a lack of engagement or participation from stakeholders or participants, thus, resulting in wasted resources including time, money, and effort.

2. **Different epistemological assumptions:** Disciplines may have varying assumptions about knowledge, reality, and research methods, requiring careful consideration and integration. Different epistemological assumptions refer to the various underlying beliefs and perspectives that shape how researchers approach knowledge and understanding. Positivism, interpretivism, realism, constructivism and pragmatism are the key epistemological assumptions. Positivism means assuming that knowledge can be obtained through observation and experience, and that reality can be understood through empirical evidence.

   Interpretivism assumes that knowledge is constructed through interpretation and understanding of social and cultural contexts, whereas realism assumes that reality exists independently of human perception, and that knowledge can be obtained through observation and experience. Constructivism assumes that knowledge is constructed through social and cultural interactions, and that reality is shaped by individual and collective perspectives. Pragmatism assumes that knowledge is obtained through practical experience and experimentation, and that truth is determined by its usefulness and effectiveness.

3. **Funding and resource constraints:** Interdisciplinary research often requires additional resources, including funding, manpower, and infrastructure. Insufficient funding can limit the scope, duration and quality of research. Funding agencies may prioritize certain research areas or topics over others, influencing the types of

projects that receive funding. The competition for grants can be intense, making it challenging for researchers to secure funding. Funding agencies may have strict timelines for project completion, which can create pressure for researchers to produce results quickly.

4. **Institutional and cultural barriers:** Academic institutions and disciplines may have entrenched cultures and practices, making it difficult to adopt interdisciplinary approaches. Complex administrative procedures and regulations can slow down research progress. Research institutions may prioritize certain areas of research over others, influencing the types of projects that receive support. Institutional structures and incentives may not support interdisciplinary research, making it challenging for researchers to collaborate across disciplines. Limited opportunities for career advancement can discourage researchers from pursuing certain areas of research.
5. **Evaluating interdisciplinary research:** Assessing the quality and impact of interdisciplinary research can be challenging, as traditional evaluation metrics may not be applicable. Lack of clear evaluation criteria, difficulty in identifying relevant reviewers, research quality, balancing depth and breadth, and addressing conflicting values and methods are some of the challenges in evaluating interdisciplinary research.

Strategies for Integrating Interdisciplinary Research

1. **Developing common languages and frameworks:** Establishing shared vocabularies and conceptual frameworks can facilitate communication and collaboration among researchers. Common languages and frameworks facilitate integration across disciplines.
2. **Creating interdisciplinary research teams:** Assembling teams with diverse expertise and backgrounds can foster collaboration and innovation.
3. **Using mixed-methods approaches:** Combining quantitative and qualitative research methods can provide a more comprehensive understanding of social issues.
4. **Engaging stakeholders and communities:** Involving stakeholders and communities in the research process can ensure that findings are relevant, applicable, and effective.
5. **Providing training and capacity-building programs:** Offering training and capacity-building programs can help researchers develop the skills and knowledge needed for interdisciplinary research.

Examples of Interdisciplinary Research

1. **Sustainable development:** Integrating insights from environmental science, economics, sociology, and politics to develop sustainable solutions for environmental challenges.
2. **Public health:** Combining knowledge from epidemiology, sociology, psychology, and policy studies to address complex public health issues, such as obesity and mental health.
3. **Urban planning:** Integrating perspectives from architecture, urban planning, sociology, and economics to design and develop sustainable, equitable, and livable cities.

4. **Climate change:** Bringing together researchers from atmospheric science, economics, policy studies, and sociology to develop comprehensive solutions for mitigating and adapting to climate change.
5. **Social inequality:** Combining insights from sociology, economics, psychology, and policy studies to understand and address social inequality, including issues related to poverty, education, and healthcare.

Date: 15.04.2025

Dr. Santosh Dhar
Dr. Upinder Dhar

About the Editors

Dr. Santosh Dhar is Rector & Dean - Faculty of Doctoral Studies and Research at Shri Vaishnav Vidyapeeth Vishwavidyalaya, Indore. She has been engaged in teaching, research, corporate training and consultancy for the last forty two years. She has widely published her work and has more than 460 publications to her credit. Her earlier assignments have been Professor, Shri Vaishnav Institute of Management, Indore; Professor, Amity Business School, Amity University, Greater Noida campus; Professor, Institute of Management and Dean – Research, JK Lakshmipat University, Jaipur; Senior Professor, OB/HR, Jaipuria Institute of Management, Jaipur; Professor and Chairperson – OB/HR Area, Institute of Management, Nirma University, Ahmedabad and Guest Faculty at IIM Kolkata and MICA Ahmedabad. Many research scholars have been awarded Ph.D degree under her supervision. She has designed and conducted management development programs for the executives of several business houses, such as Grasim Industries, JK Tyre, Bridgestone, Hindustan Motors, ONGC and GAIL to name a few. She has been on the Panel of Reviewers of Oxford University Press and Tata McGraw-Hill. She was Managing Editor of Prestige Journal of Management and Research and Prestige Research Abstracts. She has been Chairperson of Indian Society for Training and Development (Indore and Jaipur Chapters) and was on the Editorial Board of Indian Journal of Training and Development. She has presented papers in several national and international conferences/seminars and had the opportunity to visit Kathmandu (Nepal), Male (Maldives), Bangkok (Thailand), Beijing, Shangai, Guanzhou, Shenzen, Hong Kong (China), Seoul (South Korea) Dubai (UAE), Tumu (Myanmar), Poland, United States, Italy and France in connection with various professional and academic assignments.

Dr. Dhar had coordinated the implementation of a project on the *Empowerment of Women through Enterprise* in North India (2000–2002), which was funded by Canadian International Development Agency (CIDA). She has completed the research projects on *Problems of Women Trainers in India* and *Quality of Work Life as a Determinant of Mental Health in Pharmaceutical Industry*. She has also been principal investigator for Asian Development Bank funded and Rajasthan Government sponsored RUIDP Consultancy project on *Capacity Building of ULBs* of Different Towns of Rajasthan. She has twice been chairperson of Indian Society for Training and Development Jaipur and Indore Chapter & Chairperson of the Best Paper Award of the Indian Society for Training and Development, New Delhi. Dr. Dhar was conferred *National Fellowship* for her contributions to HR by the Indian Society for Training and Development in 2006–07. She is life member of Indian Society for Training and Development (ISTD), National Human Resource Development Network (NHRDN), and Indian Society for Technical Education (ISTE).

Dr. Upinder Dhar is First Vice Chancellor of Shri Vaishnav Vidyapeeth Vishwavidyalaya (Indore). Earlier, he was Group Additional Vice Chancellor and Pro-Vice Chancellor (Academics), Amity University (Noida); First Vice Chancellor of JK Lakshmipat University (Jaipur); Director - Institute of Management, Dean - Faculty of Management, and Dean - Faculty of Doctoral Studies and Research, Nirma University (Ahmedabad); Director - Prestige Institute of Management and Research (Indore); Professor of Management at NITIE (Now IIM Mumbai). He has conducted 811 management and faculty development programs for the executives of major business houses and faculty members of academic institutions respectively. He has also been Guest Faculty at IIM Calcutta, IIM Indore, IIM Trichy and IIT Roorkee. Besides undertaking consultancy assignments, he has authored/co-authored/edited 880 publications. Forty-Six (46) scholars have been awarded Ph.D. degree under his supervision by various universities.

A Fellow of ISTD and a strong proponent of Case Method, Dr. Dhar was conferred **Ravi J. Matthai National Fellow Award** by the *Association of Indian Management Schools in 2018,* and **AIMA-Kewal Nohria Award for Academic Leadership in Management Education – 2022** by the *All India Management Association* in 2022. He has been on the Panel of Reviewers of number of international journals, such as International Journal of Training and Development, Human Resources International, Journal of Global Business and Technology, and South Asian Journal of Management. He has also been on the Panel of Experts maintained by the NAAC (Bangalore), NBA (Bangalore); ICSSR (New Delhi); and SAQS (Hyderabad). He was President of Anthropological and Behavioral Sciences Section of the Indian Science Congress Association in 2007–08, Indian Society for Training and Development in 2008–09 and Association of Indian Management Schools in 2014–15. He has also been Member of the Council of Management of AIMA, Member of ATMA, All India Board of Management Studies of AICTE, Rajasthan State Productivity Council, Governing Board of DELNET, and Member of the Executive Board of AMDISA.

Dr. Dhar was awarded Commonwealth Fellowship twice to present his papers at the South Asian Management Forums held at Royal Institute of Management, Bhutan and Lahore University of Management Science, Lahore. He was invited by the American Society for Engineering Management as resource person for Case Method during its international annual Conference held at Minnesota in 2013. He has also been resource person in the Leadership for Academicians Program (LEAP) sponsored by MHRD and organized by IIT Roorkee in 2018 and BHU Varanasi in 2019. He was invited to deliver *keynote address* in the International Conference of ITAM at Montpellier Business School, France and University of Cagliari, Italy in July 2024. He had the opportunity to visit. Ivy league institutions like Harvard Business School, MIT Sloan School of Management, and Yale University School of Management. He has also visited 20 countries for professional and academic interest.

Dr. Dhar has been on the high powered Expert Committees constituted by MHRD, UGC and AICTE. Hon'ble Governor of Uttar Pradesh had nominated him as Chairman of the Search Committee for the appointment of Vice Chancellor – Awadh University. He was President of the International Simulation and Gaming Association (2021–22), and a Member of the *Standing Committee on Specification of Degrees u/s 22* of the *UGC Act,*

1956; Expert Group constituted for Implementation of NEP 2020, and Governing Council of the Association of Indian Universities. Currently, he is a member of the Executive Board of AMDISA (2022–24). He is nominee of AICTE as a subject expert on the Board of Governors (BoG) of Xavier Institute of Development and Studies, Jabalpur and Asian Business School, Noida. He is the Co-Chair of *India Case Research Centre (ICRC)* of AIMA, New Delhi. Besides his professional engagements, Dr. Dhar has been a dedicated Rotarian since 1997. He was instrumental in setting up three Rotaract Clubs and one Interact Club. He was President of RCI Indore Uptown for the Rotary Year 2023–24. Currently, he is Rotary District 3040 New Generation Service Exchange Chair.

Dr. Anjali Gupta has more than 20 years of experience in teaching in the field of Electronics and Communication Engineering. She is currently working as Assistant Professor in Department of Electrical and Electronics Engineering at Shri Vaishnav Institute of Technology & Science, Shri Vaishnav Vidyapeeth Vishwavidyalaya, Indore. She received her B.E. Degree in Electronics & Communication Engineering from Rajasthan University in 2003. She did her M.E. in Digital Communication from IET DAVV, Indore in 2009 and Ph.D. in Electronics & Telecommunication from DAVV, Indore. Her research interests include signal processing, wireless communication, and IoT. She has number publications in international journals and conferences. She is a member of the Board of Studies for Electrical and Electronics Engineering Department and member of the Institution's Innovation Council (IIC) of SVVV.

Dr. Gupta has participated in number of workshops related to IOT, Robotics, and communication systems. She has qualified NPTEL-SWAYAM Online Certification course on "Principles of Communication – Part I & II", and "Discrete Time Signal Processing". She has received Certificate for Online Certification course on "Signals and Systems" offered by IIT BombayX. She has been the book editor for (i) Industry 5.0 and Paradigm Shift: Emerging Challenges, February 2023, ISBN: 978-93-90951-50-5, (ii) Innovative and Sustainable Developments in Electrical and Electronics Engineering May 2022, ISBN: 978-93-90951-41-3. She has reviewed a number of technical papers and served as Paper Reviewer for 2nd International Conference on Emerging Trends In Engineering, ICETE 2023, University College of Engineering, Osmania University, Hyderabad, India, Publication Partner Atlantis Press (part of Springer Nature).

Dr. Gupta has been continuously contributing to the university. She had served as the coordinator of various National events such robotics competetion *Navyantram*, project competition *Navarachana*, and National conference *Sanmantrana*. She has been working as Co-Coordinator of Rotaract Club of SVVV since 2022. She had organized online lecture series '*Parisamwad*' and '*Udbhavana*' in 2021–22. Dr. Gupta has been the Co-Coordinator of International Conference on "Innovative and Sustainable Developments in Electrical and Electronics Engineering", PRAGYATA 2022. Also been the Co-Coordinator of Conference hosted and organized by SVVV in collaboration with Madhya Pradesh Vigyan Sammelan and IIT Indore, 22nd to 25th Dec. 2021. She has also worked as an Assistant Exam Superintendent. She has successfully organized Alumni Meet - *Confluence* 2018, and Committee member of various institute building as well as student activities.

Contents

Prologue .... *v*

About the Editors .... *ix*

1. A Comparative Analysis of Health and Nutritional Status in Professional Women Across Indore's Educational Institutions 1
   Manisha Dubey and Dipali Saxena
2. A Comprehensive Review of Digital Storytelling in Shaping Emotional and Mental Well-being in Children 7
   Ekta Rathi and Upinder Dhar
3. Solar Air Heater Performance Using Various Artificially Roughened Components: A Review 16
   Sunil Chaurasia and Sumit Chandak
4. A Survey on Intrusion Detection System in IoT Environment using Deep Learning 22
   Bhagyashri B. Kotame and Jigyasu Dubey
5. Achieving Financial Inclusion Through Political, Economic and Social Empowerment Among Women: An Empirical Attestation 34
   Aditi Sharma and Pragati Tomar Solanki
6. *Agrobacterium tumefaciens*-Mediated Transformation (ATMT) of Soybean Anthracnose Pathogen *Colletotrichum truncatum*: A Novel Approach for Functional Genomics 43
   Niharika Sharma and K.N. Guruprasad
7. Aligning Biometric Data Usage with Global Sustainability Goals and Indian Data Protection Laws: A Business Perspective 49
   Poorva Vaishnav and Ashutosh Bairagi
8. Analysis of Charging and Discharging Patterns in Solar Rechargeable Wireless Sensors 59
   Amit Holkar and Swapnil Jain
9. Analysis of Defects and Faults in Quantum-Dot Cellular Automata (QCA) Circuits: A Case Study on Full Adder 67
   Preet Jain and Namit Gupta
10. Analysis of Palmar Creases for Personal Identification 74
    Ayushi Beragi and Swati Dubey Mishra
11. Consumer Attitude Towards Green Packaging on Food Products in Indore 82
    Riya Sadawana and Aditi Naidu
12. Content Analysis of Central University Library Websites in Uttar Pradesh: A Comparative Study 93
    Ashish Tiwari and Pankaja Tiwari

13. Evaluating the Efficiency of V2V and V2I Communication in Vehicular Networks 102
Rani Singh and Anand Rajavat

14. Evolution in Restoration of Fire Damaged Documents 114
Krati Singh Chauhan and Richa Rohatgi

15. Green Buildings Synergizing Renewable Energy to Achieve Urbanization in Tier-II Cities 123
Anshul Jain and Ananda Babu K.

16. Leveraging Third Level Fingerprint Details to Overcome Challenges in Fingerprint Examination 131
Akanchha Kumari and Richa Rohatgi

17. Machine Learning-Based Vulnerability Assessment for Intelligent Devices 141
Romil Rawat and Anand Rajavat

18. Navigating AI Threats in IT Laws 149
Muskan Neekey and Ashutosh Bairagi

19. Optimizing Cloudlet Placement in Cloud-Integrated WOBAN: A Comparative Study of Connectivity Index and K-Means Clustering Approaches 158
Mausmi Verma and Uma Rathore Bhatt

20. Phytoremediation—An Eco-Friendly and Sustainable Technique for Wastewater Treatment 164
Vijayant Panday and Ananda Babu K.

21. SEAPIRD Model for Analysing Covid Dynamics 171
Shilpa Umdekar and Anand Prakash

22. Succession of Insect-pests on Chickpea in Solapur District (MS) 180
Samadhan P. Javalage and Yuvraj A. Shinde

23. The Impact of Fintech on Financial Regulation: A Comparative Analysis Across Regulatory Frameworks 185
Shaily Jhawar and Vikas Rathore

24. To Study the Antecedents of Political Participation 192
Sakshi Jhawar and Varsha Upadhyaya

25. To Study the Impact of Abusive Supervision on Employee Well-being: A Study of the Hospitality Sector 206
Palak Sukhija and Dimple Sukhija

26. Urban Agriculture: Potential Way for Achieving SDGs 215
Richa Sharma and Suhas Mane

Epilogue 223

Subject Index 227

Author Index 231

A Comparative Analysis of Health and Nutritional Status in Professional Women Across Indore's Educational Institutions

Manisha Dubey[1] and Dipali Saxena[2]

ABSTRACT: In the modern world, women's nutritional and health status is a major concern because of the various roles they play, which can lead to major nutritional issues. They don't give proper attention to their diet and health. Therefore, present study was taken to investigate the dietary pattern of professional women working in different education sectors in Indore city. RDA (Recommended Dietary Allowance) is considered as a major determinant of health. A random sample of 500 women (School Teachers - 250 and College Teachers - 250) in the age group of 30–45 years were chosen from Indore. A comparison was made as both study groups have different work demands which could lead to different nutritional choices. Which may have an impact on their health. According to the findings of this study, the health condition of school teachers and college teachers differed considerably in terms of RDA. The authority provides a set of recommendations for daily nutrient intake levels that are believed to be sufficient to meet the nutritional needs of most healthy individuals. Comparison revealed that most of the professional women were not taking their daily meals and according to RDA, this leads to medical issues like underweight, overweight hypothyroid etc. The paper concludes that food choices, lifestyle, and dietary habits have a significant impact on professional women, especially in terms of their physical health and well-being.

Keywords: *Dietary Habits, Lifestyle, Nutritional Status, Obesity, Recommended Dietary Allowances.*

1. INTRODUCTION

In India, women constitute nearly half of the population, playing crucial roles in families, communities, and the economy. However, their health and nutritional status remains a significant concern due to a myriad of factors, including socio-economic disparities, cultural practices, and limited access to healthcare services. Women's health in India is shaped by various determinants, including maternal health, reproductive health, and non-communicable diseases. High maternal mortality rates and undernutrition are critical issues, exacerbated by inadequate healthcare infrastructure and gender inequalities. Conditions such as anemia are prevalent, affecting women of all ages, particularly during reproductive years.

---

[1] Research Scholar, Department of Food and Nutrition, Shri Vaishnav Institute of Home Science, Shri Vaishnav Vidyapeeth Vishwavidyalaya, Indore, India.
E-mail: dubeymanisha22@gmail.com

[2] Assistant Professor, Department of Food and Nutrition, Shri Vaishnav Institute of Home Science, Shri Vaishnav Vidyapeeth Vishwavidyalaya, Indore, India.

Nutrition is a fundamental aspect of health, yet many Indian women face malnutrition in its various forms such as under-nutrition, over-nutrition, and micronutrient deficiencies. Traditional dietary practices, coupled with limited education and awareness about nutrition, contribute to suboptimal dietary habits. The prevalence of anemia, particularly iron deficiency anemia, is alarmingly high, affecting women's productivity and overall well-being. Elevated blood pressure is a major risk factor for cardiovascular disease globally, accounting for 19% of fatalities worldwide each year (Forouzanfar *et. al.,* 2015).

Women's productivity and participation in the economic system is adversely affected by malnutrition. The dual responsibility workload, poor nutritional status and due to culture of eating last leads to fatigue and results in depression, irritation and mood swing etc. To improve the quality of life it is necessary to maintain a good nutritional status which will increase the working capacity of women. The fundamental element which affects health maintenance is dietary life. Various environmental factors such as age, residence, education, job, economic level influence individual dietary life (Vasantha. *et. al.,* 2015). The prevalence of overweight and obesity among Indian women has dramatically increased over the last ten years. The health and nutritional status of Indian women did not significantly improve, according to the NFHS-5 study. Nutrition improves health and lowers illness risk factors. A balanced diet can help avoid weight gain and play a crucial role in the treatment and management of numerous diseases by substituting foods high in nutrients for those high in sugar and fat (McClelland *et. al.*, 2002).

2. RESEARCH OBJECTIVE

Given the critical importance of understanding the health and nutritional status of women, this study aims to assess nutritional knowledge, dietary practices, health outcomes and quantities of servings of macro nutrients in accordance with RDA. The RDA is set by health authorities, such as the Institute of Medicine (IOM) in the United States, and it provides guidance for the general population to ensure they get adequate nutrition.

3. RESEARCH METHOD

A comparison between school teacher and college teacher working in different educational sectors was conducted using a random selection of 500 women (250 School teachers and 250 college teachers) teaching in various educational institutions of Indore. The subject's age was estimated to be the closest whole figure. A self-designed questionnaire was used to gather information on the socio-demographic profile (type of work, family structure, age, educational level, and anthropometric measurements like height and weight and medical history). The questionnaire was distributed at different schools and colleges of Indore between September 2023 to November 2023. After recording socio-demographic details, physical activity and eating pattern detail, details of three days dietary recall was obtained from each participant and macro nutrients intake was calculated and after calculation daily intake of nutrients were compared with Recommended Dietary Allowances (RDA) proposed by ICMR (Indian Counselling Medical Research) Expert committee. To obtain an estimate portion size/utensil, commonly used glasses, bowls and spoons of different sizes were taken for assessment of food frequency. However, all utensils are of different sizes, hence weight of spoons, bowls and glasses were taken.

The World Health Organization (WHO) defines the Recommended Dietary Allowance (RDA) as the average daily intake of a nutrient that is considered adequate to meet the nutritional needs of nearly all healthy individuals in a specific life stage and gender group. It refers to the daily intake level of a nutrient considered to be sufficient to meet the nutritional needs of 97–98% of healthy individuals in a specific age and gender group.

The RDA includes:

- **EAR (Estimated Average Requirement):** The amount of a nutrient that is estimated to meet the needs of 50% of the population.
- **AI (Adequate Intake):** A recommended intake level when there's insufficient evidence to establish an RDA.
- **UL (Tolerable Upper Intake Level):** The highest level of nutrient intake that is unlikely to cause harmful effects.

Body mass index (BMI) is a person's weight in kilograms divided by the square of height in meters. The number generated from this relation is the individual's BMI number. The National Institute of Health (NIH) now uses BMI to define a person as underweight, normal weight, overweight, or obese. BMI is an inexpensive and easy screening method for weight category.

Observations

Table 1: Age Distribution of Respondents

Age Distribution	*Number of School Teachers*	*% of School Teachers*	*Number of College Teachers*	*% of College Teachers*
30–34	88	35.2%	85	34.0%
35–39	87	34.8%	87	34.8%
40–45	75	30.0%	78	31.2%
Total	**250**	**100%**	**250**	**100%**

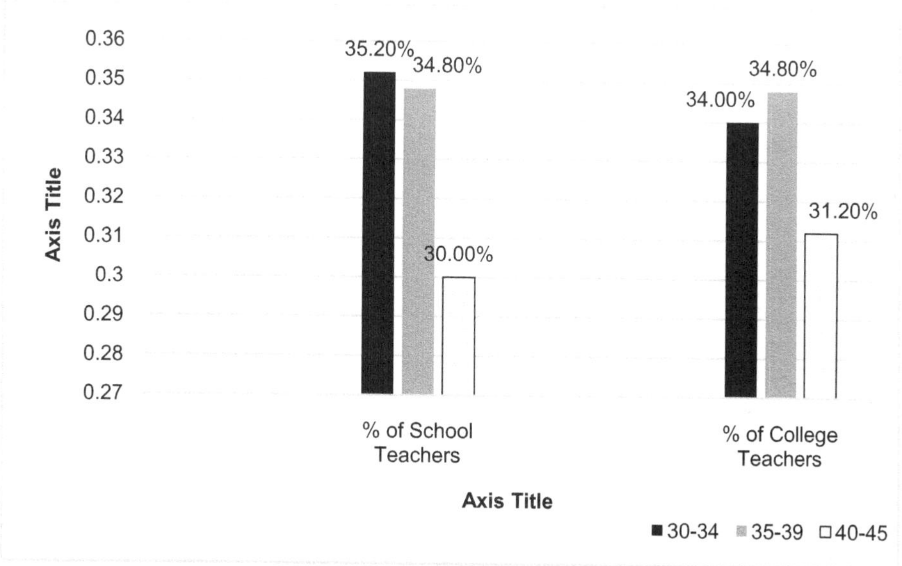

Figure 1: Graphical Representation of Age Distribution

Table 2: Family Structure of Respondents

Family Structure	*Number of School Teachers*	*% of School Teachers*	*Number of College Teachers*	*% of College Teachers*
Nuclear family	165	66.0%	168	67.2%
Joint family	85	34.0%	82	32.8%
Total	**250**	**100%**	**250**	**100%**

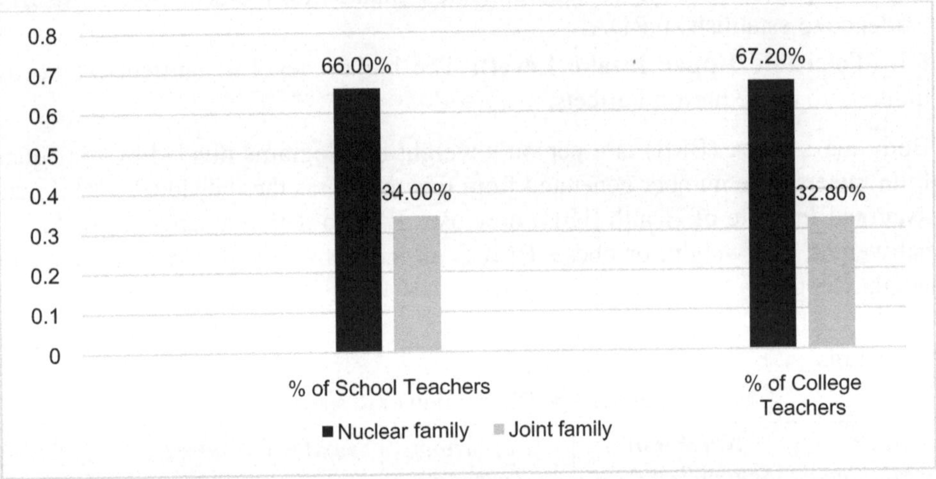

Figure 2: Graphical Representation of Family Structure

Table 3: Marital Status

Marital Status	*School Teacher*	*%*	*College Teacher*	*%*
Married	200	80.0%	190	76.0%
Unmarried	50	20.0%	60	24.0%
Total	**250**	**100%**	**250**	**100%**

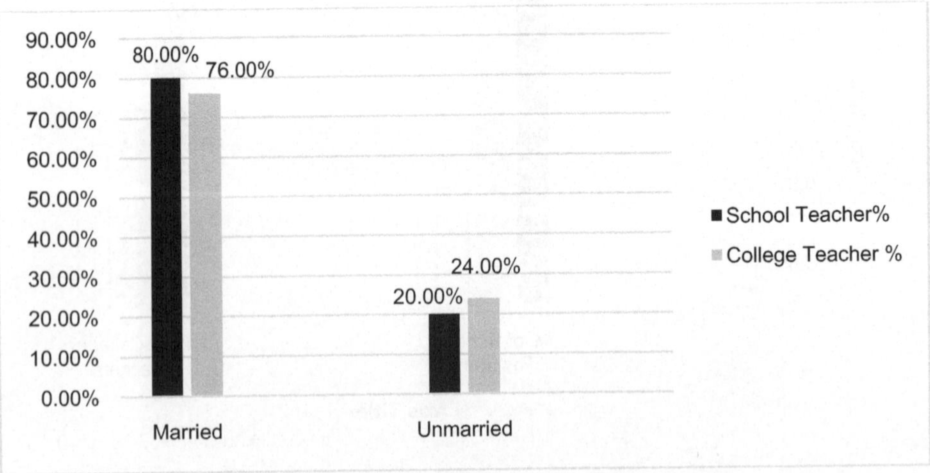

Figure 3: Graphical Presentation of Marital Status

Table 4: Categorization of Respondents According to BMI

	School Teacher	***College Teacher***
Under weight	28.0%	20.4%
Normal weight	35.2%	36.8%
Overweight & Obese	37.8%	42.8%
Total	**100%**	**100%**

Table 5: Meal Consumption Per Day

	School Teacher		***College Teacher***	
	Underweight	***Overweight***	***Underweight***	***Overweight***
2 Time	42.8%	24.0%	19.6%	27.1%
3 Time	37.1%	31.5%	21.6%	30.0%
4 Time	20.0%	33.6%	41.2%	26.1%
More than 4 Time	–	10.8%	17.6%	16.8%

Table 6: Calorie Consumption (1660 Kcal/day)

Category	***More than RDA (1700± 50kcal/day)***	***Less than RDA (1450 ± 50kcal/day)***	***According to RDA (1660 ± 50kcal/day)***	***Total***
School Teacher	113 (45.2%)	83 (33.2%)	34 (13.6%)	250
College Teacher	131 (52.4%)	46 (18.4%)	48 (19.2%)	250

Table 7: Protein Consumption (36.3 gm/day)

	More than RDA (38 ± 3 gm/day)	***Less than RDA 30 ± 3 gm/day***	***According to RDA (36.3 ± 3 gm/day)***	***Total***
School Teacher	40 (16.0%)	159 (63.6%)	51 (20.4%)	250 (100%)
College Teacher	56 (22.4%)	146 (58.4%)	48 (19.2%)	250 (100%)

Table 8: Fat Consumption (20 gm/day)

	More than RDA (23±2gm/day)	***Less than RDA (17±2gm/day)***	***According to RDA (20±2gm/day)***	***Total***
School Teacher	101 (40.4%)	82(32.8%)	67 (26.8%)	250 (100%)
College Teacher	126 (50.4%)	68 (27.2%)	56 (22.4%)	250 (100%)

4. RESULTS AND DISCUSSION

The current study investigated Recommended Dietary Allowance (RDA) of school teachers and college teachers. We found that both the groups are conscious and have knowledge about healthy diet but because of workload at home and working place they are unable to take meal on time sometimes they skip the meal. The data suggests that majority of teachers, particularly college teachers, tend to consume more calories than recommended, while a smaller percentage is under-consuming or meeting the RDA specifications. The present study will help to examine factors influencing this intake.

Overall, the findings suggest that while many teachers exceed their caloric and fat intake, a significant number do not meet the protein intake recommendations, highlighting areas for potential improvement in dietary habits.

5. CONCLUSION

Food is a necessity of life as it helps us to maintain our body functions. Health means the well-being of an individual in physical, emotional, and social condition. Women have a special position in society and if they have knowledgeable about nutrition, they will not only keep their families healthy but also themselves. The present paper gives an important insight into the health status of women in Indore and around. The percentage of fat intake was seen to be high in the diet while protein and energy intake was low than the recommended dietary specifications. To address these health concerns, it is essential for educational institutions to implement wellness programs that promote healthy lifestyles, including physical activity and nutritional education. Supporting teachers in maintaining a healthy dietary pattern can improve their overall quality of life and enhance their professional performance. Future research should continue to explore the factors influencing these trends and assess the effectiveness of interventions designed to promote healthier behaviors among educators. Factors contributing to these trends may include differences in work environments, physical activity levels, and stress management practices. Further research is warranted to explore these variables in depth and develop tailored interventions that can support teachers in maintaining a healthier lifestyle.

REFERENCES

Kaur, G.; Bains, K. and Kaur, H. (2012). Body composition, dietary intake and physical activity level of sedentary adult Indian women. *Food and Nutrition Sciences, 3*(11), 1577–1585.

Monga, S. and Choudhary, S. (2008). Efficacy of nutrition counselling on the knowledge, attitude and practices of working women. *Studies on Home and Community Science, 2*(2), 99–102.

Priyadarshini, V. (2015). Concern and dissatisfaction about body image and body weight among the urban adolescent girls. *Asian Journal of Home Science, 10*(1), 155–160.

Ray, B.S. and Sil, P. (2013). A comparative study of health and nutritional status among housewives and working women of North Bengal. *International Journal of Behavioral Social and Movement Sciences, 2*(4), 35–40.

Raza, S.A.; Ahmed, S. and Khan, M.A. (2017). Comparison of dietary practices and body mass index among educated housewives and working women in Karachi. *Journal of Ayub Medical College Abbottabad, 29*(2), 293–297.

Roday, S. (2007). *Food science and nutrition* (2nd ed.). Oxford University Press.

Sodha, S.; Jadeja, R. and Joshi, H. (2015). Anthropometric assessment of nutritional status of adolescent girls of Porbandar city of Gujarat state. *International Journal of Applied Social Science, 2*(3&4), 78–83.

Thilagamani, S. and Mageshwari, U. (2010). Risk appraisal for cardiovascular disease among selected young adult women in Coimbatore, India. *Indian Journal of Science and Technology, 3*(6), 672–675.

Vasantha, S.; Vijaylakshmi, S. and Kiran, P. (2015). Review on impact of changing lifestyles on dietary pattern. *International Journal of Current Research & Academic Review, 3*(6), 135–147.

World Health Organization. (1998). *The world health report 1998: Life in the 21st century – A vision for all*. World Health Organization.

A Comprehensive Review of Digital Storytelling in Shaping Emotional and Mental Well-being in Children

Ekta Rathi[1] and Upinder Dhar[2]

ABSTRACT: Digital storytelling has become a potent teaching tool that helps kids develop important emotional and cognitive abilities. By combining multimedia components with conventional storytelling, this approach empowers kids to actively participate in the creation and dissemination of stories. According to studies, digital storytelling helps kids visualise information, organise events, and relate stories to their own experiences, all of which improve literacy, critical thinking, and cognitive engagement. Emotionally, it fosters empathy and self-awareness in kids as they express their individuality and investigate various viewpoints. Additionally, digital storytelling supports the objectives of Social-Emotional Learning (SEL), assisting kids in expressing their feelings and building resilience. It establishes a cooperative setting where kids may develop their communication skills, build strong peer relationships, and acquire confidence. Digital media use also reflects contemporary communication trends, giving kids 21st-century abilities like ethical decision-making and digital literacy. According to research, this integrative approach improves mental health by lowering stress and raising emotional intelligence while fostering creativity and curiosity. Despite its potential, more study is needed to evaluate long-term developmental consequences and optimise storytelling strategies. Digital storytelling, however, combines education, creativity, and emotional development to provide a transforming tool for holistic childhood development.

Keywords: *Childhood Development, Cognitive Engagement, Digital Literacy, Emotional Development, Social-Emotional Learning.*

1. INTRODUCTION

Classrooms are increasingly using digital storytelling, a technique that combines contemporary digital resources with conventional narrative techniques. Digital storytelling incorporates multimedia components including videos, audio clips, photos, and text to produce dynamic narratives, in contrast to traditional storytelling, which only uses spoken or written communication (Robin, 2008). This method improves children's social, emotional, and cognitive development in addition to improving the way they tell stories.

Giving kids the tools they need to successfully navigate and use digital media is essential in the modern digital age, where it greatly influences their life. Children can express themselves, discover different viewpoints, and interact with a variety of content

[1] Research Scholar, Shri Vaishnav Institute of Architecture, Shri Vaishnav Vidyapeeth Vishwavidyalaya, Indore, India. E-mail: ektapurandare@gmail.com

[2] Vice Chancellor, Shri Vaishnav Vidyapeeth Vishwavidyalaya, Indore, India.

through digital storytelling (Leu *et. al.*, 2011). With an emphasis on social interactions, emotional intelligence, cognitive development, and the development of critical 21st century abilities like digital literacy and moral decision-making, this paper attempts to investigate the diverse ways that digital storytelling affects children's growth.

2. RESEARCH METHOD

The method employed in this study involved several key steps:

- The topic for investigation was carefully chosen to focus on the mental well being of children which is the need of the hour.
- Research papers collection was conducted over a period of two decades, with a specific emphasis on the years 2000 to 2023. Various sources were utilized to gather relevant information and insights. Existing literature and studies on the subject were reviewed to gain a comprehensive understanding of the topic.

Bibliometric Analysis was done. The collected data and information underwent a rigorous screening process to ensure its relevance and reliability. Non-relevant or outdated papers were eliminated, and the remaining sources were carefully examined for accuracy and quality. This process helped to refine the database of papers and ensure the inclusion of reliable and up-to-date information

3. RATIONALE OF THE STUDY

The growing number of youngsters experiencing mental health issues highlights the critical need for creative and easily obtainable methods to promote emotional and psychological wellbeing. In a time when digital technologies are pervasive in children's life, incorporating them into developmental practices offers a special chance to successfully manage mental health issues. There is a lot of promise in this area with digital storytelling, a methodology that combines contemporary multimedia components with conventional narrative techniques. The following factors serve as the foundation for the reasoning for this study:

3.1 Growing Mental Health Needs in Children

Global statistics show that children are experiencing an increase in stress, anxiety, and emotional challenges. Addressing these issues requires early treatments that support self-expression, resilience, and emotional control. To address these needs, digital storytelling offers a fun and healing medium.

3.2 Integration of Education and Emotion

Although digital storytelling is acknowledged for its educational advantages, its contribution to the development of emotional intelligence, empathy, and stress reduction is not as well studied. By emphasising its benefits for mental health, this study fills a significant knowledge vacuum about its comprehensive effects on kids' development.

This study aims to improve knowledge of digital storytelling as a transforming tool by concentrating on children's emotional and mental health, providing useful information for educators, parents, and mental health specialists.

4. RESEARCH OBJECTIVES

- **Assess the Therapeutic Potential:** Examine how digital storytelling can help children develop emotional regulation and resilience by providing a platform for self-expression and emotional release.
- **Examine the Benefits for Mental Health:** Examine how digital storytelling helps kids feel less stressed, relax, and think more clearly.
- **Develop Emotional Intelligence and Empathy:** Recognise how developing and disseminating multimedia storytelling fosters emotional awareness, empathy, and perspective-taking.
- **Emphasise the Role of Creativity in Mental Health:** Investigate how digital storytelling's creativity relates to mental health and self-esteem.
- **Suggest Future Research Directions:** Describe the gaps in the existing literature and suggest topics for more study, especially in order to comprehend the long-term developmental effects of digital storytelling.

The goal of this review is to provide a comprehensive understanding of how digital storytelling can be used as a transformative tool to improve children's emotional and mental health and support their overall development.

5. EMOTIONAL WELL-BEING THROUGH DIGITAL STORYTELLING

5.1 Encouragement of Self-Awareness and Empathy

Digital storytelling offers the perfect setting for developing emotional intelligence and empathy. Children are taught to investigate various viewpoints and comprehend the feelings of others through the process of developing characters and stories (Bergen, 2016). Children learn about the feelings and experiences of others through stories told from the perspectives of a variety of characters, which develops empathy. Children who write stories about characters who are struggling gain a deeper comprehension of their own feelings, according to research. Children can reflect on their own experiences and express their own emotions in a creative and safe setting by delving into the emotional journeys of their characters (Haven, 2007). As youngsters learn to recognise, comprehend, and control their emotions, this exercise aids in the development of emotional intelligence. Additionally, by using digital storytelling to create stories that represent their own personalities, interests, and experiences, kids may express their uniqueness. Children get self-awareness and a good sense of identity through this self-expression process (Greenberg & Abenavoli, 2017).

5.2 Supporting Social-Emotional Learning (SEL)

The development of critical abilities including empathy, emotional control, and interpersonal communication is a component of social-emotional learning (SEL). Children can reflect on their emotions, express their sentiments, and share their stories with others through digital storytelling, which is strongly aligned with SEL (Zhao, 2016). Children are taught to analyse their own emotional reactions through digital storytelling, which enhances resilience and emotional regulation. Children can also learn how to handle difficult emotional situations and explore a variety of social situations through digital storytelling. Characters that overcome obstacles and show resiliency teach kids important life lessons that can help them deal with their own problems. A child might, for example, write a novel about a character who triumphs over hardship, teaching the author and readers how to deal with difficulties in real life.

5.3 Building Resilience and Emotional Regulation

Children can develop emotional resilience by reading stories about characters who overcome adversity. Children can absorb complicated emotions and learn coping mechanisms through storytelling Greenberg & Abenavoli (2017). In this sense, digital storytelling helps kids develop resilience by giving them a secure environment in which to try out different ways of expressing their emotions and coping strategies. Children gain a sense of optimism and agency by creating stories where characters struggle and eventually succeed. Children can experiment with various outcomes and learn how to handle their own challenges in real life by using these stories as a kind of emotional practice (Bergen, 2016).

5.4 A Creative Outlet for Emotional Release

Complex emotions are frequently difficult for kids to express, particularly under stressful situations. Children can externalise their ideas and feelings through multimedia narratives thanks to digital storytelling, which offers an organised but imaginative platform for self-expression. Children can acquire insight and lessen emotional pain by creating stories that are reflective of their own experiences (Banaszewski, 2005). A child who is anxious, for instance, might write a narrative about a character conquering their anxieties, which would allow them to express their feelings in a creative and secure environment. This procedure is in line with therapeutic approaches that promote mental clarity and emotional healing through artistic expression (McLeod & McLeod, 2011).

5.5 Building Emotional Awareness and Resilience

Children gain vital emotional control abilities by learning to recognise, categorise, and process their emotions through digital storytelling. According to research, storytelling improves children's resilience and problem-solving skills by helping them frame difficult situations in a positive light (Greenberg & Abenavoli, 2017). Digital storytelling iterative nature, which allows kids to go back and edit their stories, promotes introspection and personal development. With time, this process develops a sense of agency, enabling kids to see themselves as competent people who can handle the difficulties of life.

5.6 Enhancing Emotional Intelligence

Children gain self-awareness and social skills by considering the reasons and feelings of characters. Children learn how to identify and express their own emotions, comprehend emotional triggers, and resolve social disputes in a positive way through digital storytelling (Robin, 2008).

5.7 Fostering Empathy and Emotional Intelligence

Children are encouraged to develop characters and settings that examine a range of experiences and viewpoints through digital storytelling. By putting kids in other people's shoes, this activity helps them develop empathy, which is a key component of emotional intelligence (Davis, 2013). A youngster might, for example, write a tale about a family of refugees, which would encourage them to think about the feelings and difficulties that displaced people encounter. Healthy social interactions and relationships depend on children's ability to comprehend and relate to others, which is improved by such activities.

6. MENTAL WELLBEING THROUGH DIGITAL STORYTELLING

6.1 Creativity as a Mental Health Resource

Children who are creative have a feeling of purpose and a channel for self-expression, which is beneficial to their mental health. Children are inspired to try out novel concepts and formats by digital storytelling, which fosters creativity and imagination. Emotional well-being depends on both intrinsic motivation and a sense of accomplishment, which are fostered by this creative freedom (Banaszewski, 2005). Furthermore, telling and sharing tales fosters self-worth and confidence. Children's self-worth and efforts are validated when they witness their stories valued by adults or peers (Greenberg & Abenavoli, 2017).

6.2 Stress Reduction and Mental Relaxation

Storytelling has been demonstrated to lower stress levels by providing a positive and entertaining diversion from everyday demands. By fusing the interactive engagement of technology with the therapeutic advantages of storytelling, digital storytelling amplifies this effect. Through creative immersion, storytelling exercises have been shown to reduce cortisol levels, a biological indicator of stress, and encourage relaxation (Banaszewski, 2005). Digital storytelling also promotes a sense of community and belonging in group settings, which is important for reducing anxiety and feelings of loneliness. Children that have strong social ties receive emotional support and encouragement, which protects their mental health (Davis, 2013).

7. COGNITIVE BENEFITS OF DIGITAL STORYTELLING

7.1 Enhancing Literacy and Language Skills

Digital storytelling's capacity to raise literacy levels is among its best-established advantages. It has long been known that traditional storytelling improves language development; adding digital components elevates this to a new level (Banaszewski, 2005). Children interact with the story more deeply when they produce digital stories. In order to strengthen language abilities, they are required to write scripts, choose images and sounds, and modify content. Students' reading and writing skills significantly improve when they take part in digital storytelling programs, according to research (Schneps & Colflesh, 2015).

Children must actively use their language abilities to arrange ideas rationally, speak clearly, and participate in group discussions when choosing and organising the story in a multimedia manner. They practise verbal expression while they tell their experiences, which increases their confidence and fluency (Haven, 2007). Additionally, digital storytelling accommodates various learning preferences, guaranteeing that the process is advantageous to both visual and aural learners. By using spoken language and visual signals, children who might find it difficult to complete traditional writing projects can succeed in digital storytelling, which strengthens their understanding and expressiveness (Mayer, 2009). A more inclusive learning environment is offered by this multimodal approach, which enables pupils to absorb language in a range of ways.

7.2 Cognitive Engagement and Critical Thinking

Children are encouraged to think critically and evaluate the information they are providing through digital storytelling. Children must plot their narrative, arrange their ideas, and determine the most effective way to use multimedia components to deliver their message in order to produce an engaging story. They must use higher-order thinking skills to do this, such as analysing, synthesising, and making conclusions (Leu *et. al.*, 2011). The fact that kids are more than just passive information consumers is a crucial component of digital storytelling. They are active makers instead, combining word, sound, and visuals to convey their thoughts and create meaning. Because students are forced to consider how to narratively and graphically communicate complicated ideas, this method promotes a deeper grasp of the material.

Children must, for example, synthesise their knowledge, pose critical questions, and decide how best to present the information in an interesting and cohesive way while writing a story about historical events or scientific ideas (Banaszewski, 2005). Additionally, studies indicate that using digital storytelling can enhance one's ability to solve problems. Children must use critical thinking to come up with original ideas when they struggle to organise their stories. For instance, students may have to fix technological problems, modify their narrative for a different format, or settle disputes that come up during group assignments. These kinds of exercises promote resilience and cognitive flexibility (Schneps & Colflesh, 2015).

7.3 Visualization of Information

Digital storytelling's use of visual components fosters the growth of visualisation abilities, which are crucial for comprehending abstract ideas. Research indicates that visual aids enhance understanding and memory, particularly in disciplines like physics and maths (Mayer, 2009). Children are required to convert abstract ideas into visual representations in digital storytelling, which aids in their comprehension and retention of the subject matter. A student working on a digital story on the water cycle, for instance, might illustrate the steps with animated graphics or short videos. Children have a deeper comprehension of difficult concepts by producing or engaging with such visuals. As adolescents learn to manipulate and arrange visual elements to express a clear and correct message, this ability to visualise information also improves their problem-solving abilities.

8. SOCIAL DEVELOPMENT THROUGH DIGITAL STORYTELLING

8.1 Enhancing Communication Skills

A dynamic setting for improving written and spoken communication abilities is offered by digital storytelling. Through oral presentations and written narratives, children are encouraged to express their thoughts succinctly and precisely. Students must collaborate to create a coherent tale, discuss topic options, and share ideas with their classmates when working in groups. According to Banaszewski (2005), this improves both expressive and receptive communication abilities, which are essential for success in school and in social situations. Additionally, students are encouraged to use technology as a communication tool through digital storytelling, which is crucial in the modern digital world. They gain useful abilities in media literacy and digital communication as they learn how to use digital platforms.

8.2 Fostering Peer Relationships and Collaboration

A crucial component of many digital storytelling initiatives is collaboration. Youngsters must cooperate to create the story, exchange ideas, and settle disputes when working in groups. Important social skills including leadership, teamwork, and conflict resolution are developed through this cooperative process (Roth, 2017). Children learn to value many viewpoints, respect the contributions of others, and form wholesome peer connections as they collaborate to create digital stories. Children's social contact during collaborative digital storytelling also contributes to their sense of belonging and community. Children build relationships and fortify their social ties by telling their tales to their peers, which promotes a healthy classroom environment (Zhao, 2016).

9. 21ST CENTURY SKILLS AND DIGITAL LITERACY

9.1 Digital Literacy and Ethical Decision-Making

Children must acquire good digital literacy abilities in a world where digital media is taking over more and more. Children can learn how to use technology in an ethical and responsible way through digital storytelling. Children who use digital media develop their ability to navigate online spaces, respect intellectual property, and make thoughtful choices about the content they produce and distribute (Leu *et. al.*, 2011). Additionally, because kids are forced to think about how their stories may affect other people, digital storytelling promotes moral decision-making. Children are encouraged to think critically about the messages they convey through digital media by, for instance, reflecting on how their stories depict various cultures or societal issues.

9.2 Creativity and Innovation

Because digital storytelling allows kids to try out various media formats including audio, video, and animation, it also encourages creativity. As kids discover new ways to use technology to express their stories, this creative flexibility fosters creativity and problem-solving skills (Mayer, 2009). Additionally, children gain a sense of agency and self-assurance in their creative ability through the process of generating digital stories, which is essential for success in the twenty-first century.

10. CONCLUSION

Through the integration of social, emotional, and cognitive development into a single framework, digital storytelling provides a revolutionary approach to early childhood education. Digital storytelling promotes literacy, creativity, empathy, and critical thinking by fusing traditional storytelling with contemporary multimedia tools. In addition to teaching kids critical 21st century skills like computer literacy and moral decision-making, it gives them priceless chances for self-expression, teamwork, and emotional control. Even though digital storytelling has many advantages, further study is required to completely comprehend its long-term effects on children's development and to maximise its use in a variety of educational contexts.

With its integrative approach that integrates social, emotional, and cognitive development into a single framework, digital storytelling marks a paradigm change in educational approaches. Children are engaged in active, meaningful learning experiences through digital storytelling, in contrast to traditional pedagogical approaches that frequently emphasise rote learning. It not only revitalises the way children engage with narratives but also introduces them to a variety of skills essential to their overall development by fusing the age-old craft of storytelling with modern multimedia resources like animations, sounds, photos, and videos.

Fundamentally, digital storytelling promotes critical thinking and literacy. Children must carefully consider the tales they want to tell, arrange their ideas coherently, and successfully communicate those ideas using a mix of written, spoken, and visual components. This multimodal method accommodates a variety of learning styles while giving students the opportunity to practise critical communication skills. For example, visual and auditory learners can interact with the material in ways that suit them, making the learning process inclusive and accessible. Beyond literacy, digital storytelling fosters innovation and creativity by giving kids the flexibility to try out various media types to make their stories come to life. Digital storytelling is an effective means of self-expression and emotional control on an emotional level. It gives kids a secure environment in which to express their emotions, think back on their own experiences, and explore their feelings.

Children can gain greater emotional awareness and resilience, for example, by telling stories about conquering obstacles or illustrating situations that call for empathy. Children develop a deeper feeling of individuality and self-worth when they are given the opportunity to express their distinct viewpoints. Digital storytelling has potential advantages outside of the classroom. According to studies, it can enhance mental health by lowering stress and fostering emotional stability. A lifelong love of learning is fostered by the creative process of storytelling, which arouses curiosity and awe. It also makes studying interesting and pleasurable by bridging the gap between education and entertainment.

Digital storytelling does have some intriguing benefits, but there are drawbacks as well that need more research. For instance, little is known about this approach's long-term developmental effects. Further research is needed to answer questions about how digital storytelling impacts social relationships, memory retention, and attention spans in the digital age. In a similar vein, tailoring storytelling techniques to various socioeconomic, linguistic, and cultural contexts is essential to guaranteeing its broad appeal. To sum up, digital storytelling is a transformative medium that redefines how kids learn, express themselves, and engage with the world. It is more than just a teaching tool. The integration of cognitive, emotional, and social aspects of development gives kids the tools they need to prosper in a world that is becoming more interconnected and dynamic by the day. This strategy must be developed, modified, and improved upon by educators and researchers in order to reach its full potential and maintain its status as a pillar of holistic early childhood education.

REFERNCES

Banaszewski, T. (2005). The power of digital storytelling in the classroom. *Journal of Educational Multimedia and Hypermedia*, 14(3), 281–290.

Bergen, D. (2016). The role of story in emotional development: How storytelling fosters empathy and emotional regulation in children. *Early Childhood Education Journal*, 44(4), 361–367.

Chen, T.; Ou, J.; Li, G. and Luo, H. (2024). Promoting mental health in children and adolescents through digital technology: A systematic review and meta-analysis. *Frontiers in Psychology*, 15, Article 1356554.

Clarke, R. and Adam, A. (2012). Digital storytelling in Australia: Academic perspectives and reflections. *Arts and Humanities in Higher Education*, 11(1–2), 157–176.

Greenberg, M.T. and Abenavoli, R.M. (2017). Social and emotional learning in schools: From programs to strategies. *The Future of Children*, 27(1), 13–32.

Haven, K. (2007). Storyproof: The science behind the startling power of story. Pearson Education.

Hull, G.A. and Katz, M. (2006). Crafting an agentive self: Case studies of digital storytelling. *Research in the Teaching of English*, 41(1), 43–81.

Lambert, J. (2013). Digital storytelling: Capturing lives, creating community (4th ed.). New York, NY: *Routledge.*

Leu, D.J.; Kinzer, C.K.; Coiro, J.; Castek, J. and Henry, L.A. (2011). New literacies: A dual-level theory of the changing nature of literacy, instruction, and assessment. *Journal of Education*, 191(3), 1–18.

Mayer, R.E. (2009). Multimedia learning. *Cambridge University Press.*

Ohler, J. (2008). Digital storytelling in the classroom: New media pathways to literacy, learning, and creativity. *Thousand Oaks,* CA: Corwin Press.

Ribeiro, P. and Silva, J. (2021). Digital storytelling and the promotion of socio-emotional skills in primary school children. *Digital Education Review*, 39, 58–72.

Robin, B.R. (2008). Digital storytelling: A powerful technology tool for the 21st-century classroom. *Theory into Practiî*, 47(3), 220–228.

Robin, B.R. (2008). The educational uses of digital storytelling. *In Proceedings of the Society for Information Technology & Teacher Education International Conference* (pp. 709–716).

Robin, B.R. (2016). The power of digital storytelling to support teaching and learning. *Digital Education Review,* 30, 17–29.

Roth, B. (2017). Collaborative learning through digital storytelling in elementary education. *International Journal of Educational Technology in Higher Education, 14*(4), 227–245.

Sadik, A. (2008). Digital storytelling: A meaningful technology-integrated approach for engaged student learning. *Educational Technology Research and Development*, 56(4), 487–506.

Sanchez, J. and Khan, M. (2020). A digital storytelling approach to enhance empathy and foster global citizenship. *International Journal of Educational Technology in Higher Education*, 17(5), 1–15.

Smeda, N.; Dakich, E. and Sharda, N. (2014). The effectiveness of digital storytelling in the classrooms: A comprehensive study. *Smart Learning Environments*, 1(6), 1–21.

Zhao, Y. (2016). The impact of digital tools on the development of social and emotional learning. *Journal of Educational Psychology*, 108(2), 224–235.

Solar Air Heater Performance Using Various Artificially Roughened Components: A Review

Sunil Chaurasia[1] **and Sumit Chandak**[2]

ABSTRACT: Many researchers have carried out studies on artificially roughed solar radiation collection devices. Transfer of heat is well acquired by researchers experimentally and theoretically. The effects of different rib shapes on thermal hydraulic performance are studied by CFD analysis. Inclined, arc-shape, transverse, and V-shape ribs this type of rib are commonly use in SAH. These ribs are critically examined based on the developments in design resulting in increased performance Present growth of the topic authentically overviews by this review. This paper presents a study of the heat transfer rate through different roughness that occur on the hot wall of a SAH.

Keywords: *Fluid Flow, Friction Factor, Heat Transfer, Non-Conventional Energy, Thermo-hydraulic Performance.*

1. INTRODUCTION

In the coming times, human dependence on non-conventional energy sources such as solar energy, tidal energy, wind etc. will increase, because non-renewable energy sources such as coal and petroleum are getting depleted rapidly. Non-renewable based devices have high efficiency as the energy is in concentrated form. On the other side, renewable-based devices, such as solar air heaters, have low alternation efficiency as energy is available in the prevalent form. Solar energy can be seen as a source of energy in future devices because it is a never-ending energy (Hani *et. al.,* 2023).

Solar air heaters use thermal energy to heat air using flat plate collectors is shown in Figure 1. The sun's radiation energy is transferred to the air flowing inside the duct through the thermal energy absorbing surface. This hot air can be used for various useful purposes like drying crops, heating cold places etc. However, Heat transfer is not good between the air and the absorber plate. Through various efforts researchers have improved the heat transfer from the absorber plate. Among all these ways to further improve the performance of this device, rib-roughing on the plate of absorber is the widely used approach (Borah *et. al.,* 2023).

[1] Research Scholar, Department of Mechanical Engineering, Shri Vaishnav Vidyapeeth Vishwavidyalaya, Indore, India. E-mail: sunilchaurasia@svvv.edu.in

[2] Associate Professor, Department of Mechanical Engineering, Shri Vaishnav Vidyapeeth Vishwavidyalaya, Indore, India.

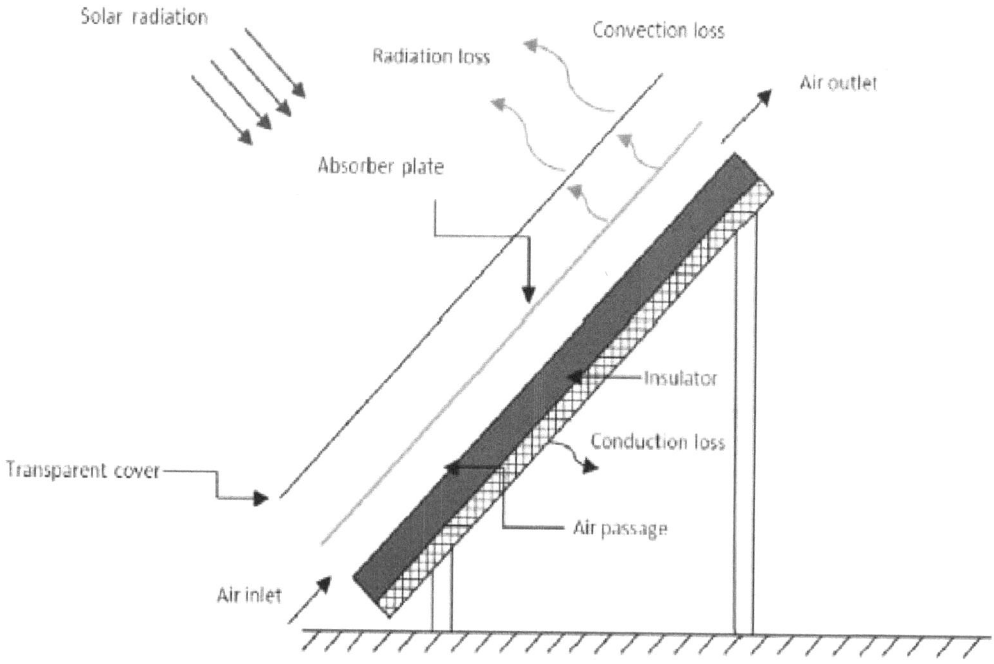

Figure 1: Solar Air Heater Model (Hiwa *et. al.,* 2023).

2. PERFORMANCE OF SOLAR COLLECTOR

Thermal Performance

Heat transfer between the absorber surface and the working medium in SAH is by convective heat transfer Figure 1. In traditional SAH channel η thermal is lower because the convective heat transfer coefficient is low caused by at the heated surface creation of a laminar sublayer. In other words, η thermal is used to presumption of thermal performance (Yadav *et. al.,* 2023).

$$Qu = A_P F_R [I (\tau\alpha)_e - U_L (T_i - T_o)]$$

Nomenclature

Qu	useful heat gain, W
A_P	area of heated surface, mm^2
F_R	factor of heat removal for collector
I	solar intensity, W/mm^2
$(\tau\alpha)_e$	effective transmittance-absorptance
U_L	overall heat loss coefficient, W/mm^2 K
T_o	temp of air at the outlet, K
T_i	temp of fluid at the entrance, K

3. EARLY STUDIES TO IMPROVE PERFORMANCE OF A SAH

SAH-Configuration	*Boundary-Conditions and Results*
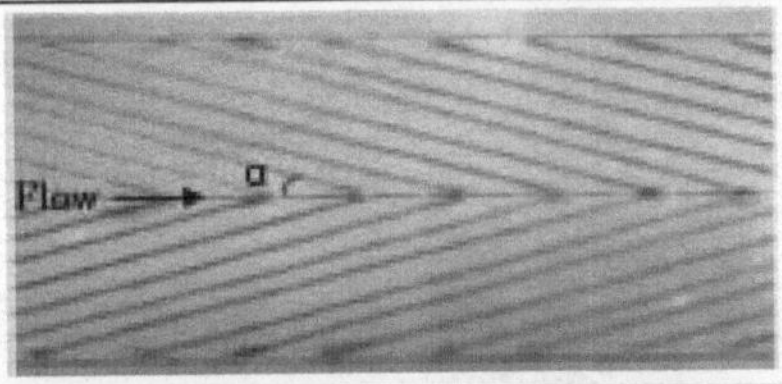	Hani *et. al.,* (2023) (wire-roughened absorber plate) The use of a surface roughness pattern consisting of artificial wires arranged in a V-shape enables improved heat transfer within the SAH.
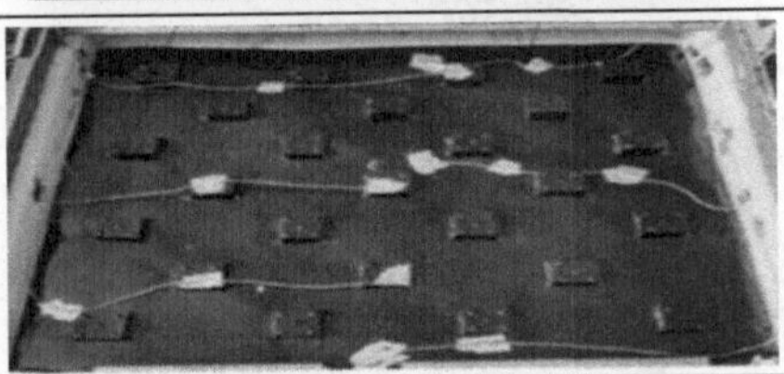	Partha *et. al.,* (2023) (square obstacles with threaded pin fins). The maximum enhancement in efficiency value is obtained as 31.62% for the collector tilt angle of 30◦ and flow rate of 0.0094 kg/s
	Jamal-Eddine *et. al.,* (2023) As the number of ribs increases, the number of primary vortices increases, while the strength of the primary vortices, the pitch of the primary vortices, and the length of the redeveloped inter-rib thermal layer decrease.
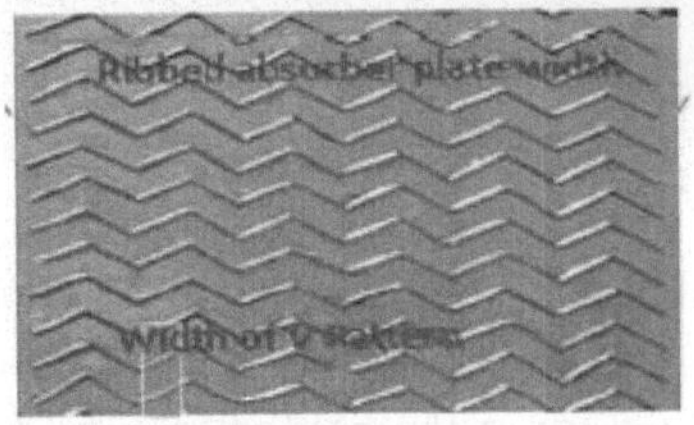	Amitesh *et. al.,* (2023) Based on experimental trials presented in this article, there is a considerable enhancement in Nu and f in the rectangular duct with multi-V-shaped ribbed impinging air jet solar heater compared to conventional SAH.
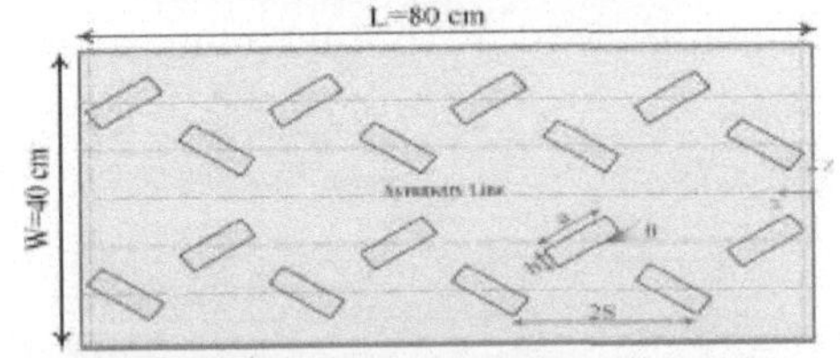	Parsa *et. al.,* (2021) The thermo-hydraulic performance factor of the proposed baffled is up to 17.5% better compared with the performance of the best design reported in the literature.
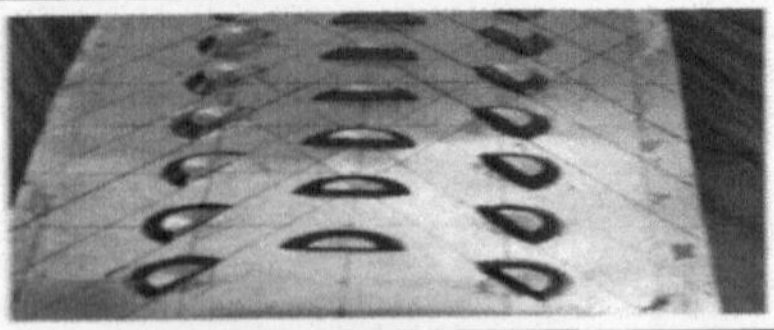	Bezbaruah *et. al.,* (2021) The performance is evaluated for an appropriate range of Reynolds number (3500–16000)
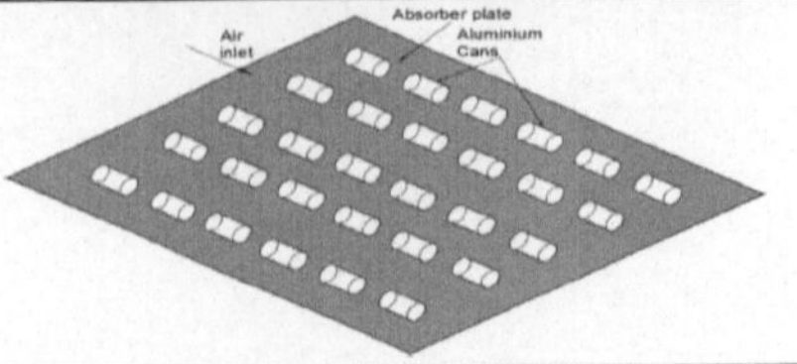	Arun *et. al.,* (2020) Finally concluding remarks and the future scope for additional enhancement in the performance of solar air heater is proposed.

	Rajesh *et. al.,* (2016) Author obtained Nu 3.6 times to the smooth duct.
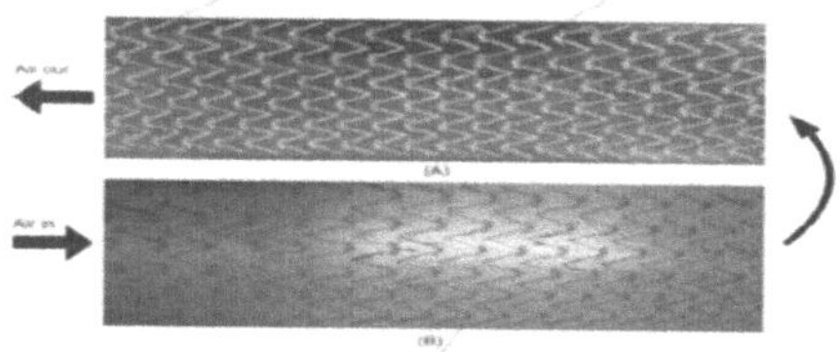	Kant *et. al.,* (2016) Based on the investigation, it is observed that heat transfer rate has found to be increased significantly through a double pass channel of a SAH.
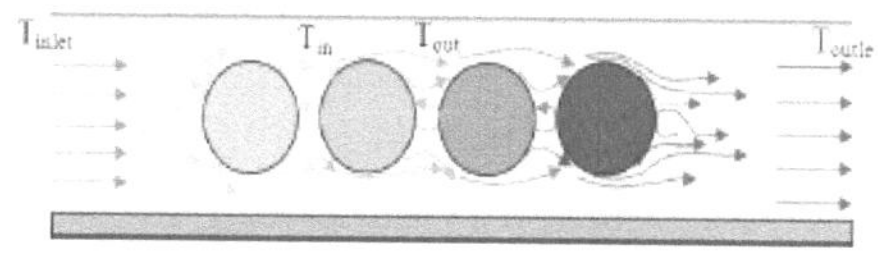	Alkilani *et. al.,* (2011) Author found paraffin wax-aluminium composite best.

Figure 2: SAH-Configuration

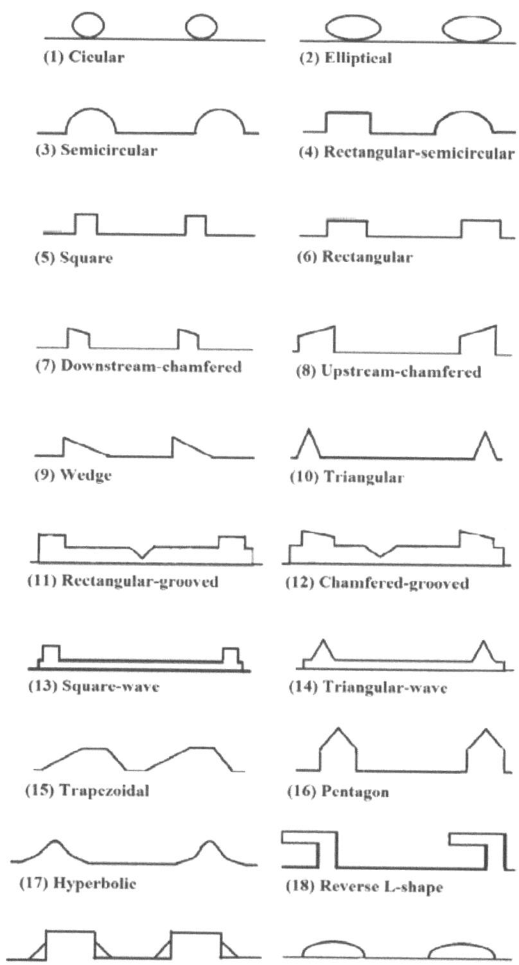

Figure 3: All Possible Cross-Sections Studied in Literature

4. CONCLUSION

Performance parameters as Friction Factor and Nusselt Number of rib-roughened air channel have been investigated. The following conclusions are listed below:

1. V-pattern dimpled rib, grooves in V-pattern rib, protrusion rib and V-pattern rib on the heated wall is a good technique to increase the heat transfer.
2. Various forms of roughening such as adding wire ribs of small diameter, machining of ribs in different shapes, wire-mesh, and creation of dimples etc. have been investigated for performance enhancement in SAH.
3. Constant pumping power is used to improve the roughness and flow parameters on the rib-roughness. So as to find the optimum V-pattern rib arrangement, by managing the pressure loss penalty and heat transfer rate.
4. Heat transfer is enhanced by managing vortices upstream and downstream by dimpled ribs and protrusion ribs. Local wall turbulence is enhanced by secondary flow, roughness angle, conducting heads which leads to improved heat transfer.
5. The V-pattern dimpled rib has long angled rib and inclined rib with protrusion rib which helps in formation of secondary flow cells give a higher heat transfer. Improvement in heat transfer can be achieved by creating turbulence in the fluid by creating grooves in the V-pattern ribs.

REFERENCES

Bezbaruah, P.J.; Das, R.S. and Sarkar, B.K. (2021). Experimental and numerical analysis of solar air heater accoutered with modified conical vortex generators in a staggered fashion. *Science Direct, Renewable Energy* (180) 109–131.

Borah, P.P. and Pathak, K.K. (2023). Experimental study of a solar air heater with modified absorber plate through square obstacles with threaded pin fins. *Science Direct, Applied Thermal Engineering* (228) 120544.

Chhaparwal, G.K.; Srivastava, A. and Dayal, R. (2019). Artificial repeated-rib roughness in a solar air heater – A review. *Science Direct, Solar Energy* (194) 329–359.

El-Sebaii, A.A.; Aboul-Enein, S.; Ramadan, M.R.I.; Shalaby, S.M. and Moharram, B.M. (2011). Investigation of thermal performance of-double pass-flat and v-corrugated plate solar air heaters. *Science Direct, Energy* (36) 1076–1086.

Hani, A. and Abdulmohsen, O.A. (2023). Heat transfer and air flow friction in solar air heaters: A comprehensive computational and experimental investigation with wire-roughened absorber plate. *Science Direct Case Studies in Thermal Engineering* (48) 103148.

Hiwa, A.M. and Mohammad, S. (2023). Hybrid thermal and optical modeling of a solar air heater with a non-flat plate absorber. *ScienceDirect, Energy Reports* (9) 6102–6113.

Jamal-Eddine, S. and Ahmed, A.M. (2023). Three-dimensional analysis of a novel solar air heater conception, for an improved heat transfer and energy conversion. *ScienceDirect, Energy Conversion and Management* X (19) 100386.

Kant, R. and Saini, R.P. (2016). Experimental investigation on performance of a double pass artificial roughened solar air heater duct having roughness elements of the combination of discrete multi-V shaped and staggered ribs. *Science Direct, Energy* (116) 507–516.

Kumar, H.S.A.; Karanth, K.V. and Kumar, S. (2020). Review on the design modifications of a solar air heater for improvement in the thermal performance. *Science Direct, Sustainable Energy Technologies and Assessments* (39) 100685, 1–18.

Mahmud, M.A.; Kamaruzzaman, S. and Sohif, M. (2011). Fabrication and Experimental Investigation of PCM Capsules Integrated in Solar Air Heater. *American Journal of Environmental Sciences* (7) 542–546.

Maithani, R. and Saini, J.S. (2016). Heat transfer and friction factor correlations for a solar air heater duct roughened artificially with V-ribs with symmetrical gaps. *Science Direct, Experimental Thermal and Fluid Science* (70) 220–227.

Nidhul, K.; Yadav, A.K.; Anish, S. and Kumar, S. (2021). Critical review of ribbed solar air heater and performance evaluation of various V-rib configuration. *Science Direct, Renewable and Sustainable Energy Reviews* (142) 110871, 1–20.

Parsa, H.; Saffar-Avval, M. and Hajmohammadi, M.R. (2021). 3D simulation and parametric optimization of a solar air heater with a novel staggered cuboid baffles. *Science Direct, International Journal of Mechanical Sciences* (205) 106607, 1–16.

Sharma, A. and Thakur, S. (2023). An integrated active-passive solution for strengthening the functionality of a solar air heater. *Taylor and Francis, Energy Sources, Part A: Recovery, Utilization, and Environmental Effects* (45) 1–17.

Yadav, A.K. and Choudhary, M. (2023). Assessment of solar air heater performance using a variety of artificiallyroughened components. *ScienceDirect, Materials Today: Proceedings (Proceedings).*

A Survey on Intrusion Detection System in IoT Environment using Deep Learning

Bhagyashri B. Kotame[1] and Jigyasu Dubey[2]

ABSTRACT: Cyberattacks frequently cause network data to leak, therefore safeguarding this information is essential. Intrusion Detection Systems (IDS) are designed to find weaknesses that exploit a target computer, network, or application. When the IDS monitoring system discovers harmful behavior, it issues alerts. It also detects suspicious activities. Internet of Things is a network of interconnected devices that exchange data and communicate with one another. IoT devices, which are embedded with sensors and software, can include digital and industrial machinery in addition to consumer goods. Many different industries and businesses are using Internet of Things (IoT) to increase productivity, improve customer service, make better decisions, and increase the value of their business. Without the need for human intervention, data can be transferred over a network thanks to IoT. It also has a significant impact on smart agriculture, smart cities, and smart homes. Intrusion detection systems must be developed for the IoT environment because a significant amount of data is transmitted to end users via IoT devices. As IoT applications have grown, there has been a significant increase in network data and a high computing complexity across all of the connected devices. The information contained in IoT devices is valuable and enables individuals or industries to make important decisions that impact their daily lives. Numerous IoT devices are limited in terms of memory, CPU speed, and energy storage capacity. Because these devices are unable to run current general-purpose security software, they are susceptible to cyberattacks. To target the IoT ecosystem, attackers develop attacks and transmit data via IoT sensor devices. Several deep learning models are created and implemented to identify intrusion behavior in the IoT environment. This survey article describes the data sets used in the Internet of Things (IoT) environment for the deep supervised and unsupervised learning model and the intrusion detection system.

Keywords: *Cyberattacks, Ecosystem, Productivity, Sensor Devices, Unsupervised Learning Model.*

1. INTRODUCTION

With the emergence of Industry 4.0, the integration of intelligent IoT sensors is now required to maintain the newest enterprise environment functioning properly. Rapid improvements in communication technology have made it possible to extend networks' reach from persons to objects. IoT devices have become more and more popular in recent years because of their enticing connectivity, communication, and decision-making

[1] Research Scholar, Department of Information Technology, Shri Vaishnav Vidyapeeth Vishwavidyalaya, Indore, India. E-mail: bhagyashrikotame@gmail.com

[2] Professor, Department of Information Technology, Shri Vaishnav Vidyapeeth Vishwavidyalaya, Indore, India.

capabilities. Technical improvement has prompted the novel gradient making unmistakable products learned in Internet of Things (IoT). It fills as an insight to expand the quantity of actual products, used in regular routines into computerized overlap making the unmistakable articles around in an ecosphere of data. The IoT has purchased all demonstrations of help to be delivered at doorsteps giving superior client support whenever, for anyone, from any place (Mehedi *et. al.*, 2024).

On the embedded platform, an enabling innovation erodes the connection between the entire set of truly seen items and the internet. This would imply that the Internet of Things would be powered by a vast number of internet-enabled devices. IoT is used to find, control, and provide the necessary solutions for the needs or advancements of the internet-enabled real world. The sensors are made visible as a component of the Internet of Things throughout the process of assembling the data through detection. In order to monitor the ongoing changes in the real world, Wireless Sensor Networks (WSNs) are a collection of highly sensitive detection components along with communication, computation, actuation, and power-accumulating devices. These wirelessly empathetic sensor groups have several advantages, such as low cost, low power consumption, high adaptability to harsh and unresponsive environments, controlling the cost of being connected to the Internet of Things to become a part of it, and the ability to track real changes in internet-enabled objects. In addition to using more energy, traditional methods of establishing the foundation between WSNs and the Internet of Things are more likely to result in delays, network lifespan, and bundle conveyance (Raj & Basar, 2019).

An intrusion detection system (IDS), a hardware/software protection architecture, is designed to alert managers to any anomalous activity on computers or networks. Intrusion Prevention Systems (IPS) are a type of system that can try to prevent interruptions and block any threats. Organisations should be mindful, though, that false positives from an IPS can prevent real action. Based on its scope, an IDS can be categorised as host-based, network-based, or hybrid. Host-based Intrusion Detection Systems (HIDS) scan and keep an eye on computer systems, including operating system audit logs, application logs, and important framework documents, for possibly suspicious activity. Network-based intrusion detection systems (NIDS) monitor the network for suspicious behaviour and alert users to any major issues or other concerns (Paxson, 1999; Roesh, 1999). By employing the hybrid technique, an IDS may differentiate between threats originating from both host and organisation sources. Anomaly-based strategies and abuse signature-based detection are the two categories into which an intrusion detection system's detection techniques fall. Before employing the signature-based approach, install an antivirus program that can recognise patterns, or signatures. For attacks that are already being perceived, this kind of discovery has a high degree of accuracy and a low false positive rate; nevertheless, without an example, it can be difficult to detect new attacks.

The anomaly-based approach compares the new traffic design to either a class of anomalous exercises developed using processes such as machine learning or a model of normal and abnormal workouts to detect hidden assaults. The disadvantages of this approach include a longer detection time for abnormalities and a higher false positive rate. Anomaly-based interruption identification shows more promise than host-based attacks in identifying network attacks, according to the scattered academic literature that is still in existence (Atefinia & Ahmadi, 2021).

Machine learning and information mining have been widely and successfully applied in a variety of situations where training data may be obtained to predict future outcomes

(Weiss, 2016). Nonetheless, a lot of machine learning techniques work effectively when it is assumed that there are no testing or preparation data in the highlight space or comparison probability distribution function. When this probability distribution function shifts, it is anticipated that the majority of the models will have to be rebuilt from the ground up utilising freshly created and merged data. In many situations, it is either impractical or expensive to review the useful preparation information to change the models. In these circumstances, knowledge sharing or transfer learning between the many fields would be required.

By shifting the important boundaries, transfer learning is utilised to enhance a classifier's performance from one space to another (Agarwal *et. al.,* 2021). Models based on deep transfer learning, which addressed a number of nonlinear issues, may show to be a promising technique in order to create a dependable IDS for the IoT environment, especially given the rapid development of IoT companies and the emergence of new threat kinds. A more robust security framework is required for heterogeneous IoT applications, particularly in light of Industry 4.0. A reliable interruption detection framework is therefore necessary to detect hostile movement within any heterogeneous IoT network. The steadiness execution assessment includes highlights of competencies, flexibility, and accessibility. How effectively an IDS model works with less computer complexity and how frequently it is available determine its efficiency. Similarly, scalability refers to the ability to handle additional data streams from a wider range of IoT devices.

2. REVIEW OF LITERATURE

Finding out more about the use of ML and DL for intrusion detection, specifically in IoT devices, was the aim of the literature review. This section examines the various methods currently in use for IoT intrusion detection. Mehedi *et. al.,* (2024) developed a dependable intrusion detection system on the basis of deep transfer learning together with enhanced performance in contrast with various other prevailing techniques. The first step of this system was pre-processing of data, which has two steps, namely cleaning and integration of data. Then, the data was transformed for achieving more effective resultant practices as well as understanding the patterns simply. The validation and training data from the current datasets were combined into a single dataset using a Python script. At last, the attack instances were classified within several heterogeneous IoT networks. This approach had the ability to classify the normal and abnormal attack situations precisely devoid of any form of malfunction or experience an action of renovation that kept the accessibility. Additionally, this method improved the scalability characteristics by incorporating multiple diverse and dependable data sources from a huge range of Internet of Things sensors into the training dataset with the highest stability.

Shahrzad *et. al.,* (2024) proposed three methods for anomaly detection with five IoT datasets ML, one DL, and five One-Class Classification. They found that supervised ML and DL methods proved superior performance, while some OCC methods exhibit bit less performance. Their research found that the Decision Tree proves most accurate algorithm among all, and Deep Robust One Class Classification and Local Outlier Factor also proves as the most accurate and consistent One-Class Classification. Decision Tree is the fastest among all methods, while DROCC and LOF are the second and third fastest among OCCs in terms of Execution time. In order to improve the prediction accuracy of IDS in IoT networks, Hamza *et. al.,* (2024) suggested a study that starts with a thorough analysis of multiple machine learning algorithms. They apply models and evaluate their efficacy using the ToN-IoT dataset. The results demonstrate the superior performance of ensemble methods, especially Random Forest and XGBoost, highlighting their potential for use in protecting IoT ecosystems from malevolent intrusions.

The architecture of an intrusion detection system for streaming data analysis is presented by (Souad *et. al.,* 2023). They used Apache Spark to develop our IDS and implemented it in a fog computing architecture. The outcomes of their application of various machine-learning algorithms to the NF-ToN-IoT-v2 dataset were encouraging. A methodology proposed by (Raj & Basar, 2019) combines neural network clustering with a simple fuzzy rule-based system backed by shortest-path finding to guarantee route entrenchment with lower power consumption and better QOS metrics. A performance analysis was conducted regarding the energy usage and packet delivery ratio, sensor network lifetime, and latency in order to show off its faultless functioning. Paxson *et. al.,* (1999) presented a standalone system BRO for passively observing a network link through which the intruder's traffic travels in order to detect network intruders in real-time. The design of the system placed a strong emphasis on real-time notification, high-speed (FDDI- rate) monitoring, and extensibility. A "policy script interpreter" decodes event handlers written in a specific language used to represent a site's security policy, and a "event engine" that breaks down a stream of kernel-filtered network data into a sequence of higher-level events. The four integrated programs, Finger, FTP, Port mapper, and Telnet, were analyzed by the proposed system.

When monitoring small TCP/IP networks to look for signs of attacks, Roesch *et. al.,* (1999) developed a packet sniffer and logger called snort for lightweight intrusion detection for the networks. They discussed a use case for this system as a component of integrated network security. It is a highly capable, compact, and adaptable system for both small and large networks. Atefinia & Ahmadi (2021) presented a multi-architectural modular deep neural network model in an attempt to lower the number of intrusion detection systems that mistakenly identify intrusions based on anomalies. The two recurrent modules, feed-forward module, stack of restricted Boltzmann machine modules, aggregator module that receives these modules' output weights, and module that outputs the model's result make up the proposed model. The CSE-CIC-IDS2018 dataset was used to test the model, and the results suggest that the model could be used in an IDS to thwart new attacks or generate alerts. The experimental results showed an improvement with up to 100% accuracy in detecting different types of network attacks compared to similar research. Transfer learning has essentially been surveyed (Weiss *et. al.,* 2016). Information on recent solutions is provided, and applications used for transfer learning are reviewed. The terms "hybrid based transfer learning", "parameter based transfer learning", "relational based transfer learning", "asymmetric features based transfer learning", and "homogeneous transfer learning" are defined.

Agrawal *et. al.,* (2021) recognized the need that for training data as well as testing data there is need to build high-performance classifiers. Deep learning is useful when enough data is not available in target domain, but large data set is available in source domain. Transfer learning along with its categorization is explained and some examples and perspective in association of transfer learning has been provided. Negative transfer learning along with its effects on accomplishment of learning in target domain has been explained. Chen *et. al.,* (2010) proposed an efficient filtering scheme to filter the traffic packets insteadof processing all the traffic packets which also leads to reduce the systems workload. Accordingly, Lightweight Network Intrusion Detection (LNID) is efficient on data detection and workload reduction.

Hoz *et. al.,* (2015) proposed a classification strategy for anomaly detection that combines statistical methods with SON. For feature selection and noise reduction, Principal Component Analysis (PCA) and Fisher Discriminant Ratio (FDR) were employed. To differentiate between the normal and anomalous connection they used probabilistic self-organized maps PSOM. By modifying the unit's activations probabilities detection capabilities of the system can be modified. Al-Yaseen, *et. al*., (2017) developed multilevel hybrid intrusion detection model that makes use of super vector machines and extreme learning machines to increase the effectiveness of identifying both known and unknown threats. The K-means algorithm was modified and used to create a training data set of superior quality. The K-means algorithm was altered. Kevric *et. al.,* (2017) created a combining classifier model using tree-based algorithms to detect network intrusions. To evaluate the performance NSL-KDD dataset was used. 41 features were used to classify weather incoming traffic is attack or normal. They used combination of random tree and NB Trees algorithm, and detection accuracy of 89.24% was achieved.

3. INTRUSION DETECTION SYSTEM

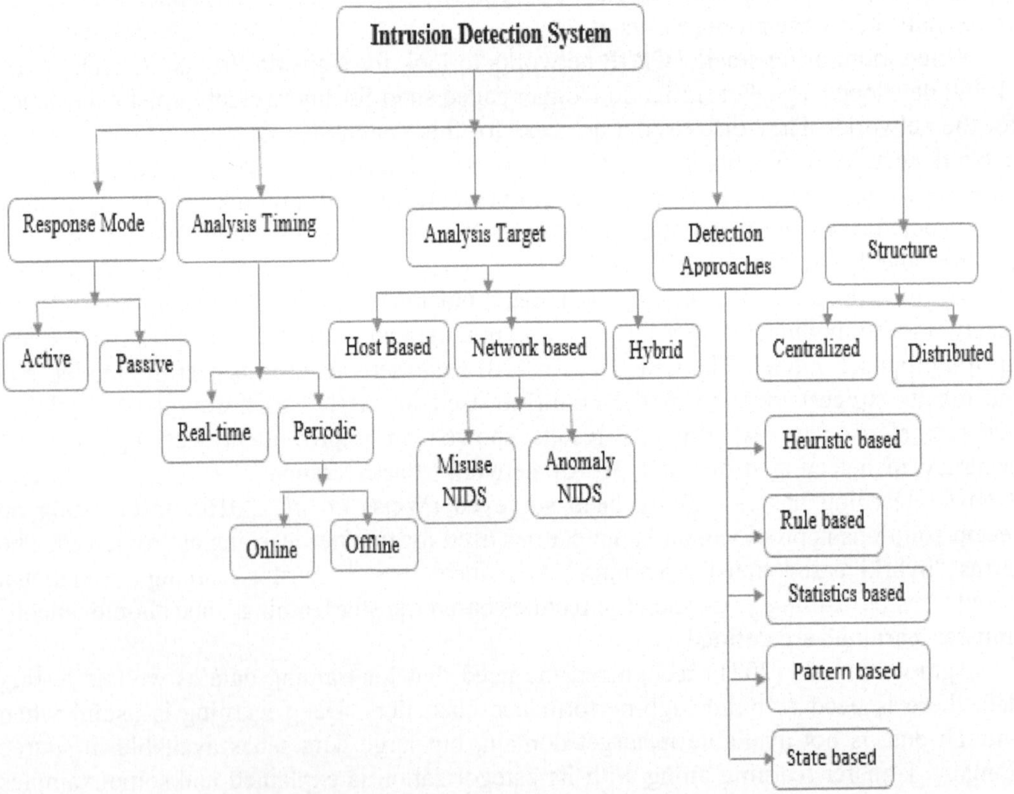

Figure 1: An Intrusion Detection System IDS

Figure 1 shows the generic structure for intrusion detection. Network traffic is monitored by Intrusion Detection Systems (IDS) to look for malicious transactions, and when they are found, they quickly send out notifications. Software called as an intrusion detection system looks for malicious activities on a network or system. Every violation or unlawful activity is regularly monitored centrally by the system or reported to the management. It guards against unauthorised access from internal users and intruders and keeps an eye out for questionable activity on a network or system. It gives a brief view of how the IDS works. The IDS is basically classified into five categories: Response mode, Analysis Timing, Analysis target, Detection Approach and the structure.

3.1 Response Mode

When the assault is detected, the IDS reacts, and it may do so passively or actively. While a passive response is static and only involves logging and informing staff, an active response that blocks the attack may alter the environment:

- **Active IDS**. Active intrusion detection systems log and alert staff, but they can also alter the environment to stop or block an attack. It can alter firewalls' access control lists (ACLs) in order to stop malicious traffic, terminate processes on a system that were the source of the attack, or redirect the attack to a secure location like a honeynet or honeypot.
- **Passive IDS**. An alert can be raised, and the attack is recorded by a passive intrusion detection system. A large number of IDSs are passive by default. Emails, texts, pop-up windows, and notifications on a central monitor are just a few of the various formats it might take.

3.2 Analysis Timing

Real-time IDS is the moment an attacker tries to attack the network or a system and finding or reporting the malicious activity at that time.

- **Offline IDS**. It detects any attack analyses pre-logged data.
- **Online IDS**. In addition to utilising continuously updated new data, online intrusion detection systems (IDS) are offline intrusion detection systems that examine previously logged data to identify intrusions.

3.3 Analysis Target

Host Based IDS. As shown in Figure 2 Host-based intrusion detection systems monitor network traffic flow, incoming TCP connection attempts, login credentials, and resource usage, including CPU, memory, and RAM. Additionally, it identifies harmful communication coming from the host itself in the event that the host is infected with malware and trying to spread to other systems.

Network Intrusion Detection System (NIDS). Installing a network intrusion detection system allows it to monitor all traffic, both inbound and outbound, to and from every device on the network as given by Figure 3. It keeps an eye on the overall network's patterns or behaviours.

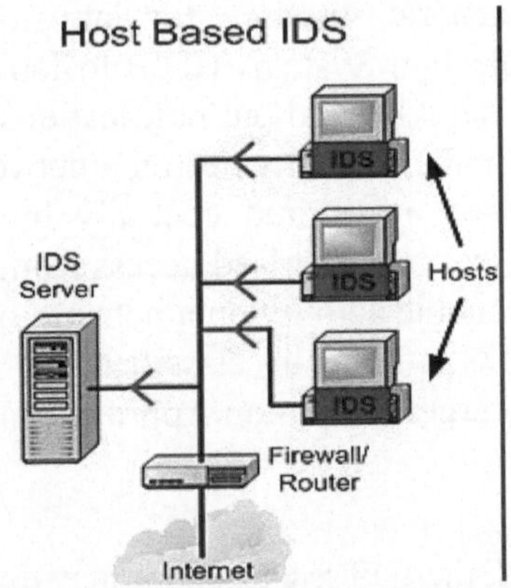

Figure 2: Host Based IDS (Othman *et. al.*, 2018)

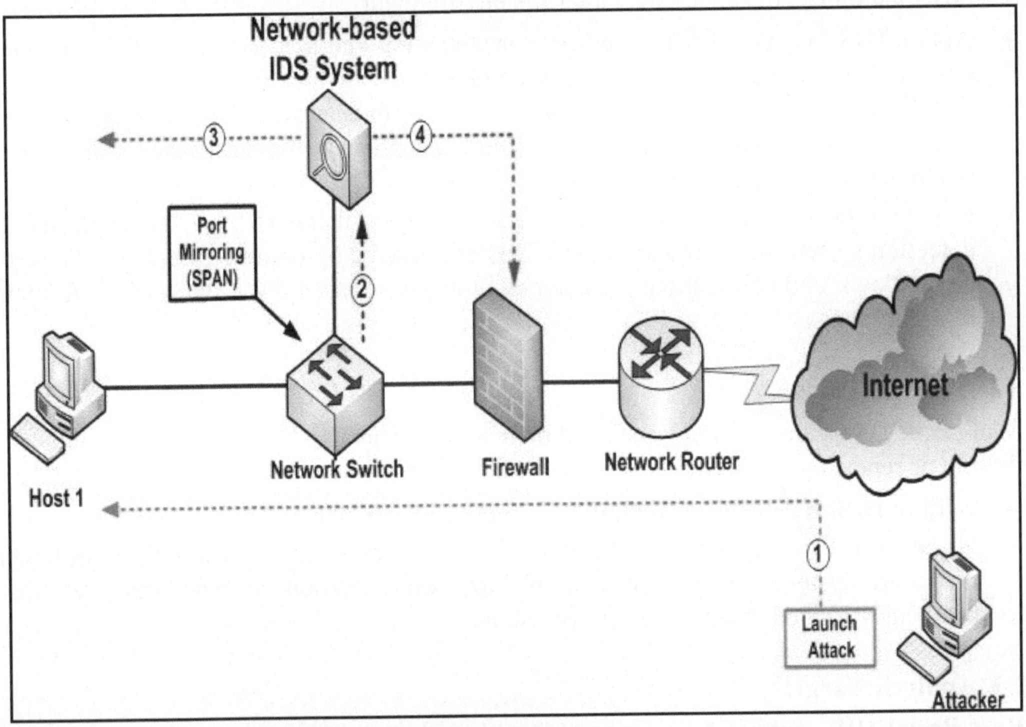

Figure 3: Network Based IDS (Othman *et. al.*, 2018)

Hybrid IDS merges two or more NIDS that are specification-based, anomaly-based, or signature-based into a single system given by Figure 4. It minimises its shortcomings while maximising the benefits of the two methods used together. This approach combines both specification-based and signature-based approaches to achieve their benefits and to remove the false alarm rate associated with anomaly-based detection.

Two Categories

- **Sequence-based:** In this case, an alternative technique is used after applying anomaly or misuse detection.

- **Parallel-based:** In this case, several detectors are used concurrently, and several output sources are used to make the final decision.

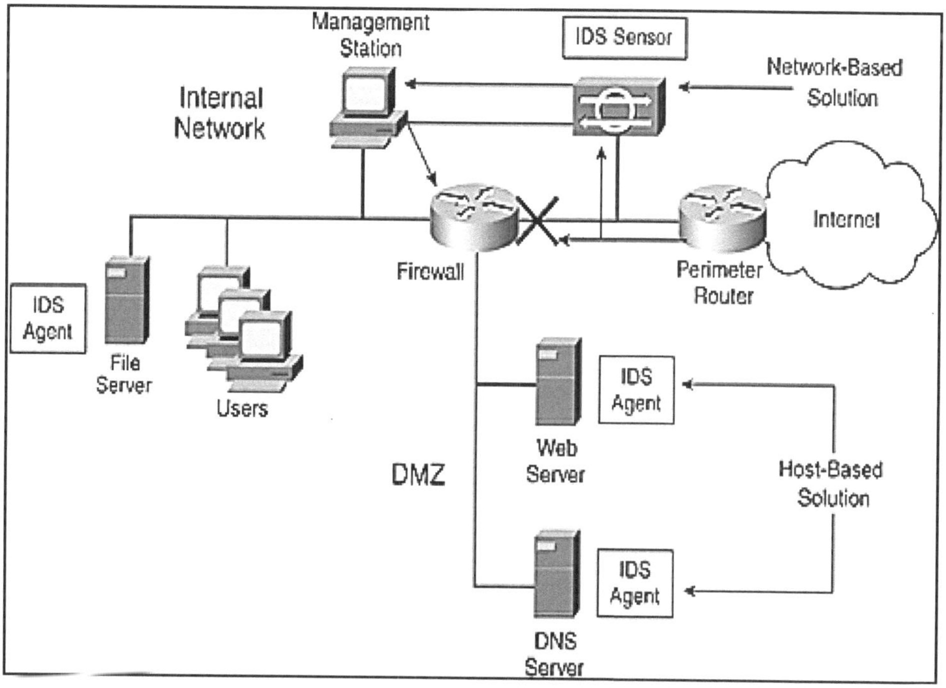

Figure 4: Hybrid or Mixed IDS (Othman *et. al.*, 2018)

3.4 Detection Approaches

- **Heuristic based IDS**. A system that can brilliantly inspect for malicious behaviour from a program inside the system, or outsider trying to access the system.
- **Rule-based** techniques apply set of rules to detect whether given pattern of activity is normal or suspicious, it observes the events within the system. It can characterize approaches like anomaly detection or penetration identification, Rule-based anomaly detection and statistical anomaly detection are similar in their approach.
- **A Statistics based IDS**. In order to identify low-probability events and categorise them as potential intrusions, a statistics-based intrusion detection system first develops a unique distribution model for a typical behaviour profile. The main factors taken into account by statistical intrusion detection systems include statistical metrics such as the mean, mode, median, and standard deviation of packets. Instead of analysing data traffic, each packet is recorded, indicating the fingerprint of the flow. Statistical IDS are used to identify any deviations from the norm in the present behaviour.
- **Pattern based IDS**. The five modules that make up the pattern-based Intrusion Detection System are the capture, decode, detection, known attack pattern, and action modules. An Intrusion Detection System that using patterns tracks network packets and compares them to a database of known malicious threat attack patterns.
- **State-based IDSs** either determine the typical behaviour of the Cyber Physical System or work similarly to rule-based techniques. These techniques, like rule-based

techniques, are unable to directly counteract attacks that cause odd transitions or time intervals.

3.5 Structure

- **Centralized IDS**. Data is analysed in a set of independent monitored hosts and locations by centralized intrusion detection systems (Modi *et. al.,* 2013). Here, the security application is keeping an eye on the network's data packet delivery rate and control packet overhead. When the application notices a change among the semetrics' statistical characteristics, it considers the network to be under attack. In contrast to a distributed system, the maintenance and administration costs for the Centralized IDS are lower. The main console was in charge of each and every IDS activity is direct.
- **Distributed IDS**. Network monitoring is made possible by distributed IDS, which consists of several IDS that exchange messages with one another and/or a central server and detects Denial-of-Service (DoS) attacks on fast networks (Figure 5) (Modi *et. al.,* 2013).

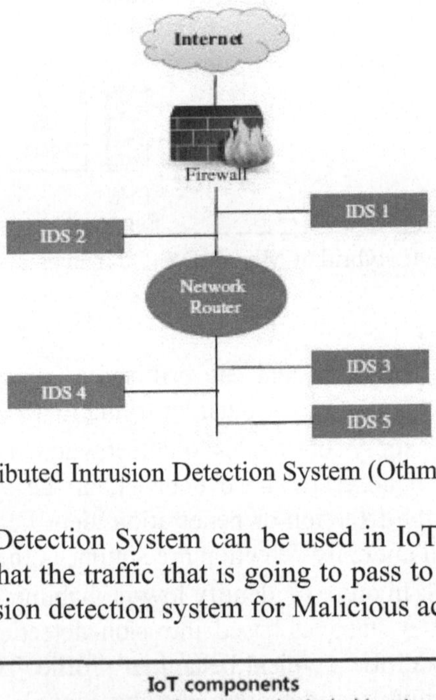

Figure 5: Distributed Intrusion Detection System (Othman *et. al.,* 2018)

The above Intrusion Detection System can be used in IoT environment with proper Interaction or linking so that the traffic that is going to pass to and from IoT devices can be monitored by the Intrusion detection system for Malicious activities.

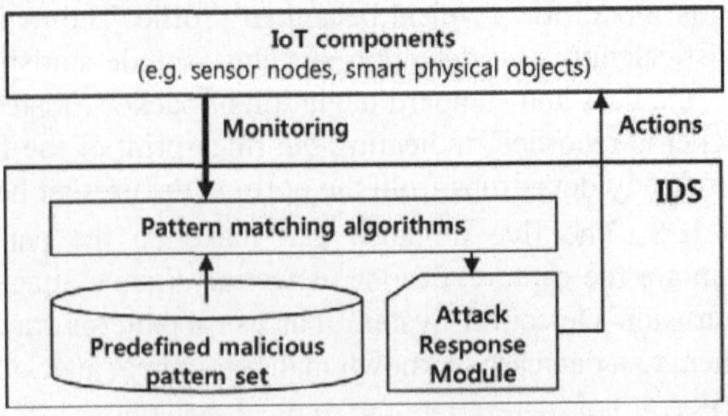

Figure 6: Intrusion Detection in IoT

Figure 6 shows that the entire IDS Module is providing the security to the IoT module. Monitoring of the traffic to and from the IoT devices is done by IDS and the action i.e., whether the traffic is genuine or it is a request from attacker, some malicious activity is send back to the IoT device.

4. PROPOSED SYSTEM

For better IoT intrusion detection, feature normalisation techniques and cluster head selection must be optimised. The following methods can be used to implement the Intrusion Detection Technique for Internet of Things devices.

- **Cluster head selection and routing:** Cluster head selection and base station routing should be performed using the new optimisation algorithm. Several cluster head selection algorithms will be studied before the new optimisation algorithm is proposed.
- **Intrusion detection at base station:** The intrusion detection should be performed at the base station as follows. At the beginning, the data will be collected and is fed to the next stage.
- **Feature normalization:** Feature normalization should be performed by using some standard normalization technique for normalizing the feature which gives the best results.

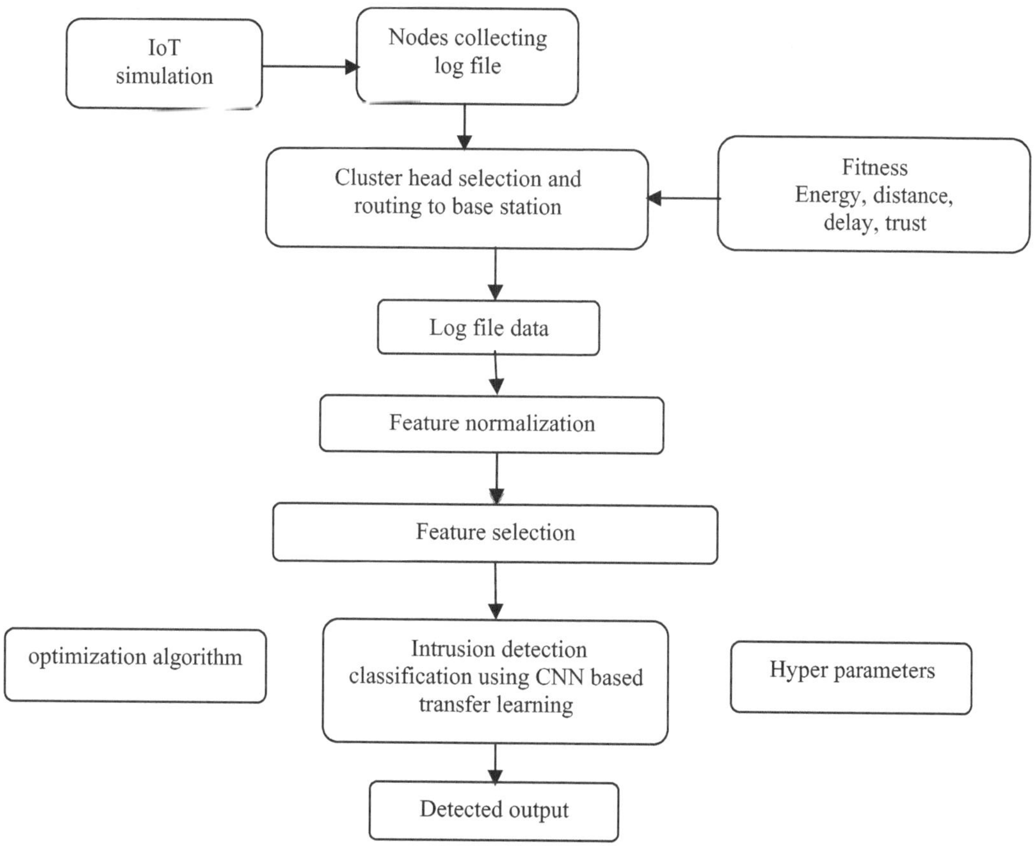

Figure 7: Proposed System Architecture

- **Feature selection:** Consequently, feature selection should be performed wherein most important features will be extracted by using the distances, and some feature selection technique.
- **Intrusion detection:** Intrusion detection can be performed using Convolution Neural Network (CNN)/Recurrent Neural Network (RNN) with transfer learning where CNN will be used with the hyper parameters from trained models (Al-Yaseen *et. al.,* 2017).

6. CONCLUSION

IoT devices have gained popularity in the past few years due to their enticing features for communication, decision-making, and connectivity. The intrusion detection technology is one important technique that has become a challenging topic in the study of IoT security. The security issues surrounding IoT have drawn more attention to the need to ensure network security. This study presents a novel optimisation algorithm for network traffic identification in the Internet of Things environment. At first, the IoT will be simulating, then the nodes will collect log file. After that, there will be a cluster head selection and routing to the base station. Finally, the CNN will be used with the hyper parameters from trained models. This model will be using the characteristics of the new optimization algorithm to be able to achieve better performance. The energy, precision, recall, and F-measure metrics of this work will be measured, and the suggested method's performance will be contrasted with that of the current approaches.

REFERENCES

Agarwal, N.; Sondhi, A.; Chopra, K. and Singh, G. (2021). Transfer learning: Survey and classification. *Smart Innovations in Communication and Computational Sciences*, 145–155.

Al-Yaseen, W.L.; Othman, Z.A. and Nazri, M.Z.A. (2017). Multi-level hybrid support vector machine and extreme learning machine based on modified K-means for intrusion detection system. *Expert Systems with Applications, 67*, 296–303.

Atefinia, R. and Ahmadi, M. (2021). Network intrusion detection using multi-architectural modular deep neural network. *The Journal of Supercomputing, 77*(4), 3571–3593.

Chen, C.M.; Chen, Y.L. and Lin, H.C. (2010). An efficient network intrusion detection. *Computer Communications, 33*(4), 477–484.

De la Hoz, E.; Ortiz, A.; Ortega, J. and Prieto, B. (2015). PCA filtering and probabilistic SOM for network intrusion detection. *Neurocomputing, 164*, 71–81.

Hamza, K.; Shaibal, D.; Rishikesh, B.; Amairanni, S.; Jason, S.; Steve, C.C.; Ahmed, F.A. and Mostafa, M.F. (2024). Evaluating the performance of machine learning-based classification models for IoT intrusion detection. *IEEE Opportunity Research Scholars Symposium (ORSS)*.

Kevric, J.; Jukic, S. and Subasi, A. (2017). An effective combining classifier approach using tree algorithms for network intrusion detection. *Neural Computing and Applications, 28*(1), 1051–1058.

Mehedi, S.T.; Anwar, A.; Rahman, Z.; Ahmed, K. and Rafiqul, I. (2024). Dependable intrusion detection system for IoT: A deep transfer learning-based approach. *IEEE Transactions on Industrial Informatics*.

Modi, C.; Patel, D.; Borisaniya, B.; Patel, A. and Rajarajan, M. (2013). A survey of intrusion detection techniques in cloud. *Journal of Network and Computer Applications, 36*(1), 42–57.

Othman, S.M.; Alsohybe, N.T.; Ba-Alwi, F.M. and Zahary, A.T. (2018). Survey on intrusion detection system types. *International Journal of Cyber-Security and Digital Forensics (IJCSDF), 7*(4), 444–462.

Paxson, V. (1999). Bro: A system for detecting network intruders in real-time. *Computer Networks, 31*(23–24), 2435–2463.

Raj, J.S. and Basar, A. (2019). QoS optimization of energy-efficient routing in IoT wireless sensor networks. *Journal of ISMAC, 1*(1), 12–23.

Roesch, M. (1999). Snort: Lightweight intrusion detection for networks. In *LISA*, 99(1), 229–238.

Shahrzad, G. and Dwight, M. (2024). Exploring unsupervised one-class classifiers for lightweight intrusion detection in IoT systems. *IEEE Conference on Distributed Computing in Smart Systems and the Internet of Things (DCOSS-IoT).*

Souad, A.; Chaimae, S. and Haibaba, C. (2023). Design of a distributed detection system for streaming data in IoT environment. *9th International Conference on Optimization and Applications (ICOA).*

Weiss, K.; Khoshgoftaar, T.M. and Wang, D. (2016). A survey of transfer learning. *Journal of Big Data, 3*(1), 1–40.

Achieving Financial Inclusion Through Political, Economic and Social Empowerment Among Women: An Empirical Attestation

Aditi Sharma[1] and Pragati Tomar Solanki[2]

ABSTRACT: Financial inclusion and empowerment are closely related concepts. When we take it from a woman's perspective, its importance will be doubled. In India, FI is recent concept that helps in the sustainable growth of the economy. As women form two-fifths of the labor force, women have extremely restricted access to the formal financial channels. The government and RBI have both made efforts to raise the number of financially integrated women, but the results have not yet been fully determined. Women contributed 50% of the total population and likewise to the economy of the country. Even after their important contribution, women are facing different types of privation. In the Madhya Pradesh District of India, women's empowerment is not satisfactory (Tyagi *et. al.,* 2010). To analyze a detailed picture of the situation of women they tried to identify how the empowerment of women helps in the financial inclusion in M.P. state. Purposive sampling and regression analysis were used to analyse the results. Data was collected from February 2023 to December 2023. Data was gathered from Indore, Ujjain, and Bhopal cities of Madhya Pradesh. The findings suggested that social and economic empowerment plays an important role in developing the understanding and usage of financial inclusion among women whereas it has no significant impact of political empowerment on inclusion. This study is useful for government, financial institutions, and society.

Keywords: *Banking System, Financial Channels, Illiteracy, Life Insurance, Nationalization.*

1. INTRODUCTION

Around one billion people across the globe live on less than $1.25 per day (World Bank, 2011). Despite this grim reality, there is hope that providing financial services to rural, underdeveloped, and low- to middle-income households can significantly reduce poverty and bring about meaningful social and economic transformation. Financial inclusion has emerged as a critical issue in today's economic scenario, drawing attention from Indian and global scholars, as well as the Government of India (GOI). The concept of financial inclusion is gaining momentum in India, as evidenced by the nationalization of 14 major commercial banks in 1969 to extend credit to underserved populations. However, despite such efforts, a significant portion of the population still lacks access to

---

[1] Research Sholar, Shri Vaishnav School of Management, Shri Vaishnav Vidyapeeth Vishwavidyalaya, Indore, India. E-mail: gaykwad.aditi@gmail.com

[2] Associate Professor, Shri Vaishnav School of Management, Shri Vaishnav Vidyapeeth Vishwavidyalaya, Indore, India.

formal banking services. As per a recent World Bank estimate, half of the world's adults do not have basic bank accounts, and in India alone, about 65% of adults out of a population of approximately 1.23 billion remain unbanked (World Bank, 2012). Factors such as low income, poverty, illiteracy, and lack of awareness contribute to financial exclusion.

Recognizing the challenges, the Government of India, along with financial institutions and policymakers, has prioritized financial inclusion to ensure that economic growth benefits all sections of society. One of the most prominent initiatives is the Pradhan Mantri Jan Dhan Yojana (PMJDY), launched on August 28, 2014. This nationwide financial inclusion scheme aims to provide every household with basic banking services, including bank accounts, debit cards, and insurance coverage. The scheme's ambitious goal was to open bank accounts for every household within a year, offering benefits like accident insurance, life insurance, and a no-collateral overdraft facility. On the first day alone, 15 million accounts were opened, and by January 2015, more than 100 million households had been integrated into the formal banking system.

Financial inclusion is increasingly recognized as a fundamental tool for promoting inclusive economic growth and reducing poverty. The World Bank's global goal of achieving universal financial access by 2020 underscores the importance of this mission. Financial inclusion entails ensuring affordable access to essential financial services for low-income and vulnerable groups, facilitating timely and adequate financing as needed. Empowering women is also an essential aspect, involving economic, social, and political dimensions that enhance their ability to make informed decisions and actively participate in society. Various financial services, including savings, loans, insurance, credit, and payments, play a vital role in helping disadvantaged communities overcome poverty. While microfinance and microcredit have seen considerable success, other financial services must also achieve similar outcomes.

Financial exclusion can arise due to issues related to access, cost, marketing, or self-exclusion due to negative experiences or perceptions. Addressing these challenges requires building a diverse financial ecosystem. Empowerment and accountability are interlinked concepts, both crucial for enabling individuals to hold those in power accountable while also fostering their participation in governance and decision-making processes. Social and economic empowerment, particularly for women, is fundamental for building sustainable and inclusive growth. Women's economic empowerment not only enhances household and community economies but also contributes to national progress. Addressing gender disparities, discrimination, and exclusion is essential for creating an equitable and just society.

Although women make up a significant portion of the labor force in India, their access to formal financial services remains limited. Despite initiatives by the government and the Reserve Bank of India (RBI), the financial inclusion of women is still far from adequate. The situation is particularly concerning in regions like Madhya Pradesh, where women's financial empowerment and inclusion remain low. Understanding the link between women's empowerment and financial inclusion, especially in Madhya Pradesh, is crucial for formulating effective policies. While numerous studies have explored financial inclusion in India, few have examined its correlation with women's empowerment. The current study seeks to analyze the relationship between financial inclusion and various dimensions of women's empowerment, with a particular focus on Madhya Pradesh. This research aims to bridge the gap by investigating how enhancing women's financial inclusion contributes to their broader empowerment.

2. REVIEW OF LITERATURE

Murillo (2020) concluded that the situation in good financial management starts with using a positive financial attitude towards the country in which they live Researchers worked on cognitive learning and how and when people gain knowledge about finance which shapes their financial behavior. Elzahi & Ali (2019) investigated empowering women in Comoros through Islamic financial inclusion. The women surveyed included payment, borrowing, savings and investments, and insurance financial inclusion where they found that women have a weak ability to participate in all the dimensions.

Aiman & Ebrahim (2019) found in their research that women invest less than men for a variety of reasons. Women deliberately refrain from making financial decisions because they cannot understand investing. The main sources of investment for individual investors are bank deposits, and the main purpose of investing is for children's education, marriage, and post-retirement security. The ability of financial professionals to deal with the psychological aspects of their clients and relationship and behavioral problems has become an important factor associated with creating and implementing a financial planning framework. Bhatia & Singh (2019) concluded that financial inclusion and women's empowerment are closely related and analyzed the awareness about government schemes related to women's empowerment. Datta & Singh (2018) studied the secondary data to determine the extent of financial inclusion, the phenomena of urbanization, and the growth of cities in women empowerment.

Ozili (2018) draws attention to several issues, including the degree of financial inclusion that is ideal or excessive, the transmission of systemic risks to the formal financial sector as a result of financial inclusion, and whether financial inclusion or exclusion is pro-cyclical in response to changes in the economic cycle. The results show that the degree of financial innovation, levels of poverty, stability of a financial sector, financial strength, financial literacy, and regulatory frameworks that vary between nations all have an impact on and are influenced by financial inclusion. Bakar & Sulong (2018) analyzed the role of financial inclusion on economic growth and concluded that financial inclusion is a driving engine toward growth economy in several dimensions with various methods used to assess this link and increase in financial system needs of the world. Monalisa (2015) analyzed the condition of FI in the rural areas of the district of Hisar and came up with measures to speed up the process of financial inclusion. The problems faced by the respondents in the selected sample with the present banking system and suggestions given by them to tackle the problems. The sample size consists of 367 respondents. The methodology used in the research for selecting a respondent as a sample is convenient and random sampling. The study found that 65.67% of households in rural areas of the district, Hisar, have been financially included. Wrigley-Asante (2012) studied gender wise differences in empowerment.

Sharma (2016) concluded that there is a positive impact of financial inclusion on economic growth based on empirical studies. Datta & Sahu (2017) researched the significance of microfinance institutions in the empowerment of women. Zulfiqar & Bilal

(2016), and Mutang *et. al.*, (2017) found that financial attitudes have a positive impact on financial well-being. Nanda & Kaur (2016) conclude that financial inclusion contributes to economic growth through the value creation of small businesses with positive spillover effects on human development indicators such as health, education, and reduction of inequality and poverty. Sahay (2015) concluded that increased use of these services by women and increased access to various banking services for businesses and households have a significant positive influence on economic growth. Kabeer (1999) highlighted the three dimensions of women's empowerment. Zanvar (2015) studied that age, qualifications, and income level affect the level of risk-tolerant investors and, hence, their investment decisions. Basu (2006) found, after studying 100 SHGs in Hooghly District, that women empowerment is formed in weak form using saving and incomes as an indicator. Ghosh (2013) examined different themes for promoting financial inclusion. Bold (2012) analyzed that and concluded that financial inclusion helps to improve the level of social inclusion in many societies. Nigam & Thakur (2012) studied the historical background of financial inclusion, recent developments, and government initiatives taken for financial inclusion in Madhya Pradesh. Ghosh (2011) concluded that several important empirical studies have shown that both poverty and inequality are negatively associated with access to formal financial services.

Hannig & Jansen (2010) examined the impact of financial inclusion on financial stability, suggesting that increased financial inclusion offers better opportunities to strengthen financial stability. They noted that, despite the risks posed at the institutional level, the potential costs of financial inclusion are outweighed by the significant long-term benefits that contribute to financial stability through a diversified financial system.

Chatterjee *et. al.*, (2018) investigated the role of medium enterprises in supporting the sustainability of self-help groups (SHGs). Similarly, Massey (2010) emphasized that financial institutions in developing nations play a pivotal role in promoting financial inclusion. The proactive involvement of capital market participants, particularly financial institutions, can significantly support government initiatives aimed at expanding and deepening financial inclusion. Rai (2006) explored financial deepening and inclusion within the Indian banking system, highlighting the crucial role of financial institutions in achieving inclusive growth.

3. RESEARCH GAP

The gap was identified after the substantial literature review. It was found that factors of financial inclusion, access, and usage of financial services have been majorly studied by the researchers. However, the specific study to understand women's empowerment through financial inclusion is still an area where there is less research, and a specific study considering financial inclusion and women's empowerment in Madhya Pradesh gives a new dimension to researchers for research. The present study has been undertaken with an objective: To study the relationship between Financial Inclusion and different dimensions of Women's Empowerment (Economic, Social, and Political).

4. RESEARCH METHOD

The research was descriptive. Purposive sampling was adopted to obtain the results. The study was conducted in Indore, Jabalpur, Bhopal, and Ujjain, Cities of Madhya Pradesh

District of India. These cities are the largest and contribute majorly to the income of Madhya Pradesh. The questionnaire developed by Bhatia & Singh (2019) was adopted to collect the data. The earlier questionnaire was used in the Punjab state of India. But in this study, it is used for Madhya Pradesh state, which has a different literacy, employment, and education scenario. The Demographic profile of the respondents was also collected. The questionnaire was distributed among 250 women, required as per design from chosen cities. 199 responses were collected, which were fair and accurate for further analysis. Data was collected both in hard and soft form. The data sources for this study are both primary and secondary. Secondary data was used from published research papers and published material. The impact was checked with the help of Regression Analysis. The dependent variable was financial inclusion, whereas the independent variables were Economic, Social, and Political Empowerment.

Hypotheses

H_{01}: There is no significant relationship between financial inclusion and economic empowerment of women.

H_{02}: There is no significant relationship between financial inclusion and social empowerment of women.

H_{03}: There is no significant relationship between financial inclusion and the political empowerment of women.

5. RESULTS AND DISCUSSION

Table 1 shows the demographic profile of the respondents.

Table 1: Demographic Profile

Age (in years)	21–30	74
	31–40	53
	41–50	42
	above 50	30
Educational Qualification	Below Higher Secondary	44
	Graduation	72
	Post`graduation & above	83
Marital status	Married	121
	Unmarried	78
Employment status	Working	136
	Non-working	63

Reliability

Cronbach's alpha is a measure of internal consistency, that is, how closely related a set of items are as a group. A Cronbach's alpha of 0.70 or more is considered to be satisfactory. The value is 0.824 which indicates the data is reliable.

Cronbach's Alpha	*No. of Items*
0.824	4

Regression Analysis

To identify the impact of financial inclusion regression analysis was used. The dependent variable was financial inclusion whereas the independent variables were Economic, Social, and Political Empowerment. Model summary denotes the variations in the financial inclusion described by the regression model.

Table 2: Regression Analysis

Model Summary				
Model	*R*	*R Square*	*Adjusted R Square*	*Std. Error of the Estimate*
1	0.632[a]	0.399	0.381	0.60019

Predictors: (Constant), Political Empowerment, Social Empowerment, Economic Empowerment.

Table 2 displays the overall fit of the model. The value of R square here is 0.399 which means 33.9%. This shows value is more than 10% and the model is a good fit for the analysis. 33.9% of the variations in financial inclusion may be explained by three factors of empowerment. Empowerment is the independent variable considered as a predictor in the study.

Table 3: Showing ANOVA Summary

ANOVA						
Model		*Sum of Squares*	*D_f*	*Mean Square*	*F*	*Sig.*
1.	Regression	23.005	3	7.668	21.288	0.000[b]
	Residual	34.582	96	0.360		
	Total	**57.587**	**99**			

a. *Dependent Variable:* Financial Inclusion.

b. *Predictors:* (Constant), Political Empowerment, Social Empowerment, Economic Empowerment.

The R-value is 0.632 which denotes that good correlation exists between financial inclusion and empowerment. Model significance was tested by using ANOVA. The ANOVA table for the regression model is explained below in Table 3. It indicates that the F ratio is 21.28. The higher value of F denoted that the model is good. The noted value of p is 0.000 which is lower than the critical value of 0.05 showing that the regression model results in financial inclusion with factors of empowerment viz. political, economic, and social. In brief, the regression model predicts empowerment among women with financial inclusion.

Findings: The empowerment component viz. economic, political, and social predicts inclusion and influences the financial inclusion of women.

Table 4: Showing Coefficients

Model	*Unstandardized Coefficients*		*Standardized Coefficients*	*t*	*Sig.*
	B	*Std. Error*	*Beta*		
(Constant)	1.122	.342			
Economic Empowerment	.417	.090	.490	4.637	.000
Social Empowerment	.243	.106	.236	2.298	.024
Political Empowerment	.030	.093	.034	.319	.750

a. Dependent Variable: Financial Inclusion.
Table 4 defines the model equation Y = á + âx + å
Financial inclusion (FI) = $á_0 + â_1x_1 + â_2x_2 + â_3x_3$
Financial inclusion = 1.122+0.417 (economic) + 0.243 (social) + 0.030 (political).

The relationship between financial inclusion and women's empowerment is explained by the value of â. If coefficient â is positive which denotes a positive relationship exists between predictor and outcome and a negative value of the coefficient indicates a negative relation midst the variables. All three predictors mentioned above denoted positive â which shows the relationship is positive. Hence it can be projected that an increase in economic empowerment leads to an increase in her financial inclusion as well. An increase in social empowerment leads to an increase in her financial inclusion. Ultimately, an increase in political empowerment will lead to an increase in financial inclusion. Table 4 indicates that economic empowerment (0.490) is the most important and this makes financial inclusion followed by social empowerment (0.236) and finally political empowerment (0.034).

- **Economic empowerment:** (â = 0.417): from the equation, it was interpreted that 1 unit of change in economic empowerment causes a 0.417-unit change in financial inclusion among women. This is correct only if the effects of social and political empowerment remain constant.
- **Social empowerment:** (â = 0.243): from the equation, it was interpreted that 1 unit of change in social empowerment causes a 0.243-unit change in financial inclusion among women. This is correct only if the effects of economic and political empowerment remain constant.
- **Political empowerment:** (â = 0.030): from the equation, it was interpreted that 1 unit of change in economic empowerment causes a 0.030-unit change in financial inclusion among women. This is correct only if the effects of social and economic empowerment remain constant.

The results of hypotheses testing is given below:

H_{01}: There is no significant relationship between financial inclusion and economic empowerment of women.

As the result shows in Table 4, the null hypothesis was rejected as the p-value is 0.000, which is less than 0.05. It indicates that financial inclusion and economic empowerment have a close relationship, and economic empowerment helps in the growth of women by making them financially literate and aware.

H_{02}: There is no significant relationship between financial inclusion and the social empowerment of women.

As the result shows in Table 4, the null hypothesis was rejected as the p-value is 0.024, which is less than 0.05. It indicates that financial inclusion and social empowerment have a close relationship. Socially empowered women are more prone to financial inclusion.

H_{03}: There is no significant relationship between financial inclusion and the political empowerment of women.

As the result shows in Table 4 the null hypothesis was accepted as the p-value is 0.750, which is more than 0.05. It indicates that financial inclusion and political empowerment do not have a close relationship. A woman may participate in political issues and aspects but does not have financial awareness and literacy.

This study looked at the relationship between financial inclusion and women's empowerment in terms of social, political, and economic empowerment. The findings corroborated the idea that was put out. The result of the study depicted that a positive relationship was found between social and economic empowerment with financial inclusion. The result of the study matched with (Wrigley-Asante, 2012). In summary, this study advances the knowledge of women's financial inclusion in the Madhya Pradesh District of India very empowerment metric that reflects the theories in this study and previous research related to women's empowerment. The research also shows that women who have greater access to and use of financial services like opening bank accounts and purchasing insurance are also more empowered on the social, political, and economic fronts. This has ramifications for raising women's empowerment by giving them more negotiating leverage, political decision-making autonomy, financial decision-making authority at work, and familial decision-making authority.

This study acknowledges that women's empowerment can influence various financial inclusion procedures, which is consistent with the body of literature (Chatterjee *et. al.*, 2018; Basu, 2006). Likewise, the result depicted from economic and social empowerment is matched with the result of Datta & Sahu (2017); Kabir (1999). Given these variations, impoverished women's lifestyles varied greatly from one another. To close this gap, a systematic understanding of these households' financial situations is required, and the delivery method must be tailored to be both scalable and reasonably priced. Therefore, to develop a more inclusive financial system for women living in Madhya Pradesh, new information-gathering points must be established.

6. CONCLUSION

The study helps to understand the relationship between Financial Inclusion and women empowerment. The study results depict that economic and social empowerment helps women to grow in society and is a strong push for their financial inclusion. Financial inclusion is an important aspect for developing countries like India, especially in their underdeveloped states. There is a substantial need for women to be empowered so that they can participate in their financial decisions and make themselves financially independent. There should be a formal financial system to enhance the scale of financial inclusion. The study has some limitations. Only Madhya Pradesh state was considered for the study, a new study can be performed on other states or in the country. The research is cross-sectional and does not consider a longitudinal structure and hence may not be suitable for the long term.

REFERENCES

Bhatia, S. and Singh, S. (2019). Empowering Women Through Financial Inclusion: A Study of Urban Slum, *The Journal for Decision Makers,* 44(4), 182–197.

Bold, C.; Porteous, D. and Rotman, S. (2012). Social cash transfers and financial inclusion: Evidence from four countries, *Consultative Group to Assist the Poor*, 77, 1–28.

Chatterjee, S.; Dutta, A.; Gupta, S. and Upadhyay, P. (2018). Empowering women and stimulating development at bottom of pyramid through micro entrepreneurship, *Management Decision*, 56(1), 160–174.

Datta, S. and Sahu, T.N. (2017). An empirical study on the impact of microfinance on women empowerment: Evidence from West Bengal, *Indian Journal of Commerce and Management Studies*, 8(3), 53.

Datta, S.K. and Singh, K. (2018). Aspects of inclusion and peoples' empowerment related to national rural employment Guarantee Scheme in India, *International Journal of Public Administration*, 41(2), 83–94.

Elrahman, A. and Elzahi, S. (2019). Empowering Women Through Financial Inclusion: Some Evidence from Comoros, *International Journal of Asian Social Sciences*, 9(2), 256–270.

Ghosh, J. (2013). Microfinance and the challenge of financial inclusion for development, *Cambridge journal of economics*, 37(6), 1203–1219.

Ghosh, S. (2011). Does financial outreach engender economic growth? Evidence from Indian states. *Journal of Indian Business Research*, 3(2), 74–99.

Hannig, A. and Jansen, S. (2010). Financial inclusion and financial stability: Current policy issues. *Asian Development Bank Institute Working Paper*, 259, 1–29.

Kabeer, N. (1999). Resources, agency, achievements: Reflections on the measurement of women's empowerment. *Development and Change,* 30(3), 435–464.

Melisa, M.; Pilar, F. and Diego, R. (2020). The role of cognitive abilities on financial literacy: New experimental evidence. *Journal of Behavioral and Experimental Economics*, 84.

Nanda, K. and Kaur, M. (2016). Financial inclusion and human development: cross-country evidence. *Management and Labour Studies*, 41 (2), 127–153.

Sahay, R.; Cihák, M.; Diaye, P. and Barajas, A. (2015). Rethinking financial deepening: stability and growth in emerging markets. *Staff Discussion Notes*, 15(8), 73–107.

Sharma, D. (2016). Nexus between financial inclusion and economic growth: evidence from the emerging Indian economy. *Journal of Financial Economic Policy*, 8(1), 13–36.

Sulong, Z.B. (2018). The Role of Financial Inclusion on Economic Growth: Theoretical and Empirical Literature Review Analysis. *Business Finance*, 356.

Tyagi, M.; Mahor, Y. and Tyagi, C. (2010). Women Status in MP and Planned Interventions — A Gender Review, 1–21.

Wrigley-Asante, C. (2012). Out of the dark but not out of the cage: Women's empowerment and gender relations in the Dangme west district of Ghana. *Gender, Place & Culture*, 19(3), 344–363.

Agrobacterium tumefaciens-Mediated Transformation (ATMT) of Soybean Anthracnose Pathogen *Colletotrichum truncatum*: A Novel Approach for Functional Genomics

Niharika Sharma[1] and K.N. Guruprasad[2]

ABSTRACT: *Agrobacterium tumefaciens*-mediated transformation (ATMT) has emerged as a promising tool for genetic manipulation in plant-associated fungi, including plant pathogens. This study explores the application of ATMT for transforming *Colletotrichum truncatum*, the causal agent of soybean anthracnose, a destructive fungal disease impacting soybean crops worldwide. By utilizing ATMT, we successfully introduced the *Green Fluorescent Protein (GFP) gene* as a reporter using a binary vector into *C. truncatum,* facilitating the generation of stable transformants. High level expression of GFP protein was obtained both in spores and in mycelia as detected by fluorescence microscopy. The successful integration of GFP allows for easy visualization of transformed fungal colonies and provides a reliable marker for confirming transformation efficiency. The work establishes a standardized ATMT protocol for *C. truncatum* using GFP as a visual tool, which can be extended to future experiments aimed at exploring the molecular mechanisms of pathogenesis, offering potential strategies for targeted disease management in soybean and crop protection.

Keywords: *Agrobacterium tumefaciens, Fluorescence Microscopy, Fungus, Gene, Pathogenesis.*

1. INTRODUCTION

Soybean (Glycine max) is a vital global crop, providing essential protein and oil for human consumption and livestock feed. Among the numerous diseases that afflict soybean crops, anthracnose, caused by the fungal pathogen *Colletotrichum truncatum*, represents a major threat to crop yield and quality. The pathogen is responsible for significant economic losses, as it leads to seed and pod rot, blight, and defoliation, particularly under favorable conditions of high humidity and temperature (Abd-Elsalam *et. al*., 2020). Effective management of *C. truncatum* has been challenging, as conventional methods such as fungicide applications and resistant cultivars often fall short, particularly

---

[1] Research Scholar, Department of Life Science, Shri Vishnav Institute of Science, Shri Vaishnav Vidyapeeth Vishwavidyalaya, Indore, India. E-mail: niharikasharma400@gmail.com

[2] Professor, Dean Science, Shri Vishnav Institute of Science, Shri Vaishnav Vidyapeeth Vishwavidyalaya, Indore, India.

due to the complex nature of the host-pathogen interaction and the limited genetic resources available for pathogen control (Nejad *et. al.*, 2021). Thus, a deeper understanding of the molecular mechanisms underlying pathogenicity and virulence is crucial to developing more effective management strategies.

Colletotrichum truncatum is a member of the *Colletotrichum* genus, a group of filamentous fungi known for their ability to cause anthracnose in a variety of plants, including many economically important crops (Dean *et. al.*, 2012). While other species in the genus, such as *C. acutatum* and *C. gloeosporioides*, have been studied extensively, *C. truncatum* has received relatively little attention in comparison. This is primarily due to the difficulty of genetically manipulating this pathogen, which has hindered the investigation of genes involved in its pathogenicity and virulence. Understanding these genes is critical for unraveling the complex molecular interactions between the pathogen and its host plant, which could ultimately inform new strategies for disease management.

Traditionally, research on fungal pathogens has been limited by the lack of reliable genetic transformation techniques. While *C. truncatum* and other fungi have been subject to various forms of genetic manipulation, the tools available have often been inefficient or difficult to implement (Hollomon *et. al.*, 2018). However, advances in genetic engineering techniques have allowed for the development of more effective approaches to fungal transformation. One of the most promising methods for genetic modification of *Colletotrichum* species is Agrobacterium tumefaciens-mediated transformation (ATMT), a method that uses the natural ability of the soil bacterium *A. tumefaciens* to transfer DNA into plant and fungal cells.

Agrobacterium tumefaciens has long been known for its ability to transfer a portion of its Ti (tumor-inducing) plasmid into plant cells, where the transferred DNA integrates into the plant genome (Gelvin, 2003). This process has been harnessed for genetic transformation in a wide range of plant species, but more recently, ATMT has been adapted for use in fungi (Tzfira *et. al.*, 2004). The ability of *A. tumefaciens* to mediate efficient and stable transformation in fungi, including *C. truncatum*, presents a powerful tool for functional genomics studies. This technique enables researchers to introduce foreign genes into the fungal genome, allowing for the study of gene function in a more direct and systematic manner than traditional knockout approaches.

In *Colletotrichum* species, ATMT has already been successfully applied to species such as *C. gloeosporioides*, *C. acutatum*, and *C. higginsianum* (Liu *et. al.*, 2017; O'Connell *et. al.*, 2012). These studies have demonstrated that ATMT is an effective method for creating stable transformants, allowing for the functional analysis of genes involved in fungal development, virulence, and host interaction. For example, the transformation of *C. gloeosporioides* using ATMT has led to the identification of critical virulence factors, including secreted effector proteins that play a role in the establishment of infection in host plants (Huguet-Tapia *et. al.*, 2016). Moreover, ATMT has been used to generate strains for functional analysis of genes involved in secondary metabolism and stress responses, further expanding its utility for investigating the biology of *Colletotrichum* species.

Despite the growing body of research on ATMT in *Colletotrichum*, there has been limited exploration of its application in *C. truncatum*, a pathogen that poses a unique set of challenges. The study aims to fill this gap by developing and optimizing an ATMT protocol specifically for *C. truncatum*. The successful establishment of a transformation system for the pathogen will significantly enhance the ability to probe the molecular mechanisms underlying its pathogenicity. By introducing foreign genes, researchers can examine the functions of specific genes involved in infection, virulence, and the host immune response, thus opening new avenues for targeted genetic interventions.

Moreover, transforming *C. truncatum* will enable the identification of candidate genes that could be used as targets for novel fungicides or resistance genes in soybean. Given the economic importance of soybean and the persistence of anthracnose as a limiting factor in production, the potential for using genetic engineering to develop more resistant soybean varieties or more effective control methods is immense. Additionally, the ability to manipulate *C. truncatum* genetically could facilitate the development of biocontrol strategies or new diagnostic tools for early disease detection.

The research seeks to establish an Agrobacterium tumefaciens-mediated transformation (ATMT) protocol for *Colletotrichum truncatum*, with the ultimate goal of advancing our understanding of the molecular mechanisms involved in soybean anthracnose. By leveraging the power of functional genomics, we aim to uncover key factors involved in the pathogenicity of *C. truncatum* and provide a foundation for developing more effective disease management strategies. The successful transformation of this pathogen will not only contribute to the broader field of fungal molecular biology but also have significant implications for crop protection and food security.

2. MATERIALS AND METHOD

Procurement of fungal material: Colletotrichum truncatum culture was procured from ICAR-Indian Agricultural Research Institute, Regional station, Indore, India.

Fungus growth conditions: *C. truncatum* mycelial colony was propagated on potato dextrose agar (PDA) medium Figure 1. The fungal cultures were incubated at 25°C with a 12 h day/night cycle under cool white fluorescent lamps. Every 7–10 days, fungal isolates were transferred to fresh PDA plates. The authenticity of the cultures was confirmed by colony morphology.

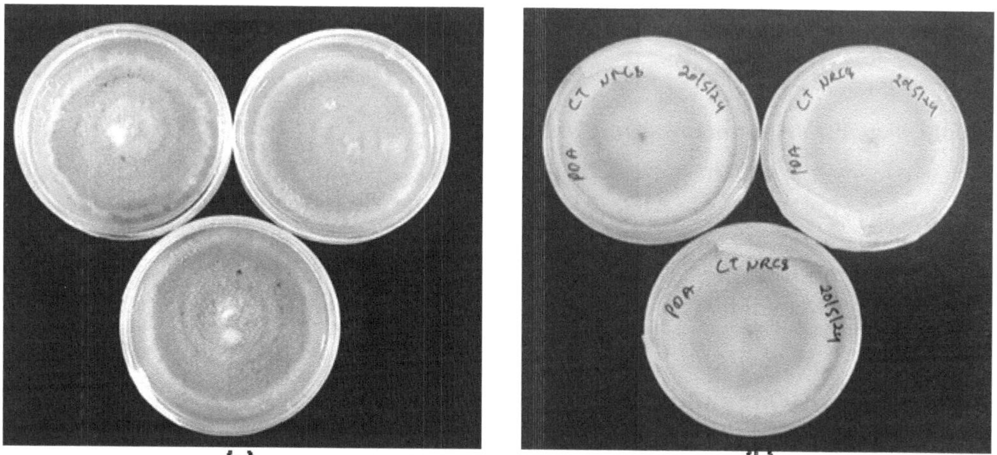

(a) (b)

Figure 1: *Colletotrichum truncatum* on PDA, Ten Days Post Inoculation, (a) From Above; (b) From Below

Agrobacterium tumefaciens-mediated transformation (ATMT) of Colletotrichum truncatum

A. tumefaciens strain GV3101 containing the pBIF-GFP vector was grown on an LB agar plate supplemented with 30 μg/ml rifampicin and 100 μg/ml kanamycin at 28 C for 2 days. A single colony was picked from the LB agar plate and grown in LB containing 30 μg/ml rifampicin and 100 μg/ml kanamycin at 28°C, 150 rpm, for 16 hr or until the OD_{600} reached 0.8–1.0. From the above culture, 25 μl was inoculated in 25 ml LB media, containing rifampicin (30 μg/ml) and kanamycin (100 μg/ml) and incubated under the same conditions until the OD_{600} reached 0.4–0.5. The culture was centrifuged at 6600 rpm for 5 min at RT. The supernatant was discarded and pellet was diluted in 1 ml Induction Medium (IM) with acetosyringone to acquire an OD_{600} of 0.15. The culture was incubated at 28°C and 150 rpm for 6hr. the above tertiary culture was centrifuged at 6600 rpm for 5 min at RT. Supernatant was discarded and pellet was resuspended in 1 ml Induction Medium (IM) to make OD_{600} up to 0.3–0.6. *C. truncatum* conidia were harvested by adding sterile MQ water to the 14-day-old plate and rubbing the surface with the end of a sterile micropipette tip.

Conidial suspension was filtered through muslin cloth. The conidial suspension was washed twice with one ml of IM and resuspended in IM to establish a final concentration of 1×10^7 conidia/ml. The 100 μl of IM-suspended Agrobacterium culture was mixed with 100 μl of *C. truncatum* conidial suspension. The mixed suspension (200 μl) was added to petri plates containing Induction Medium agar & cellophane membrane and co-cultivated at 28°C for 72 hrs. The membrane was transferred to PDA plates containing hygromycin (50 μg/ml), cefotaxime (100 μg/ml), chloramphenicol (100 μg/ml); plates were incubated at 25°C. Discs were removed after an additional 48 hours of co-cultivation at 25°C. The transformants that arose after 7–10 days of transfer were moved to fresh selection plates and were further purified by single spore culture on PDA plates containing hygromycin, cefotaxime, chloramphenicol to eliminate any Agrobacterium contamination.

3. RESULTS

3.1 Microscopic Method

Sample preparation for microscopic analysis:

For microscopy, the conidia were obtained form 14-day-old *C. truncatum* and transformed *C. truncatum* in 1 ml sterile MQ. The conidia were filter-sterilized using Muslin cloth. The conidia suspensions were diluted to optimum concentration. 10 μl of this suspension were allowed to grow on sterile glass coverslip incubated at 25°C for 24 h in dark. The grown hyphae were further investigated through inverted and confocal laser scanning microscopy.

Confocal laser scanning microscopy:

For microscopic studies, A1+ Ti2 confocal laser scanning microscope (Nikon, Japan) was used. The excitation and detection wavelengths of the laser channels utilised for fluorescence microscopic investigation are listed in Table 1. The control of microscopy and processing of the confocal images we accomplished by the NIS-Elements Ar (Nikon, Japan) software.

Table 1: Lasers Used for the Excitation and Detection Wavelength for A1+ Ti2.

Detection	*Excitation Wavelength*	*Detection Wavelength*	*Laser Type*
GFP	488 nm	515 nm	White light laser

Agrobacterium tumefaciens*-mediated transformation (ATMT) of *Colletotrichum truncatum: To transform *C. truncatum*, we used pBIF-EGFP vector. Co-cultivation of *A. tumefaciens* cells (carrying GFP) with conidia from *C. truncatum* was performed in the presence of varying amounts of acetosyringone. The co-cultivation let to the emergence of colonies after 3–4 days of membrane transfer from co-cultivated medium to selection plate as shown in Figure 2.

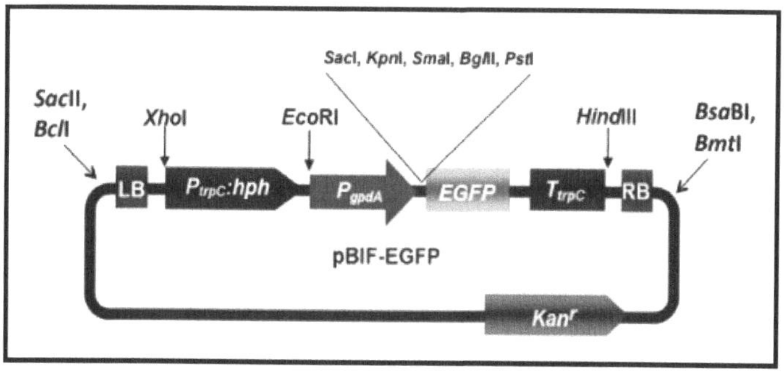

Figure 2: Binary Vector pBIF-EGFP Used in this Study

Expression analysis of GFP in the *C. truncatum:* To evaluate the expression of EGFP in the trans- formed C. truncatum, mycelia from transformants were directly harvested from the selection plate and observed with fluorescence microscopy. The green fluorescent mycelia were easy to detect in all transformants of C. truncatum. To further analyze germination and fungal morphology, conidia from 14-day-old plates were harvested and studied at 24 hr germination on a glass cover slip. Confocal microscopy studies clearly indicate the expression of EGFP in different stages of fungal development (i.e., germ tube, conidia) (Figure 3).

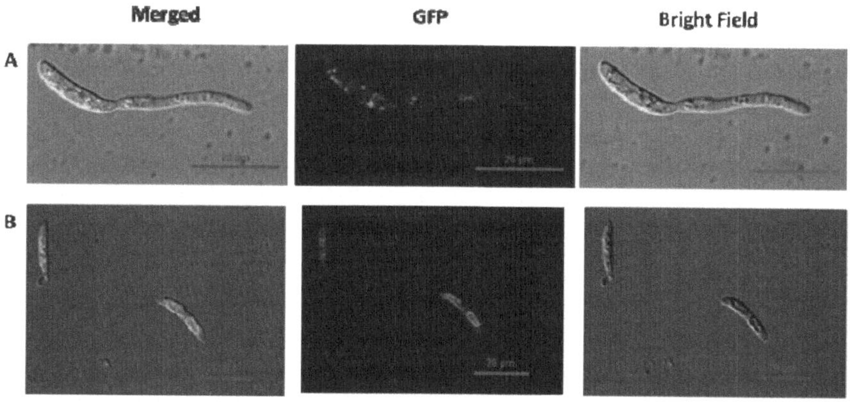

Figure 3: Fluorescence Images of C. truncatum Showing Expression of GFP at Different Development Stages. (a) Germinating Conidia, and (b) Conidia. Each Bar Represents 20 μm

4. CONCLUSION

The study demonstrates the successful application of *Agrobacterium tumefaciens*-mediated transformation (ATMT) to introduce the GFP gene into *Colletotrichum truncatum*, providing a valuable tool for visualizing fungal transformation. The establishment of a standardized ATMT protocol for *C. truncatum* facilitates the generation of stable transformants, allowing for the easy tracking of fungal colonies and confirming transformation efficiency. The use of GFP as a reporter offers significant potential for future research into the molecular mechanisms of pathogenesis and paves the way for the development of targeted strategies to combat soybean anthracnose and improve crop protection. This approach represents a significant advancement in genetic manipulation techniques for plant-associated fungi and holds promise for enhancing our understanding of fungal biology and disease management in agricultural systems.

REFERENCES

Abd-Elsalam, K.A.; Omar, M.R.; Aly, A.A. and Mohamed, E.M. (2020). Colletotrichum truncatum and its impact on soybean production: A review. *Plant Pathology Journal, 36*(3), 179–187.

Dean, R.; Kan, V.J.A.L.; Pretorius; Z.A., Hammond-Kosack, K.E.; Di Pietro, A.; Spanu, P.D.; Rudd, J.J.; Dickman, M.; Kahmann, R.; Ellis, J. and Foster, G.D. (2012). The genome of the plant pathogen *Colletotrichum gloeosporioides* reveals mechanisms for living on plant surfaces. *Nature Communications, 3*, 1073.

Gelvin, S.B. (2003). Agrobacterium-mediated plant transformation: The biology behind the "gene-jockeying" tool. *Microbiology and Molecular Biology Reviews, 67*(1), 16–37.

Hollomon, D.W.; Brent, K.J. and Wheeler, I.E. (2018). Advances in the control of plant fungal diseases: The application of genetic modification technologies. *Annual Review of Phytopathology, 56*, 1–21.

Huguet-Tapia, J.C.; Soto-Arredondo, J.; Lozano-Contreras, M. and Ibarra-Laclette, E. (2016). Functional analysis of the secreted proteins in *Colletotrichum gloeosporioides* and their role in pathogenesis. *Frontiers in Plant Science, 7*, 623.

Liu, T.; Zhang, W.; Wang, H.; Chen, X. and Liu, X. (2017). Agrobacterium-mediated transformation of *Colletotrichum acutatum* and functional characterization of a gene involved in pathogenicity. *Fungal Genetics and Biology, 99*, 1–9.

Nejad, M.S.; Karimi, H. and Bahramnejad, B. (2021). Challenges in managing soybean anthracnose and current strategies. *Journal of Phytopathology, 169*(4), 213–225.

O'Connell, R.J.; Thon, M.R.; Hacquard, S. and Gotz, M. (2012). Agrobacterium-mediated transformation of *Colletotrichum higginsianum* for functional genomics. *Fungal Genetics and Biology, 49*(3), 225–233.

Tzfira, T.; Tian, G.; Lacroix, B. and Citovsky, V. (2004). Agrobacterium-mediated transformation of fungi. *Nature Biotechnology, 22*(11), 1489–1494.

Aligning Biometric Data Usage with Global Sustainability Goals and Indian Data Protection Laws: A Business Perspective

Poorva Vaishnav[1] and Ashutosh Bairagi[2]

ABSTRACT: Biometric data has become a crucial asset for businesses, enhancing security, efficiency, and user experience. However, its increasing use poses challenges around privacy, ethical handling, and environmental sustainability. The Digital Personal Data Protection Act 2023 (DPDP Act) in India establishes stringent guidelines for managing sensitive biometric data, requiring businesses to ensure compliance while aligning with global sustainability frameworks like the United Nations Sustainable Development Goals (SDGs). This paper investigates how businesses can responsibly manage biometric data while contributing to SDG 9 (Industry, Innovation, and Infrastructure), SDG 12 (Responsible Consumption and Production), and SDG 16 (Peace, Justice, and Strong Institutions). It highlights the importance of adopting sustainable data management strategies, such as energy-efficient storage systems and ethical data lifecycle practices, while adhering to key DPDP Act principles like informed consent, data minimization, and purpose limitation. Through case studies of businesses successfully integrating sustainability with data protection, the research offers practical insights into balancing innovation with environmental responsibility. Recommendations include embracing sustainable technologies, enhancing privacy measures, and fostering partnerships for ethical data governance. By aligning biometric data practices with the DPDP Act and global sustainability goals, businesses can ensure legal compliance, promote environmental stewardship, and build a foundation for a resilient digital economy.

Keywords: *Data Governance, Digital Personal Data Protection Act 2023, Environmental Stewardship, Ethical Data Management, Resilient Digital Economy.*

1. INTRODUCTION

In the digital age, data has become a resource as valuable as oil, driving competition and innovation among businesses and nations. Like crude oil, raw data must be refined through analysis to unlock its potential, producing insights that span health, financial, and personal domains. While public data is openly accessible, private data such as browsing histories, account details, and biometric information requires stringent protection due to its sensitive nature. The increasing misuse of personal data globally, including in India, highlights the urgent need for robust legislative frameworks. The Digital Personal Data Protection Act 2023 (DPDP Act) seeks to address these challenges by establishing

[1] Research Scholar, Shri Vaishnav Institute of Law, Shri Vaishnav Vidyapeeth Vishwavidyalaya, Indore, India. E-mail: poorvavaish11@mail.com

[2] Professor, Shri Vaishnav Institute of Law, Shri Vaishnav Vidyapeeth Vishwavidyalaya, Indore, India.

regulatory protocols to protect privacy, mitigate electronic surveillance risks, and ensure responsible data collection.

Biometric data, a subset of personal data, has emerged as a cornerstone of secure identification systems. Biometric technologies, including fingerprint, facial, voice, and iris recognition, provide reliable methods for verifying identity and enhancing privacy. Unlike conventional virtual identifiers such as passwords, biometrics offer a superior solution for authentication, leveraging the uniqueness of physiological and behavioral traits inherent to individuals. Historically, biometrics has been used to identify individuals, but modern advancements enable precise, rapid, and secure identification. These technologies play a pivotal role in safeguarding identity in the digital realm while aligning sustainability goals through their potential for efficiency and resource optimization. This paper explores the alignment of biometric data usage with the DPDP Act and global sustainability objectives, emphasizing the need for ethical and secure data management to foster trust and resilience in a rapidly digitizing world. Biometric data refers to unique biological characteristics used for identifying individuals, such as fingerprints, facial features, iris patterns, and voice recordings. These traits are digitized into storable formats for efficient matching and recognition, forming the backbone of secure identification systems.

The origins of biometric identification date back to ancient civilizations. For example, the Babylonian empire recorded fingerprints on clay tablets for identity verification as early as 500 BC. Over time, methods evolved from physical transcriptions of faces and fingerprints to advanced digital systems. Today, biometrics is integral to modern life, enabling secure access to devices, authentication of official documents, and enhanced identity verification. Understanding the historical development of biometric data underscores its contemporary relevance, particularly in the context of data protection. In alignment with the Digital Personal Data Protection Act 2023, biometric data management must balance security, privacy, and sustainability to ensure ethical and responsible usage in the digital era. Biometric data pertains to the measurement and analysis of human physical and behavioral characteristics for identification or verification purposes. Biometrics encompasses two primary categories: physiological traits and behavioral patterns.

1.1 Physiological Biometrics

These include stable, physical attributes such as fingerprints, iris patterns, facial structures, vein geometry, and even DNA or odor. Such features are generally unchanging over time unless altered by factors like injury, medical intervention, or prolonged manual labor.

- **Fingerprints:** One of the most established biometric methods, fingerprints utilize the unique ridge patterns on an individual's fingers. Modern scanners process these patterns digitally for accurate identification, replacing traditional ink methods. Despite challenges like skin elasticity variations, fingerprints remain a reliable tool for identity authentication in devices and systems.
- **Finger/Hand Veins:** Vein pattern recognition uses infrared imaging to capture the unique vascular patterns under the skin. Its resistance to forgery and replication makes it a highly secure method.

- **Iris Recognition:** The iris's distinct patterns and colorations offer a robust basis for identity verification. However, environmental factors like lighting and eye angle can affect accuracy. Advanced imaging systems analyze features such as crypts and striations to create a unique biometric template.
- **Facial Recognition:** Facial recognition examines features such as the distance between eyes and facial contours. Approaches like feature-based analysis and Eigenface methodology enable automated, high-precision identification, with applications ranging from security to personal device authentication.
- **Voice Recognition:** Voice biometrics analyze both physiological traits (vocal tract structure) and behavioral patterns (tone and speech dynamics) to create a unique vocal signature. Factors like illness, however, can impact consistency.
- **DNA Matching:** DNA-based biometrics compare genetic samples (e.g., saliva or blood) to verify identity. DNA's inherent uniqueness makes it highly reliable for personal identification and lineage verification.

1.2 Behavioral Biometrics

Behavioral biometrics identify individuals by analyzing unique patterns in their actions, such as typing rhythms, walking styles, or voice modulation. These patterns, shaped by physiological factors like body proportions or hand dexterity, are recorded and compared to user profiles for authentication. Innovations in this field extend to involuntary actions like heart rhythms, which exhibit individual-specific patterns and broaden the scope of behavioral analysis.

- **Gait Analysis:** Gait biometrics measure unique walking patterns using imaging technology, making it effective for remote and large-scale surveillance.
- **Lip Movement:** Lip movement biometrics analyze the motion patterns of the lips during speech, providing a secure method for identity verification, especially when integrated with speech-based systems.
- **Signature Recognition:** This technique evaluates factors like pressure, stroke dynamics, and spatial dimensions during handwriting. It is used in both offline and digital environments for identity authentication.
- **Keystroke Dynamics:** Keystroke biometrics analyze typing patterns, such as speed and rhythm, to enhance traditional password security.

1.3 Key Features of Biometric Data

Biometric identifiers must be:

- **Unique:** Distinct to an individual.
- **Measurable:** Capable of being quantified and analyzed.
- **Consistent:** Remaining stable over time.
- **Digitally Convertible:** Processable by algorithms for integration into databases.

Unlike traditional identifiers (keys, IDs, passwords), biometric identification is intrinsic to an individual, enhancing security by eliminating reliance on external objects or memorized codes.

Biometric data holds a unique legal and regulatory position. It is categorized as sensitive personal data under frameworks like the GDPR, which demands robust technical processing and stringent privacy protection. Similarly, Indian e-governance policies define biometric data as any data derived from biometric characteristics, reflecting its critical role in secure identification systems. By integrating advanced algorithms and evolving technologies, biometrics represents a pivotal tool in modern authentication, surpassing conventional methods in both precision and reliability.

1.4 Biometric Identification Technologies and Techniques

Biometric authentication employs advanced technologies to ensure precision and reliability. Key methods include:

- **Fingerprint Technology:** Fingerprint systems analyze unique friction ridge patterns to authenticate identities. Digital scanning has replaced traditional ink methods, enabling high-resolution image processing. While fingerprint identification is highly accurate, real-time processing and handling variations due to skin elasticity remain technical challenges.
- **Hand Geometry Authentication:** Based on the shape and dimensions of hands, this method uses optical scanners to capture data, often in 2D or 3D formats. Although effective for access control, its inability to differentiate between individuals limits its applicability.
- **Vein Pattern Recognition:** Vein recognition captures vascular patterns using infrared imaging, offering robust security. Techniques like feature extraction and neural networks improve accuracy during the authentication process.
- **Facial Recognition:** Facial biometrics utilize software to map facial features or analyze Eigenface patterns. The latter focuses on variations in facial features and achieves high accuracy by reconstructing facial templates with advanced algorithms.
- **Iris Technology:** Iris recognition analyzes the intricate patterns of the iris, including features like crypts and striations. Though sensitive to external factors like lighting and focus, it remains one of the most secure biometric methods.

Biometric systems provide a sophisticated layer of security by combining physiological and behavioral uniqueness. While challenges persist, ongoing advancements in technologies such as neural networks and image processing continue to enhance reliability, making biometric authentication a cornerstone of modern identity verification systems.

2. RESEARCH METHOD

The research methodology for this study involves a comprehensive approach aimed at examining the impact of Biometric Data Protection in Corporations after the enactment of the Digital Personal Data Protection Act in India. This research employed a keyword-based search method to locate relevant studies concerning Biometric data protection and DPDP Act. The search utilized the following keywords: Biometric Data protection, Corporate Operations, Digital Personal Data Protection Act, etc. The main source of data handling is both primary and secondary data and is collected to examine the intentions and to answer the questions of the research from various research papers, books, case laws, websites, legal documents, news articles, and industry reports on the DPDP Act and biometric data protection.

3. REVIEW OF LITERATURE

The literature review delves into a broad array of scholarly works, encompassing books, articles, and research publications that address the intersection of biometric data protection and the Digital Personal Data Protection Act, 2023. It draws upon diverse sources, including law journals, legal literature databases (e.g., SCC Online, Research Gate, Hein Online), and statutory frameworks, providing a well-rounded understanding of the subject.

Jain *et. al.,* (2011) critically analyzed biometric systems, categorizing vulnerabilities and discussing proposed countermeasures in their book titled "Introduction to Biometrics". Chaudhari *et. al.,* (2013) provided an account of the historical development of biometric authentication systems in their study that was published in the International Journal of Engineering, Research, and Technology. Wijegunawardhana (2019) discussed the importance of protecting biometric identity, emphasizing the need for regulations to ensure high-level security in biometric identification.

Juma'h & Alnsour (2020) analyzed the ramifications of data intrusions on company operations, highlighting significant implications on metrics such as DDROA and DDROE. Bisztray *et. al.,* (2020) examined the landscape of privacy and data protection within biometric identification systems, emphasizing regulatory frameworks and risk assessments. Metekia *et. al.,* (2020) explored the legal protection of biometric data, highlighting the unique vulnerabilities associated with such data. Their study identified risks ranging from system design flaws to surveillance concerns, emphasizing the need for comprehensive legal safeguards. Uppal (2019) highlighted India's legal recognition of biometric data as sensitive under Privacy Rules and the Aadhaar Act, specifying its use for authentication purposes.

Burman (2023) scrutinized India's Data Protection and Privacy Act of 2023 (DPDP Act), emphasizing its significance while expressing concerns over the broad discretionary powers granted to the central government. Similarly, Kodandaram (2023) provided a detailed examination of the DPDP Act of 2023, underlining its importance in safeguarding personal data and privacy rights.

4. GLOBAL SUSTAINABILITY GOALS AND BIOMETRIC DATA USAGE

SDG 9: Promoting Innovation Through Biometric Authentication in Digital Solutions

This goal emphasizes building resilient infrastructure, promoting inclusive and sustainable industrialization, and fostering innovation. Biometric technologies play a pivotal role in advancing innovation by providing secure, reliable digital identification methods. They enable seamless access to digital financial services, e-governance platforms, and healthcare systems. Innovations in biometrics, such as fingerprint or iris recognition, have been integrated into mobile banking applications, improving accessibility in remote areas and reducing fraud. These advancements foster digital inclusion while supporting sustainable industrial growth.

SDG 12: Adopting Sustainable Data Lifecycle Management

Biometric systems generate vast amounts of data, necessitating efficient and sustainable data management practices. SDG 12 calls for responsible consumption and production patterns, which can be applied to the lifecycle of biometric data. Sustainable data lifecycle management ensures minimal environmental impact by reducing energy consumption during data storage, processing, and transfer. Data centers hosting biometric information can adopt energy-efficient technologies, utilize renewable energy sources, and follow policies for the ethical deletion and recycling of outdated data.

SDG 16: Ensuring Peace, Justice, and Strong Institutions via Secure Identity Management Systems

Biometric technologies contribute to SDG 16 by enabling secure and transparent identity verification, reducing corruption, and ensuring equal access to public services. In regions plagued by identity fraud, robust biometric systems help maintain electoral integrity, improve law enforcement efficiency, and streamline refugee management. These systems ensure that individuals receive benefits such as subsidies, healthcare, and education, fostering trust in public institutions and promoting justice.

4.1 Challenges of Biometric Data Usage in Meeting Sustainability Goals

- **Environmental Impact of Data Storage Systems:** Biometric data storage systems are resource-intensive, requiring significant energy for data centers to operate. The environmental footprint of these facilities includes high electricity usage for powering servers and cooling equipment, contributing to greenhouse gas emissions. Addressing this challenge involves shifting toward green data centers that leverage renewable energy sources and advanced cooling technologies. Implementing edge computing and data compression techniques can reduce the volume of biometric data transmitted and stored, further minimizing environmental impact.
- **Ethical Concerns in Developing Regions:** The adoption of biometric technologies in developing regions raises ethical concerns, including potential misuse of data and lack of informed consent. Inadequate infrastructure and limited access to digital literacy programs can exacerbate inequalities. For example, marginalized groups may face challenges in accessing biometric systems due to technological or systemic barriers, leading to their exclusion from critical services. Ensuring ethical deployment requires clear policies on data protection, education initiatives to enhance public understanding, and collaboration with local communities to address unique cultural and socio-economic contexts.

4.3 Legal Framework: DPDP Act 2023

- **Classification of Biometric Data as "Sensitive Personal Data":** The Digital Personal Data Protection Act (DPDPA) 2023 recognizes biometric data as "sensitive personal data," a classification that highlights the need for enhanced protection due to the potential risks associated with misuse or unauthorized access.
- **Consent Requirements for Data Collection and Processing:** The Act mandates explicit consent from individuals for the collection and processing of biometric data. Organizations are required to obtain informed consent before utilizing biometric information for any purpose, ensuring individuals retain control over their data.
- **Data Minimization and Purpose Limitation Principles:** In line with data protection principles, the Act enforces data minimization, which means only the

minimum necessary biometric data can be collected. Additionally, the processing of biometric data is strictly limited to the specific purpose for which consent was granted, preventing unnecessary or excessive use of personal information.

- **Cross-Border Data Transfer Restrictions:** The DPDPA imposes restrictions on the cross-border transfer of biometric data, ensuring that data is not transferred to countries that do not meet adequate data protection standards. This aims to safeguard individuals' biometric data from being subjected to potentially lax or conflicting regulatory environments.

The Digital Personal Data Protection Act 2023 takes a step towards aligning India's data protection framework with global standards, particularly the European Union's General Data Protection Regulation (GDPR). Both frameworks emphasize the need for clear consent, robust data protection, and individual rights over personal data. However, the DPDPA does not fully mirror the GDPR's comprehensive provisions, especially concerning the categorization of sensitive data and the rights afforded to individuals, signaling a gap in India's alignment with international best practices for data protection.

5. ALIGNING BIOMETRIC DATA PRACTICES WITH SUSTAINABILITY AND COMPLIANCE

The Digital Personal Data Protection Act (DPDP Act) 2023 introduces significant changes that impact corporate operations, particularly in the management of biometric data. Companies must align their biometric data practices with the sustainability goals and compliance requirements set forth by the Act. This ensures not only legal adherence but also builds consumer trust and safeguards privacy rights. The following points highlight key practices for aligning biometric data handling with the DPDP Act's provisions:

- **Stringent Compliance Requirements:** Corporations must adopt rigorous data management practices for biometric data, ensuring explicit consent, accurate data collection, and secure processing. Non-compliance may lead to penalties, reinforcing the need for robust data governance frameworks.
- **Transparent Data Handling:** Corporations must overhaul their data handling practices to align with the Act's principles. This includes securing explicit consent, implementing data minimization strategies, and ensuring transparency in data collection, storage, and usage.
- **Biometric Data Consent and Control:** The DPDP Act mandates that individuals provide clear, informed, and revocable consent for biometric data collection. Corporations must ensure this consent is obtained voluntarily, empowering individuals to control their personal biometric information.
- **Purpose Limitation and Data Minimization:** Biometric data must only be collected for specific, legitimate purposes, preventing misuse. Corporations must adopt data minimization practices, ensuring only essential data is processed to reduce exposure and enhance privacy protection.
- **Accuracy and Integrity:** Maintaining the accuracy and integrity of biometric data is essential. Regular verification processes should be implemented to prevent inaccuracies, ensuring that the data remains reliable and up-to-date.

- **Enhanced Security Measures:** Corporations handling biometric data must implement robust security protocols such as encryption, access controls, and secure storage to protect against breaches and unauthorized access, ensuring data privacy.
- **Data Subject Rights:** Individuals must have the right to access, rectify, delete, or port their biometric data. Corporations should create mechanisms that enable individuals to exercise these rights easily, fostering greater transparency and control over personal data.
- **Cross-Border Data Transfers:** The Act imposes restrictions on cross-border transfers of biometric data. Corporations must ensure compliance by implementing safeguards and obtaining necessary consent for international transfers, maintaining data protection standards globally.
- **Corporate Accountability and Transparency:** Companies must demonstrate accountability in managing biometric data, appointing data protection officers, conducting privacy impact assessments, and ensuring transparency in data processing activities. This enhances consumer trust and aligns with legal expectations.
- **Penal Measures for Non-Compliance:** Corporations must be aware of the penalties for non-compliance with biometric data protection standards, including fines and legal actions. Ensuring adherence to data protection measures minimizes reputational and financial risks (Kodandaram, 2025).

By aligning biometric data practices with the DPDP Act, corporations can ensure legal compliance, protect individual privacy rights, and contribute to sustainable data management practices. This approach will not only mitigate legal and reputational risks but also foster greater trust among consumers and stakeholders.

6. SUGGESTIONS AND RECOMMENDATION

Overcoming the challenges and ensuring the success of the DPDP Act initiatives in India requires several corrective actions. To enhance the effectiveness of the DPDP Act, the following recommendations are proposed:

1. Implement comprehensive awareness campaigns to educate businesses, organizations, and the general public about the provisions and implications of the DPDP Act. This will help foster a culture of data protection and encourage compliance with the law.
2. Provide specialized training and capacity-building programs to equip businesses, data fiduciaries, and regulatory authorities with the knowledge and skills necessary to implement the DPDP Act effectively. This includes training on data handling practices, compliance requirements, and cybersecurity measures.
3. Strengthen regulatory oversight mechanisms to ensure proactive enforcement of the DPDP Act. This involves establishing dedicated regulatory bodies with adequate resources and authority to monitor compliance, investigate violations, and impose penalties for non-compliance.
4. Foster collaboration and partnership between government agencies, industry stakeholders, and civil society organizations to address challenges and share best practices in data protection. Collaborative efforts can facilitate the exchange of knowledge, resources, and expertise to support the implementation of the DPDP Act.

5. Encourage technological innovation and investment in advanced data protection solutions to address emerging threats and vulnerabilities. This includes the development of encryption technologies, data anonymization techniques, and privacy-enhancing technologies to safeguard personal data.
6. Conduct regular public consultations and stakeholder engagements to gather feedback, address concerns, and incorporate diverse perspectives into the implementation of the DPDP Act. Engaging stakeholders in the decision-making process promotes transparency, inclusivity, and legitimacy in data protection efforts.
7. Simplify and streamline compliance processes to reduce the administrative burden on businesses and data fiduciaries. Clear guidance, standardized procedures, and online compliance tools can help facilitate compliance with the DPDP Act while minimizing regulatory complexities.
8. Collaboration between different sectors, including academia, industry, government, and civil society, should be fostered to leverage interdisciplinary expertise and resources in data protection. Such collaboration can facilitate knowledge sharing, innovation, and the development of holistic approaches to addressing data protection challenges.

7. CONCLUSION

The DPDP Act 2023 marks a significant step toward personal data protection in India, particularly in regulating biometric data usage within corporate operations. While it provides essential legal frameworks, its successful implementation will depend on the evolving regulatory landscape and the government's commitment to privacy protection. The law's pragmatic approach, with its relatively lower costs for businesses, allows for a balance between operational efficiency and privacy protection, although discretionary powers vested in the central government pose uncertainties. In the context of biometric data, the DPDP Act emphasizes the importance of robust privacy frameworks and compliance with legal obligations. Corporations must prioritize accountability, transparency, and proactive privacy measures, including consent management, purpose limitation, data minimization, and enhanced data security. Aligning biometric data usage with global sustainability goals and Indian data protection laws requires a comprehensive, ethical, and legally compliant approach. Corporations that foster a culture of privacy awareness, adhere to international standards, and implement responsible data governance can mitigate risks while maintaining consumer trust. By balancing innovation with ethical considerations, businesses can become responsible stewards of biometric data in the digital age, contributing to a secure, sustainable, and privacy-conscious future.

REFERENCES

Biometrics Institute. (n.d.). Physiological and behavioural biometrics.

Bisztray, T.; Cseh, G. and Pelle, A. (2020). Data protection impact assessment in identity management with a focus on biometrics. *Interdisciplinary Description of Complex Systems,* 18(1), 72–85.

Burman, A. (2023). Understanding India's new data protection law. *Carnegie Endowment for International Peace.*

Chaudhari, R.D.; Pawar, A.A. and Deore, R.S. (2013). The historical development of biometric authentication techniques: A recent overview. *International Journal of Engineering Research and Technology.*

Devi, T. (2021). Biometric data, identification and authentication in India – Legal framework, challenges and impact. *International Journal of Law Management & Humanities*, 4(3).

Jain, A.K.; Ross, A.A. and Nandakumar, K. (2011). Introduction to biometric. Springer.

Juma'h, A.; Al Shobaki, M.; El Talla, S.A.; Abu-Naser, S.S. and Amuna, Y.M. (2020). The effect of data breaches on company performance. *International Journal of Accounting and Information Management,* 28(4), 723–748.

Kodandaram, M.G. (2023). A detailed analysis of the Digital Personal Data Protection Act, 2023.

Matekja, J.; Fialova, E.; Krausova, A.S. and Hazan, H. (2020). Biometric data and its specific legal protection. Institute of State and Law, Czech Academy of Sciences.

Samim, S.A. and Zai, M.E.A. (2023). Navigating data protection in India: Key laws and regulations for protecting personal information. Trinity Law Review, 3(2). ACS Publisher.

Uppal, A. (n.d.). Biometric data: Regime in India. AZB & Partners.

Wijegunawardhana, P.K.D.P. (2019, November). Protecting bio-metrics identity in the world. *In IEEE Conference Proceedings.*

Analysis of Charging and Discharging Patterns in Solar Rechargeable Wireless Sensors

Amit Holkar[1] and Swapnil Jain[2]

ABSTRACT: Wireless sensor networks (WSNs) have emerged as a crucial technology for various applications, including environmental monitoring, industrial automation, and smart cities. The integration of solar energy harvesting capabilities into WSN nodes has gained significant attention due to its potential to extend network lifetime and reduce maintenance costs. This study presents a comprehensive simulation-based analysis of solar-powered wireless sensor networks using MATLAB. The simulation model incorporates 100 solar rechargeable sensor nodes, each with distinct charging and discharging time constants to reflect real-world variability. The primary objective of this research is to evaluate the network's performance under different scenarios of energy depletion, specifically when 10%, 20%, and 50% of the total number of rechargeable solar nodes fall below a predefined threshold voltage level. The simulation framework allows for the assessment of various network parameters, including node longevity, energy consumption patterns, and overall network reliability. This approach provides insights into the system's behavior under different stress levels, mimicking real-world conditions such as prolonged periods of low solar irradiance or increased energy demand. The insights gained from the simulation results can inform the design of adaptive energy management strategies, optimized node placement, and improved solar harvesting technologies for WSNs.

Keywords: *Lifetime, Network Reliability, Perpetual Network, Sensor Networks, Solar Harvesting.*

1. INTRODUCTION

Wireless Sensor Networks (WSNs) have gained significant importance in various applications, including environmental monitoring, industrial automation, smart cities, and precision agriculture (Chowdary *et. al.*, 2023). One of the primary challenges in WSNs is the energy constraint due to battery limitations. Energy-efficient solutions are crucial to extending the network's lifetime and reducing maintenance efforts. Solar energy harvesting presents a promising solution by harnessing renewable energy to power sensor nodes. However, challenges such as variability in solar irradiance and effective energy management need to be addressed (Sah *et. al.*, 2023).

2. RESEARCH OBJECTIVES AND CONTRIBUTIONS

Yadav & Kumar (2023) addressed the primary problem of understanding how energy depletion impacts the performance of solar-powered WSNs. There is a knowledge gap in comprehending the network's resilience to node failures caused by energy depletion

---

[1] Research Scholar, Shri Vaishnav Institute of Technology & Science, Shri Vaishnav Vidyapeeth Vishwavidyalaya, Indore, India. E-mail: amitholkar@gmail.com

[2] Assistant Professor, Shri Vaishnav Institute of Technology & Science, Shri Vaishnav Vidyapeeth Vishwavidyalaya, Indore, India.

under varying conditions. In this paper, various scenarios for the WSN have been considered and comparison has been drawn for a WSN without recharging facility and with the provision of rechargeable sensor nodes.

The primary objective of this research is to evaluate the performance of a solar-powered WSN under different energy depletion scenarios using MATLAB simulations. Specific objectives include:

- Modelling a WSN with solar-powered nodes, incorporating realistic charging and discharging characteristics (Rahman *et. al.*, 2019).
- Simulating the network's behaviour when 10%, 20%, and 50% of nodes fall below a critical voltage threshold.
- Assessing network parameters such as node longevity, energy consumption, and network reliability.
- Analyzing the impact of charging and discharging time constants on network performance (Fan *et. al.*, 2008).

The contributions of this research are:

- Providing insights into the network behaviour under different operating conditions.
- Informing the design of adaptive energy management strategies.
- Suggesting optimized node placement and improved solar harvesting technologies.
- Offering a foundation for future research into hybrid energy harvesting systems (Akyildiz *et. al.*, (2002).

3. REVIEW OF LITERATURE

WSNs comprise sensor nodes that communicate wirelessly to collect and transmit data. These networks are used in various applications, from environmental monitoring to industrial automation. Challenges include energy constraints, scalability, and reliability (Raghunathan *et. al.*, 2002).

Solar Energy Harvesting for WSNs

Research on solar energy harvesting techniques for WSNs has explored various solar panel technologies and their efficiency. Energy storage solutions, such as batteries and supercapacitors, are crucial for storing harvested energy (Park & Chou, 2006).

Energy Management Strategies in WSNs

Different energy management protocols and algorithms, such as adaptive duty cycling, sleep scheduling, and dynamic voltage scaling, are employed to balance energy consumption across the network (Rahman *et. al.*, 2019).

Simulation Tools used for Analysis

Simulation tools like MATLAB, NS-3, and OMNeT++ are used in WSN research. MATLAB is chosen for this study due to its advantages in modelling energy systems and performing numerical analysis (Fan *et. al.*, 2008).

Related Work on Energy Depletion Analysis

Studies have investigated the impact of node failures on WSN performance, focusing on network resilience and fault tolerance. There is limited research on analyzing solar-powered WSNs under varying energy depletion scenarios (Akyildiz *et. al.*, 2002).

4. RESEARCH METHOD

Simulation Environment

- Platform: MATLAB Simulation Environment
- Area: 100 × 100 cm square region
- Simulation Duration: 5000 timesteps
- Base Station Location: Center of the area (50,50)
- Initial Node Energy: 1000 mJ
- Threshold Energy Level: 80% of initial energy (800 mJ)

Network Model

- Network Size: 50 wireless sensor nodes
- Node Distribution: Random uniform distribution
- Energy Model:
- Distance-dependent energy consumption
- Linear discharge rate proportional to distance
- Discharge coefficient: 1.0
- Energy consumption formula:

$$\text{discharge\_rate} = 1.0 \times \left(\frac{\text{distance}}{\text{area\_size}}\right) \times \frac{\text{initial\_energy}}{100}$$

Energy Model

1. *Base Energy Parameters*

- Initial Node Energy: 1000 mJ
- Threshold Level: 800 mJ (80% of initial)
- Maximum Energy Cap: Cannot exceed initial energy

2. *Energy Consumption Factors*

- Distance-dependent discharge
- Linear relationship with distance
- Normalized by area size
- Base discharge coefficient: 1.0

3. *Recharging Mechanism*

- Recovery rate: 20% of discharge rate
- Continuous recharging
- Upper limit: Initial energy level
- Net energy change = Recharge – Discharge

4. *Energy States*

- Full Energy: 1000 mJ
- Operational Threshold: 800 mJ
- Critical State: Below threshold
- Dead State: 0 mJ

This energy model effectively captures:

- Distance-based energy depletion
- Threshold-based performance monitoring
- Recharging dynamics
- Energy conservation constraints
- Network lifetime characteristics

Simulation Scenarios

Scenario 1: Non-rechargeable Nodes

- Continuous energy depletion based on distance
- No energy recovery mechanism
- Nodes permanently fall below threshold when energy depletes

Scenario 2: Rechargeable Nodes

- Energy depletion based on distance
- Recharging capability at 20% of discharge rate
- Continuous energy recovery mechanism
- Maximum energy capped at initial energy level

Performance Metrics

Number of nodes above threshold energy

Time to reach critical network degradation points:

- 10% node degradation (45 nodes remaining)
- 20% node degradation (40 nodes remaining)
- 30% node degradation (35 nodes remaining)
- 50% node degradation (25 nodes remaining)

Network lifetime analysis

- Energy depletion patterns
- Node survival rate over time
- Impact of distance on energy consumption
- Network sustainability metrics

These parameters and configurations allow for comprehensive analysis of network behavior under both scenarios, providing insights into the effectiveness of recharging mechanisms and their impact on network longevity.

5. RESULTS AND DISCUSSION

The simulation results are presented through three key figures that demonstrate the behavior and performance of the wireless sensor network under both non-rechargeable and rechargeable scenarios.

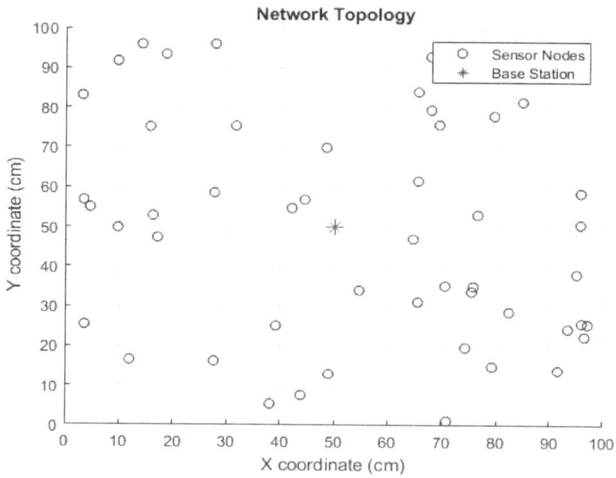

Figure 1: Network Topology

The network topology visualization as given by Figure 1 shows the random distribution of 50 sensor nodes across the 100 × 100 cm area, with the base station positioned at the center (50, 50). This spatial distribution is crucial as it directly influences the energy consumption patterns of individual nodes based on their distance from the base station.

Figure 2 illustrates the network degradation pattern for non-rechargeable nodes. The graph shows a steady decline in the percentage of nodes above the threshold energy (80% of initial energy). Key observations include:

- The 10% degradation point occurs relatively early, indicating rapid energy depletion of the furthest nodes

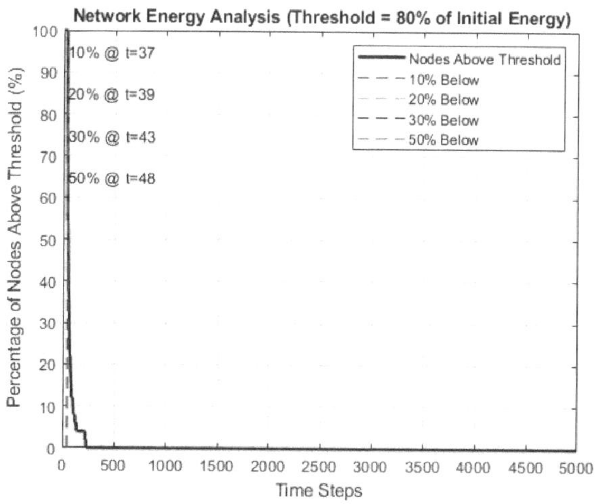

Figure 2: Network Energy Analysis - Non-Rechargeable Scenario

- A steeper decline between 20% and 30% degradation points
- The 50% mark shows significant network deterioration
- The curve demonstrates the classic energy-hole problem where outer nodes deplete faster.

The introduction of recharging capability Figure 3 shows markedly different behaviour:

- More gradual decline in node energy levels
- Extended time intervals between degradation points
- Higher sustainability in network operation
- Reduced impact of the energy-hole problem
- Some nodes maintain stable energy levels due to the 20% recharge rate

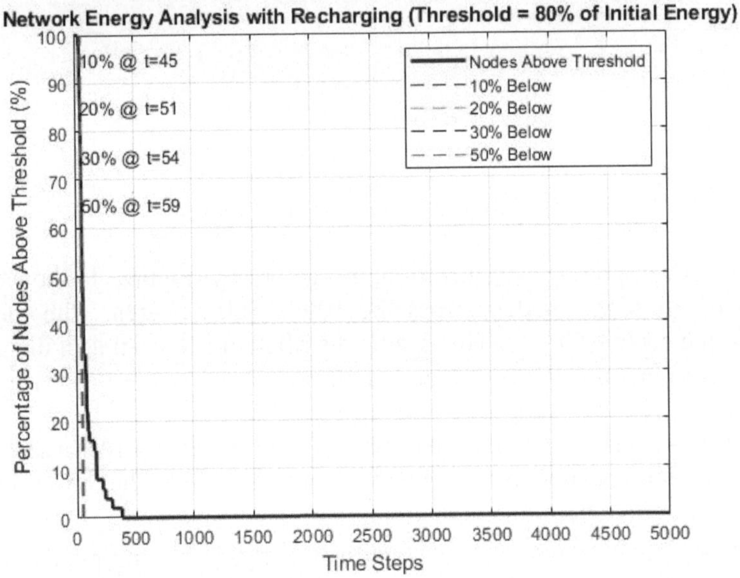

Figure 3: Network Energy Analysis with Recharging

The comparison between non-rechargeable and rechargeable scenarios reveals:

1. Network Lifetime: Significant extension in the rechargeable scenario
2. Degradation Pattern:
   - Non-rechargeable: Sharp, consistent decline
   - Rechargeable: Gradual decline with potential stabilization
3. Spatial Impact: Distance-based energy consumption remains a factor, but recharging provides a compensatory mechanism.
4. Threshold Maintenance: More nodes maintain above-threshold energy levels in the rechargeable scenario.

These results demonstrate the substantial impact of incorporating recharging capability in wireless sensor networks, particularly for long-term deployments. The 20% recharge rate provides a meaningful extension of network lifetime while maintaining operational integrity above the 80% threshold for longer periods.

Summarise analysis without recharging:

- Time when 10% nodes below threshold: 37 (Nodes remaining: 45)
- Time when 20% nodes below threshold: 39 (Nodes remaining: 40)
- Time when 30% nodes below threshold: 43 (Nodes remaining: 35)
- Time when 50% nodes below threshold: 48 (Nodes remaining: 25)

Summarise analysis with recharging:

- Time when 10% nodes below threshold: 45 (Nodes remaining: 45)
- Time when 20% nodes below threshold: 51 (Nodes remaining: 40)
- Time when 30% nodes below threshold: 54 (Nodes remaining: 35)
- Time when 50% nodes below threshold: 59 (Nodes remaining: 25)

6. CONCLUSION

The simulation demonstrates the non-uniform energy depletion pattern in wireless sensor networks, where nodes farther from the base station deplete their energy more rapidly. This creates an energy hole problem, particularly affecting outer nodes first. The 80% threshold analysis provides valuable insights into network lifetime and degradation patterns, which can be crucial for network planning and maintenance scheduling. Future implementations could benefit from adaptive transmission power control or clustering mechanisms to achieve more uniform energy consumption across the network.

REFERENCES

Akyildiz, F.; Su, W.; Sankarasubramaniam, Y. and Cayirci, E. (2002). Wireless sensor networks: A survey. *Computer Networks*, 38(4), 393–422.

Chowdary, R.P.; Priyadarsini, C.I.; Reddy, V.J.; Devi, P.A.; Chandrakanth, A. and Aditya, T.N. (2023). Solar powered sensors for efficient routing without power constraints. *In 2023 3rd International Conference on Innovative Practices in Technology and Management (ICIPTM)* (pp. 1–5). Uttar Pradesh, India.

Fan, K.W.; Zheng, Z. and Sinha, P. (2008). Steady and fair rate allocation for rechargeable sensors in perpetual sensor networks. *In Proceedings of the 6th ACM Conference on Embedded Network Sensor Systems (SenSys '08)* (pp. 239–252). Raleigh, NC, USA.

Hill, J.; Szewczyk, R.; Woo, A.; Hollar, S.; Culler, D.E. and Pister, K.S.J. (2000). System architecture directions for networked sensors. *ACM SIGOPS Operating Systems Review*, 34(5), 93–104.

Kansal, A.; Hsu, J.; Zahedi, S. and Srivastava, M.B. (2007). Power management in energy harvesting sensor networks. *ACM Transactions on Embedded Computing Systems,* 6(4), 32–38.

Mottola, L. and Picco, G.P. (2011). Programming wireless sensor networks: Fundamental concepts and state of the art. *ACM Computing Surveys*, 43(3), 1–51.

Park, J. and Chou, P.H. (2006). AmbiMax: Autonomous energy harvesting platform for multi-supply wireless sensor nodes. *In Third Annual IEEE Communications Society Conference on Sensor, Mesh and Ad Hoc Communications and Networks* (pp. 168–177). Reston, VA, USA.

Raghunathan, V.; Schurgers, C.; Park, S. and Srivastava, M.B. (2002). Energy-aware wireless microsensor networks. *IEEE Signal Processing Magazine*, 19(2), 40–50.

Rahman, B.; Bakhtawar, N.; Saleem, F.; Ahmad, F. and Rizwan, M. (2019). Energy optimization in wireless rechargeable sensor networks. *International Journal of Scientific and Research Publications,* 9(4), 477–483.

Sah, D.K.; Hazra, A.; Mazumdar, N. and Amgoth, T. (2023). An efficient routing awareness-based scheduling approach in energy harvesting wireless sensor networks. *IEEE Sensors Journal,* 23(15), 17638–17647.

Sharma, A.; Mishra, A. and Singh, M. (2010). Energy efficient strategies for wireless sensor networks: A survey. *International Journal of Computer Applications*, 6(2), 12–18.

Vullers, R.; Van Schaijk, R.; Visser, H.; Penders, J. and Hoof, C. (2010). Energy harvesting for autonomous wireless sensor networks. *IEEE Solid-State Circuits Magazine*, 2(2), 29–38.

Yadav, K. and Kumar, A. (2023). The smart analysis of prolong lifetime in industrial wireless sensor networks. *In 2023 International Conference on Distributed Computing and Electrical Circuits and Electronics (ICDCECE),* pp. 1–6, Ballar, India.

Analysis of Defects and Faults in Quantum-Dot Cellular Automata (QCA) Circuits: A Case Study on Full Adder

Preet Jain[1] and Namit Gupta[2]

ABSTRACT: Quantum-dot Cellular Automata (QCA) is an emerging nanotechnology that offers a promising alternative to traditional CMOS technology for digital circuit design due to its ultra-low power consumption, high-density integration, and novel computational paradigms. However, like any technology, QCA circuits are prone to defects and faults that can affect their reliability and performance. This paper investigates various types of defects and faults in QCA-based digital circuits, including vacancy cells, Interstitial cells, and cell defects due to manufacturing limitations. A comprehensive comparative analysis is conducted to evaluate these faults against those found in circuits designed with other existing technologies, such as CMOS, highlighting key similarities and differences in fault manifestation, detection, and impact. This paper provides a critical foundation for advancing QCA circuits, paving the way for more robust digital systems in nanotechnology.

Keywords: *CMOS, Digital Circuits, High Density Integration, Interstitial Cells, Nanotechnology.*

1. INTRODUCTION

The continuous scaling of CMOS technology, as per Moore's Law, is reaching fundamental physical limits, necessitating exploration of alternative paradigms. QCA emerges as a viable option due to its unique operational principles based on electron tunnelling within quantum dots. Unlike CMOS circuits, which rely on current flow, QCA leverages the position of electrons within quantum dots to represent binary information, enabling ultra-low power consumption and high-speed operation.

1.1 QCA Basics

Quantum-dot Cellular Automata's basic building block is the QCA cell. Four quantum dots are inserted at the corners of the square construction. Columbic interaction allows quantum mechanical particles like electrons to tunnel between quantum dots. Columbic interactions between cells are used to convey information between cells. Four quantum dots are placed in the corners of a square in a QCA cell's layout. There are four quantum

[1] Research Scholar, Department of Electrical & Electronics Engineering, Shri Vaishnav Institute of Technology and Science, Shri Vaishnav Vidyapeeth Vishwavidyalaya, Indore, India.
E-mail: preetjain@gmail.com

[2] Director and Dean Engineering, Shri Vaishnav Institute of Technology and Science, Shri Vaishnav Vidyapeeth Vishwavidyalaya, Indore, India.

dots in every cell, and electrons go from one quantum dot to the next. After polarization, two electrons are introduced into the cell. Figure 1 shows the two electrons resting on a diagonal owing to their columbic interaction with QCA cells, which causes tunnelling.

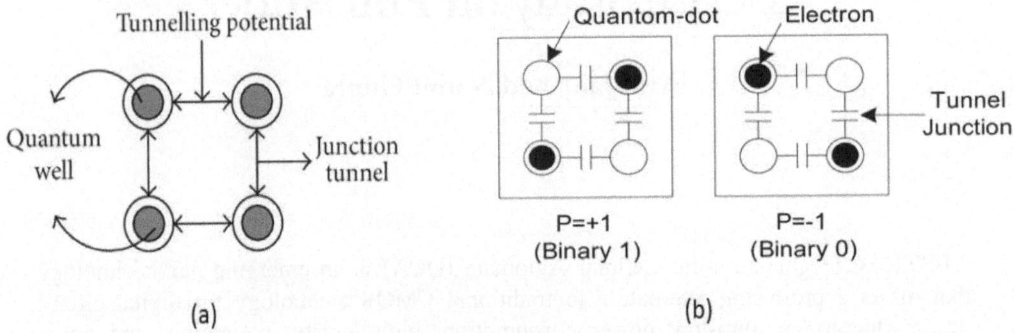

Figure 1: (a) QCA Cell (b) Binary Representation as per Polarization of Quantum Dots

In order to construct QCA-based storage components, logic gates, and connections, one has only to employ these fundamental components. Figure 1(a) depicts a QCA cell with four quantum dots. While Figure 1(b) represents the logic 1 and logic 0 in terms of Quantum cell polarization. Despite its advantages, QCA's reliance on precise nanoscale fabrication introduces susceptibility to defects and faults, impacting its performance and reliability. Understanding these faults and developing robust fault-tolerant designs are critical for the practical deployment of QCA-based systems.

1.2 Defects and Faults in QCA Circuits

Defects and faults are concepts in electronic systems design and manufacturing, particularly relevant in the context of reliability and performance. A defect refers to a physical imperfection or anomaly in the manufacturing process of a circuit or device. It is a tangible flaw at the hardware level that can potentially affect the circuit's behaviour. While a fault refers to a deviation in the intended behaviour of a circuit or system caused by defects. Faults represent the logical or functional consequence of a defect on the circuit's operation.

1.3 Types of QCA Defects

Even Quantum cell automata designs are also vulnerable to manufacturing defects. Most of the reports presented by Tahoori *et. al.,* (2004), Momenzadeh *et. al.,* (2005) & Dysart *et. al.,* (2005) related to structural defects in QCA circuits show displacement and misalignment of the cells.

In general, the manufacturing deficiencies may be separated into four distinct categories.

- As shown in Figure 2a cells that have been rotated about their axis are the root cause of the dislocation problems.
- A QCA cell has a dopant fault if it contains one or more additional dots or if it is missing dots altogether as illustrated by Figure 2b.
- The illustration in Figure 2c represents an interstitial fault, A cell is misplaced in either the horizontal or the vertical direction.

- Figure 2d shows the "vacancy defect" refers to the situation in which a complete cell is missing.
- QCA circuits rely on a four-phase clocking scheme to propagate signals. Any irregularity in clock generation or application can lead to faults.

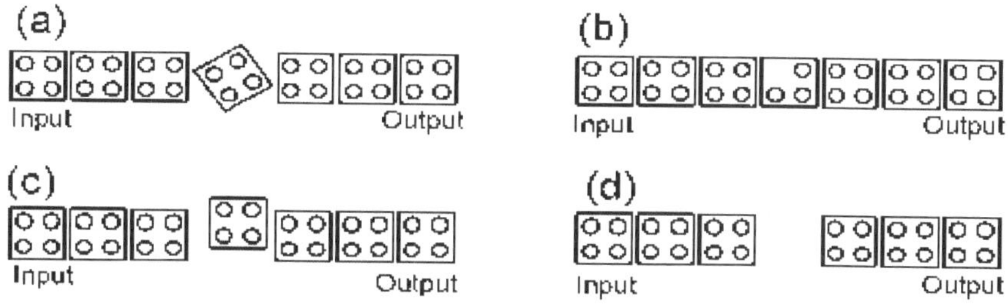

Figure 2: Structural Defects: (a) Dislocation, (b) Dopant, (c) Interstitial and (d) Vacancy

2. REVIEW OF LITERATURE

Quantum-dot-Cellular Automata (QCA) is emerging as a potential option for integrated circuit technology, eliminating the need for transistors and potentially replacing CMOS technology. However, QCA devices operate at the molecular scale, making flaws more prone to develop. This necessitates the development of suitable fault models and test generation schemes for QCA-based designs. Tahoori *et. al.,* (2004) conducted research on testing QCA-based designs, demonstrating that coupling mechanisms and behavior of flaws at the logic level differ from those in standard CMOS. They found that majority voters require a fixed number of test vectors to achieve 100% fault coverage. A design-for-test strategy was also discussed, leading to a more concise test set.

Momenzadeh *et. al.,* (2005) investigated deposition faults in devices and circuits composed of QCA for molecular implementation. They found that missing cell deposition defects have a more significant impact than increased cell deposition defects. The straight shape offers superior resistance to single cell deposition faults, while the L-shaped wire has only one fault in functionality. The author proposed the design, testing, and characterization of a new complex QCA logic gate called the AOI gate, which proved to be resistant to fluctuations in the manufacturing process. They also addressed testing at the logic level and built suitable test sets. Gupta *et. al.,* (2007) introduced the first thorough testing approach for combinational QCA circuits, developing fault collapse theorems for majority circuits. They demonstrated that even if an SSF test finds every single SSF in a circuit, it does not guarantee it will find all simulated QCA flaws in the gates that make up the majority.

Adineh-Vand *et. al.,* (2008) introduced a partitioning methodology for evaluating Quantum-dot Cellular Automata circuits, which improves controllability, observability, and testability. Mohammedi *et. al.,* (2012) investigated a testable implementation of reversible QCA circuits, using the partitioning capacity and multilayer property to find faults. Dhare & Mehta (2016) implemented the QCA combinational circuit and half adder, analysing faults produced by single missing cell deposition problems at both layout and logic levels. Mukherjee *et. al.,* (2016) studied the single electron fault (SEF) in QCA, finding that it is not comparable to ordinary faults of QCA. Dhare & Mehta (2018) focused on defect analysis, construction of fault models, and derivation of characteristics for the QCA Majority Voter (MV) to efficiently build test patterns for QCA circuits. They showed that Multiple Missing Cell (MMC) defects cause significant differences in functionality compared to Single Missing Cell (SMC) defects and thus need to be considered when tests are being generated. Verilog fault models were suggested for functional verification, timing verification, and activation of faults produced by MMC defects. Dhare & Mehta (2019) aimed on test generation for QCA combinational circuits, using the expansion of the basic Automatic Test Pattern Generator (ATPG) to illustrate MV-based circuits in the testing process. Tiwari & Dhare (2022) developed an algorithm for automatic test pattern generation (ATPG) based on D-algorithm to test stuck-at faults in QCA circuits. Yang *et. al.,* (2022) presented a novel approach to designing QCA testing circuits to reduce total consumption space.

3. FAULT MANIFESTATION USING FULL ADDER

Faults in QCA circuits manifest differently than in CMOS due to the nature of information representation and propagation. In QCA, defects often lead to improper polarization states or signal disruptions, whereas CMOS faults typically result in open circuits, short circuits, or parametric deviations. Here we are presenting our analysis and observations using Full adder design implemented in QCA. Figure 3a shows one such full adder given by Safaiezadeh *et. al.,* (2023). Three major kinds of defects i.e., 1. Cell Displacement, 2. Cell Rotation and 3. Cell Omission defects were introduced on the possible fault sites as shown in Figure 3b in the QCA Designer tools and its impacts are observed.

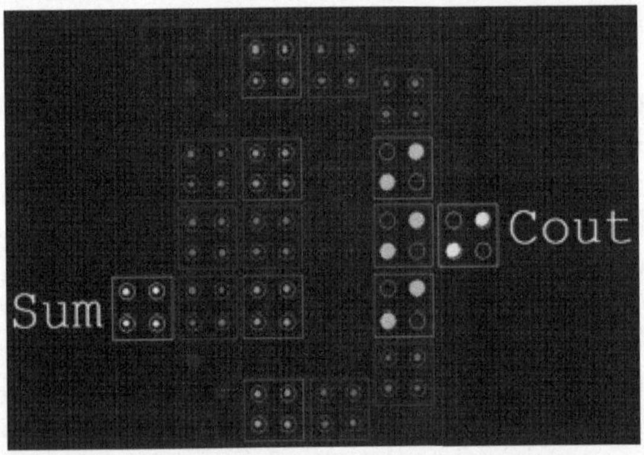

Figure 3a: Full Adder Design

11	12	13	14	15	16	17	18
21	22	23	24	25	26	27	28
31	32	33	34	35	36	37	38
41	42	43	44	45	46	47	48
51	52	53	54	55	56	57	58
61	62	63	64	65	66	67	68
71	72	73	74	75	76	77	78
81	82	83	84	85	86	87	88
91	92	93	94	95	96	97	98

Figure 3b: Tentative Fault Site

To develop a better understanding all the cell sites were numbered, the blue cells in Figure 3b show the original QCA cell's location of the Full adder design and Orange colored cells show the tentative fault location. The table shows the results of the simulation carried out using QCA Designer tool developed by the University of Calgary and Notre-Dam as proposed by Walus *et. al.,* (2004).

Table 1: Fault Analysis for Displaced Cells

Displaced Cell	***Output***	***Inference***
24 → 14, 24 → 23, 25 → 15,	Correct	As cell Radius of effect is 65 nm, thus it has no effect on output, even if the Cell 32 is displaced to 3 cell location
36 → 26, 36 → 37, 46 → 47, 46 → 45, 66 → 67, 66 → 65	Correct	
76 → 77, 76 → 88, 76 → 88	Correct	
85 → 86, 85 → 75, 85 → 95	Correct	
84 → 94, 84 → 83, 33 → 32, 43 → 41	Correct	
62 → 61	Correct	Stuck at Zero, 001,010,100,111 need to be applied on inputs for testing
57 → 58	Incorrect	Stuck at Zero, 011,101,110,111 need to be applied on inputs for testing
64 → 65, 44 → 45	Incorrect	Random, 101 need to apply as Cout should be 1, but it will provide zero on test
73 → 83	Incorrect	Stuck at B, 011 will be applied
73 → 72	Incorrect	Output Sum behaving Randomly, Test Case 011
55 → 45, 55 → 65	Incorrect	Outputs Inverted. Test cases are 000,001,010,100,101,110,111

Rotated cell	***Output***	***Inference***
33, 24, 25, 36, 66, 84, 85, 53, 43, 54, 55	Correct	Stuck at B, 011 will be applied
56	Incorrect	Output Carry behaving Randomly, Test Cases are 001, 000
57	Incorrect	Stuck at Gnd, 011, 101, 110, 111
73	Incorrect	Carry inverted, Test Cases are 001, 010, 011, 100, 101, 110, 111
63	Incorrect	Sum behaving Randomly, Test Cases are 001, 010, 100
62	Incorrect	Sum Stuck at Gnd, Test cases are 001, 010, 100, 111
44, 64	Incorrect	Cout Stuck at 1, Test Cases are 001, 010, 100

Omitted cell	*Output*	*Inference*
33	Incorrect	Carry Inverted, Test Cases are 100, 010, 000, 001 will be applied
24, 25, 36, 46, 66, 76, 85, 84, 54, 43, 53	Correct	
56	Incorrect	Random Carry Out Test Cases are 001, 101
57	Incorrect	Carry Output missing Test Cases are 001, 010, 011, 100, 101, 110, 111
62	Incorrect	SUM Output missing Test Cases are 001, 010, 011, 100, 101, 110, 111
73	Incorrect	Missing A Random output, Test Cases are 000, 100
55(B Missing), 64, 44	Incorrect	Cout Stuck at 1, Test Cases are 001, 010, 100
63	Incorrect	Sum behaving randomly, Test cases are 100, 101, 001

4. RESULTS

- **Omitted Cell Faults:** These faults generally have a significant impact on the functionality of the adder, leading to incorrect outputs such as inverted carries, missing outputs, and random behavior. The critical cells identified include 33, 56, 57, 62, 73, and 63.
- **Rotated Cell Faults:** These faults also have a significant impact on the functionality of the adder, leading to incorrect outputs such as random carry behavior and stuck-at faults. The critical cells identified include 56, 57, 73, and 62.
- **Displaced Cell Faults:** These faults have varying impacts on the functionality of the adder. Some displacements do not significantly impact the functionality, while others lead to incorrect outputs such as stuck-at faults and random behavior. The critical cells identified include 62, 57, 64, 44, 73, and 55.

5. CONCLUSION

Above mentioned faults such as Cell Omission faults, Displacement Fault, Cell Rotation faults have been investigated manually on Full Adder. Some of the faults are following standard model that are found in CMOS technology like Stuck at Zero, Stuck at one and Stuck at pin. But there are various faults which are behaving randomly, so there is need for further investigation on other types of QCA circuits. Comparing to CMOS technology the fault sites increase enormously with the increase in QCA circuit complexity, and thus manual procedure of fault identification becomes time consuming, so there is a need of development of fault identification algorithm with the help of that the test procedure can be applied on other QCA circuits to reduce the overall time.

REFERENCES

Adineh-Vand, A.; Latif-Shabgahi, G. and Azghadi, M.R. (2008). Increasing testability in QCA circuits using a new test method. *Proceedings of the 3rd International Design and Test Workshop (IDT 2008)*, 40–44.

Dhare, V. and Mehta, U. (2016). Fault analysis of QCA combinational circuit at layout & logic level. *2015 IEEE International WIE Conference on Electrical and Computer Engineering (WIECON-ECE)*, 22–26.

Dhare, V. and Mehta, U. (2019). Test pattern generator for majority voter-based QCA combinational circuits targeting MMC defect. *2019 IEEE European Test Symposium (ETS)*, 1–2.

Dhare, V. and Mehta, U.S. (2018). Multiple missing cell defect modeling for QCA devices. Journal of Electronic Testing, *34*(6), 623–641.

Dysart, T.J.; Lohmer, D.J. and Kogge, P.M. (2005). Missing cell patterns causing circuit failures in densely packed molecular QCA wires. *Proceedings of IEEE International Symposium on Defect and Fault Tolerance in VLSI Systems*, 1–14.

Gupta, P.; Jha, N.K. and Lingappan, L. (2007). A test generation framework for quantum cellular automata circuits. *IEEE Transactions on Very Large-Scale Integration (VLSI) Systems, 15*(1), 24–36.

Momenzadeh, M.; Huang, J. and Lombardi, F. (2005). Defect characterization and tolerance of QCA sequential devices and circuits. *Proceedings of IEEE International Symposium on Defect and Fault Tolerance in VLSI Systems,* 199–207.

Momenzadeh, M.; Huang, J.; Tahoori, M.B. and Lombardi, F. (2005). Characterization, test, and logic synthesis of AND-OR-Inverter (AOI) gate design for QCA implementation. IEEE Transactions on Computer-Aided Design of Integrated Circuits and Systems, *24*(12), 1881–1892.

Momenzadeh, M.; Ottavi, M. and Lombardi, F. (2005). Modeling QCA defects at molecular level in combinational circuits. *Proceedings of IEEE International Symposium on Defect and Fault Tolerance in VLSI Systems*, 208–216.

Mukherjee, R.; Tripathi, S.; Sen, S. and Sen, B. (2016). Characterization and analysis of single electron fault of QCA primitives. *International Conference on Microelectronics, Computing and Communications (MicroCom 2016).*

Safaiezadeh, B.; Haghparast, M. and Kettunen, L. (2023). Novel efficient scalable QCA XOR and full adder designs.

Tahoori, M.B.; Huang, J.; Momenzadeh, M. and Lombardi, F. (2004). Testing of quantum cellular automata. *IEEE Transactions on Nanotechnology, 3*(4), 432–442.

Tahoori, M.B.; Momenzadeh, M.; Huang, J. and Lombardi, F. (2004). Defects and fault characterization in quantum cellular automata. *NSTI Nanotechnology Conference and Trade Show - NSTI Nanotech* 2004, *3*, 190–193.

Tiwari, A. and Dhare, V. (2022). Development of test pattern generation for QCA-based circuits. *Proceedings of International Conference on Advances in Computing and Data Sciences*, 801–811.

Walus, K.; Dysart, T.J.; Jullien, G.A. and Budiman, R.A. (2004). QCADesigner: A rapid design and simulation tool for quantum-dot cellular automata. *IEEE Transactions on Nanotechnology, 3*(1), 26–31.

Yang, Y.; Li, K. and Luo, Z. (2022). A new design for testability of the circuits based on quantum-dot cellular automata to reduce total consumption area. *Optik, 262*, 169266.

Zahra Mohammadi, M.H. and Mohammadi, M. (2012). Designing testable reversible QCA circuits using a new reversible Mux2x1. *Journal of Advanced Computer Research, 3*(1), 51–64.

Analysis of Palmar Creases for Personal Identification

Ayushi Beragi[1] and Swati Dubey Mishra[2]

ABSTRACT: Palmar creases or flexion creases are the lines or wrinkles found on the palms of the hands formed during foetal development around the 12th week of gestation. These creases aid in grasping objects and have a unique, persistent pattern for everyone. Along with fingerprints, palmar creases serve as a valuable tool in personal identification due to their distinctiveness and longevity. They can be effectively utilized in forensic investigations and biometric systems to establish an individual's identity. The purpose of this study is to explore the potential of palmar creases as a reliable biometric feature for personal identification particularly in criminal and forensic contexts.

Keywords: *Biometrics, Flexion Creases, Forensic Investigation, Gestation, Persistent Pattern.*

1. INTRODUCTION

Palmprints are the unique patterns found on the palm of the hand have emerged as a vital tool in forensic science. They cover a larger surface area compared to fingerprints providing a more extensive array of ridge patterns, minutiae and creases. This richness increases the probability of capturing usable prints at crime scenes. Palmprints are often left unintentionally on various surfaces such as weapons, windows, and other objects handled during the commission of a crime making them a valuable source of forensic evidence. They are crucial evidence in identifying individuals and building connections between suspects and victims. Palmar flexion creases are the folds or wrinkles formed on the palm of the hand that appear because of the skin's underlying anatomical structure during fetal development. They serve as markers for joint movements caused by muscle contractions around the various joints of the fingers and palm. Palmar Creases are categorized into three types: major, minor, and secondary creases.

1.1 Major Creases

These are the most prominent and deep creases on the palm. They form early in foetal development and are associated with major movements of the hand. The three primary major creases are:

- **Proximal Transverse Crease** (also known as the Head Line):
  - Located near the base of the fingers.
  - Associated with the flexion of the fingers.

[1] Research Scholar, Shri Vaishnav Institute of Forensic Science, Shri Vaishnav Vidyapeeth Vishwavidyalaya, Indore, India. E-mail: aberagi2017@gmail.com

[2] Associate Professor, Shri Vaishnav Institute of Forensic Science, Shri Vaishnav Vidyapeeth Vishwavidyalaya, Indore, India.

- **Distal Transverse Crease** (also known as the Heart Line):
  - Found closer to the centre of the palm.
  - Related to the movement of the fingers and thumb.
- **Radial Longitudinal Crease** (also known as the Life Line):
  - Arches around the base of the thumb.
  - Connected with thumb movements and wrist flexion.

1.2 Minor Flexion Creases

These creases formed the second category of palmar creases show greater variability in length, prominence, and presence compared to major creases (Ashbaugh, 1999).

- **Longitudinal or Finger Creases**

  Running from the base of the fingers towards the centre of the wrist these minor creases are named after the corresponding digits: little finger, ring finger, middle finger, and occasionally the index finger crease (Ashbaugh, 1999).
- **Accessory Distal Transverse Crease**

  Located between the base of the fingers and the distal transverse creases, these creases may be simple or complex, often extending beneath the third, fourth, or fifth digits.
- **"E" Lines**

  Found between the distal transverse crease and the base of the little finger along the ulnar border of the palm. These short and parallel wrinkles typically form an "E" shape when viewed in a print.
- **Hypothenar Crease**

  A single small crease located in the hypothenar region of the palm, usually concave and oriented toward the ulnar side.

1.3 Secondary Creases

As the third category of flexion creases secondary creases include all remaining creases that do not fall under the major or minor categories. These creases can appear anywhere on the palmar surface. Common examples include the checker creases on the thenar eminence, wrist hatch creases located just above the wrist, and hatch creases along the margin of the hypothenar region. Quantitative and qualitative analyses of these features are employed to establish individuality and correlations with genetic or pathological conditions. Palmar creases can be used to supplement palmprint ridge patterns in forensic investigations. While ridge patterns provide detailed minutiae for identification, the broader patterns of palmar creases can help confirm identities especially in cases where the ridge details are insufficient or partially damaged.

The formation of palmar creases is influenced by both genetic and environmental factors during fetal development. This can make them useful in identifying individuals with certain genetic disorders or syndromes which often present distinct crease patterns. For instance, individuals with Down syndrome commonly exhibit a single transverse palmar crease which can aid in medical and forensic identification. In forensic scenarios palmar creases can be especially useful when partial prints are recovered. Even if ridge details are incomplete the patterns of the creases can assist in narrowing down potential matches. Additionally palmar creases can provide context about the orientation and positioning of the hand when the print was made offering insights into the actions of individuals at a crime scene.

2. REVIEW OF LITERATURE

Palmar flexion creases have long been studied for their significance in medicine, genetics, anthropology, and forensic science. This review systematically examines key studies from historical to contemporary research, highlighting the role of palmar creases in understanding human variability, ethnic diversity, genetic inheritance, and forensic identification.

The exploration of palmar creases dates back to the late 19th and early 20th centuries. Carrara (1893) was among the first to study simian creases in Italian soldiers, laying the groundwork for morphological studies. Bettman (1932) extended this work to French soldiers and German university students respectively providing evidence of variability in crease patterns across populations. Longdon-Down (1909) and other early researchers identified the potential of palmar creases in medical and genetic studies. Subsequent works by Rittmeister (1936) and Portius (1937), emphasized their relevance in population studies and ethnic variation. Buchi (1954) further advanced the field by studying Indian communities and highlighting the morphological variability of palmar creases. Palmar creases have been shown to hold diagnostic significance. Sharma (1989) observed a connection between crease morphogenesis and mental retardation. Rawat & Bali (1980) analysed criminal populations, studying attributes such as crease surface area, transversality, length, breadth, and base points. These studies underscored the potential of creases as markers of behavioural and genetic traits.

The hereditary nature of palmar creases has been a focus of several researchers. Khatoon *et. al.*, (1990) studied genetic inheritance patterns, while Bali (1971, 1990) explored hereditary behaviours in Indian populations. Das (1981) and Sharma (1989) conducted population-specific studies, contributing to a deeper understanding of the genetic basis of crease formation. Sarkar (1961) analysed palmar flexion creases in anthropoid apes and monkeys, providing comparative insights into human evolution. Lestrange (1966, 1968, 1969) established creases as tools for ethnographic studies, particularly in European populations demonstrating their utility in studying ethnic variability. Similarly, Chaube & Bali (1976) observed bimanual and bisexual differences in bracelet creases among populations in Madhya Pradesh, India.

Palmar creases have gained significant importance in forensic investigations. Ashbaugh (1999) highlighted two landmark cases where palmar flexion creases played a crucial role in solving crimes. In Sulphur Springs, Texas, a suspect was convicted based on the analysis of palmar creases in a bloody palm print, marking a significant advancement in North American forensic science. Similarly, In Canada the "St. John's Newfoundland" case involved the use of palmar flexion creases to identify a suspect in the 1996 murder of a 51-year-old woman. Blood and two palm prints found on a bedroom wall led to the defendant's conviction, making it the first case in Canada to rely on palmar flexion crease evidence. The advent of digital imaging and computational techniques has revolutionized the study of palmar creases. Chen *et. al.*, (2001) developed algorithms for accurately extracting crease patterns from palmprint images, underscoring their importance in biometric identification due to their stability over time.

Roszaharah *et. al.*, (2019) refined biometric identification by focusing on specific regions of interest such as the hypothenar and interdigital areas enhancing accuracy through detailed crease pattern analysis. Daniel *et. al.*, (2022) investigated palmar crease patterns among Ethiopian students, identifying significant factors influencing crease variability, including sex, ethnicity, handedness, and primary crease origin points. Their findings highlighted sex-based differences with males more likely to exhibit simian and Sydney creases and noted the influence of handedness on crease types. Omuruka *et. al.*, (2022) examined the distribution of middle longitudinal creases among the Isoko and Urhobo tribes, suggesting common ancestry and tribal affiliations based on crease patterns. Attar *et. al.*, (2023) further highlighted the use of palmar creases in personal identification and sex determination emphasizing their forensic relevance.

3. CHARACTERISTICS OF PALMAR CREASES AS BIOMETRIC TOOL

Biometric traits are unique biological characteristics used for identification and verification purposes in various applications including security systems, personal identification, and access control. For a trait to be considered effective as a biometric identifier, it must possess several key characteristics (Clark, 1994) such as universality, uniqueness, permanence, collectability, distinctiveness, robustness and acceptability. Each of these characteristics plays a vital role in ensuring that biometric systems function reliably to protect user privacy and provide accurate identification and verification capabilities. Addressing these traits helps in developing robust biometric systems used across various applications from security to personalized services the following biometric feature must also be easily repeatable and dependable in order to be accepted as evidence in a forensic application.

- **Universal:** Most people have two or three creases on their palms but some have only one crease. This is referred as "Simian crease", it is sometimes associated with conditions such as Down syndrome, Foetal Alcohol syndrome, and Aarskog syndrome (Alhaji *et. al.*, 2015). Therefore, according to the literature available palmar creases are not universal in nature.
- **Uniqueness:** The formation of palmar flexion creases is influenced by genetic factors which means they can differ significantly from one person to another. According to Bansal *et. al.*, (2024) this genetic diversity implies that some crease patterns can be inherited leading to unique configurations in individuals. Researchers like Almudhahka *et. al.*, (2016), Esan *et. al.*, (2013), and Gao *et. al.*, (2003) highlighted in their studies that palmar creases provide unique and distinctive insights into an individual's characteristics.
- **Distinctive:** The pattern and formation of palmar creases are unique to each person. Variations in their length, depth, and curvature provide distinct identifiers that are difficult to replicate or alter. These patterns are influenced by genetic and developmental factors resulting in significant variations even among closely related individuals. This uniqueness provides an additional layer of differentiation in biometric identification.
- **Persistency:** Once palmar flexion creases are formed, they remain stable and produce limited changes with age barring any significant trauma to the skin. This permanence allows them to serve as a reliable trait for identity verification and biometric

applications. Unlike fingerprints which can be altered by environmental factors palmar creases remain viable indicators of identity throughout life (Bansal *et. al.*, 2024). The stability and uniqueness of palmar creases make them highly suitable for biometric identification. These features offer a reliable and distinct basis for differentiating individuals (Ashbaugh, 1999; Roszaharah, 2017).

- **Collection:** The collection of palmprints involves well-established, reliable and accurate methods. Techniques such as the ink and roller method, stamp pad method and palmprint scanners are commonly employed. Capturing palmar crease data can be performed quickly and efficiently using non-contact imaging techniques. They can be captured using cameras or scanning devices enabling contactless and non-invasive imaging. This ensures convenience and upholds personal hygiene (Kumar & Xu, 2016; Michael *et. al.*, 2011).
- **Acceptance:** Palmar creases can serve as supplementary evidence in forensic contexts aiding in the identification of victims or suspects (Ashbaugh, 1999). Palmar creases have been established as useful identifiers in forensic investigations particularly when other forms of biometric evidence such as fingerprints are not available. Studies indicate that approximately 25% of all crime scenes contain only latent palm prints, emphasizing the importance of palm print evidence in criminal cases (Jain & Demirkus, 2008). Moreover, the recognition and analysis of these creases contribute to the robustness of forensic biometrics, enhancing the pool of identification methods available to forensic analysts.
- **Circumvention:** Palmar flexion creases significantly enhance forgery resistance in biometric authentication systems. Research by Cook *et. al.*, (2013) demonstrates their efficacy in palmprint identification, achieving high genuine acceptance rates and low false acceptance rates making them invaluable for accurate identification.

4. RESEARCH METHOD

The analysis of palmar crease patterns for personal identification involves a systematic approach that combines data collection, classification, and pattern recognition techniques.

Table 1: Steps Followed for Methodology

S. No.	*Steps*	
1.	Data Collection	- Palm prints collected from individuals using ink or digital scanners.
		- Ensure high-quality, clear impressions for accurate analysis.
2.	Sample Selection	- Selection of a diverse sample group (age, gender, ethnicity) to analyse variability in palmar creases.
		- Define inclusion/exclusion criteria (e.g., individuals with hand injuries or skin conditions).
3.	Analysis Tools	- Use of manual comparison and automated software for crease analysis.
		- Implementation of image enhancement techniques to improve the quality of crease patterns.

S. No.	*Steps*	
4.	Crease Classification	- Identification of major, minor, and secondary flexion creases.
		- Categorization based on the type, depth, and location of creases.
5.	Pattern Recognition	- Classification of crease patterns (e.g., parallel, curved, zigzag) for individual identification.
		- Use of algorithms for pattern matching and comparison across samples.
6.	Comparison with Other Identification Methods	- Compare palmar crease patterns with fingerprint patterns for validation of identification accuracy.
7.	Statistical Analysis	- Statistical methods to assess the uniqueness of palmar crease patterns and their reliability.
		- Calculation of inter-individual variation and intra-individual consistency.
8.	Validation of Findings	- Cross-check results with known forensic cases or historical datasets to validate findings.
9.	Ethical Considerations	- Ensure informed consent from participants.
		- Maintain confidentiality and privacy of the individuals' biometric data.

4.1 Forensic Identification Repositories

Palmar crease patterns have been included in various biometric repositories to enhance forensic investigations. These repositories store high-resolution images, 3D models, and associated metadata, aiding pattern recognition and statistical analyses.

4.2 Medical Case Research

Longitudinal studies have documented correlations between specific crease patterns and genetic disorders, providing a resource for medical diagnostics. Case studies also explore the variability of creases across age groups and populations.

4.3 Anthropological Research Data

Comprehensive datasets compiled from diverse populations have facilitated cross-cultural comparisons and evolutionary studies, offering insights into genetic and environmental influences on crease formation.

5. CONCLUSION

The analysis of palmar creases for personal identification represents a compelling intersection of biometric technology and forensic science. Palmar creases as a biometric trait offer a unique blend of stability, specificity, and practical application in both forensic science and biometric technology. Their inherent characteristics not only improve security measures but also facilitate a deeper understanding of human genetics and development. So palmar creases for personal identification serves as an innovative approach to enhancing security measures and improving forensic methodologies. Continued research in this area will likely lead to advancements in identification technologies offering even greater reliability and applicability in diverse fields including criminal justice and access control. As the focus on contactless identification methods grows the importance of palmar creases as a biometric trait will undoubtedly expand, further contributing to our understanding of human physical characteristics.

6. FUTURE DIRECTIONS

The future of palmar crease analysis in personal identification lies in its integration with other biometric methods, such as fingerprint analysis and palm vein recognition. Combining these technologies could create more robust and accurate identification systems, leveraging the strengths of each modality to improve reliability and security. Advancements in artificial intelligence (AI) and deep learning offer significant potential to enhance crease-based identification systems. These technologies could enable automated, large-scale analysis of palmar creases, increasing both the speed and accuracy of matching processes. With AI algorithms capable of learning complex patterns, the identification system could become more efficient in recognizing subtle variations in crease patterns. Moreover, ongoing research into the genetic factors influencing palmar crease formation could further broaden its application. Understanding how genetics play a role in the development of these creases might open new avenues for diagnosing certain medical conditions or genetic disorders. This could lead to the use of palmar crease analysis in both forensic and medical diagnostics.

REFERENCES

Alhaji, M.M.; Timbuak, J.; Umana, E. and Tanko, M. (2015). Palmar Creases and Handedness in Hausas of Northern Nigeria: A Cross -Sectional Study, *Asian journal of biological and medical sciences,* 1(2), 6–13.

Ashbaugh, D. (1999). Quantitative-Qualitative Friction Ridge Analysis: An Introduction to Basic and Advanced Ridgeology. CRC Press.

Attar, S.B. and Vinod, N.K. (2023). Implementation of accurate personal identification by using palm print image processing. *International Journal of Engineering Technology and Management Sciences*, 7(1), 120–130.

Bali, R.S. (1971). Palmar creases and schizophrenia. *Proceedings of the International Symposium on Human Genetics,* Waltair, India.

Bali, R.S. (1990). Creases in population studies. *Proceedings of the International Conference on Progress and Trends in Dermatoglyphics Research,* Calcutta.

Bansal, R., Goyal, R., Chhabra, U., Kaur, H. and Kalyan, G. (2024). Dermatoglyphic palmar pattern variations in congenitally deaf and mute subjects, *International Journal of Community Medicine and Public Health.*

Bettman, S. (1932). *Anatomy and Development,* 25, 98.

Buchi, E.C. (1954). The simian crease in India. *Bulletin of the Department of Anthropology,* 3(1), 139.

Clarke. R. (ed.) (1994). Human Identification in Information Systems: Management Challenges and Public Policy Issues, Cannberra: Xamax Consultancy Pvt. Ltd.

Crookshank, F.G. (1924). *The Mongol in Our Midst: A Study of Man and His Three Faces.* Dutton & Co.

Das, B.M. and Das, R. (1981). Intra- and inter-tribal variation in palmar flexion creases: A population study. *Indian Journal of Physical Anthropology and Human Genetics,* 7, 173.

Eshwaraiah, G. and Bali, R.S. (1976). Palmar flexion creases and dermatoglyphics in diabetic patients. *American Journal of Physical Anthropology,* 47(1), 11–13.

Gilchrist, R.J. (2010). Forensic Human Identification of the Living Based Upon the Palmar Flexion Creases of the Hand. Axis 2: 32–3.

Jain, A.K. and Demirkus, M. (2008). On Latent Palmprint Matching, technical report, Michigan State University.

Khatoon, S., Khan, M.F.H., Choube, R. and Bali, R.S. (1990). Inheritance of transverse palmar flexion creases. *Proceedings of the International Conference on Progress and Trends in Dermatoglyphics Research,* Calcutta.

Lestrange, M. de. (1966). Étude des plis de flexion de la main: Le pli transverse chez les habitants de Plozevet (Finistère sud, France). *Cahiers de C.R.A., Bulletin et Mémoires de la Société d'Anthropologie de Paris,* 10(11), 103–116.

Lestrange, M. de. (1967). Le pli transverse: Nouvelle étude de sa répartition chez les habitants de Plozevet. *Bulletin et Mémoires de la Société d'Anthropologie de Paris,* 2(3–4), 183.

Lestrange, M. de. (1969). The transverse crease in Europe: Index and comparative study of different samples cited in the literature. *American Journal of Physical Anthropology,* 30, 173.

Longdon-Down, J.L.H. (1909). Mongoloid imbecility. *British Medical Journal,* 12, 665.

Michael, G., Connie, T. and Teoh, A. (2011). A Contactless Biometric System Using Palm Print and Palm Vein Features.

Omuruka, T.C.; Osunwoke, E.A.; Edibamode, I., and El Bouchti, I. (2022). Palmar creases and ancestry prediction, *Scholars International Journal of Anatomy and Physiology*, 5(2), 41–49.

Portius, W. (1937). Beitrag zur Frage der Erblichkeit der vierfingerfurche. *Zeitschrift für Morphologie und Anthropologie,* 36, 382.

Rathee, R., Kamal, N., Kumar, A., Vashist, M. and Yadav, R. (2014). Dermatoglyphic Patterns of Acute Leukemia Patients. *International Research Journal of Biological Sciences*, 3(6), 90–93.

Rawat, S.K. (1980). The study of palmar dermatoglyphics and palmar creases among murderers. In *Human Biology: Recent Advances*, 2, 401–412.

Rawat, S.K. and Bali, R.S. (1980). Morphogenesis of creases among murderers. *South Asia Regional Symposium of International Association of Human Biologists, Seventh Annual Conference of Indian Society of Human Genetics,* Ranchi, India.

Rittmeister, J.F. (1936). Über die Affenfurche (vierfingerfurche) mit besonderer Berücksichtigung der Mikrodegenerationen und des Problems des Mongolismus. *Zeitschrift für Anatomie und Entwicklungsgeschichte,* 106(2), 276.

Sarkar, S.S. (1961). The simian crease. *Zeitschrift für Morphologie und Anthropologie,* 51(2), 212.

Sharma, A.N. (1989). The study of crease morphogenesis among mentally retarded children. In *Crease Anthropology*, 63–83. Northern Book Centre Publishers.

Sharma, A.N. and Yadav, D.K. (1989). Longitudinal flexion crease specificity in three Indian populations. In *Crease Anthropology*, 101–108. Northern Book Centre Publishers.

Consumer Attitude Towards Green Packaging on Food Products in Indore

Riya Sadawana[1] and Aditi Naidu[2]

ABSTRACT: This study investigates customers' attitudes toward green packaging for food products in Indore, India, due to growing concerns about the environment and the rising demand for sustainable consumption. Eco-friendly packaging, which is defined by its use of biodegradable, recyclable and reusable items, play a vital role in reducing environmental impacts and encouraging environmental responsibility. The research attempts to understand consumer awareness, preference and willingness to pay for eco-friendly packaging, along with the effect of Demographic variables like age, gender, income level, and education. Using a systematically designed questionnaire filled in by a group of 50 volunteers, the research looks at consumer sentiment in three categories: general attitude towards green packaging, its perceived effectiveness in providing protection and convenience, and the role it plays in product purchasing and buying choices. The results indicate a fairly positive preference for green packaging among the young and the highly educated displaying increased sensitivity towards environmental problems. However, the study also underscores obstructive factors such as limited brand recognition, concerns regarding packaging effectiveness, and aversion to spending more money on environmentally friendly options. Further the study reveals that customers are increasingly more open to sustainable alternatives. Therefore, more stress must be laid on education, branding, and affordability. This research can assist policymakers and businesses in coming up with strategies that promote adoption of green packaging in new urban economies like Indore.

Keywords: *Biodegradable, Consumer Awareness, Consumer Behaviour, Eco-Friendly Packaging, Sustainable Consumption.*

1. INTRODUCTION

Consumer attitudes towards green packaging of food products are becoming increasingly important in today's world. As there is growing awareness of ecological problems and sustainability, increasingly more individuals look for products in line with their worldviews. Green Recyclable or renewable content packaging that is acceptable to be recycled or composted is considered to be a cleaner option that helps to ease waste management reduction and diminishes carbon footprints. These sentiments significantly influence purchasing decisions and brand loyalty. Comprehending consumer viewpoints allows food corporations to make careful choices in packaging and efficiently communicate environmental benefits to their customers.

[1] Research Scholar, Shri Vaishnav School of Management, Shri Vaishnav Vidyapeeth Vishwavidyalaya, Indore, India. E-mail: riyasadawana5@gmail.com

[2] Associate Professor, Shri Vaishnav School of Management, Shri Vaishnav Vidyapeeth Vishwavidyalaya, Indore, India.

1.1 Sustainable Packaging

Green packaging refers to the use of reusable, biodegradable, or compostable materials in packaging, wrapping, and shipping products. It also includes production processes that aim at recycling and minimizing pollution. "Green Packaging" refers to packaging made from materials that are safe for the environment and harmless to living organisms (Mahmoud *et. al.,* 2022). Robert Holdway and David Walker, the co-founders of Giraffe Management Consultancy, and Mark Hilton, a senior environmental consultant at Enviros Aspinwall, defined the goal of eco-design is "To minimize total lifespan impacts while maintaining performance and cost-effectiveness". Eco-design packaging in the packaging sector includes key aspects like source reduction, reuse, recycling, and waste elimination (Holdway *et. al.,* 2002).

Packaging is a container for protection which physically comes into direct contact with a product needed to contain, safeguard, apply, identify, and advertise it (Giovannetti, 1995). As an advertising tool, packaging is known to be both brand and product structure. Package structure has over the recent past undergone tremendous modifications due to escalated consumer awareness and enhanced information accessibility. Contemporary consumers, knowing the environmental consequences of packaging and the depletion of resources, look for solutions that suit their sustainability objectives. Hence, sustainable packaging is now an integral component, where the call is for packaging materials that can be recycled, minimize waste, and reused or recycled post-consumption (Sandu, 2014).

1.2 Importance of Sustainable Packaging

The importance of environmental protection worldwide has grown significantly in recent years. According to the above assumption, eco-green packaging is extremely important to waste reduction, prevention of pollution, and sustainable development. Also often named as "eco-green packaging," "eco-friendly packaging," "sustainable packaging," or "recyclable packaging," it involves the application of eco-friendly materials and ensuring the protection, safety, and efficacy of products concerning human health and the environment. Packaging plays a critical role in protecting consumers whether the products are food or otherwise and therefore is a critical component of marketing. Further, protection, packaging serves as a good medium of communication between business firms and customers.

In the present day world, packaging must be protective but, simultaneously, eco-friendly. It must balance environment responsibility with basic product needs. From a marketing standpoint, packaging performs four basic functions. It mainly ensures the safety and protection of the product. Also, it aids in the marketing of the product by engaging and informing customers. Further, it encourages recycling, thus reducing environmental impacts. Finally, it enhances consumer convenience, as products are easy to use and handle. The Association of Plastic Manufacturers asserts that packaging constitutes the largest portion of plastic use worldwide, at 39.6%, followed by construction at 20.3% and the automotive industry at 8.5%. Globalization has connected markets in a record way; however, it has also brought serious challenges, one of which is the extensive use of packaging that poses environmental hazards. In Asia and Europe, plastic packaging ends up in landfills, where it can stay for decades, inflicting huge harm on ecosystems. Green packaging is a workable alternative way which offers many advantages including recyclability, biodegradability, and energy efficiency. In spite of these benefits, companies are reluctant to abandon traditional packaging due to fear of costs and potential risks.

2. RATIONALE

Green packaging is one of the key drivers of consumer choice, with environmental concern and sustainability being placed at the top of corporate agenda. Green packaging consists of biodegradable, recyclable, and reusable materials to reduce the environmental footprint while maintaining product quality and ease of use. Although there is growing global emphasis on sustainable consumption, green packaging is perceived differently by consumers depending on how much they believe in the brand and packaging price and their present awareness of eco-friendly alternatives. The research considers Indore because there is not a lot of information related to consumer attitude towards green packaging applied on food items. Consumer knowledge levels along with willingness to pay and green packaging benefits identification will provide key findings that are valuable for business processes and policymaking. The study explains key variables supporting the employment of green packaging. It would support the use of green packaging, while enhancing awareness about business applications.

3. OBJECTIVES OF THE STUDY

- To examine the consumers' views about packaging of environmentally sustainable foodstuffs in Indore.
- To examine consumers' views on green packaging concerning its functionality for food preservation and convenience.
- To examine consumer opinion regarding the effect of green packaging on the sale of merchandise for consumption.

4. REVIEW OF LITERATURE

Anh (2017) noted that although minimal-material packaging is mostly praised for being environmentally friendly, there are issues with its durability. Some consumers have raised concern that this kind of packaging is not strong enough to protect pollution or damage products. Despite how great the environmental benefits of sustainable packaging are, cost is still a vital component that influences the purchasing habits of consumers. Credibility of packaging information largely influences consumer behavior by making products more appealing and the purchase process easier. Gheorghe *et. al.,* (2018) implemented a quantitative survey with 268 Romanian consumers to explore their attitudes towards sustainable packaging. The central purpose of the study was to identify the attitudes of consumers toward the effects of environmentally friendly packaging in encouraging sustainable behavior.

The study tested consumers' perceptions of various forms of environmentally friendly packaging, drivers of their shopping behavior, and how awareness affects encouraging sustainability. The findings uncovered that the majority of the respondents recognize the environmental effects of packaging, with their primary reasons for selecting environmentally friendly products being environmental conservation, recyclability and a feeling of duty (Fatma, 2023). First choice packaging ingredients were paper, glass, and cardboard, although plastic and wood were selected for less. Singh & Pandey (2019) examined green packaging from a process viewpoint, focusing on economic considerations involved in the development of a green packaging system. They utilized a system dynamics model to analyze their results in three glass bottle manufacturers' firms. The study determined that even though the initial remanufacturing cost due to collection processes and reverse logistics is high, the cost decreases as the system comes to equilibrium. Overall, remanufacturing is more economically viable compared to manufacturing new material for a long duration of time.

Popovic *et. al.,* (2019) observed that there was a notable scarcity of research that accounted for the demographic characteristics of consumers purchasing food products using eco-friendly packaging. Their evidence indicated that younger Indian consumers are more environmentally conscious and a strong emphasis on sustainability. Gender has a significant impact on consumer decision-making, with considerable differences in purchasing. The study discovered that less educated individuals place more importance on the product itself than on its packaging, with more educated individuals having higher awareness of sustainable packaging options. Wandosell *et. al.,* (2021) explored the implications of green packaging from the perspectives of consumers and companies. Their research included many factors, including sustainable packaging materials and design, economics, marketing strategies, corporate social responsibility, and the importance of green packaging to waste management and the circular economy.

The survey captured a growing interest among researchers and scholars in the two fields, as evidenced by the growing number of journal articles on green packaging. The study emphasized the practical implications of going for green packaging solutions, in light of the increasing consumer and business concern for sustainable development. Gupta (2021) examined the determinants influencing the Indian consumer choice for green packaging to minimize environmental impacts. Environmental awareness, sustainable packaging attitude, and willingness to pay for green options were identified as three independent variables by the research (Boz *et. al.,* 2020). The research concluded that all three variables positively influenced the dependent variable buyers' intent to purchase green-packaged products. This shows that as there is increased awareness and positive attitudes towards green packaging, there is an increased intent to support eco-friendly options.

4.1 Research Gap

Few studies have specifically targeted urban areas, with a bias to ignore the studies of consumer sentiments in Indore, a Tier-II city. The present study seeks to fill the research gap by carrying out a localized study. The literature on green packaging adoption has highlighted gaps in its analysis of demographic factors influencing perceptions of green packaging and consumer willingness to pay a premium for sustainable packaging in terms of gender background and educational attainment and levels of income. The psychological drivers of buying decisions about environmentally friendly packaging continue under researched such that scholars get to understand the psychological and behaviour factors consumers adopt sustainable packaging measures or the lack thereof. Numerous companies perceive the cost of green packaging as too high while the customers question the quality and operating life. The study explores the issues by looking at consumer perceptions of acceptance and trust.

5. RESEARCH METHOD

5.1 Questionnaire Development

A self-developed questionnaire was used to conduct this quantitative study. It has three distinct parts:

- **Consumer Attitudes towards Green Packaging:** This segment explored how consumers view the effectiveness of green packaging in fulfilling its three main functions, with focus on protection and convenience aspects.
- **Demographic Information:** This segment collected important data about the participants, including age, gender, educational attainment, occupation, and gross yearly income.
- The final segment assessed consumer attitudes towards green packaging according to its influence on the marketing and promotion of food items.

5.2 Data Collection

The questionnaire was designed to give the respondents the convenience and spontaneity of response. For the pilot study, 50 people were sampled. Primary data were collected through a questionnaire given to people of Indore. The secondary data collection involved an extensive search of different published and unpublished research papers, peer-reviewed journals, and web sources to support evidence of the study. The questionnaire contained 13 well-structured questions, some of which used a Likert scale, to assess consumer opinions. The questions were framed to be in line with the research objectives and provide valuable insights into consumer perceptions of eco-friendly packaging.

5.3 Data Analysis & Findings

Demographic: This study talks about the consumer opinion regarding eco-friendly packaging of food items. The findings of the survey data indicated that the sample population was comprised of 46% females and 54% males. The findings show that the greatest demographic (48%) are individuals aged 18–24 years, which reflects the active participation of young consumers in the food market. Additionally, 32% of the respondents were between 25–34 years and 12% between 35 and 44, and 8% were between the ages of 45 and 54. By educational qualifications, 36% of the interviewees had a bachelor's degree or were included in undergraduate studies, 44% held a master's degree, and 20% were working professionals.

With regards to environmental consciousness, 44% of the interviewees showed concern for the preservation of the environment. In addition, 38% had once bought foodstuffs with environmentally friendly packaging, 42% preferred environmentally friendly packaging over plastic packaging, In addition, 52% of the respondents prefer products that utilize refillable or reusable packaging. These findings echo an increasing consumer trend of favouring sustainability and eco-friendly packaging.

CATEGORY 1: CONSUMER ATTITUDE TOWARDS GREEN PACKAGING

Descriptive Statistics

The below table shows the descriptive statistics of consumer attitude towards green packaging. The mean scores indicate the general direction of the responses, and the standard deviations indicate the level of variability of the participants.

Table 1: Descriptive Statistics (Mean & Standard Deviation)

Statement	*Mean*	*Std. Deviation*
I prefer green product packaging while I shop.	3.32	1.392
I am aware of the fact that various brands provide green packaging.	2.72	1.325
I am familiar with the advantages of green packaging for the environment and human health.	2.84	1.434

Interpretation

Preference for Green Packaging: The average of 3.32 shows that there is a moderate preference for green packaging among consumers. The standard deviation of 1.392 shows variation in opinions. Awareness of Brands That Offer Green Packaging: The average score of 2.72 is quite low, showing that consumer awareness about the brands that provide green packaging is low. The standard deviation of 1.325 shows a moderate range of responses. Familiarity with Green Packaging Benefits: The average score of 2.84 shows that familiarity with the benefits of green packaging is slightly higher than brand awareness. However, the standard deviation of 1.434 shows varying opinions on the topic.

Table 2: Frequency Distribution

Response Category	*I Prefer Green Packaging (%)*	*Aware of Brands Providing Green Packaging (%)*	*Familiar with Green Packaging Benefits (%)*
Strongly Disagree	12	20	24
Disagree	20	30	22
Neutral	20	22	16
Agree	20	14	22
Strongly Agree	28	14	16

Implications

A substantial percentage (48%) of respondents agree or strongly agree with the use of eco-friendly packaging in their shopping experiences, reflecting a potential market opportunity for green packaging alternatives. The awareness of eco-friendly packaging companies is relatively low as only 28% showed their consent. This means that businesses must more promote themselves more and make people aware of their sustainability. Conservative estimates place environmental consciousness of green packaging at a moderate 38% agreeing or strongly agreeing. More campaigns of education will be needed to continue educating consumers and have increased adoption.

The findings suggest that while customers are keen on green packaging, they are not aware of specific brands and the benefits related to them. Firms must make the most of this by increasing marketing and informing customers of the benefits of eco-friendly packaging options.

CATEGORY 2: CONSUMER ATTITUDE TOWARDS GREEN PACKAGING IN PROVIDING PROTECTION AND CONVENIENCE TO CONSUMERS

Descriptive Statistics

The results in this category examine consumer attitude towards the effectiveness and convenience of green packaging. The mean scores reflect a moderate agreement with most of the statements, which means that consumers recognize the benefits of green packaging, some concerns about its functionality persist.

Table 3: Descriptive Statistics (Mean & Standard Deviation)

Question	*Mean*	*Std. Deviation*
Packaging made from green material (i.e., recycled, biodegradable materials) is as beneficial as plastic packaging.	3.42	1.486
I believe in the recycle/reuse of products and their packaging.	3.04	1.324
Products packed with minimal material lack the ability to keep the products fresh and in good quality.	2.96	1.442
I prefer purchasing products that are more informative about their packaging.	3.06	1.268
I would go for products with packaging that can be refilled	2.92	1.441

Table 4: Frequency Distribution

Response Category	*Green Material as Beneficial as Plastic (%)*	*Believe in Recycling/ Reuse (%)*	*Minimal Packaging Affects Quality (%)*	*Prefer Informative Packaging (%)*	*Prefer Refillable Packaging (%)*
Strongly Disagree	18	16	24	12	20
Disagree	10	18	14	26	24
Neutral	16	30	22	20	22
Agree	24	18	22	28	12
Strongly Agree	32	18	18	14	22

Interpretation

Perception of Green Packaging vs. Plastic Packaging

- 56% of the respondents strongly agree or agree that green materials are as useful as plastic, showing a general positive attitude.
- Nevertheless, 28% disagree or strongly disagree with the statement.

- The mean score of 3.42 reflects a moderate level of confidence in the use of green packaging materials.

Belief in Recycling and Reuse

- 36% of the respondents agree or strongly agree with recycling and reuse, and 34% disagree.
- A strong neutral response of 30% means that a high percentage of consumers might not be actively involved, but they are receptive to involvement.
- A mean of 3.04 suggests a fairly evenly balanced position.

Perceived Effectiveness of Minimal Packaging

- 40% are of the view that little packaging influences product quality, whereas 38% disagree, showing divergent views.
- The average score of 2.96 indicates that consumers are evenly split on whether less packaging affects product quality.

Preference for Informative Packaging

- 42% agree or strongly agree, and 38% disagree or strongly disagree, reflecting a moderate tendency towards detailed packaging information.
- The mean of 3.06 reveals some extent of regard for informative packaging.

Preference for Refillable Packaging

- 34% favour refillable packaging, while 44% oppose it, showing lower acceptance.
- The mean of 2.92 suggests a weak endorsement, with potential problems regarding convenience or usability.

The findings show that customers are cognizant of the benefits of green packaging, but there is doubt as to whether it affects the quality of the product. There is moderate backing for recycling packaging and refill packaging, but not everyone is entirely convinced. Increasing awareness to the working ways and advantages of green packaging is likely to augment acceptance and implementation levels among citizens.

CATEGORY 3: CONSUMER ATTITUDE TOWARDS PROMOTING PRODUCTS WITH GREEN PACKAGING

Table 5: Descriptive Statistics (Mean & Standard Deviation)

Question	*Mean*	*Std. Deviation*
I can pay more if the product is wrapped in eco-friendly packaging as it will be less harmful to the environment and human health.	2.98	1.505
I look for 'green' packaging on the label due to its benefits.	3.12	1.380
I find green packaging more attractive than plastic ones.	3.16	1.299
I look for a green label first when choosing a green product.	3.20	1.385
I recognize packaging products by their color, size, and shape.	3.00	1.340

Table 6: Frequency Distribution

Question	*Strongly Disagree (%)*	*Disagree (%)*	*Neutral (%)*	*Agree (%)*	*Strongly Agree (%)*
I can pay more if the product is wrapped in eco-friendly packaging as it will be less harmful to the environment and human health.	22	20	22	10	26
I look for 'green' packaging on the label due to its benefits.	14	26	14	26	20
I find green packaging more attractive than plastic ones.	12	18	34	14	22
I look for a green label first when choosing a green product.	18	12	22	28	20
I recognize packaging products by their color, size, and shape.	18	18	26	22	16

Interpretation

Category 3 findings tell us how consumers feel about selling products with green packaging.

- **Willingness to Pay More:** Shoppers are divided regarding paying extra for eco-friendly packaging (Mean = 2.98, SD= 1.505. Although 26% strongly agree, 42% (22% SD + 20% D) disagree, indicating cost remains an issue.
- **Looking for Sustainable Labels:** Most are searching for green packaging labels actively (Mean = 3.12, SD = 1.38), but 40% (14% SD + 26% D) do not find this significant.
- **Attraction of Green Packaging:** Green packaging is more desirable than plastic packaging (Mean = 3.16, SD = 1.299), although 34% are undecided.
- **Preference for Green Labels:** A relatively stronger inclination is seen for initially considering green labels (Mean = 3.20, SD = 1.385), with 48% in agreement and only 30% in disagreement.

Recognition by Packaging Attributes

- Consumers identify packaging by shape, size, and color (Mean = 3.00, SD = 1.340), with views being approximately evenly split and indicating that unique eco-friendly attributes should take precedence in branding initiatives.
- In general, consumers are cognizant of the benefits of green packaging, but cost factors and absence of strong preference remain barriers to complete adoption.

6. CONCLUSION

The study validates the consumer sentiment for green packaging to be moderately positive with varying degrees of awareness, preference, and willingness to adopt green options. In Category 1 (General Consumer Attitude), consumers are interested in green packaging; however, their awareness about its availability and benefits is relatively low. Category 2 (Perceived Protection & Convenience) captures consumers' scepticism toward the efficacy of minimalist and biodegradable packaging since most are uncertain whether it will preserve product quality. Lastly, Category 3 (Promotion & Purchase Behavior) reveals a divided willingness to pay extra for green packaging, with packaging design and labeling playing a large role in determining consumer purchasing behavior. While greater awareness and predisposition toward sustainable packaging solutions exist, concerns about cost, performance, and accessibility imply greater consumer education, greater packaging innovation, and better market positioning are required to realize greater acceptance.

7. FUTURE SCOPE

Subsequent research on environmentally friendly packaging must investigate consumer attitudes toward environmentally sustainable packaging outside the current districts and states to determine regional patterns. Temporal analysis can lend firmness to analysis of changing consumer attitudes. research design to track sustainable awareness development over time periods. The study analyzes the impacts of government policies that control consumer responses and business adoption of green packaging alternatives. Corporate difficulties in going green with sustainable packaging and how they market their products should be dealt with from a business perspective. Researchers should consider how environmentally friendly packaging measures up to sustainability compared to zero-waste shopping and carbon footprint reduction processes in food manufacturing.

REFERENCES

Boz, Z.; Korhonen, V. and Sand, C.K. (2020). Consumer considerations for the implementation of sustainable packaging: A review. *Sustainability*, 12(6), 2192.

Fatma, I. (2023). To understand the mentality of the consumer towards the products packaging in favor of protect the planet. *Journal for Re Attach Therapy and Developmental Diversities*, 2254–2266.

Gupta, R.K. (2021). Exploring the factors affecting purchase intention towards green packaged products of Indian consumers. *3rd International Conference on Design and Manufacturing Aspects for Sustainable Energy (ICMED-ICMPC 2021),* 309, 01084.

Jerda, H. and Sahayaselvi, S. (2018). Green packaging: An emerging need for sustainable development. *Environmental Science, Business*.

Mahmoud, M.A.; Tsetse, E.K.K.; Tulasi, E.E. and Muddey, D.K. (2022). Green packaging, environmental awareness, willingness to pay and consumers' purchase decisions. *Sustainability*, 14(23), 16091.

Mintel (2024). Consumer perspectives on eco-friendly packaging: An Indian context.

Orzan, G.; Cruceru, A.; Bălăceanu, C. and Chivu, R.-G. (2018). Consumers' behavior concerning sustainable packaging: An exploratory study on Romanian consumers. *Sustainability*, 10(6), 1787.

Popovic, I.; Bossink, B.A.G. and van der Sijde, P.C. (2019). Factors influencing consumers' decision to purchase food in environmentally friendly packaging: What do we know and where do we go from here? *Sustainability*, 11(24), 7197.

Singh, B.P. and Mehra, R. (2019). A study on consumer awareness towards green marketing with special reference to Indore region. *Journal of the Gujarat Research Society, ISSN: 0374-8588*, 21(16).

Wandosell, G.; Parra-Meroño, M.C.; Alcayde, A. and Baños, R. (2021). Green packaging from consumer and business perspectives. *Sustainability*, 13(3), 1356.

Xin, W.K., Kar Sen, Y. and Rajendran, S.D. (2019). A study on the benefits of eco-friendly packaging on sustainable supply chain management in fast moving consumer goods industry. *International Conference on Building Energy Conservation, Thermal Safety and Environmental Pollution Control*, 136, 04092.

Content Analysis of Central University Library Websites in Uttar Pradesh: A Comparative Study

Ashish Tiwari[1] and Pankaja Tiwari[2]

ABSTRACT: University library websites play an important role in providing students and scholars with academic resources, digital teaching tools and research support. This study analyzes the content of library websites of Central Universities of Uttar Pradesh, evaluating their structure, accessibility, resource availability and user engagement. The research uses a systematic framework to assess key aspects such as online catalogs, e-resources, user support services, accessibility compliance. Variations in accessibility and compliance have been highlighted. While some libraries offer seamless access to extensive digital repositories and academic databases, others lack important features like interactive user support, mobile responsiveness etc. Based on the analysis, this paper offers recommendations for enhancing digital library services to ensure greater accessibility and usability for students and researchers

Keywords: *Academic Databases, Accessibility Compliance, Digital Repositories, e-Resources, Online Catalogs.*

1. INTRODUCTION

In the digital age, university library websites serve as essential platforms for academic research, information dissemination, and student support. Libraries in higher education institutions have transformed from mere physical spaces to digital knowledge centers providing access to a vast collection of e-books, journals, research databases, and institutional repositories. This study focuses on analyzing the content of library websites of central universities in Uttar Pradesh and evaluating their effectiveness in providing digital resource services.

Key Aspects Analyzed Include

- Availability of online catalogs (OPACs).
- Access to e-resources such as e-books, journals and research databases.
- User support services, including help desks and FAQs.
- Website accessibility and mobile responsiveness.

2. OBJECTIVES OF THIS STUDY

To assess how well these websites support academic and research activities and identify gaps that need improvement. The study also aims to provide insights into best practices that can enhance digital library services.

---

[1] Research Scholar, Shri Vaishnav Institute of Social Sciences, Humanities & Arts, Shri Vaishnav Vidyapeeth Vishwavidyalaya, Indore, India. E-mail: librariantiwari@gmail.com

[2] Assistant Librarian, Shri Vaishnav Institute of Social Sciences, Humanities & Arts, Shri Vaishnav Vidyapeeth Vishwavidyalaya, Indore, India.

Research Questions

To guide this analysis, the following research questions are considered:

- What are the common features available on the library websites of central universities in Uttar Pradesh?
- How accessible and user-friendly are these websites for students and researchers?
- What improvements can be recommended for enhancing the effectiveness of these library websites?

By analyzing and comparing the content and structure of these library websites, this study seeks to highlight strengths, weaknesses, and areas for improvement, ultimately contributing to the enhancement of digital library services in higher education institutions.

3. REVIEW OF LITERATURE

Library websites have become a critical component of academic institutions, serving as a gateway to knowledge and research materials. The evaluation of these digital platforms through content analysis has been widely explored in past studies, focusing on aspects such as usability, accessibility, resource availability, and user engagement. This section reviews existing literature on academic library website evaluation, content analysis methodologies, and best practices in digital library services.

Brahma & Verma (2022) identified the Web content available on the websites of national libraries in Asia. In manual mode, they designed checkpoints categorized into nine parts: site description, design factor, responsibility, general information, availability of help and tools, currency, authority, file format, and Web 2.0. The author observed that most websites used graphics. In contrast, libraries used animations the least, and few had information about the regular updates of their websites, an essential element for their visibility. Khawaja (2022) assessed accessibility of library websites for users with disabilities, different types of access errors, and the relationship between community demographics and internet accessibility of 120 selected US public library websites. Furthermore, most of the library websites experienced color discrepancy errors on each page, while no correlation was found between access errors and community demographics. However, multimedia features, general information, products and services, my library and training programs, Web 2.0, linking and navigation, organization and structure, mobile library research and services were uncovered.

Ambika & Ganesan (2021) examined the online content of selected central university library websites in India, using content analysis as research methodology and design checklist for data collection. The checklist was divided into six sections, viz. (i) general information, (ii) the physical collections, (iii) library services (iv) electronic resources (v) e-learning, (vi) value added services. "Library websites did not provide sitemaps, copyright, mission information, and committee details, while only seven websites provided information about NDL and NPTEL". However, the study did not focus on multimedia assessment components/features, my library, library training programs, accuracy, relevance, organization with structure, links and navigation, and mobile library services. Rafiq *et. al.,* (2021) evaluated The quality of the library websites of the world's top ranked medical university libraries was assessed using an online checklist form, which was classified into nine main parts, i.e., appearance/design, currency of content, general information, library services/technical service, value-added services, medical e-resources, information dissemination tools, education and training information tools, and library information resources with 87 indicators. The author found that no library scored a hundred percent in the field of medicine. In contrast, two libraries (University of Cambridge and University of Washington) scored more than 90%.

Yadav & Mishra (2021) assessed the effectiveness, accessibility and effectiveness of IISER library websites using a systematic checklist divided into four main categories, ie. Basic information, services, features of library websites and access. The authors found that many library websites were relatively simple, including general information, web 2.0 features, search features, interlibrary loan, etc. However, multimedia features, my library, library training programs, accuracy, relevance, organization and structure, links and navigation and mobile library services are not included.

Anyaoku & Lucky (2020) examined the usability of university library websites in Southern Nigeria using five usability attributes, (i) usefulness, (ii) efficiency, (iii) effectiveness, (iv) learn ability, and (v) accessibility. The authors found that only one university received a high usability score of 89.5%, while the other received a low score of 26.3%. However, most university libraries scored 50% in learning skills, while only one university scored 33.3%. The scope of the study does not focus on the evaluation component, namely, multimedia, my library, library training program and mobile library services. Niazi *et. al.,* (2020) proposed a framework that includes ten dimensions of credibility, trustworthiness, usability, website design, functionality, content, page design, efficiency, webometrics, and systematic evaluation. They suggested that all these dimensions should be used with their components and indicators in the evaluation of university websites.

Saloi (2020) examined the web-based content of selected university library websites of Assam using 76 items comprising seven parts. The author found that 13 out of 25 universities have their own websites, while only 07 (53.85%) provided links to library websites on their university homepage. In addition, 12 out of 13 university libraries offered remote access to various e-resources, while nine provided plagiarism and citation guidelines for researchers. The study did not cover features such as multimedia, my library, currency, accuracy, relevance, organization and structure, links and navigation, and mobile library services. Bharti & Madhusudan (2019) set out to examine the web content of BHU and JNU library websites using qualitative (11 checkpoints) and quantitative (170 checkpoints) assessment methods. The authors found that the JNU library website scored 128 (75.29%) out of 170, above average, while the BHU library website scored 74 (43.52%) out of 170 on features. This research is one of the unique studies that should help web developers at both universities improve the quality of their library websites. The study seeks to show the features of both libraries that need improvement for ease of use and improved user interaction.

Sheshaiya & Rekha (2019) analyzed the resources, services, facilities and other information available on websites of engineering colleges in Andhra Pradesh. The checklist was classified into (i) domain structure, (ii) authorization, (iii) material description, (iv) currency, (v) appearance and beauty aspects, (vi) ease of navigation and (vii) special factors. The authors found that most college websites did not provide educational information, while only one college provided information in more than one language. Moreover, very few colleges provided navigational facilities such as search facilities or sitemap. However, the scope of study did not focus on my library, mobile library services, and search facilities.

4. RESEARCH METHOD

This study employs a systematic content analysis approach to evaluate the library websites of central universities in Uttar Pradesh. The methodology focuses on data collection, evaluation criteria, and analytical framework to ensure comprehensive assessment. The research follows a qualitative and quantitative content analysis method. Qualitative aspects include navigational structure, accessibility, and user engagement, while quantitative data covers the availability of digital resources, user support services, and compliance with accessibility standards. The study focuses on the five central universities in Uttar Pradesh:

1. Aligarh Muslim University (AMU)
2. Babasaheb Bhimrao Ambedkar University (BBAU), Lucknow
3. Banaras Hindu University (BHU), Varanasi
4. Rani Lakshmi Bai Central Agricultural University, Jhansi (RLBCAU)
5. University of Allahabad (AU), Prayagraj

4.1 Data Collection

The data was collected by visiting the official library websites of the selected universities. The following method was used:

- Manual browsing of website content.

4.2 Data Analysis

The collected data was analyzed using:

- Descriptive statistics (to quantify available resources and services).
- Comparative analysis (to identify gaps and strengths among universities).
- Thematic analysis (to assess qualitative aspects such as usability and accessibility).

5. WEBSITE CONTENT ANALYSIS CRITERIA

The content analysis of central university library websites in Uttar Pradesh is based on a structured framework that evaluates key aspects of usability, accessibility, resource availability, and user engagement. The analysis criteria are divided into four main categories: General Information and Navigability, Digital Resources and Services, User Support and Engagement and Accessibility.

5.1 General Information and Navigability

This criterion assesses how well the website provides essential information about the library and its operations. Key aspects include:

- Presence of a dedicated library website or a clearly defined library section
- Contact information (email, phone number, physical address)
- Library staff directory (names, roles, and contact details)
- Library hours of operation (updated and easily accessible)

- Ease of navigation (clear menu structure, quick links)
- Availability of a search bar for site-wide and catalog searches.

5.2 Digital Resources and Services

The primary function of a library website is to provide access to digital resources and research tools. This category evaluates:

- **Online Public Access Catalog (OPAC):** Availability of an online catalog for searching books and resources.
- Access to e-books and e-journals and Subscription to online databases.
- **Institutional Repository:** Availability of past research papers, dissertations, and faculty publications.
- **Digital thesis collection:** Access to theses and dissertations.
- **Remote access to digital resources:** Whether students/researchers can log in remotely to access e-resources.
- **Open-access resources:** Availability of free resources such as Shodhganga, DOAJ, and institutional repositories.

5.3 User Support and Engagement

This section analyzes how well the website interacts with users and supports their research needs. Key parameters include:

- **FAQs or Help Section:** Availability of a Frequently Asked Questions (FAQ) page.
- **Ask-a-Librarian or Chat Support:** Availability of live chat, email query, or chatbot services.
- **Research guides and tutorials:** Digital literacy guides, research methodology tutorials, and citation guides.
- **Library social media presence:** Facebook, Twitter, YouTube links for updates and engagement.
- **News and Announcements section:** Updates on new arrivals, digital resource subscriptions, and library events.
- **Library membership details:** Information on membership eligibility, borrowing limits, and rules.

5.4 Accessibility

A well-designed website must be accessible, responsive, and user-friendly. This category evaluates:

- **Mobile-friendliness:** Compatibility with smartphones and tablets.
- **Page loading speed:** Fast and optimized page performance.
- **Search functionality:** Effectiveness of the site-wide and catalog search bar.
- **Multilingual support:** Availability of content in multiple languages (if applicable).

6. RESULTS AND DISCUSSION

This section presents the data collection and key findings from the content analysis of central university library websites in Uttar Pradesh. The study evaluates the websites based on the predefined content analysis criteria, highlighting strengths, weaknesses, and areas for improvement. Table 1 gives a basic information about the various Central Universities in Uttar Pradesh.

Table 1: General Information of Central Universities in Uttar Pradesh

Sr. No	*University*	*Establishment Year*	*Web Site*
01	Aligarh Muslim University (AMU)	1875	https://www.amu.ac.in
02	Babasaheb Bhimrao Ambedkar University (BBAU)	1996	https://www.bbau.ac.in
03	Banaras Hindu University (BHU)	1916	https://www.bhu.ac.in
04	Rani Lakshmi Bai Central Agricultural University (RLBCAU)	2014	https://www.rlbcau.ac.in
05	University of Allahabad (AU)	1887	https://www.allduniv.ac.in

6.1 General Information and Navigability

Table 2: General Information

Evaluation Criteria	*AMU*	*BHU*	*BBAU*	*AU*	*RLBCAU*
Library Hours and Contact Information	Yes	Yes	Yes	Yes	No
Search Function for Library Resources	Yes	Yes	Yes	Yes	No

Table 2 revels that the Four universities have dedicated library WebPages excluding RLBCAU.AMU and BHU have well-organized sites with clear menus and contact details. RLBCAU lacks detailed staff directories and operational hours.AU and BBAU have functional search bars, but AU's search results are limited.

6.2 Digital Resources and Services

Table 3: Digital Resources and Services

Evaluation Criteria	*AMU*	*BHU*	*BBAU*	*AU*	*RLBCAU*
OPAC (Online Public Access Catalog)	Yes	Yes	Yes	Yes	No
Institutional Repository	Yes	Yes	No	No	No
Access to E-Journals and E-Books	Yes	Yes	Yes	Yes	No
Remote Access to Digital Resources	Yes	Yes	No	No	No

Table 3 shows that the OPAC (Online Public Access Catalog) is available in AMU, BHU, BBAU and AU but RLBCAU lacks an OPAC.AMU and BHU offer extensive e-journal access and digital repositories. BBAU and AU have institutional repositories, but content updates are inconsistent. Remote access to digital resources is fully functional in AMU and BHU but not available on the rest of websites. RLBCAU has limited digital resources compared to other universities.

6.3 User Support and Engagement

Table 4: User support and Engagement

Evaluation Criteria	*AMU*	*BHU*	*BBAU*	*AU*	*RLBCAU*
Live Chat/Ask-a-Librarian	Yes	Yes	No	No	No
FAQs and Research Help Section	Yes	Yes	No	No	No
Social Media Integration	No	Yes	No	Yes	No

Table 4 describes that the live chat/Ask-a-Librarian support is available only on AMU and BHU websites. All five universities provide email and phone contacts for assistance. BHU and AU have social media links, while rest websites lack active social engagement. FAQs and research guides are available on AMU and BHU, while other universities lack detailed user guides.

6.4 Accessibility

Table 5: Accessibility

Evaluation Criteria	*AMU*	*BHU*	*BBAU*	*AU*	*RLBCAU*
Mobile-Friendly Design	Yes	Yes	Yes	No	No
Accessibility Compliance	Yes	Yes	No	No	No
Fast Loading Speed	Yes	Yes	No	No	No

Table 5 reveals that the mobile responsiveness is well-optimized in BHU, AMU, and BBAU.BBAU and RLBCAU have slower loading speeds. BHU and AMU meet most accessibility standards (alt text, keyboard navigation). RLBCAU, AU and BBAU need improvements in screen reader support. RLBCAU lacks basic accessibility features.

6.5 Key Observations

- AMU is the oldest University in our study and RLBCAU is the youngest.
- BHU and AMU have the best library websites, offering extensive digital resources, OPAC, institutional repositories, and user support.
- AU and BBAU provide moderate digital services but lack interactive user engagement features like chat support.
- RLBCAU has the least developed library website with limited digital resources, no OPAC and poor accessibility compliance.
- Library General Information, OPAC, Access to online database and mobile friendly design are the common features available on the library websites of central universities in Uttar Pradesh.
- Only AMU and BHU websites are accessible and user-friendly.
- Well-structured websites enhance user experience. AMU and BHU perform best in this aspect, while RLBCAU needs improvements.

- Comprehensive digital resources support academic success. Universities with OPAC, e-journals, and institutional repositories provide better research support.

7. RECOMMENDATIONS

Based on the findings, the following recommendations are proposed to enhance the effectiveness of central university library websites:

- All universities should implement or improve OPAC systems for better resource accessibility.
- RLBCAU should enhance digital resources by integrating e-journals, databases, and institutional repositories.
- BBAU and AU need to introduce chat support or FAQs to improve user engagement.
- All universities should ensure incorporating screen reader support, alt text for images, and keyboard navigation.
- Universities should improve their website loading speed and mobile responsiveness for better accessibility.
- Accessibility compliance is a major gap. Universities must ensure accessibility standards to make their websites inclusive.

This study provides a benchmark for future improvements in academic library website design and functionality, ensuring better access to digital resources for students and researchers.

8. CONCLUSION

This study conducted a content analysis of the library websites of central universities in Uttar Pradesh. The findings highlight significant variations in the quality, functionality, and usability of these library websites. AMU and BHU have the most user-friendly library websites with well-structured OPAC systems, digital repositories, remote access, and strong user support. AU and BBAU have moderately developed websites but lack real-time engagement features. RLBCAU has the least developed library website, with limited digital resources and no OPAC. Accessibility remains a major challenge, except for AMU and BHU. Most universities lack user engagement tools like live chat and FAQs, reducing their effectiveness. Overall, significant improvements are needed in accessibility, resource availability, and user support across central university library websites in Uttar Pradesh.

REFERENCES

Ambika, C.A. and Ganesan, P. (2021). Central university library websites in India: Web content analysis. *Library Philosophy and Practice,* 1–15.

Anyaoku, E.N. and Lucky, O.A. (2020). Usability evaluation of university library websites in South-South Nigeria. *Library Philosophy and Practice,* 1–26.

Bharati, S.K. and Madhusudhan, M. (2019). Content evaluation of Jawaharlal Nehru University and Banaras Hindu University library websites in India. *Library Philosophy and Practice*, 1–23. https://digitalcommons.unl.ed u/libphilpr ac/ 2290.

Brahma, K. and Verma, M.K. (2022). Web content analysis of national libraries' websites in Asia: An evaluation. *International Journal of Information Science and Management,* 20(1), 427–448.

Khawaja, P. (2022). Accessibility of public library websites in the United States. *Universal Access in the Information Society*, 1–11.

Rafiq, S. *et. al.,* (2021). A Content Analysis of the Websites of the World's Top 50 Universities in Medicine. *Science and Technology Libraries,* 40(3), 260–281.

Saloi, A. (2020). Web Content Evaluation of the University Libraries of Assam. *Journal of Information Management*, Vol. 7, No. 2, 2020, 70–77.

Seshaiah, O. and Rekha, R.V. (2019). Web Pages of Engineering College Libraries in Andhra Pradesh: An Analysis. *Journal of Indian Library Association,* 55(2), 8–16.

Yadav, M.K. and Mishra, R. (2021). Usability analysis of Indian institutes of science education and research (IISERs) library websites: A study. *Library Philosophy and Practice,* 1–6.

Evaluating the Efficiency of V2V and V2I Communication in Vehicular Networks

Rani Singh[1] and Anand Rajavat[2]

ABSTRACT: Vehicular ad-hoc network (VANET) is the core of intelligent vehicles. VANETs communicate in two modes V2V (vehicle to vehicle) and V2I (vehicle to infrastructure). The communication network formed in VANET ensures accuracy and security while the vehicles are moving on the road to increase road safety and decrease traffic congestion. The capability to see around all corners in V2V communication enhances the safety features in various driving scenarios for VANET. The research aims to analyze the two types of communication network formed in VANET i.e., V2V and V2I. The simulations are performed using the QualNet network simulator. Based on the simulation result, the performance comparison of V2V and V2I is analyzed on the metrics like throughput, jitter, and end-to-end delay. Data rate i.e. data send by the client vehicle and data received by the server vehicles are also compared between V2V and V2I communication. According to the analyzed metrics, V2V communication shows a higher data rate, higher throughput and lesser delay and jitter compared to V2I communication.

Keywords: *End-to-End Delay, Jitter, Qualnet, Throughput, Traffic Congestion, VANET.*

1. INTRODUCTION

In VANET, the environment changes constantly. VANET is the core of Intelligent Smart vehicles which will be part of IoT in the coming future. VANET is used to yield suitable wireless network services (Abhale *et. al.*, 2013). The evaluation and deployment of wireless communication systems have completely altered the life of common people by offering internet services and their various applications that ultimately made human life easy and flexible while travelling. In recent times, vehicles are not simply a vehicle which is used for transportation. VANET or Intelligent vehicles of today have On board Unit (OBU) as a wireless communication device installed in the vehicle as well as vehicles are also equipped with smart technologies that gives more sensing, processing, and communicating capabilities (Taha *et. al.*, 2023) in VANET. VANET cnsures accuracy and security for communication in vehicle-to-vehicle (V2V) and vehicle-to-infrastructure (V2I) modes. In VANETs mostly two types of communication take place, vehicle to vehicle (V2V) communication and vehicle to infrastructure (V2I) communication (Singh & Rajavat., 2024).

V2I is the communication between vehicles and RSUs (Road-Side Units). RSUs are strong computing device that are placed at several locations (Hu *et. al.*, 2017). An RSU

[1] Research Scholar, Shri Vaishnav Institute of Information Technology, Shri Vaishnav Vidyapeeth Vishwavidyalaya, Indore, India. E-mail: rani.usic@gmail.com

[2] Director, Shri Vaishnav Institute of Information Technology, Shri Vaishnav Vidyapeeth Vishwavidyalaya, Indore, India.

acts as a router in VANETs. RSUs are the backbones of this network for providing several services like it collects traffic data from the nearby road or static sensing area and forwarding those collected data to the traffic management centre. So it always causes too much traffic congestion in RSUs and base stations. RSUs are situated at a minimum distance of 2 to 5 km (Singh & Rajavat, 2024). In VANET, the vehicle communicates with other vehicular user on road while travelling either for sharing safety or any urgent information. All information communicated in between the vehicles is stored in cloud server (traffic management system) through RSUs and base station. This information can be useful for other vehicles travelling with the same route. The RSUs can broadcast the information from cloud server through base station to all the vehicles within the range and the vehicles can further communicated it to those vehicles that are in its range. So this V2V and V2I communication is a good support for broadcasting the information's to the different vehicular user.

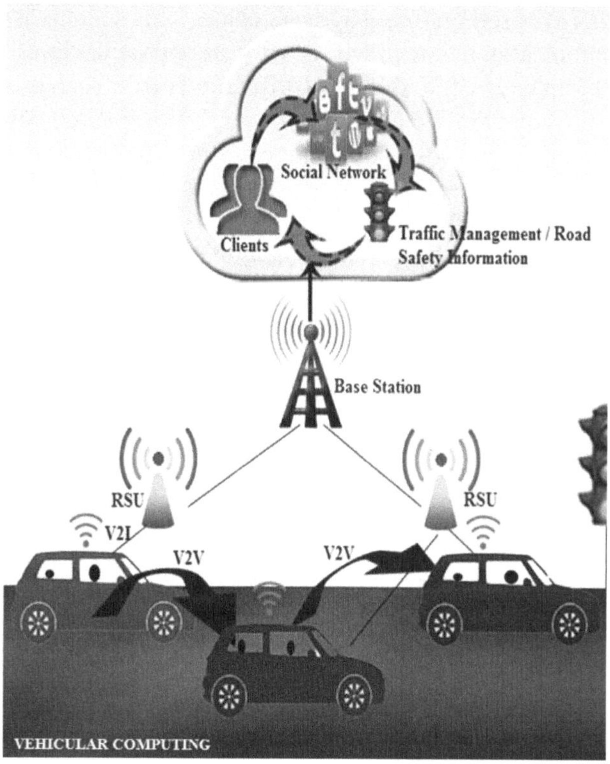

Figure 1: VANET Scenario

The objective of the research is to compare V2V and V2I communication on the parameters like throughput, jitter and end to end delay. This will make easier to decide, while the vehicles are communicating on road which communication mode to be used respective of the given parameter. As of today the biggest challenges in VANET is getting the safety and security messages as fast as possible. As in VANETs the mobile nodes (vehicles) are moving, so sending and receiving messages at right time and right place is very important.

2. REVIEW OF LITERATURE

Singh & Rajavat. (2024) have compared AODV and DSR protocols on MANET Scenarios, under different performance metrics like throughput, packet drop rate and end to end delay. Wang *et. al.,* (2011) investigated the connection between network algorithm and social behaviour in respect of VSNs (Vehicular Social Networks). Centrality concept has been introduced for Dynamic Bandwidth Allocation (DBA) in this paper. Simulation results have measured the performance in terms of throughput and average queuing delay based on the proposed Quality of Service (QoS)-aware DBA algorithm. Abbani *et. al.,* (2011) discussed the security issues for real time Vehicular Cloud Service (VCS) which combines the security issues of Body Area Sensor Network (BASN), smart phones, and V2V authentication and authorization. Three-Tier Vehicular Cloud architecture has been proposed in this paper. This paper has also introduced special concept of real time VCS like health care, resource sharing, parking, dinning etc. For the purpose of improvement in public safety and road traffic optimization, an authentication protocol is proposed (Sulaiman *et. al.*, 2013) based on one-way hash chain. This scheme is applicable for both V2V and V2I communications to achieve security and privacy. Hu *et. al.,* (2017) focused on the performance analysis of VANET in different Traffic scenarios, different routing protocols are used for comparative analysis like AODV, DSR, OLSR and AODVUU. A reverse back-off strategy is proposed by (Stanica *et. al.*, 2014) for enhancing road safety in VANET. A vehicle in a network generates messages of various priorities. To deal with this problem, a prioritized gossip algorithm is developed (Cornejo *et. al.*, 2013).

Vehicles of today are not simply a vehicle which is used for transportation from one place to another rather vehicles are equipped with smartphones that have more sensing, processing, and communicating capabilities (Wang *et. al.*, 2011). Akbar *et. al.,* (2020) mapped scheme for the V-track system is based on the Markov model and Viterbi decoding scheme is used for estimating travel time. They have further investigated the performance analysis of different protocols for V2V and V2I communication, The DSR routing protocol performs better than the FSR routing protocols in both V2V and V2I network models for throughput and end-to-end delays in all scenarios.

Almeida & Gomes (2022) did a comparative analysis on vehicular safety on two network simulation tool NS3 and Vein. For comparative analysis three metrics was considered like packet inter-reception time, packet delivery rate, and maximum communication range. Yadav *et. al.,* (2018) have presented a short summary for all the routing protocols such as proactive, reactive and hybrid routing protocols which are used in VANETs, with their merits and demerits. Firstly, a Homogeneous Continuous-Time Markov Chain (HCTMC)-based security state model is designed for VANET. The value of each state of the HCTMC is determined with a value function that incorporates the security strength of transmitted data, dynamic and randomness of the vehicular channel, and transmission delay of the current situated environment of VANETs (Wang *et. al.*, 2020). Xie *et. al.,* (2017) investigated the security and privacy issue in the transportation system and the vehicular IoT environment in SDN-enabled 5G-VANET.

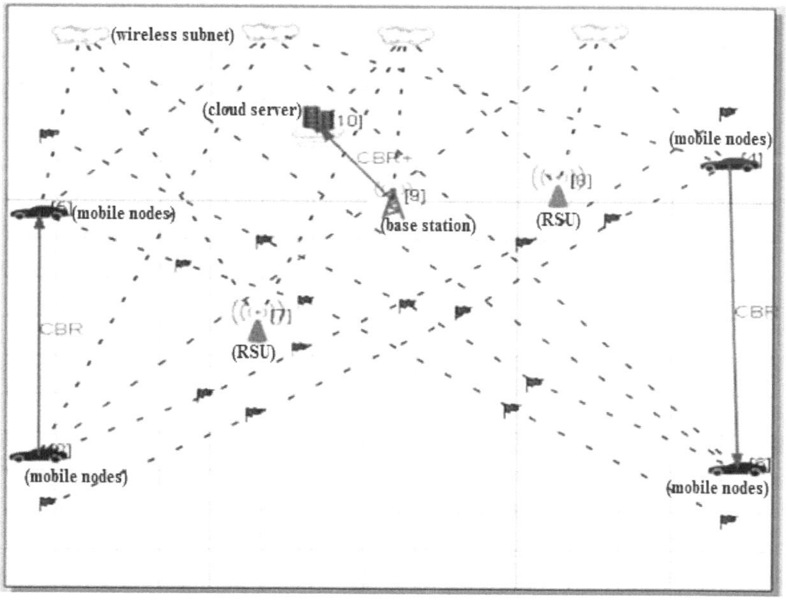

Figure 2: Architect Module of QualNet Showing the Simulation Scenario Including 4 Vehicle Nodes, 1 Base Station, 2 RSUs, and 1 Cloud Server

3. VANET SCENARIO

According to the scenario presented in Figure 2, the vehicles are connected to form a network for sharing data. The movements of the vehicles are shown using mobility waypoints. There are RSUs at regular intervals. The RSUs are connected to WiMAX base station. The vehicles are connected to the cloud via the RSUs and base station. CBR (Constant Bit Rate) links has been defined between the vehicles. The vehicles connect with other vehicles through wireless when they are in signal range of each other. When the vehicles come within the signal range of the RSUs, they can connect to the internet via the base station.

The parameters which have been used in QualNet while simulating VANET scenario are given in Table 1.

Table 1: Scenario Parameter Values

Network Simulator	Qualnet 7.1
Dimension of space	1500 m × 1500 m
Simulation Time	1000 sec
Item Size	512 bytes
Number of Channels	3
Routing Protocol	AODV
MAC Protocol for RSUS	802.11
MAC protocol For Base Station	802.16
Application Used	CBR

In Figure 2, four vehicles move according to the mobility waypoints. The routing protocol used is AODV because on-demand paths are established between the vehicles. Figure 3 shows the simulation of VANET where nodes 2, 5, 6, 4 are the vehicles, nodes 7,8 are the RSUs, node 9 is the WiMAX base station and node 10 is the cloud server can be considered as a Traffic Management system (Jain *et. al.*, 2022). Constant Bit Rate (CBR) is a traffic generator which is a UDP-based client-server application that sends data from clients to server at a constant bit. CBR links have been defined between the vehicles. Here the client may be vehicles and servers may be the vehicle itself or RSUs or base stations.

Two different scenarios have been considered here, in the first scenario the vehicles are kept closer to each other by adjusting the mobility way point. For vehicular node 4, 2 (CBR client node) and vehicular node 5, 6 (CBR server node)), the mobility way point is adjusted in such a manner that these vehicle communicate with each other in V2V communication mode and in the next scenario the mobility way points of the vehicles are adjusted in such a way that it communicate with RSUs (V2I). V2V or V2I communication takes place with the help of a special device, installed in vehicles i.e., OBU. To study the performance of VANET, depending on parameters like throughput, end-to-end delay, and jitter, a network simulation is performed using QualNet network simulator. After the simulation, performance analysis of the CBR clients and the servers has been performed. The values of the Quality of Service (QoS) parameters: throughput, average jitter and average delay have been observed from the statistics generated after the simulation.

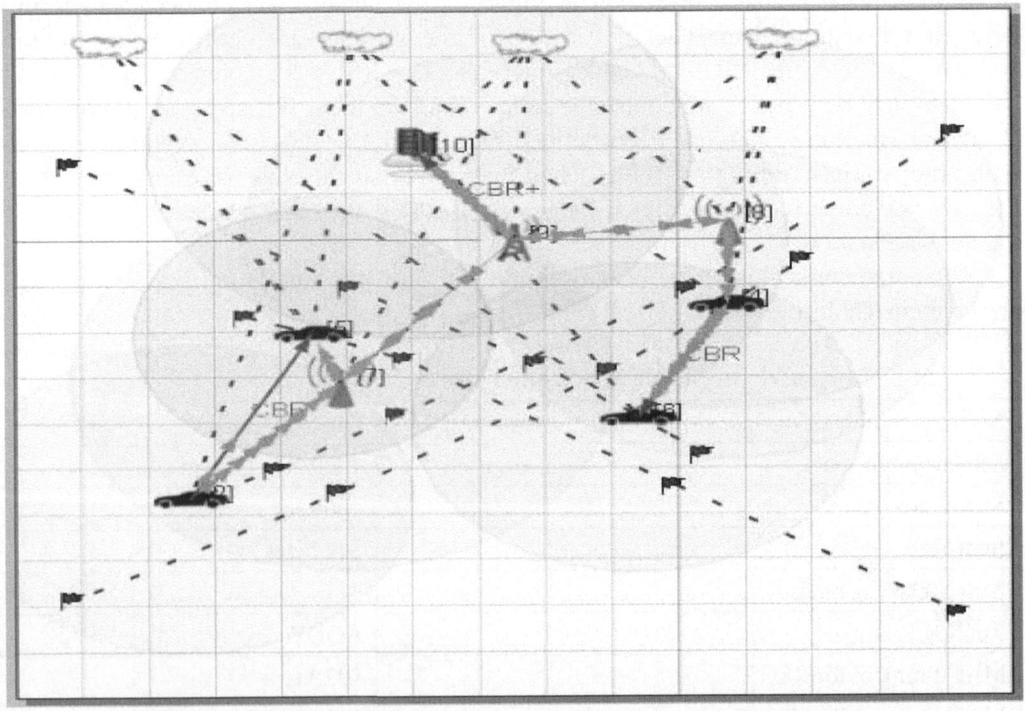

Figure 3: Architect Module of QualNet Showing the Simulation Scenario of VANET Communication

4. PERFORMANCE COMPARISON BASED ON VEHICLE MOVEMENT

In this paper a performance comparison based on vehicle movements by changing the waypoint arrival time of the vehicles is done, by adjusting the waypoint arrival time of the vehicles which leads to a variation in the time duration for which the vehicles are in the signal range of each other. This in turn affects the data received by the CBR server. In the first case, the waypoint arrival time of all the vehicles 2, 4, 6 and 5 is set as 0, 100, 300, 500 and 800 seconds. Due to closer waypoints or arrival time of the vehicles, all the vehicles arrive at their waypoints at the same instant.

When the way point arrival time set for the vehicles are less, then mostly vehicle to vehicle communication takes place i.e. vehicles moves within their ranges. In the second case, when the waypoint arrival time of vehicles 2 is set as 0, 100, 500, 1000 and 1500 seconds. The waypoint arrival time of the vehicle 5, 2, 4 is kept the same. Due to this the vehicles 2(CBR client) and 5(CBR server) moves at different instant at the waypoints. In such case, vehicles are not in range of each other. Vehicle communicates mostly via base stations and RSUs. So here V2I communication takes place. Figure 4 and Figure 5 show

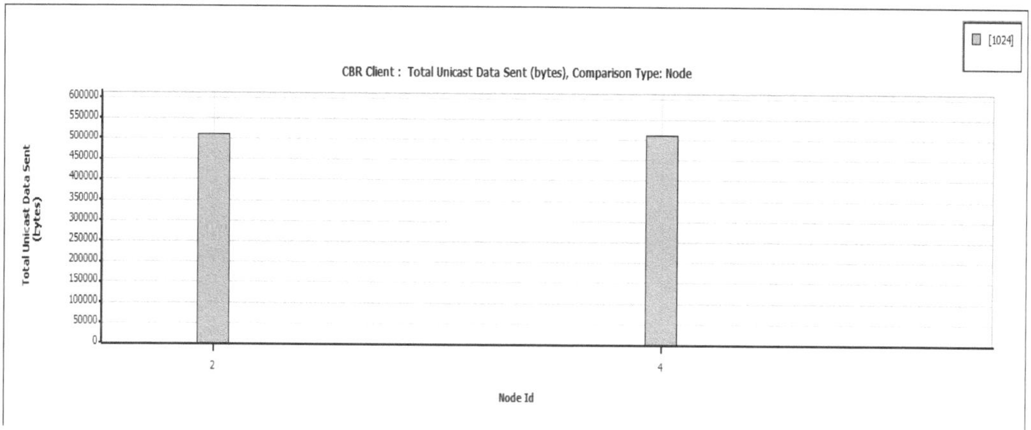

Figure 4: Total Unicast Data Sent by the CBR Client (nodes 2, 4). When the Mobility Waypoint is set as 0, 100, 300, 500, and 800 seconds

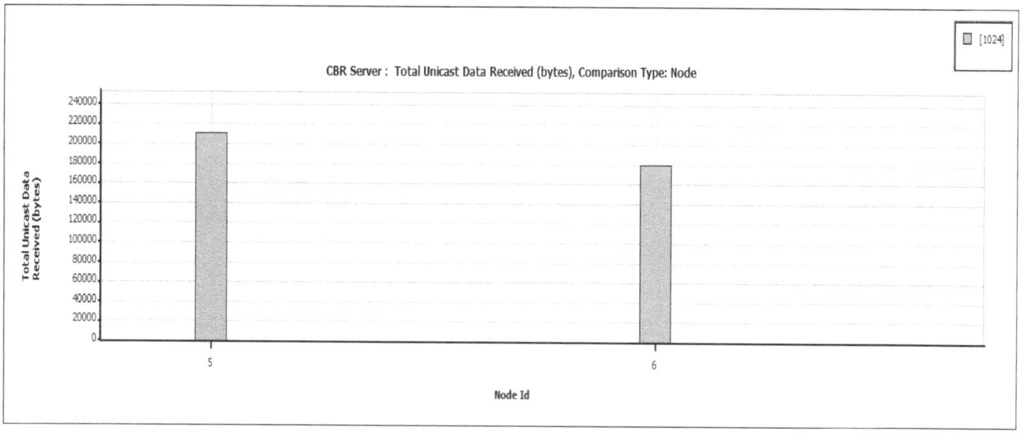

Figure 5: Total Unicast Data Received by the CBR Server (nodes 5, 6). When Mobility Waypoint is Set as 0, 100, 300, 500, 800

the CBR data sent and received in the first case. Figure 6 and Figure 7 show the CBR data sent and received in the second case. In Figure 8 and Figure 9 the graphs show the comparison between the data sent and received for the first and second cases respectively.

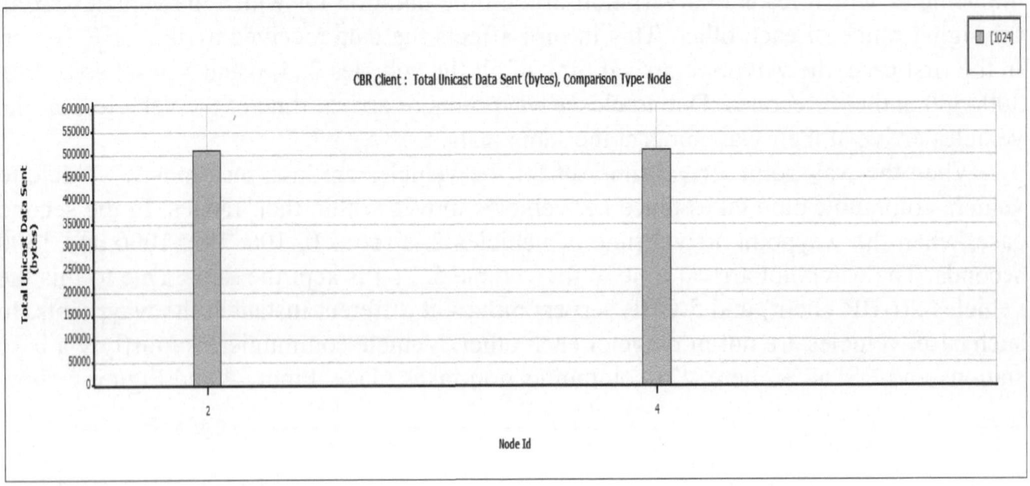

Figure 6: Total Unicast Data Sent by the CBR Clients when the Mobility Waypoint is Set 0, 100, 500, 1000 and 1500 seconds (for node 2)

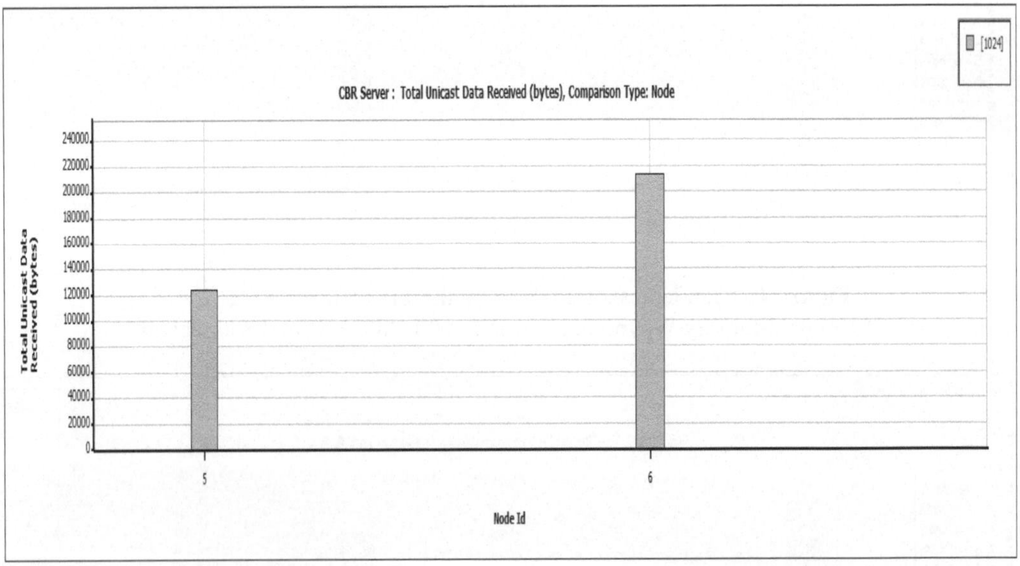

Figure 7: Total Unicast Data Received by CBR Server when the Mobility is Set as 0, 100, 500, 1000 and 1500 seconds

From Figure 6 it is observed that the data received by node 5 is more when the waypoint arrival times of vehicles 2 and 5 same are. Figure 7 depicts the second case where the arrival time at the waypoints is different for vehicles 2 and 5. It is seen that the data received by vehicle 5 is less in this case. This shows that when the vehicles are in the signal range of each other data sharing is more efficient.

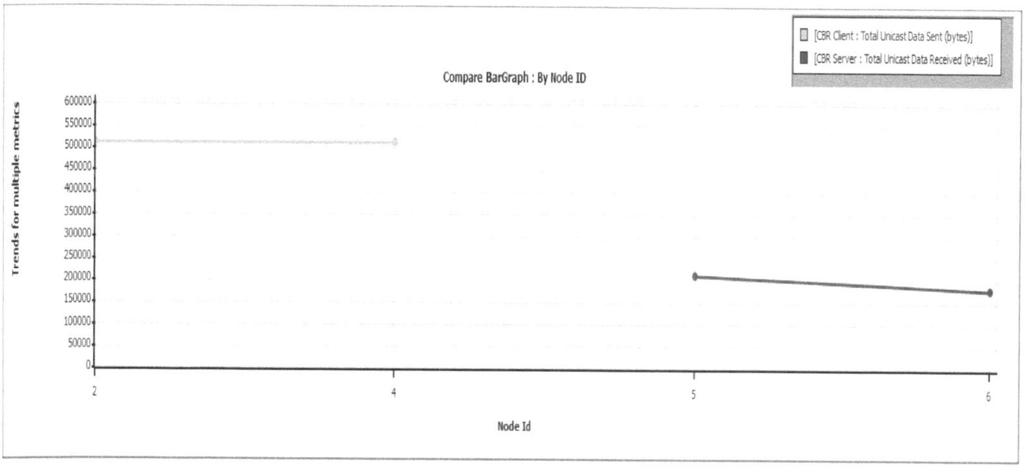

Figure 8: Comparison between Data Sent (node 2, 4) and Received (node 5, 6) between the CBR Server and Client when the Mobility Waypoints in Set as 0, 100, 300, 500 and 800 seconds

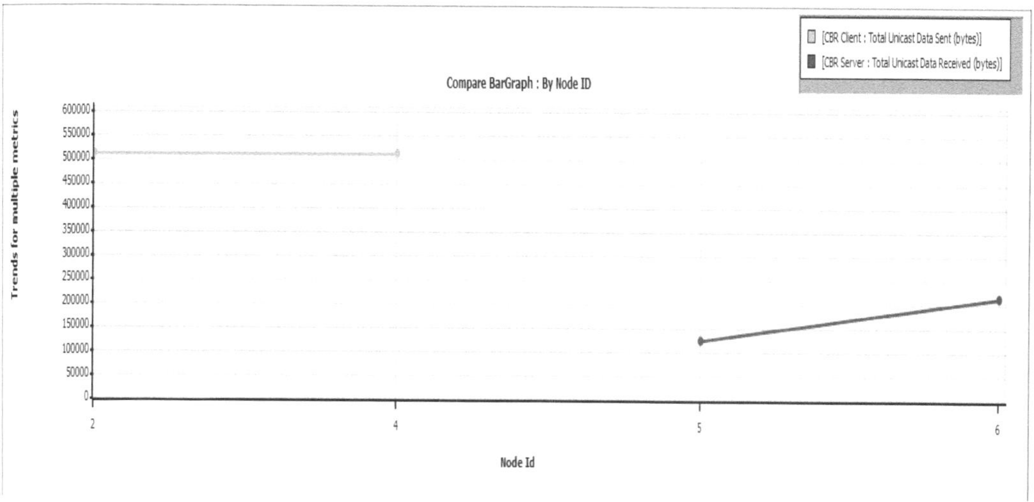

Figure 9: Comparison Between Data Sent and Received between CBR Server and Client when the Ways Points are Set as 0, 100, 500, 1000 and 1500 seconds

5. RESULTS AND DISCUSSION

5.1 Average End-to-End Delay

The end-to-end delay gives the measure of time taken by the data packet to traverse from the CBR client to the application layer of the CBR server (Yumuşak & Demirtaş, 2022). It includes all forms of delay like delays due to buffering, delays caused due to the discovery of routes, queuing latency at the interface, delays due to retransmission of packets, and delays involved in the transmission and propagation of the packets. The graph shown in Figure 10 shows the end-to-end delay of the four CBR servers i.e. nodes 5, 6, 9, and 10 in our simulation. In between node 5 and node 6 which is a mobile node (vehicles) according to our scenario, the delay of node 5 is higher than that of node 6. This is because the CBR client node 4 was within the signal range of the CBR server node 6, so communication among the vehicles takes place with fewer overheads (V2V). But node 2 and node 5 were away due to the difference in their waypoint arrival time, so here V2I communication took place. Node 9 has a maximum average end-to-end delay than all the other nodes because network conjunction is highest at this node. According to the scenario node, 9 is a base station through which the vehicle communicates to cloud storage and vice versa either for storing data or fetching some data/information. A base station is the central point of vehicular communication.

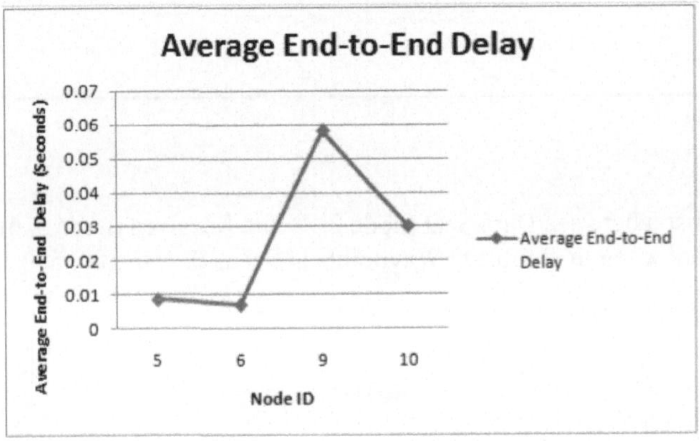

Figure 10: Average Unicast End-to-End Delay of CBR Servers

5.2 Average Jitter

Jitter is defined as the disparity in timing in the arrival of packets caused due to congestion of the network, time drift, or changes in the route (Naim & Hossain, 2019). For better performance of the routing protocol, the jitter should be less. Figure 11 shows the graph of the average jitter of nodes 5 and 6. It has been observed that the jitter in case of node 5 is higher. CBR server node 5, when not in the signal range of CBR client vehicle 2, it communicates through RSUs. Therefore, delay between nodes is higher when they are communicating with RSUs and then to base stations. Base station node 9 has the highest average jitter because due to network traffic conjunction and data prioritization (Jain *et. al.*, 2022). Node 10 which is the cloud storage according to our scenario has almost negligible jitter due to constant latency with zero variation.

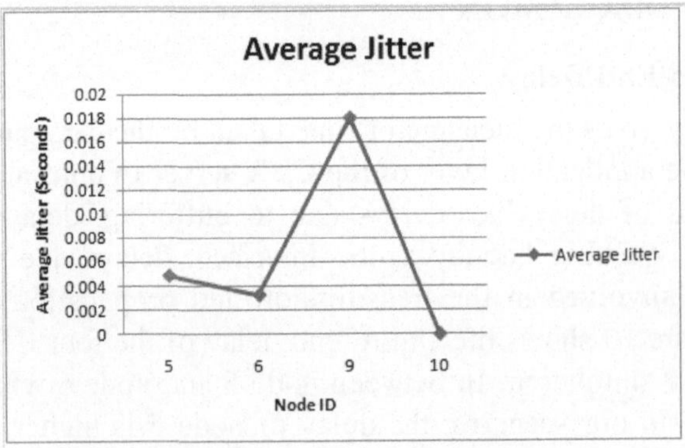

Figure 11: Average Jitter of CBR Servers

5.3 Throughput

Throughput can be defined as the rate of data received by the CBR server from the CBR client. It is expressed in bits/seconds (Naim & Hossain, 2019). Figure 12 shows the throughput of the CBR servers' nodes 5, 6, 9, and 10. Between node 5 and node 6, throughput is more in node 6 (because of V2V communication with node 4) than node 5 which show V2I communication with node 2. Data send and receive is the maximum for the cloud server and base station. Vehicles communicate to a cloud server through RSUs and base stations, and vice versa for uploading important information.

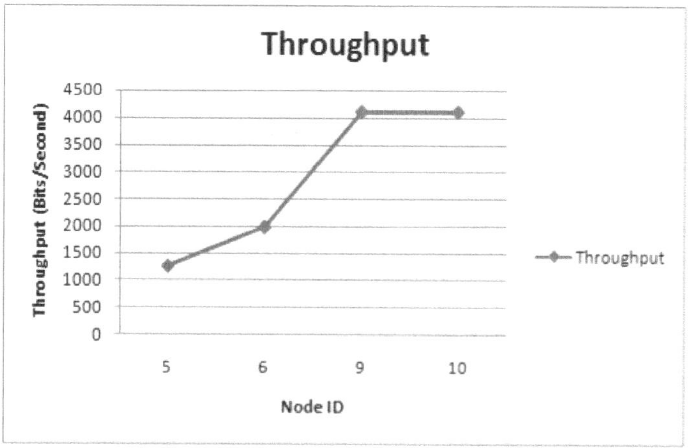

Figure 12: Through Puts of CBR Servers Depending on the Rate of Data Exchanged by CBR Clients and Servers

6. CONCLUSION

In VANET, Vehicles are the moving nodes. Additionally, urgent information like traffic congestion, accidents, roadblocks, natural calamities, and information related to utilities like hospitals, schools, cafeterias, etc. can be shared via this network. Thus, VANETs can help in mitigating several types of emergencies by providing prior information to unaware commuters. In case of natural disasters, the most used network infrastructure may collapse. In such situations, VANET can significantly contribute to disseminating information. Therefore, it is important to circulate emergency information among vehicles with lesser delay and jitter, so for that preferable V2V communication is better than V2I communication. V2V communication occurs when vehicles are within the range of each other. Otherwise, V2I communication occurs where the vehicles communicate with RSUs or though base stations.

Performance comparison of VANET communication, V2V and V2I are done on QualNet network simulator. After simulation, it is depicted that when the vehicles are closer to each other (V2V), i.e. within the range, the data exchange rate is higher with less delay and jitter. But when the vehicles are far from each other (V2I), communication includes more delay and jitter comparatively. Due to large network conjunction at RSUs and Base station as large numbers of vehicles tries to get connected with RSUs and Base station for runtime message communication, therefore conjunction is more, and data rate is less in V2I communication.

In the future, it is expected that multi-hop vehicle to vehicle communication can be established when the vehicles are not in range of each other, so that vehicular ad-hoc networks will be supporting more services and applications for increasing road safety and efficient road transportation with a faster way of communica

REFERENCES

Abbani, N.; Jomaa, M.; Tarhini, T. and Artail, H. (2011). Managing social networks in vehicular networks using trust rule. IEEE Symposium on Wireless Technology and Applications, 168-173.

Abhale, S.; Khandelwal, U. and Nagaraj, U. (2013). Shifting VANET to cloud- Survey. IJARCSSE, 3, 1056-106.

Akbar, R.Z.; Istikmal and Sussi (2020). Performance analysis FSR and DSR routing protocol in VANET with V2V and V2I models. 2020 3rd International Seminar on Research of Information Technology and Intelligent Systems (ISRITI), 158-163.

Aljabry, I.A. and Al-Suhail, G.A. (2022). A QoS evaluation of AODV topology-based routing protocol in VANETs. *2022 International Conference on Engineering & MIS (ICEMIS),* 1–6.

Cornejo, A., Newport, C., Gollakota, S., Rao, J. and Giuli, T. J. (2013). Prioritized gossip in vehicular networks. Ad Hoc Networks, 11, 397-409.

de Almeida, T.T.; de Carvalho Gomes, L.; Ortiz, F.M., Júnior, J.G.R. and Costa, L.H.M.K. (2022, January). Comparative analysis of a vehicular safety application in NS-3 and Veins. IEEE Transactions on Intelligent Transportation Systems, 23(1), 620-629.

Hu, S.; Jia, Y. and She, C. (2017). Performance analysis of VANET routing protocols and implementation of a VANET terminal. 2017 International Conference on Computer Technology, Electronics and Communication (ICCTEC), 1248-1252.

Jain, S.; Jain, V.K. and Mishra, S. (2022). Vehicular traffic offloading through intelligent RSU selection in VANET. 2022 IEEE 6th Conference on Information and Communication Technology (CICT), 1-5.

Naim, Z. and Hossain, M. I. (2019). Performance analysis of AODV, DSDV, and DSR in vehicular adhoc network (VANET). 2019 International Conference on Robotics, Electrical and Signal Processing Techniques (ICREST), 17-22.

Singh, R. and Rajavat, A. (2024). VANET security using blockchain. Fostering Multidisciplinary Research for Sustainability, 159.

Singh, R. and Rajavat, A. (2024, May). Short-lived social vehicular network. *2024 International Conference on Electronics, Computing, Communication and Control Technology (ICECCC), 1-9. IEEE.*

Stanica, R.; Chaput, E. and Beylot, A.L. (2014). Reverse back-off mechanism for safety vehicular ad hoc networks. Ad Hoc Networks, 16, 210-224.

Sulaiman, A.; Raja, S. K. and Park, S. H. (2013). Improving scalability in vehicular communication using one-way hash chain method. Ad Hoc Networks, 11, 2526-2540.

Taha, M.B.; Alrabaee, S. and Choo, K.-K.R. (2023). Efficient resource management of micro-services in VANETs. IEEE Transactions on Intelligent Transportation Systems.

Vibin, V.; Sivraj, P. and Vanitha, V. (2018). Implementation of in-vehicle and V2V communication with basic safety message format. 2018 International Conference on Inventive Research in Computing Applications (ICIRCA), 637-642.

Wang, J.; Chen, H. and Sun, Z. (2020). Context-aware quantification for VANET security: A Markov chain-based scheme. IEEE Access, 8, 173618-173626.

Wang, J.; Cho, J.; Lee, S. and Ma, T. (2011). Real-time services for future cloud computing enabled vehicle networks. International Conference on Wireless Communications and Signal Processing, 1-5.

Xie, L.; Ding, Y.; Yang, H. and Wang, X. (2019). Blockchain-based secure and trustworthy internet of things in SDN-enabled 5G-VANETs. IEEE Access, 7, 56656-56666.

Yadav, S.; Rajput, N.K.; Sagar, A.K. and Maheshwari, D. (2018). Secure and reliable routing protocols for VANETs. 4th International Conference on Computing Communication and Automation (ICCCA), 1-5.

Yumuşak, A.K. and Demirtaş, A.M. (2022). Effect of end-to-end delay on lifetime and average bit error rate in directional antenna based wireless sensor networks. 2022 International Balkan Conference on Communications and Networking (BalkanCom), 137–141.

Evolution in Restoration of Fire Damaged Documents

Krati Singh Chauhan[1] and Richa Rohatgi[2]

ABSTRACT: Document when exposed to excessive heat becomes brittle and blackened, such documents are difficult to restore and decipher eventually leading to loss of significant information present in the document. In order to preserve such documents substantial measures are taken which can further lead to the decipherment of the information present in those documents holding legal, cultural or historical significance. Currently the restoration of the charred documents is still a challenging task for the document examiners as the conventional methods used for stabilization comprise of the substances which are not entirely efficient. The stabilization method used for preservation of documents depends on the extent of burning a document exhibits which further hinders the fastening of the polymers to the document. Since ages various methods have been incorporated in the crucial task of charred document preservation. This paper discusses and summarizes the pros and cons of the existing traditional methods used for preservation and conclude which method is most suited for the restoration that can further enhance the readability of the obscured text which can be further used in the court of law.

Keywords: *Blackened, Brittle Charred Document, Decipherment, Preservation, Stabilization.*

1. INTRODUCTION

A document which is challenged on the basis of authorship, authenticity, or tampered with in any form is called as questioned document, stated by Osborn (1929). Any surface bearing marks, impressions not specific to paper is considered as a Questioned Document. To analyze these documents or surfaces to accept or refute the claims of conviction in a court of law is the role of a questioned document examiner by Koppenhaver (2007). The documents must be handled and examined shrewdly so that the evidentiary value can remain intact.

Ellen (2004) said Questioned Documents mostly occur in cases regarding forensic investigations, financial crimes and legal disputes where the examination of the documents establishes documents genuineness, claimed author of the document and also determines if any alteration has been done in the document. Before the examination of the Questioned Documents, care and handling of the documents is of utmost concern and requires careful steps to be followed by the questioned document examiner. According to

[1] Research Scholar, School of Forensic Science, National Forensic Sciences University, Delhi, India. E-mail: kratisinghchauhan@gmail.com

[2] Assistant Professor, School of Forensic Science, National Forensic Sciences University, Delhi, India.

Hilton (1940), the precautions which should be taken while collecting and preservation of the documents are:

- Any type of marking should not be done on a document
- Writing on the document should not be done
- Pencils, pens, erasures, dividers and pointers should not be used on the document
- Mutilation of the document should not be done by repeated folding, creasing, cutting and tearing
- Document should not be folded and kept in the pocket for a long period of time and should not be handled extremely
- Documents should always be kept in protecting folders and envelopes
- Documents should be kept dried and should be kept away from extreme heat and light
- Chemical examination of the documents should not be done until advised and should be done by qualified experts
- Documents should be forwarded to the laboratory or expert at earliest convenience

Many a times documents having legal importance, historical or cultural significance are destroyed in fire either accidentally or maliciously to cover an unlawful act. When done intentionally, the outlook of the culprit is turning the document into ash will finish off the evidence against him. Kelly & Lindblom (2006) mentioned that Charred documents are mostly encountered in cases of arson, financial frauds, identity theft, embezzlement where documents are considered an important piece of evidence. Although Fire has a destructive effect on the documents, but they can be prevented from complete obliteration using some scientific tools. After discovering charred documents on a scene of crime, it should be immediately covered with a box to prevent it from further burning as fire dies out in absence of air. The level of scorching which a document exhibits depends on the factors like temperature of burning, Atmospheric condition while burning, quality of the paper, storage place where the documents were stacked, type of ink used on the paper.

The extent of burning in a document aid in determining what further process needs to be followed to preserve the documents. The partially burned documents are easier to handle and recover as compared to completely burned documents but all the same they need to be handled with utmost care. Over the years different techniques for preservation and decipherment have been integrated but due to the carbonized state of the document they were rendered inefficient. Though various methods are available for restoration of the charred documents but to enhance the preservation and decipherment, a unique and new approach is needed to overcome the shortcomings of the existing ones. Therefore, this paper summarizes and highlights the positives and negatives of the existing methods used to stabilize the charred documents and what advanced practices could be incorporated for efficient preservation of the charred documents.

2. EXISTING STABILISATION METHODS USED TO PRESERVE CHARRED DOCUMENTS

2.1 Gum Arabia

A colourless solution of gum Arabia was used by Gross (1902) to stabilise the charred document in which a colourless solution is applied on the glass sheet, followed by placing the charred fragment on the sheet by pressing it gently with hands but the drawback of using Gum Arabia was that it was sticky and it does not flatten out the curled fragment instead it breaks at certain places giving it mosaic appearance.

2.2 NEATAN Treatment

The Charred documents are extremely fragile and can disintegrate with slight mishandling. In order to stabilise the charred documents, Bartha & Duxbury (1968) used NEATEN NEW (MERK) solution (used for the preservation of thin layer chromatograms) which was spread over the document using eyedropper after which the sheet became flexible and easy to handle. The method used for charring involved placing the paper on Asbestos mat and putting a wire screen on the paper to prevent it for curling. The set up was placed in controlled temperature furnace to observe burning along the time.

2.3 Lamination

Another method for stabilizing the charred document is to laminate it given by Bartha & Duxbury (1968), the document will be flattened under the pressure of the heated rollers without breaking it which will protect the document from further damage and will be easier to transport or to be photographed. The method used for burning involved placing the paper on Asbestos mat and putting a wire screen on the paper to prevent it for curling. The set up was placed in controlled temperature furnace to observe charring along the time.

2.4 Alkyl-2-cyanoacrylate ester (Superglue Fuming)

Alkyl-2-cyanoacrylate ester is the polymer given by Hirth & Royds (2012) used commercially in production of superglues. Initially Cyanoacrylate fuming was used in the development of latent fingerprints. For charred documents the superglue fuming method is used as a pretreatment to the use of polyvinyl acetate (PVA), which includes the document to be humidified first and later with the treatment of Cyanoacrylate, the document gets some strength which makes it less fragile, but it doesn't provide enough strength that PVA could be excluded as the further treatment. This method was found efficient on partial and completely charred documents.

2.5 Poly vinyl acetate

3% Poly vinyl acetate in acetone solution by Harrison (1958) is the favored plasticizer used to stabilize the charred document by spreading it with the help of a spray or a glass rod. The drawback of using PVA as a stabilizer is that it doesn't get sprayed well over the document. Before treating the document with PVA, it must be fixed on a glass sheet which should be treated with silicon water repellent so that document doesn't get stuck over the glass sheet after PVA application. The application of PVA covers the charred mass with a white coating which later hinders the decipherment of the written content and does not provide suitable plasticity to the document. The acetone evaporates after the application giving the document sufficient strength for transportation. The method was found effective for all partially to completely charred documents.

2.6 Methyl-Methacrylate

It is also known as 40% Bed Acryl and is used in stabilization of the charred document by spraying. There are numerous drawbacks to using this synthetic polymer. Firstly, it does not give the required plasticity to the document and due to presence of a white coating over the document, visibility of the written content is not very clear and since it is a chemical method, chances of examination by other non-destructive methods are reduced. The method was found effective for all partially to completely charred documents.

2.7 Cellulose Nanofibers

The documents for this method were gathered from a public library where the books were damaged due to fire and water. The charred paper exhibits structural changes after getting burned. A stabilization method was devised by (Völkel *et. al.*, 2022) in which damaged charred documents were treated with a coating of cellulose nanofibers by air brush which preserved the document efficiently rendering decipherment. The nanofibers form a flexible, transparent film which adheres to the damaged fibers of the document making it less fragile, more stable and easier to handle.

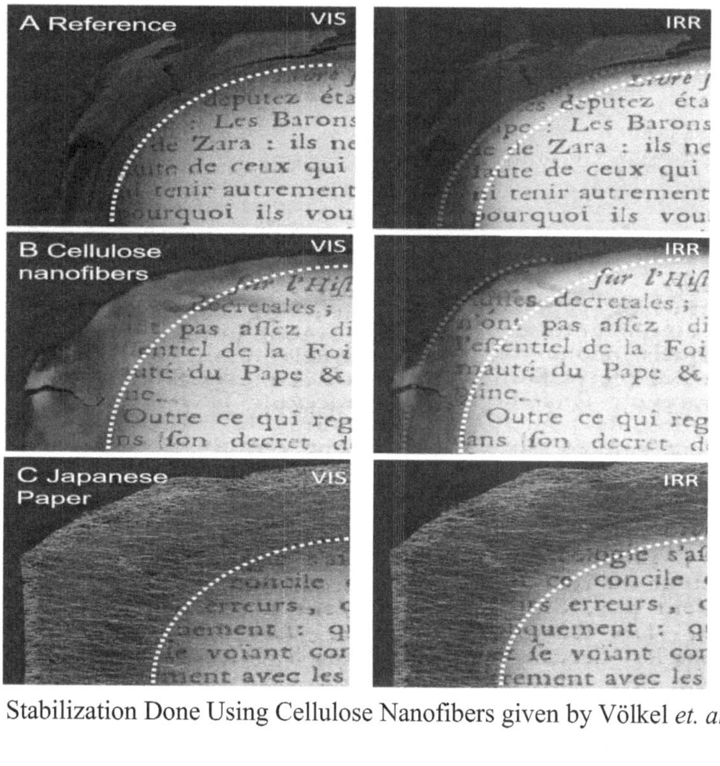

Figure 1: Stabilization Done Using Cellulose Nanofibers given by Völkel *et. al.*, (2022)

2.8 Starch based coatings

6% starch analog by Kesarwani *et. al.*, (2023) microwaved at 80^0 C was used as a coating on the charred documents which stabilized the document giving it satisfactory strength while deciphering the written content to some extent all together. The stabilized documents were analyzed using VSC (Video Spectral Comparator) and HCR (Handwriting Character Recognition) by Google lens which deciphered the text more efficiently.

6% Starch Analog		
75 g/m^2	**80 g/m^2**	**Bond paper**

Figure 2: Preservation and Decipherment Using 6% Starch Analog

2.9 Sago Seeds

Another approach of preserving documents with sago seeds involved using sago analog (Kesarwani & Tripathy, 2024) to coat the charred documents which provided appreciable strength to the document and also deciphered the content of the document. The examination of the charred document after the application of the sago analog was done by observing the document under video spectral comparator (VSC) and using a new technique i.e. optical character recognition technique using Google lens which was able to decipher the written content of the charred document noticeably. The method for charring involved preparing the samples of different papers and keeping it in muffle furnace and the charring was done from 280 to 300°C.

3. RESEARCH METHOD

Over the years many methods were developed for stabilization were developed but it was observed that no method was completely efficient in stabilizing all sorts of charred documents. Major challenges which were associated with the preservation involves severe degradation of the document due to extreme heat, completely obscured text and carbonization of the documents. Documents undergo a lot of chemical changes and exhibit different extent of burning which renders the material used for stabilization ineffective.

Table 1: Summary of Existing Stabilization Methods

S. No.	*Method*	*Description*	*Advantages*	*Drawbacks*
1.	Gum Acacia by Gross (1902)	Colorless solution applied on the glass and document is pressed on the sticky surface gently which gives mosaic appearance	It was the First method implemented for the stabilization of the charred documents	Solution is particularly sticky and breaks the document if pressure exerted is more than the required amount
2.	NEATAN by Bartha & Duxbury (1968)	NEATAN NEW (Merk) solution was applied on the document with eyedropper placed on an asbestos mat	Makes the document flexible, easy to handle	Time consuming process. Solution is applied one drop at a time and second drop is only applied after first one dries out

S. No.	*Method*	*Description*	*Advantages*	*Drawbacks*
3.	Lamination by Bartha & Duxbury (1968)	The lamination of the document is done with heat rollers which flatten out the document	Permanent record of the document can be made this way	No further examination could be done on the document which inhibits the decipherment process
4.	Cyano-acrylate fuming by Hirth & Royds (2012)	Cyano-acrylate fuming is used as a pre-treatment before the application of the plasticizer which makes the document less fragile than originally found	It makes the document less fragile	Further treatment of plasticizers is needed to strengthen the document
5.	Poly-vinyl Acetate by Harrison (1958)	A solution of Poly-vinyl Acetate when applied to the charred document gives it enough strength to be transported for the further examination	Provides strength to the document, stabilize it	Cannot be sprayed well, hinders decipherment under UV and IR
6.	Methyl-methacrylate by Harrison (1958)	The solution of Methyl-methacrylate when applied to the document makes it less fragile and strengthens it for transportation	Makes the document less fragile, stabilize it	Cannot be sprayed well
7.	Cellulose-Nanofibers by Völkel et. al., (2022)	A coating of cellulose nanofibers is applied on the document which adheres to the fibers of the damaged documents	Makes it flexible, less fragile, more stable	Only partially burned documents can be preserved this way not completely burnt documents
8.	Starch based coatings by Kesarwani et. al., (2023)	6% starch analog is used as a coating on charred documents stabilizing it and giving it sufficient strength	Stabilization and decipherment are done all together to some extent	Stabilization could vary in different sets of papers and with different writing instruments
9.	Sago seeds by Kesarwani & Tripathy (2024)	Analog of sago seeds powder was used to coat the charred document for stabilization and decipherment of the written content	Stabilization and decipherment were done all together up to an extent	Stabilization could vary in different sets of paper. Completely charred documents were not deciphered. Stabilization could also vary if, different writing instruments are used.

Following setbacks can be inferred from above discussion:

- The stabilization techniques are not fully effective in the preservation of the document and lack in either in the method of application or the effect the material have on the documents. Since all the stabilization techniques are chemical methods to preserve, it reduces the chances of non-destructive method to decipher the written content clearly. The chemical changes induced due to extreme heat changes the properties of the documents and thus making stabilising even more challenging.
- The surface properties of the paper after getting charred are not examined by any of the techniques. The changes in the fibres of the paper after getting burned and the changes induced in the ink after burning should be analysed which will enable us to devise a method which can be more efficient than the existing ones
- Existing stabilization methods does not ensure the long-term preservation of the document

5. CONCLUSION

Over the years above methods are used for the stabilization of the charred documents with continuous innovations. All the stabilization methods have been an advancement in the field of document examination and provided results up to an extent but lacked where a specific problem needs to be dealt with. Out of all the methodologies discussed above Polyvinyl Acetate by Harrison (1958) is the most prominent method currently used for preservation and the organic methods involving cellulose nanofibers by Völkel *et. al.*, (2022) and starch-based coatings by Kesarwani *et. al.*, (2023), still need to be practically explored. Quality of paper and ink, extent of burning in a document were the influencing factors which hindered the stabilization process. For preservation of the document, more research needs to be done to formulate a method which can be used for complete stabilization of the document without compromising the integrity of the document. The above discussion leads us to the conclusion that each method has been efficient up to an extent, but no single method can overcome the shortcomings of all the other methods used. The main concern in preserving charred documents is long term preservation, which needs to be focussed upon. Interdisciplinary approaches should be aimed to overcome the limitation of charred document preservation

REFERENCES

Ahluwalia, A. (2020). Forensic examination of fire and water damaged documents. *Legal Desire Media and Insights.*

Bartha, A. (1973). Restoration and preservation of typewriting and printing on charred documents. *Canadian Society of Forensic Science Journal,* (6, 111–112).

Bartha, A. and Duxbury, N.W. (1968). Restoration and preservation of charred documents. *Canadian Society of Forensic Science Journal,* (1, 1–4).

Black, D.A. (1948). Decipherment of charred documents. *Journal of Criminal Law and Criminology,* (38, 542–546).

Cutter, C. (1967). The restoration of paper documents and manuscripts. *College and Research Libraries*, (28, 387–397).

Davis, R. (1923). Action of charred paper on the photographic plate and method of deciphering charred records. *Scientific Papers of the Bureau of Standards*, (445–450).

Doud, D. (1953). Charred documents, their handling and decipherment: A summary of available methods for treating the burnt papers. *Journal of Criminal Law and Criminology*, (43, 812–826).

Doud, D. and Hilton, O. (1955). The document examiner aids the arson investigation. *Journal of Criminal Law and Criminology*, (46, 404–407).

Ellen, D. (2004). The scientific examination of questioned documents: Methods and techniques (2nd ed., 143–144). CRC Press.

Godown, L. (1964). New non-destructive document testing methods. *Journal of Criminal Law, Criminology and Police Science*, (55, 280–286).

Grant, J. (1941). Deciphering charred documents: Some recent work and a new method. *The Analyst*, (42–46).

Gross, H. (1893). Criminal investigation: A practical handbook for magistrates, police officers and lawyers (479–482).

Gupta, A.K. and Kaushal, S. (n.d.). Forensic science paper no. 8: Questioned document, module no. 22: Charred and torn documents. e-Pathshala.

Harrison, W.R. (1958). Deciphering of charred documents. In Suspect documents: Their scientific examination (110–114).

Hilton, O. (1940). The care and preservation of documents in criminal investigation. *Journal of Criminal Law and Criminology*, (31, 103–110).

Hilton, O. (1956). Scientific examination of questioned documents. *Elsevier.*

Hirth, S. and Royds, D. (2012). Stabilisation of charred documents using alkyl-2-cyanoacrylate ester (superglue fuming). *Australian Journal of Forensic Sciences*, (44, 103–105).

Kelly, J.S. and Lindblom, B.S. (2006). Scientific examination of questioned documents, (24–25). *CRC Press.*

Kesarwani, S. and Tripathy, D.B. (2021). Advancements in potential preservation and decipherment techniques of charred documents. *Indian Journal of Forensic Medicine and Pathology*, (14, 359–366).

Kesarwani, S. and Tripathy, D.B. (2024). Green approach of charred document preservation using sago seeds and its decipherment using OCR and VSC techniques. *Journal of Forensic Document Examination,* (35, 3–14).

Kesarwani, S.; Tripathy, D.B. and Kumar, S. (2023). Application of starch based coatings as a sustainable solution to preserve and decipher the charred documents. *Coatings*, 13(2).

Khan, P.M.W.; Lakhalani, P. and Pandya, S. (2023). A review on charred document decipherment, fingerprint enhancement and visualization from burnt surfaces and use of video spectral comparator for different studies. *International Journal of Biology, Pharmacy and Allied Sciences*, (12, 1109–1126).

Khasrithong, K. and Chitaree, R. (2010). Recovering written contents of a burnt paper by the IR reflected photography. *Thai Journal of Physics*, 31(2).

Koppenhaver, K.M. (2007). Restoring documents. In Forensic document examination: Principles and practice (193–195). *Humana Press.*

Minogue, A.E. (1946). Treatment of fire and water damaged documents. *JSTOR*, (17–25).

Mitchell, C.A. (1922). Documents and their scientific examination with special relevance to the chemistry involved in cases of suspected forgery, investigations of disputed documents, handwritings etc. *Charles Griffin London.*

Mitchell, C.A. (1925). The examination of charred documents (174–180). *Charles Griffin London.*

Mitchell, C.A. (1935). The use of infrared rays in examination of inks and pigments. *The Analyst,* (454–461).

Murray, H.D. (1941). Examination of burnt documents. *Nature,* 147, 199.

NICFS. (2017). A forensic guide for crime investigation (452). *National Institute of Criminology and Forensic Science.*

Osborn, A.S. (1929). Questioned documents (2nd ed.). Boyd Printing Co.

Rohatgi, S.; Gupta, S.; Sharma, M. and Shukla, S.K. (2017). A study to focus on augmentation of pre-existing methodologies for tampered document examination. *Research Journal of Pharmacy and Technology,* 10(6).

Tidke, C.R. and Kushwaha, K.P.S. (2019). Decipherment of ball point pen writings on the charred/burnt paper. *International Journal of Forensic Science*, 4(1), 21–24.

Tyrell, J.F. (1939). The decipherment of charred documents. *American Journal of Police Science,* (30, 236–242).

Völkel, L.; Beaumont, M.; Johansson, L.S.; Czibula, C.; Rusakov, D.; Mautner, A.; Teichert, C.; Kontturi, E.; Rosenau, T. and Potthast, A. (2022). Assessing fire-damage in historical papers and alleviating damage with soft cellulose nanofibers. *Small*, 18(6).

Walker, J.T. and Parker, A.G. (1951). Visualization of writing on charred paper. *Journal of Criminal Law and Criminology*, 42, 112–113.

Walls, H.J. and Taylor, W.D. (1941). A new method for the decipherment of charred documents. *Nature*, 147, 417.

Green Buildings Synergizing Renewable Energy to Achieve Urbanization in Tier-II Cities

Anshul Jain[1] and Ananda Babu K.[2]

ABSTRACT: Global urbanization is accelerating, leading to unprecedented levels of energy demand in cities, which is increasing greenhouse gas emissions. As a result, the idea of green buildings (GBs) is emerging as a viable way to meet urban energy requirements. By balancing the energy, it produces primarily from Renewable Energy (RE) sources with the energy it consumes, GB seeks to attain a net-zero energy footprint. This thorough study examines the function of RE synergies in the context of GBs in Tier-II cities covering the definition and growth of GBs, RE-synergies for achieving GBs, sustainable trends and clusters of GBs, effects of climate change on GBs, how well they perform, policy and regulatory frameworks, and problems and potential solutions pertaining to GBs. It is vital to modify GB criteria to reflect energy supply and demand, building architecture and microclimate characteristics have a significant impact on this as well. The evaluation of building energy equilibrium, occupant comfort, and interactions with the energy grid is a part of assessing the consequences of climate change and GB practices. More focus is needed on technical, policy, and socioeconomic issues to offer comprehensive solutions that will improve GBs' performance and sustainable development going forward.

Keywords: *Environmental Sustainability, Green Residential Project, Low Carbon Emission, Sustainable City, Sustainable Construction.*

1. INTRODUCTION

The buildings industry is significantly contributing to climate change as a major global source of Green House Gas (GHG) emissions and energy consumption. About 30–40% and 15–25% of the primary energy used in affluent and developing nations, respectively, is attributed to the building industry. Furthermore, 19% of the world's GHG emissions are attributable to this industry. GBs are thought to be an efficient way to combat climate change by lowering building-related energy consumption and greenhouse gas emissions (Shirinbaksh & Harvey, 2021). To achieve this, many nations, areas, and organizations have proposed a variety of policies and initiatives to support the growth of GBs. The "Building Technologies Program" of the US Department of Energy and the "Energy Performance of Buildings Directive" of the European Union are two instances of this endeavour. GB integrates with, or heavily depends upon, RE technologies to attain yearly energy balance in a building.

---

[1]Research Scholar, Department of Civil Engineering, Shri Vaishnav Vidyapeeth Vishwavidyalaya Indore, Indore, India. E-mail: jainanshul17@gmail.com

[2]Associate Professor, Department of Civil Engineering, Shri Vaishnav Vidyapeeth Vishwavidyalaya Indore, Indore, India.

These technologies typically comprise marine/ocean energy systems, geothermal, hydro, solar, wind, and biomass (Omer & Naguchi, 2020). Through evaluation and optimization, the best configurations, and capacities of the implemented RE systems in GBs must be chosen to meet the desired performance goal. The growing interest in RE applied to GBs calls for more research to consolidate current understanding and analyse the intricate interactions between various aspects (i.e., difficulties, policies, technologies, and concepts) related to GBs in urban settings. Put differently, an assessment of the viability and potential of using RE sources to convert urban buildings into energy-neutral or energy-positive entities should be conducted by synthesizing current technology breakthroughs and case studies. Moreover, government frameworks and incentives that could support integration should be explored, as well as obstacles and hurdles preventing the general deployment of RE systems in urban areas. Thus, the purpose of this research is to investigate how RE synergies function within the framework of urban GBs (Qiang *et. al.*, 2023).

2. REVIEW OF LITERATURE

2.1 GBs: Overview and Progress

The rapid increase in urbanization and population growth has intensified energy requirements, leading to heightened interest in energy-efficient structures considering pressing concerns such as greenhouse gas emissions and climate change due to reliance on fossil fuels. GB's, which include residential and commercial properties, utilize advanced sustainable construction techniques to balance energy consumption with renewable energy production. The transition from conventional fossil fuel energy practices to sustainable alternatives is essential, with the aim to design edifices that generate equivalent energy to their consumption over a designated period (Feng *et. al.*, 2023).

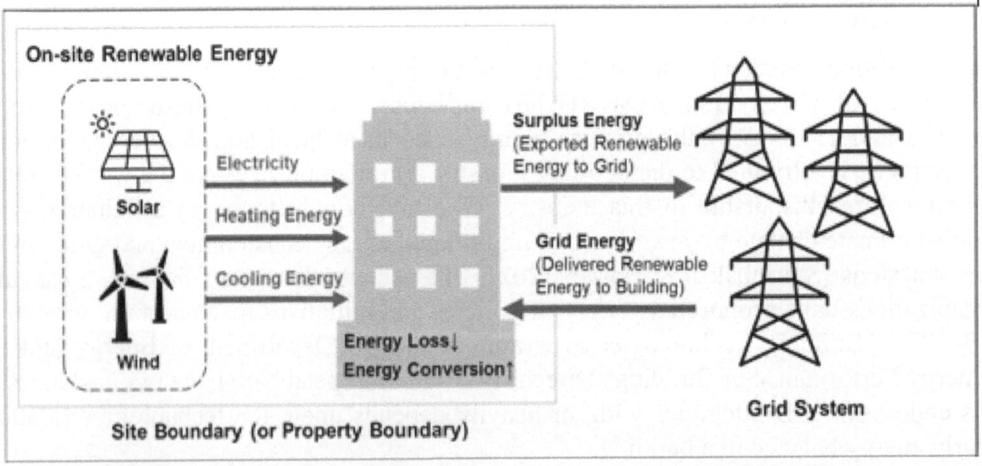

Figure 1: Configuration and Energy Flow of a Net-Zero Energy Building

Certain structures can attain energy balance by generating on-site renewable energy (RE) without external utilities and by operating active systems like biomass, geothermal heat pumps, wind turbines, and solar energy. Energy-efficient architectural design and planning can either increase or decrease a building's energy needs. The incorporation of mechanical systems such as energy-efficient HVAC systems or hot water heaters is common. For effective reduction of overall energy consumption, GB design characteristics encompass a comprehensive strategy that integrates passive design elements, such as optimizing building orientation for solar exposure, maximizing natural light, and adequate insulation (Gondal, 2021).

Numerous countries are considering the utilization of Green Buildings (GBs), with notable examples being China, the United States, and India. The global market for GBs and associated applications is projected to witness a growth of 44.5% in compound annual rate between 2014 and 2035. An exhaustive assessment of the environmental impacts of GBs throughout their lifecycle is currently receiving significant attention, with a focus on life cycle evaluation (LCA) and the embodied energy of materials. As these structures proliferate and expand, they emerge as a fundamental element in establishing a resilient and sustainable built environment for future generations, while also serving as a representation of energy efficiency (Gupta *et. al.*, 2022).

2.2 Utilizing Renewable Energy for Green Buildings

The essential roles of building energy include electricity provision, heating, cooling, ventilation, and air conditioning. To achieve net-zero energy, buildings must focus on improving energy efficiency or diminishing load consumption. RE sources, such as wind, geothermal, and solar, are critical for building functionality and represent sustainable alternatives to conventional energy systems. GBs integrate RE by either utilizing on-site resources or sourcing from external RE locations. Among various RE options, solar power is the most prevalent, offering a multitude of applications while enhancing energy efficiency through advancements in photovoltaic technology (Jain & Babu 2024).

2.3 Long-Term Patterns and Groupings of Net Zero Energy Buildings (NZEBs)

As of 2023, 35 countries, including the US and various nations in Europe and Asia, are participating in the World Green Building Council's "Advancing Net Zero" initiative aimed at decarbonizing the built environment via green buildings. Currently, very few residential homes and commercial buildings exist globally. However, interest in GBs is rapidly growing, with the market projected to exceed USD 47.4 billion by 2026. Europe leads in GB implementation due to robust energy efficiency regulations and funding for retrofits, while North America primarily focuses on single-family homes. Conversely, the development of GBs in Asia is hindered by financial and technological challenges, although China shows considerable potential for advancements in this arena. To achieve net-zero carbon emissions by 2050, the building sector must retrofit existing structures, which currently require increasing renovation rates and enhancing material energy efficiency significantly (Loveday *et. al.*, 2022).

2.4 The Effects of Climate Change on GBs

Global perception and policies for energy system consumption and planning are also altered because of the changes brought about by global climate change and related events. Various net-zero targets are being set globally. Climate change can affect the supply and demand of renewable energy sources in relation to energy equilibrium. The performance of these above-mentioned factors is to be assessed in the ensuing section. Xinya, (2023) contended that there is a chance that, given the conditions, a GB won't meet its energy-balance target in the future. Consequently, a more thorough analysis of the ways in which climate change impacts GB energy supply and demand could help to enhance overall energy supply and demand management. While several recent studies discuss minimizing the impact of the climate catastrophe, they are restricted to small-scale scenarios and situations, and do not explore mitigation strategies under ordinary or extreme future weather conditions.

2.5 Green Building Performance Assessment

Three criteria are essential for assessing a building's performance: energy consumption, environmental impact, and financial sustainability. The evaluation of green buildings should prioritize energy performance methodologies, tools, and metrics. Recent significant investigations focus on the operational phase and annual energy balance of GBs, often neglecting the implications of climate change in detailed simulations. According to Xu *et. al.*, (2021) performance assessments encompass the entire building lifecycle, which includes construction, maintenance, demolition, and production phases, while also considering embodied, operational, and recycled energy.

2.6 Frameworks for Policies and Regulations

Particularly for GBs, governance frameworks, regulations, and rules differ between locations and borders. There are differences in the way that GBs are defined and operate internationally when it comes to implementation. The goals are then applied through further federal and municipal regulations-based initiatives that provide incentives, performance certification, and similar measures. Following the significant debate in the following is a very succinct summary of the most recent policies and tactics aimed toward GB practice in the US, EU, and Asian counterparts (China and India). The objective is to attain a net-zero energy effect on the grid by balancing the amount of energy produced and consumed. Moreover, GB is certified by the US International Living Future Institute. California has set goals to adopt ZNE buildings in residential settings by 2020 and commercial settings by 2030 as part of the state's energy efficiency strategy plan. By 2030, 50% of commercial structures are expected to be retrofitted, and by 2025, 50% of newly important state building restorations are expected to become ZNE buildings (Zhong *et. al.*, 2021).

Asian cases: By adopting passive design, GBs are buildings that adjust to the location and environment, lowering the need for lighting, air conditioning, and heating. This information is provided by the Ministry of Housing and Urban-Rural Development of China. Their goal is to optimize the energy equipment efficiency by fully using RE. By 2030, the goal is to surpass the performance baseline of the 1980s and reach a complete energy efficiency level of 82% in residential buildings and 79% in commercial buildings (Ahmed *et. al.*, 2022). There are voluntary green building standards like the Passive House standard and Green Star in place, efforts toward net-zero buildings in China are now driven by individuals and volunteers rather than by explicit policies or building code regulations. Japan's GB objectives are in line with a larger plan to lower CO_2 emissions. The nation established a zero-energy target of 2050 for new residential structures and 2020 for new public buildings, with a focus on net-zero building as a central idea. Considering these efforts, the government set aside a sizeable sum of money in 2016 to support energy-efficient building and residential technologies, citing the net-zero city of Sakai and the Sekisui House Head Office as examples. The Indian government's Bureau of Energy Efficiency, Ministry of Power, has advised optimal temperature settings for building space cooling to conserve energy (Gehlot *et. al.*, 2022).

Since early 2016, there has been an increase in the use of green and energy-efficient buildings in India. To improve the energy efficiency of buildings, the Indian government has put in place several laws and regulations that encourage customers to switch to renewable energy sources and set long-term goals for zero-energy buildings. The Jawaharlal Nehru National Solar Mission, the National Mission for Enhanced Energy Efficiency, the Integrated Energy Policy, the National Mission for Sustainable Habitat, and the National Mission for a Green India are a few notable efforts. In addition, India became a leader in the operational energy reduction effort in 2019 when it unveiled the Indian Cooling Action Plan. According to Jayaswal *et. al.*, (2022) India has invested more in solar energy in 2018 than it did in all other non-RE sources combined. Due to India's dedication to energy efficiency, the country was able to avoid emitting 300 million tons of CO_2 between 2000 and 2018, which resulted in a 15% decrease in annual energy growth. The integration of RE technologies is mandated under nearly GB legislation.

In significant international regulations, this integration frequently includes traditional solutions like PV systems. However, more reassessment of international regulatory requirements is necessary to optimize RE technologies throughout the GB concept (Santos *et. al.*, 2021). In emerging nations, the adoption of general regulatory norms has been sluggish, and their viability is still up for debate. Furthermore, there is uncertainty around the shift in wealthy countries from passive to high-performance housing. It is essential to concentrate on the drivers and current barriers across multiple aspects to understand GB realization and its regulatory outlooks. Within the framework of current policy and regulatory frameworks, a comprehensive promotional strategy that builds on prior research to turn homes into nearly-GBs has been outlined. This strategy can be further divided into different themes and scales, including

1. Educational training and awareness.
2. Legislation.
3. Financial regulations, and
4. Industrial regulations.

Public awareness campaigns, industry training and education programs, increasing client and occupant knowledge, and specialist training enhancements for zero-carbon construction are all included under the category of educational training and awareness (de Luca *et. al.*, 2020). The results of earlier research, however, highlight how crucial it is that the next standard under educational training and awareness have a strong and transparent policy framework that addresses GB and global attitudes. To stimulate market demand, raising public knowledge of the benefits and necessity of zero-carbon houses should be a top priority for both the government and business sectors. Improvements covered by law include construction codes, a framework for a strategic planning policy, precise definitions of zero-carbon dwellings, broad political support, the establishment of incentive programs, and strict rules for public land development (Manco *et. al.*, 2021). To encourage the adoption of GB homes and guarantee the delivery of zero-carbon housing, it is imperative to recognize the importance of state government financial incentives. Thus, to ensure the successful design, construction, and operation of GBs, professionals in the building business must get the technical expertise and knowledge required. GB realization also requires the involvement of multiple stakeholders and a cumulative evolution of perceptions, encompassing

1. government/national-level initiatives,
2. industry-level strategies, and
3. community-level strategies,

Strategies at the Federal or State Levels

It is imperative that building decarbonization strategies and energy performance programs be integrated into nationally decided contributions at the national level. This strategy fully addresses disparities at the sectoral and national levels. To lower upfront costs for building owners and developers, the government supports RE in buildings through financial incentives like grants, tax credits, and subsidies. Policies that support requiring a certain percentage of energy in buildings to come from renewable sources also support sustainability objectives (Christopher *et. al.*, 2023). The goal of information and awareness-raising initiatives is to inform stakeholders and the public about the benefits of renewable energy and energy efficiency. Furthermore, governments can establish research and development initiatives, working in conjunction with academic and industrial partners to promote sustainable construction practices and energy-efficient technology.

Strategies at the Industry Level

GB certifications and grading systems are being implemented. Industry-level solutions must include developing GB capacity, demonstrating workable energy-saving techniques, and working with research institutes. Community-level strategies: Although actual building codes and regulations typically concentrate on individual building-level strategies, some studies emphasize the need for renewable integration or community-level adaptation of GBs as part of the standard. Energy efficiency and building management are improved by the integration of smart building technologies, such as sensors and smart meters. Energy audits offer a thorough analysis of a building's energy use and recommend ways to improve efficiency. Frequently, they are combined with a cost-benefit analysis. Using life-cycle cost analysis-based decision-making frameworks and community building energy modelling, incorporate RE production and supply integration understanding at the community level. Green roofs, energy-efficient windows, improved building envelopes, and sophisticated HVAC systems are a few examples of passive and active strategies that help preserve a comfortable internal climate while cutting energy use (Zhang *et. al.*, 2021).

2.7 Challenges

Technological advancements such as the development of smart building technologies, sophisticated energy monitoring systems, energy storage solutions, and building-integrated RE systems, which further improve performance and feasibility, can have a continuous impact on the evolution of GBs. The construction of new GBs alone cannot reach global net-zero carbon; existing buildings must be retrofitted. Building renovation rates are currently low, but they need to pick up speed to reach net-zero carbon. More focus is still needed on a few technical, policy, and socioeconomic issues to offer comprehensive solutions that will improve GB's performance and sustainable development going forward and help it meet its goals. The difficulties could be anything from applying RE technologies to achieve GBs to being vulnerable to the effects of climate change, for finding the best energy efficiency in figuring out the most effective combination of RE technologies in GBs for each climate, to load matching and grid interaction, and so on. In terms of energy equilibrium, climate change may have an impact on the supply of RE as well as the demand for building energy, therefore it is critical to determine if a GB will be able to maintain its energy balance in the future. Thus, deeper research into the ways that climate change impacts GB energy supply and demand can help to enhance overall energy supply and demand management.

3. RESULTS

The current research work focussed on the sustainable factors related to GBs along with the regulatory norms and effects on the climatic conditions due to GBs. The principal conclusions are:

1. Buildings are a major source of greenhouse gas emissions and one of the world's largest energy consumers, which makes them a big contributor to climate change.
2. GBs are thought to be a useful solution for lowering building-related energy consumption and greenhouse gas emissions as well as mitigating climate change.
3. The amount of scholarly study on GBs is gradually rising. It is also anticipated that the global market for GBs and related applications will expand.
4. GBs rely on RE technology to achieve a yearly energy balance. The best mixes of different RE systems should be used to counteract the loads and energy requirements of GBs.
5. Every nation or area must acknowledge the unique qualities of its own climate, architectural style, and energy resources and infrastructure, and must modify the concept of a GB accordingly.
6. The development of GBs is comparatively delayed in low-income nations because of financial constraints and technological restrictions.
7. Three main components can be used to assess the effects of climate change and GB practices: the building energy equilibrium, occupant temperature comfort, and interaction with the energy grid.
8. GB realization requires the involvement of multiple stakeholders and a cumulative evolution of perceptions, encompassing (i) strategies at the national or government level, (ii) strategies at the industry level, and (iii) initiatives at the community level.

REFERENCES

Ahmed, A.; Ge, T.; Peng, J.; Yan, W.C.; Tee, B.T. and You, S. (2022). Assessment of renewable energy generation towards net-zero energy buildings: A review. *Energy and Buildings, 256*, 111755.

Christopher, S.; Vikram, M.P.; Bakli, C.; Thakur, A.K.; Ma, Y.; Ma, Z.; Xu, H.; Cuce, P.M.; Cuce, E. and Singh, P. (2023). Renewable energy potential towards attainment of net-zero energy buildings status—A critical review. *Journal of Cleaner Production, 405*, 136942.

De Luca, G.; Ballarini, I.; Lorenzati, A. and Corrado, V. (2020). Renovation of a social house into a NZEB: Use of renewable energy sources and economic implications. *Renewable Energy, 159*, 356–370.

Feng, J.; Gao, K.; Khan, H.; Ulpiani, G.; Vasilakopoulou, K.; Yun, G.Y. and Santamouris, M. (2023). Overheating of cities: Magnitude, characteristics, impact, mitigation and adaptation, and future challenges. *Annual Review of Environment and Resources, 48*, 651–679.

Gehlot, M. and Shrivastava, S. (2022). Sustainable construction practices: A perspective view of Indian construction industry professionals. *Materials Today, 61*(2), 315–319.

Gondal, I.A. (2021). Prospects of shallow geothermal systems in HVAC for NZEB. *Energy and Built Environment, 2*, 425–435.

Gupta, A.; Amin, S. and Malik, F.A. (2022). An investigation of Green Buildings in India. *Neuroquantology, 20*(15), 3384–3393.

Jain, A. and Babu, K.A. (2024). Role of green buildings in the sustainable development of Tier-II cities in India. *Archives for Technical Sciences, 2*(31), 368–378.

Jayaswal, R.K., Chakraborty, S., Elangovan, D. and Padmanaban, S. (2022). Concept of net-zero energy buildings (NZEB): A literature review. *Cleaner Engineering and Technology, 11*, 100582.

Loveday, J.; Morrison, G.M. and Martin, D.A. (2022). Identifying knowledge and process gaps from a systematic literature review of net-zero definitions. *Sustainability, 14*, 3057.

Mancò, G.; Guelpa, E.; Colangelo, A.; Virtuani, A.; Morbiato, T. and Verda, V. (2021). Innovative renewable technology integration for nearly zero-energy buildings within the Re-cognition project. *Sustainability, 13*, 1938.

Omer, M.A. and Noguchi, T. (2020). A conceptual framework for understanding the contribution of building materials in the achievement of Sustainable Development Goals (SDGs). *Sustainable Cities and Society, 52*, 101869.

Qiang, G.; Tang, S.; Hao, J.; Di Sarno, L.; Wu, G. and Ren, S. (2023). Building automation systems for energy and comfort management in green buildings: A critical review and future directions. *Renewable and Sustainable Energy Reviews, 179*, 113301.

Santos-Herrero, J.M.; Lopez-Guede, J.M. and Flores-Abascal, I. (2021). Modeling, simulation, and control tools for NZEB: A state-of-the-art review. *Renewable and Sustainable Energy Reviews, 142*, 110851.

Shirinbaksh, M. and Harvey, L.D. (2021). Net-zero energy buildings: The influence of definition on greenhouse gas emissions. *Energy and Buildings, 247*, 111118.

Xinya, H. (2023). Sustainable skylines: Architecture for a greener future. *International Journal of Research and Review Techniques, 2*(2), 21–27.

Xu, J.; Ye, M.; Lu, W.; Bao, Z. and Webster, C. (2021). A four-quadrant conceptual framework for analyzing extended producer responsibility in offshore prefabrication construction. *Journal of Cleaner Production, 282*, 124540.

Zhang, S.; Wang, K.; Xu, W.; Iyer-Raniga, U.; Athienitis, A.; Ge, H.; Woo Cho, D.; Feng, W.; Okumiya, M.; Yoon, G., *et. al.*, (2021). Policy recommendations for the zero energy building promotion towards carbon neutrality in the Asia-Pacific region. *Energy Policy, 159*, 112661.

Zhong, X.; Hu, M.; Deetman, S.; Steubing, B.; Lin, H.X.; Hernandez, G.A. and Behrens, P. (2021). Global greenhouse gas emissions from residential and commercial building materials and mitigation strategies to 2060. *Nature Communications, 12*(1), 6126.

Leveraging Third Level Fingerprint Details to Overcome Challenges in Fingerprint Examination

Akanchha Kumari[1] and Richa Rohatgi[2]

ABSTRACT: Identification and individualization are key aspects in forensic cases wherein fingerprint has been crucial evidence since decades. When fingerprints are left at the crime scene, unknowingly, it might not be easily visible but can be developed using suitable fingerprint development technique and successfully studied. But in cases of partial or degraded prints, examiners face challenges in analysis and interpretation of the fingerprint evidence. A detailed review of research reflects the potential of level 3 details, specifically Poroscopy in improving identification of fingerprint. However, there are challenges in the practical implementation of fingerprint microfeatures because of variability in latent fingerprint development, inconsistency in reproducibility of sweat pore and lack of standardized protocol. The paper discusses the gaps in current literature including the need of large-scale database with level 3 details and advanced fingerprint imaging technique. Further, the scope of future research in improving fingerprint analysis by leveraging improved visualization and analysis techniques are highlighted. The exploration of sweat pore features reveals the potential of age and sex determination from fingerprint poroscopy, extensive research is required to validate and expand this in forensic usage.

Keywords: *Degraded Prints, Epidermis, Poroscopy, Reproducibility, Visualization.*

1. INTRODUCTION

One of the distinguished features found on fingertips, palms and soles is the folds of the outer skin layer, the friction ridge skin. When this friction ridge skin touches another surface, it leaves an impression behind that is known as fingerprint. Fingerprints are unique, classifiable, and immutable features of an individual that are significant tools in personal identification (Sharma *et. al.*, 2019). No two individuals have the same fingerprint, even identical twins sharing the DNA have different fingerprints. This makes fingerprint one of the most crucial types of evidence in forensic science. The uniqueness is attributed to development of fingerprint during foetal development. There is a relationship between fingerprint pattern and volar pads (Hale, 1952). Volar pads are temporary anatomical structures formed at the fingertips, between the digits, on distal side of the palm, in thenar and hypothenar area, during the 7th week of foetal development (Kücken, & Newell, 2005). From 10th to 16th week, the establishment of ridge pattern takes place through the process

[1] Junior Research Fellow, School of Forensic Science, National Forensic Sciences University, Delhi, India. E-mail: akanchha123.grd@gmail.com

[2] Assistant Professor, School of Forensic Science, National Forensic Sciences University, Delhi, India.

of regression of volar pads (Okajima, 1975). Fingerprints originate from the dermal layer of the skin which is the deeper living layer below the epidermis. The ridge pattern is supported by dermal papillae because of which the ridges are formed on the skin (Sudha *et. al.*, 2021). Thus, even in case of damage to the epidermis, the dermal layer regenerates resulting in same pattern, accounting for the permanence of the fingerprint. The characteristic of fingerprints being classifiable is attributed to the systematic grouping of fingerprints into categories based on formation and features of ridges (Cooke, 2015). Classification is important for organization and arrangement of fingerprints in databases so that it can be conveniently used for identification and matching.

1.1 History of Fingerprints

Table 1: History of Fingerprints (Barnes, 2010)

Year/Period	*Event/Development*	*Significance*
Circa 2000 BCE	Ancient Babylonian clay tablets have fingerprints as a seal for business transaction	Early evidence showing the use of fingerprint for authentication
221–206 BCE	Documents from Qin Dynasty have fingerprints on official records and clay seal (Champod, 2004)	Use of fingerprint in administration aspect
14th Century	Jaafar al-Tayyar, a Persian scholar observed the individualistic nature of fingerprint	Understanding of the uniqueness of fingerprints
1686	An Italian anatomist, Marcello Malpighi studied fingerprints under the microscope	Identification of ridge patterns but it was not associated with personal identification
1788	Johann Mayer, a German anatomist stated that every fingerprint is unique	Scientific acknowledgement of uniqueness of fingerprint
1823	Jan Evangelista Purkyně, a Czech physiologist classified fingerprints into nine categories on the basis of geometric arrangement	The foundation of fingerprint classification
1858	Sir William Herschel, a British administrator in India used fingerprints in contracts	Use of fingerprint for fraud prevention and authentication
1880	Henry Faulds, a Scottish doctor published his findings on fingerprint in Nature	Suggested the use of fingerprint in criminal identification system
1892	A British scientist, Sir Francis Galton highlighted uniqueness of fingerprint in his publication Fingerprints	Established the scientific basis of individuality and permanence of fingerprint
1896	An inspector in India, Edward Henry developed the fingerprint classification system	Formed the foundation of arrangement and indexing of fingerprint database
1901	Scotland Yard (UK) adopted fingerprint as a method of criminal identification	Widespread usage of fingerprint by law enforcement agency

Year/Period	*Event/Development*	*Significance*
1903	Post a false identification case in the United States, fingerprint replaced the Bertillon System	Demonstrated the reliability of fingerprint over the traditional anthropometric method
1908	U.S Army significantly depended on fingerprint for identification of soldiers	Expansion of fingerprint for military identification
1924	Establishment of Identification Division by FBI	Centralized the fingerprint database in the U.S.
1960–1970s	Introduction of Automated Fingerprint Identification System (AFIS)	Automated the task of fingerprint matching
2000s	Integration of fingerprint biometrics in various technologies like laptops and smartphones	Widespread usage of fingerprint for security and personal identification

1.2 Fingerprint Characteristics

The identification and comparison of fingerprints happens at three levels as shown in Figure 1. The first level is concerned with the macro features like the type of pattern, core, delta, ridge count and orientation. It is not possible to individualize the fingerprint just based on first-level details. The second level includes different ridge characteristics, called the Galton's details or minutiae. It is possible to individualize the fingerprint based on Galton's details. The third level concerns the microfeatures or intra-ridge details like edge contours, sweat pores, incipient ridges, scars, creases, friction ridge width and other features. This level of examination covers a wide range of extended features, pores being the dominant ones (Kaur & Dhall, 2023).

In some cases, forensic professionals face challenges in identifying the fingerprint or individualising the fingerprint because of various limitations. Some of the commonly encountered limitations are partial, distorted or degraded fingerprints that lack of sufficient ridge characteristics, this makes the fingerprint challenging to be used for personal identification. To work with such challenging prints, scientists are now researching the use of additional details from the poor-quality fingerprint. One such area of study is dermatoglyphic markers found in the limited area of fingerprints.

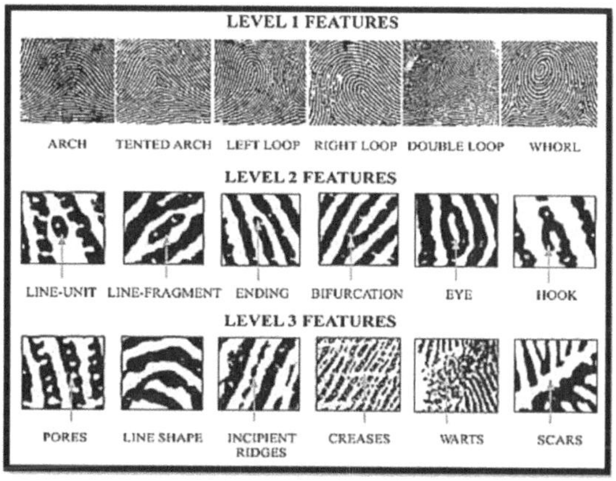

Figure 1: Fingerprint Details at Different Levels (Abhishek & Yogi, 2015)

The science of poroscopy was developed in 1912 by Sir Edmond Locard in Lyons, France. The openings of sweat glands are called sweat pores. The components released from the sweat pores are found in significant quantities on the friction ridge skin. Because of these components, the fingerprint patterns get deposited on any surface that comes in contact with the skin. The friction ridge skin has specific contour lines reflected in the fingerprint formed on the surface. Locard states that pores on the fingerprint ridges also exhibit uniqueness, permanence and immutability. This uniqueness of the sweat pores is reflected in various parameters like shape, size, type, position, interspace and number of pores, which is very challenging to mimic. Locard also stated that a mathematical agreement of 20 to 40 pores between two fingerprints is sufficient to prove the identity of the fingerprint (Sharda & Mondal, 2023).

One of the most significant factors related to the credibility of evidence in forensic science is the reproducibility of the identified trait in the evidence. More research is needed to validate the reproducibility of sweat pores and their usage in personal identification. However, studies have proved that the dermal ridges on palmer and plantar surfaces appear as the fusion of cellular areas comprising the sweat pore openings. Since the boundaries of sweat pores are elevated, they appear as white space in the inked fingerprint. The shape of the white space varies depending on the shape of the sweat pores (Oklevski *et. al.*, 2019). Publications in this regard are available, but the application in a practical setting is not fully explored.

2. REVIEW OF LITERATURE

Kuhn (1994) stated that the science of poroscopy was developed in 1912 by Sir Edmond Locard in Lyons, France. The openings of sweat glands are called sweat pores. The components released from the sweat pores are found in significant quantities on the friction ridge skin. Because of these components, the fingerprint patterns get deposited on any surface that comes in contact with the skin. The friction ridge skin has specific contour lines reflected in the fingerprint formed on the surface. Locard states that pores on the fingerprint ridges also exhibit uniqueness, permanence and immutability. This uniqueness of the sweat pores is reflected in various parameters like shape, size, type, position, interspace and number of pores, which is very challenging to mimic. He also stated that a mathematical agreement of 20 to 40 pores between two fingerprints is sufficient to prove the identity of the fingerprint. Although the science of poroscopy was developed in 1912 but there were limited advances in this field for over two decades because of the minute size of pores and the difficulty in studying such minute structure.

Later, in 1953 Salil Kumar Chatterjee published a book titled *Finger, Palm and Sole Prints* and an article in 1962 titled *Edgeoscopy* in which he highlighted his findings. In the article he stated that specific ridge shape and its characteristic can be used for individualization of fingerprint and thus establish the person's identity. Like ridges and pores, the edges of ridges also have the potential for individualization because of its uniqueness and persistence. The ridge shapes defined by him include straight, peak, convex, concave, angle, table and pocket (Ashbaugh, 1999). Chatterjee's contribution in dactyloscopy is recognized for highlighting the third levels details and its usage for personal identification. His idea was based on the friction ridge skin and minutiae arrangement in combination with edge formation variability to aid in individualization and personal identification. He gave specific names to some shapes that reappeared frequently on the friction ridge edges. The characteristics encountered were described as straight edge, convex edge, concave edge, pocket – the edge appears like a pocket with narrow opening, table – the edge appears like a protrusion with broad flat and narrow base, angle and infinite characteristics of friction ridge edges. Further studies in the field of Edgeoscopy revealed that the different characteristics encountered along the ridges can fit in one of the highlighted characteristics.

In 1982, David Ashbaugh, a Canadian police officer coined the term Ridgeology. He defined Ridgeology as the process of quantitative and qualitative analysis for friction ridge identification. He proposed two methods for comparison of pore location and its usage for individualization. The first method is of relative pore location wherein the position of the pores in respect to each other on the ridges are analyzed. The second method is of geometric transformation in which mathematical calculation is used for alignment and comparison of pore arrangement between the fingerprints. In 1999, Ashbaugh wrote a book titled *Quantitative - Qualitative Friction Ridge Analysis: An Introduction to Basic and Advanced Ridgeology*, which is considered to be an important resource for latent print professionals. The book provides a history and summary of fingerprint identification along with specific focus on pressure distortion, poroscopy, Edgeoscopy and challenging print examination. The terms level one, level two and level three were created by Ashbaugh and today it is widespread term in the fingerprint domain. Another significant contribution of Ashbaugh is the introduction of ACE-V methodology of fingerprint identification which is an abbreviation of analysis, comparison, evaluation and verification.

Stosz & Alyea (1994) introduced an automated fingerprint authentication system that integrate sweat pore details with friction ridge pattern to improve biometric security. The traditional fingerprint authentication system largely depended on Galton's details and neglected pores in spite of its uniqueness and potential for personal identification. By combining ridge and pore details, the authors have presented a multilevel verification approach that has better accuracy than the traditional systems. Bindra *et. al.*, (2000) conducted a study on fingerprint and palm prints of 100 individuals. The plain and rolled print of the participants were collected on white sheet following the standard method described by Henry. The findings reveal that the shape of the pores varies, and the most frequently found shapes were rhomboid, followed by round, elliptical and rectangular shapes. The authors concluded that although challenging, the study of microscopic sweat pores is a reliable and accurate method for personal identification.

Kryszczuk *et. al.*, (2004) did research to understand the problems that might be encountered while studying fingerprints at level 2 and level 3 in the fragments of fingerprint. The authors have also proposed the use of score matching or measurement technique for study of level 2 and level 3 features in small fingerprint fragment. It was found that as the size of fingerprint fragment decreases, the correlation score increases, in case the two prints are from same origin. The authors further concluded that the use of level three details can provide at least a comparable recognition potential even from small fingerprint fragment similar to how level 2 details provide for larger fingerprint area.

Gupta & Sutton (2010) examined the reliability of using sweat pore area for personal identification and focused on both direct microscopic image and 500 ppi livescan image. Pore features have shown to be discriminatory similar to second level friction ridge details. The study focuses on understanding whether pore area is reproducible across different conditions and imaging techniques. Direct microscopic images provided better precision of pore area for measurement wherein the variation in the same day remained in the acceptable limit. But when measurements were taken on multiple days, significant differences were observed that suggest influence of physiological, environment and other factors on pore size Figure 2.

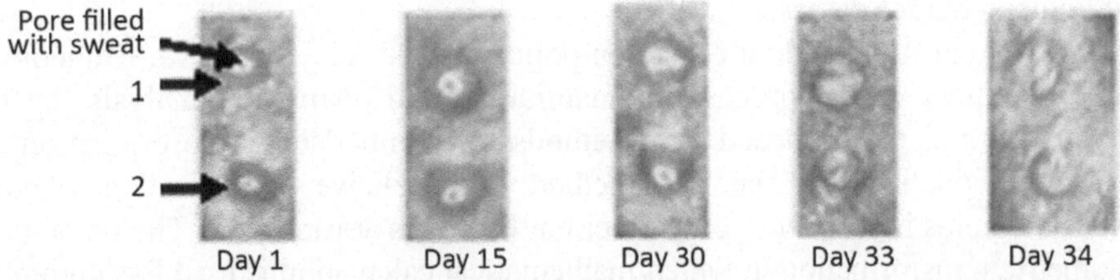

Figure 2: Different Sweat Pore Size in Direct Microscopic Images (Gupta & Sutton, 2010)

Anthonioz & Champod (2014) investigated the integration of fingerprint pore details in the examination of fingerprint evidence while focusing on the evidential value in comparison to level 2 details. Even after the uniqueness and permanence of pores, it has limited usage in forensic science because of variability in fingerprints and lack of agreement among the professionals on the specific method for usage of poroscopy. The contribution of pores is quantified in the article using likelihood ratio as the statistical approach.

Oklevski *et. al.*, (2019) researched different aspects of poroscopy in latent fingerprints. The study aimed to understand the relationship between the time interval of taking inked fingerprints and the visibility of second and third-level fingerprint details in the print. Different areas of the first fingers/thumbs were recorded for this study. Further, latent fingerprints on various surfaces like unfired cartridges were developed using suitable techniques, and the developed fingerprint was recorded for further analysis. Post analysis, the authors found that the visibility of pores in the central zone of the fingerprint was better even when taking prints at fixed time intervals. They also found that the visibility of the pores present in the developed fingerprints from different surfaces showed considerable differences because of the surface and method used for fingerprint development. However, when the openness or closeness of the pores were considered at various time intervals, no significant differences were seen.

Kaur & Dhall (2022) conducted a study aimed at evaluating assessing the reproducibility of the microfeatures of fingerprint. The microfeatures that they considered for the study include pore area, angle and inter distance present in the fingerprint obtained on both sticky side of adhesive tape and on glass surface. The analysis was done for ten consecutive days. Photomicrographs were taken and four pores having clearly defined margins and lying on the same ridge were chosen from the central area of the fingerprints. This study highlighted the reproducibility and reliability of pore inter-distance and angle and supports their application in fingerprint matching.

Chen *et. al.*, (2022) have chalked out different sweat pore parameters to be used for personal identification and fingerprint matching involving level three details. The parameters like pore density, pore location, interspace, pore size, pore area and pore to pore angle have also been discussed in previous works along with the focus on understanding the reliability and accuracy of these parameters. The authors have proposed a new parameter, frequency distribution of the distance between sweat pores (FDDasp) that aims to describe the location of a pore in respect to the adjacent pores.

Quispe *et. al.*, (2023) aimed at understanding the protocol that could be useful in incorporating level three details in fingerprint analysis. The study population included 26 men and 54 women from whom 800 fingerprint impressions and 800 direct fingerprints were collected using fingerprint powder and sensor respectively. The analysis revealed that the fingerprints captured using black powder showed characteristic points, but the pores were not identified. But in case of sample captured using sensors, the pores were also identified. This reflects the potential of poroscopy to be used in automated fingerprint identification system.

Anjana *et. al.*, (2024) did a study to observe and analyze the presence and abundance of sweat pores in left thumbprint of the target population to understand any correlation between sweat pores and gender of the individual. 50 individuals were included in the study from whom fingerprint samples were collected. The analysis of the sample revealed significant difference between the average number of pores in males and females. The authors concluded that sweat pore parameters like shape, type and frequency can be used as a presumptive stage for gender determination from fingerprints. Kaur & Dhall (2024) also explored the potential of poroscopy in sex determination to narrow down the potential suspects. Their study comprised of 396 participants which included 205 females and 191 males in the age group of 18 to 35 years. The frequency of sweat pore in 3×3 mm^2 randomly selected area was counted and the data was analyzed using SPSS tool. The findings revealed that males have less pores than females in the same fingerprint area. Thus, suggesting the potential of poroscopy for gender determination.

3. RESEARCH METHOD

Various methodologies have been proposed by researchers to leverage the potential of poroscopy in fingerprint examination. Bindra *et. al.* (2000) studied unit centimetre friction ridge on the collected plain and rolled print of 100 individuals and they stated that the average pore number varied between 8 to 25 per centimetre of friction ridge which is in agreement of the statement of Locard "number of pores along a centimetre of ridge varies from 9 to 18" (Wilder & Wentworth, 1918). The methodology designed by Chen *et. al.*, (2022) includes Frequency Distribution of the Distance between Sweat Pores (FDDasp) which is a statistical representation of the distance between sweat pores on the fingerprint. The distribution analyses the spatial arrangement of sweat pores Figure 3. The importance of this parameter lies in the highly identifiable potential which the authors highlighted through implementation of this parameter to differentiate between two fingerprint fragments. Figure 4 shows that the pore-to-pore distance (FDDasp) is not consistent in the two fingerprint fragments. The minutiae in this case however appear to be similar and it is challenging to reach a conclusion just by using second level details. But with the help of level three features, the authors gave the opinion that the two fingerprint fragments are from different source. It shows the potential of poroscopy to help in examination of fingerprints that would otherwise be challenging if only first and second level details are used.

Recent studies include correlation between pore features and gender of the individual. Anjana *et. al.*, (2024) stated that the average number of pores in females was 156.12 ± 68.41 per 25 mm square whereas in males it was 105.12 ± 77.47 per 25 mm square. Kaur & Dhall (2024) reported that males are likely to have ≤ 45 pores/9 mm^2 and females are likely to have ≥ 49 pores/9 mm^2. Thus, suggesting the potential of poroscopy for gender determination.

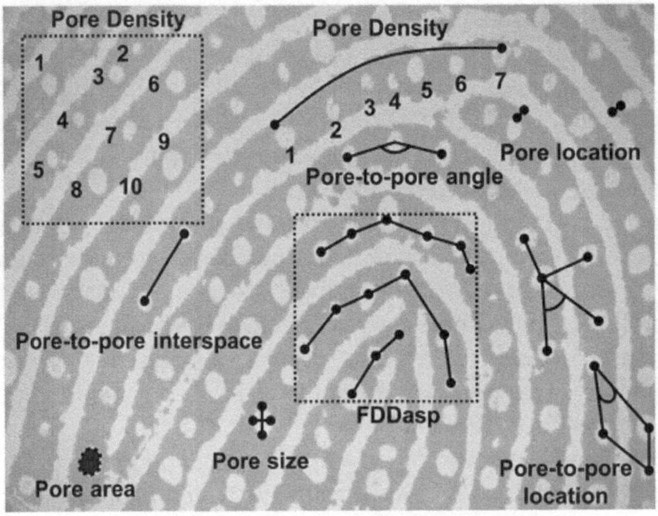

Figure 3: Schematic Measurement of Sweat Pore Parameters (Chen *et. al.*, 2022)

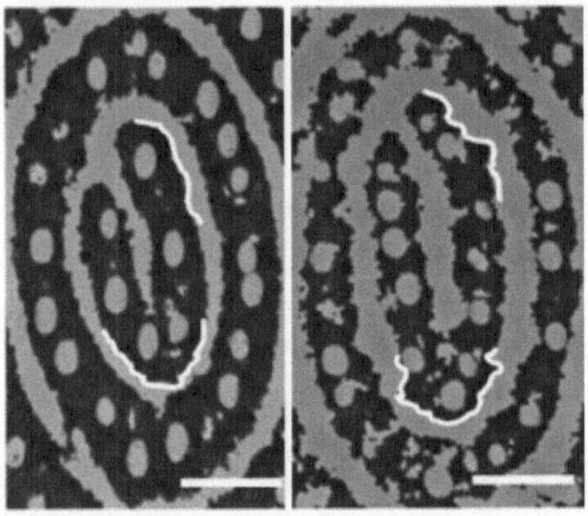

(a) (b)

Figure 4: Segments of Two Fingerprint Differentiated Based on FDDasp

4. RESULTS AND CONCLUSION

The review of literature reveals that poroscopy has the potential to overcome the challenges associated with examination of partial, degraded or other such difficult fingerprints. However, not sufficient standard protocol is available in this regard. Locard (1912) developed the concept of poroscopy in 1912 and Chatterjee (1953) introduced the concept of Edgeoscopy. Poroscopy can be used to improve small print identification ability and strengthen the value of fingerprint in cases of challenging fingerprints (Kryszczuk *et. al.*, 2004; Anthonioz & Champod 2014). Pore area is an unstable parameter of sweat pores whereas pore distance and angle are stable parameters as stated by (Gupta & Sutton 2010; Kaur & Dhall 2022). Pore frequency distribution proposed by Chen *et. al.*,

(2022) is a novel metric to be used as a reliable sweat pore parameter. Sweat pore has the potential for gender identification of an individual. The studies conducted by Anjana *et. al.*, (2024) and Kaur & Dhall (2024) agree with the correlation between sweat pore and gender.

From early studies by Nehemiah Grew and Marcello Malpighi to modern forensic identification approaches, the uniqueness, permanence and classifiable nature of fingerprints are greatly leveraged by forensic researchers and professionals. The classification of fingerprints and its levels of details, i.e. level one, level two and level three are thoroughly explored, highlighting the importance of these features in personal identification and criminal investigation. The traditional techniques largely depend on pattern type and minutiae, but recent studies dive into the potential of ridge edges and sweat pores for improvement in accuracy of fingerprint identification. However, the difficulties like inconsistency in latent print development, variability in pore area and lack of standardized approach limits the application of poroscopy in routine forensic work. The scope of future studies includes the potential of advances in automated fingerprint identification system (AFIS), forensic application of poroscopy for age and sex determination, improved visualization method and large-scale database for level 3 details. Inclusion of advanced technologies have potential to enhance the pore-based fingerprint identification but there is need to standardize the usage of these technologies. Future studies can improve fingerprint-based identification systems' forensic applicability, efficiency, and dependability by filling in these gaps, ensuring increased precision in the security and law enforcement fields.

REFERENCES

Abhishek, K. and Yogi, A. (2015). Minutiae count based method for fake fingerprint detection. *Procedia computer science*, *58*, 447–452.

Anjana, C.D.; Priyatha, C.V. and Prasad, M.S. (2024). A comparative study on friction ridge pore features of males and females. *International Journal of Biometrics*, *16*(2), 158–175.

Anthonioz, A. and Champod, C. (2014). Integration of pore features into the evaluation of fingerprint evidence. *Journal of forensic sciences*, *59*(1), 82–93.

Ashbaugh, D.R. (1999). *Quantitative-qualitative friction ridge analysis: an introduction to basic and advanced ridgeology*. CRC press.

Barnes, J.G. (2010). Fingerprint sourcebook-chapter 1: History. *US department of Justice, Office of Justice Programs, national institute of Justice*, 1–16.

Bindra, B.; Jasuja, O.P. and Singla, A.K. (2000). Poroscopy: A method of personal identification revisited. *Anil Aggrawal's Internet Journal of Forensic Medicine and Toxicology*, *1*(1).

Chen, H.; Ma, R. and Zhang, M. (2022). Recent progress in visualization and analysis of fingerprint level 3 features. *ChemistryOpen*, *11*(11), e202200091.

Cooke, T.G. (2015). Henry Faulds, Finger-Print Pioneer. *Journal of Forensic Identification*, *65*(4).

Gupta, A. and Sutton, R. (2010). Pore sub-features reproducibility in direct microscopic and livescan images—their reliability in personal identification. *Journal of forensic sciences*, *55*(4), 970–975.

Hale, A.R. (1952). Morphogenesis of volar skin in the human fetus. *American Journal of Anatomy*, *91*(1), 147–181.

Jain, A.; Chen, Y. and Demirkus, M. (2006, August). Pores and ridges: Fingerprint matching using level 3 features. In *18th International Conference on Pattern Recognition (ICPR'06)* (Vol. 4, pp. 477–480). IEEE.

Kaur, J. and Dhall, M. (2022). Reproducibility of fingerprint microfeatures. *Egyptian Journal of Forensic Sciences,* 12(1).

Kaur, J. and Dhall, M. (2023). Useless or used less? Poroscopy: The evidence of sweat pores. *Heliyon*, *9*(7), e17927.

Kryszczuk, K. M., Morier, P. and Drygajlo, A. (2004). Study of the distinctiveness of level 2 and level 3 features in fragmentary fingerprint comparison. In *Biometric Authentication: ECCV 2004 International Workshop, BioAW 2004, Prague, Czech Republic, May 15th, 2004. Proceedings* (pp. 124–133). Springer Berlin Heidelberg.

Kücken, M. and Newell, A.C. (2005). Fingerprint formation. *Journal of theoretical biology*, *235*(1), 71–83.

Kuhn, K. (1994). The Fingerprint Science and Ridgeology. *DIRECTOR*, *909*, 627–1594.

Okajima, M. (1975). Development of dermal ridges in the foetus. *Journal of Medical genetics*, *12*(3), 243–250.

Oklevski, S.; Jasuca, O.M. and Singh, G. (2019). Poroscopy as a Method for Personal Identification: Issues and Challenges. *Turkish Journal of Forensic Science and Crime Studies*, 1(1).

Quispe, A.N.A., Acosta, A.F.L., Naupari, L.M.S. and Neyra-Rivera, C.D. (2023). Comparative Pilot Study between Dactyloscopy Identification and Poroscopy for Human Identification Purposes in Peru. *International Journal of Morphology*, *41*(5), 1400–1410.

Roddy, A.R. and Stosz, J.D. (2022). Fingerprint feature processing techniques and poroscopy. In *Intelligent biometric techniques in fingerprint and face recognition* (35–105). Routledge.

Sharda, S. and Mondal, P. (2023). A bimanual comparison of variation in sweat pores with sex and age: a brief dermatoglyphic survey of population in Delhi-NCR. *Egyptian Journal of Forensic Sciences*, 13(1).

Sharma, B.K.; Bashir, R.; Hachem, M. and Gupta, H. (2019). A comparative study of characteristic features of sweat pores of finger bulbs in individuals. *Egyptian Journal of Forensic Sciences*, *9*, 1–6.

Stosz, J.D. and Alyea, L.A. (1994). Automated system for fingerprint authentication using pores and ridge structure. In *Automatic systems for the identification and inspection of humans* (2277, 210–223). SPIE.

Sudha, P.I., Singh, J. and Sodhi, G.S. (2021). The dermal ridges as the infallible signature of skin: An overview. *Indian Journal of Dermatology*, 66(6), 649–653.

Machine Learning-Based Vulnerability Assessment for Intelligent Devices

Romil Rawat[1] and Anand Rajavat[2]

ABSTRACT: Conventional techniques, such as power consumption tracking or signature-based detection, may miss new, vulnerable behaviours on smart devices. A technique for identifying Suspicious Script Codes (SSC) in smart device apps that use the Echo State Network (ESN) is presented in this article to analyse the attributes of apps on smart devices. Alerts and permissions are required by the Application Programming Interface (API). The Malware Memory Analysis (CIC-MalMem-2022) dataset is used to evaluate our method. The testing assessments show that the Deep Learning Approach (DLA) performs better than other methods in several aspects, with an accuracy of 99.7 percent.

Keywords: *Echo State Network, Malware Memory, Smart Device, Static Analysis, Suspicious Script Codes.*

1. INTRODUCTION

The number of people using cellphones is increasing more quickly than has ever been done. About 4.3 billion smart devices on the earth by 2022 (Carrier *et. al.*, 2022). Moreover, almost 76% of regular cellphones use the Smart Device operating system. Moreover, cellphones with smart devices seldom ever have antivirus software installed (Wang *et. al.*, 2024). It might not be particularly effective in identifying illnesses, even for those that install it (Ramalakshmi *et. al.*, 2024). These features may make the smart device system more alluring to Online Vulnerability Actors (OVA) because of the enormous number of users and the quantity of crucial information that can be accessed on these devices.

The quantity of useful information that an OVA may access increases with the number of users. Using a program that has already been added to Google Play, the threat agent could be able to get unauthorized access (Vatambeti *et. al.*, 2024. After installation, the victim unintentionally grants the attacker access (Khazane *et. al.*, 2024; Mary & Mahalakshmi, 2024). After 2023, there were over 2.87 million smart devices apps found for download on smart devices (Kantola *et. al.*, 2012). Moreover, 513,568 SSC programs every month, or around 17,700 per day, were found (Rawat *et. al.*, 2024). Due to high quantity of malignant software, much advanced SSC tracing systems are necessary. Three different kinds of SDSD approaches exist: hybrid, dynamic, and static analysis (Huang *et. al.*, 2022). Features are extracted from smart device applications using static analysis (Ramalakshmi *et. al.*, 2024).

---

[1] Research Scholar, Shri Vaishnav Institute of Information Technology, Shri Vaishnav Vidyapeeth Vishwavidyalaya, Indore, India. E-mail: Rawat.romil@gmail.com

[2] Director, Shri Vaishnav Institute of Information Technology, Shri Vaishnav Vidyapeeth Vishwavidyalaya, Indore, India.

Abnormal or suspicious behaviour has to be watched closely. Although it may achieve a high degree of feature coverage, it has certain disadvantages, such as dynamic code loading and code obfuscation. By running the characteristics on a smart device machine, dynamic analysis extracts the qualities (Wang *et. al.*, 2024). Through the identification of extra features or risks that static analysis might miss, this approach may perform better than static analysis. Static analysis is more efficient than dynamic assessment towards time and smart resources (Xu *et. al.*, 2023). Static and dynamic analysis are combined to provide hybrid analysis. It is more successful and efficient in the detecting process (Liu *et. al.*, 2024). The present methodology is based on a static examination.

Essentially, it has been demonstrated in several studies (Sharma *et. al.*, 2021; Bhardwaj *et. al.*, 2024; Rawat *et. al.*, 2023) that both Machine Learning (ML) approaches and DLA are effective in detecting SSC, whether in smart device application analysis or other cyber security domains. This study looked at how well five categorising techniques performed. Support Vector Machines (SVM) and Generative Adversarial Networks (GANs) are utilised in recognising smart device SSC. Next, we contrasted its outcomes with the DLA-ESN technique using the CIC-MalMem-2022 dataset (Elsaeidy *et. al.*, 2020). The feature extraction and selection process on the dataset provides both API-IA features and permissions, as SSC requires certain permissions and API-Threat-Alarm not available in benign apps (Sharma *et. al.*, 2021).

2. REVIEW OF LITERATURE

Hackers who produce malicious software have developed new techniques to target owners of smart devices (Wang *et. al.*, 2024). As a result, a large number of scholars have affirmed the value of current methods or suggested brand-new ones that would be more effective at identifying malicious programs (Khazane *et. al.*, 2024).

Sharma *et. al.,* (2021) proposed a new mechanism for detecting malignant Smart Device apps by using pseudodynamic analysis and creating an API-IA (Ramalakshmi *et. al.*, 2024; Vatambeti *et. al.*, 2024) graph (Khazane *et. al.*, 2024) for each execution path (Kantola *et. al.*, 2012). The mechanism is based on a DLA and model that was built and trained on a data set consisting of approximately 25,000 benign and 30,000 malignant apps. Nonetheless, in order to depict every execution route that SSC may take during its lifespan, the researchers built an API-IA tree. It changed towards a low-dimensional-vector feature set of numbers so that the deep neural network (DNN) could utilise it. Additionally, they concentrated on optimising network performance by contrasting and evaluating distinct embedding strategies and modifying various network configuration parameters to guarantee that the ideal hyperparameter was attained for accuracy (Huang *et. al.*, 2022).

Alazab *et. al.,* (2020) introduced a parallel-ML-based categorisation approach to detect smart device SSC. A total of 179 training attributes were gathered and divided into instructions pertaining to API-IA and 54 characteristics, based on authentic SSC samples and benign applications, and used DLA to generate a composite classification framework from a sequence of heterogeneous system classifiers. The classifiers performed better with accuracy. A lightweight ML system that can distinguish between benign and malignant applications was proposed by (Mishra *et. al.*, 2024). They also extracted features for applications using both static and dynamic techniques. Additionally, they offer a brand-new method for feature dimensionality reduction that has been successfully used for feature selection. By lowering the dimensions using both the SVM framework and the newer model that was proposed, their study demonstrated a high degree of efficiency in recognising SSC. This paved the way for them to enhance with a higher and a lower detection rate. In every one of these studies, conventional methods for recognising SSC in the Smart Device App worked better.

The present study stands out from the research mentioned above because it uses up-to-date data. In this paper, the identification of Smart Device SSC apps using normal categorisation algorithms versus DLA is tested.

3. RESEARCH METHOD

Combining innocuous Smart Device Application Package (APK) files with SSC files taken from a publicly available dataset is the initial stage in this work (Elsaeidy *et. al.*, 2020). The Jupyter notebook (Vatambeti *et. al.*, 2024; Khazane *et. al.*, 2024) environment's built-in Python script (Mary & Mahalakshmi, 2024) is then used to extract the static characteristics (AlMasri *et. al.*, 2023). Permission and API-IA are 2 of the attributes. To use in the training procedure, attributes are created and saved in the data frame in a CSV (Comma-Separated Values) file. Lastly, we compute the required metrics for the assessment and test each classifier using 10-fold cross-validation (Liu *et. al.*, 2024). The Figure 1 shows the SSC detection phases.

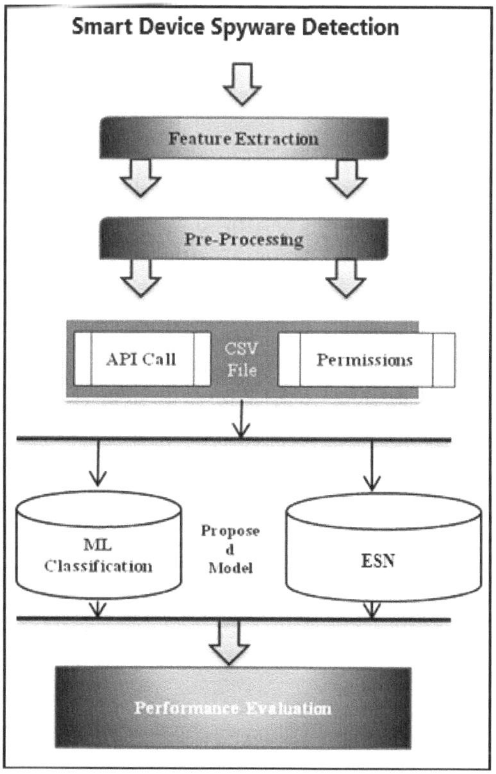

Figure 1: SSC Detection Phases

3.1 Dataset

In order to examine and evaluate the SDSD system utilising DLA and framework, a sizable and reliable dataset is needed. Therefore, a portion of the CIC-MalMem-2022 (Carrier *et. al.*, 2022; Wang *et. al.*, 2024) dataset designed is available on the Canadian Institute of Cyber Security website (Alazab *et. al.*, 2020) was used in this work. The dataset employs debug mode (Alazab *et. al.*, 2020) for the memory dumping procedure to avoid the dumping process (Bhardwaj *et. al.*, 2024) showing up in the memory dumps. It was put together utilising actual experiments (Mary & Mahalakshmi, 2024). The collection includes 365 SSC samples and 347 examples of innocuous Smart Device applications; the SSCs are categorised into four families: Ransomware, Scareware, SMSware (Vatambeti *et. al.*, 2024), and Adware.

3.2 Preprocessing and Feature Extraction

When it comes to classification, it's important to choose attributes that indicate the class to which the new record belongs. Permissions and API-IA for all Smart Device apps are extracted from this viewpoint and added to the dataset as features. The fully functional tool Androguard (Wang *et. al.*, 2024) for working with smart device files can only be accessed in Python environments (Sharma *et. al.*, 2021). It may be applied to reverse engineering and decompile certain apps for smart devices. Androguard is an application that extracts the DEX file permissions for every APK file separately to evaluate APK files (Vatambeti *et. al.*, 2024). Consequently, a data frame consisting of attributes and applications was produced (rows), whereby each column denotes a different license or API-IA (Elsaeidy *et. al.*, 2020) with binary values (Mishra *et. al.*, 2024), and rows signify both benign APK (Sharma *et. al.*, 2021) and SSC.

3.3 Classifiers Framework

Generally, traditional ML classifiers perform well when working with labelled data. Some ML classifiers are SVM (Sharma *et. al.*, 2021) and GANs (Bhardwaj *et. al.*, 2024). To assess the classifiers and choose the best values that can yield an optimal outcome, many metrics have been developed. F-measure, recall, and precision scores and accuracy are examined in the evaluation; they are calculated using the formulas below, as seen in Figure 2.

⇨ $TPR = \frac{TP}{TN + TP}$	⇨ $FPR = \frac{FP}{TP + FN}$
⇨ $precision = \frac{TP}{TP + FP}$	⇨ $recall = \frac{TP}{TP + FN}$
⇨ $F - Measure\ (F1 - Score) = 2 * \frac{precision * recall}{precision + recall}$	

Figure 2: Evaluating Parameters

A metric used to assess categorisation models is accuracy, which is the proportion of correct predictions the model makes. The precision of a result may be evaluated by dividing the entire count of positive outcomes containing those that were incorrectly recognized by the count of correctly identified positive results. Furthermore, recall is calculated by dividing the total count of samples correctly recognised by the number of correctly identified findings. Another way to think of precision is as an indicator of a classifier's accuracy, where a low precision would suggest a high rate of false positives. While high recall indicates that classifiers are comprehensive, low recall suggests many false negatives. The accuracy and recall balance are represented by the F-measure, which may be used to select the metrics.

3.4 ESN-Architecture

ESN has been utilised to build a binary categorisation model. A particular type of Recurrent Neural Network (RNN) intended to effectively handle sequential input is called ESN. These are implemented in Python as a reservoir computing framework, which consists of a "reservoir," or fixed, randomly initialised recurrent layer. The output of an ESN is produced by linearly mixing the input and reservoir states. They differ in that the reservoir weights stay fixed and only the output layer is trained. This variant of RNN features a sparsely linked randomised hidden layer. The only portion of the network that is trainable is the weight of the output neurons. This is a recurrent neural network type that is well-known for its easy training procedure and capacity to simulate a wide range of issues, particularly those requiring time-series data. This study demonstrated the efficacy of ESN in detecting and reducing smart device threats. Figure 3 depicts the ESN architecture.

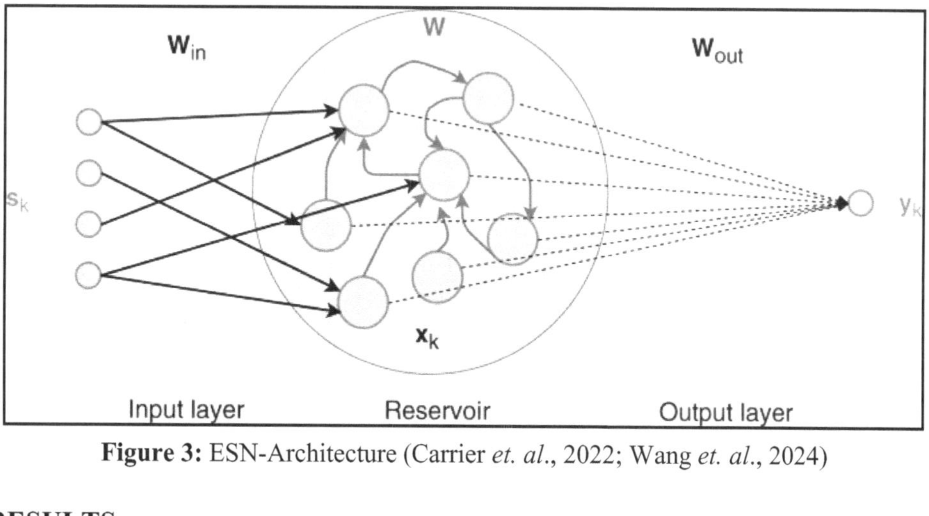

Figure 3: ESN-Architecture (Carrier *et. al.*, 2022; Wang *et. al.*, 2024)

4. RESULTS

The study employed two different kinds of models: conventional DLA classifiers. The classifiers are trained on the dataset first, and then they are tested and assessed. Both research' categorisations are predicated on attributes gleaned from permissions and API queries.

4.1 ML Approach

We chose SVM and GANs in particular because we wanted to create a useful model for finding SSC applications, keeping in mind that both methods are part of supervised learning. These tools are easy to set up and operate, and they may be used for both regression and classification tasks. Table 1 shows about Smart Devices SSC Metrices. and Figure 4 shows about the threat metrics.

Table 1: Smart Device – SSC Metrices

Metrics	*SVM*	*GANs*	*ESN*
Precision (%)	98.9%	99.6%	97.7%
F-measure (%)	97.8%	98.7%	98.8%
Accuracy (%)	98.3%	99.7%	99.8%
Recall (%)	96.6%	98.6%	99.8%

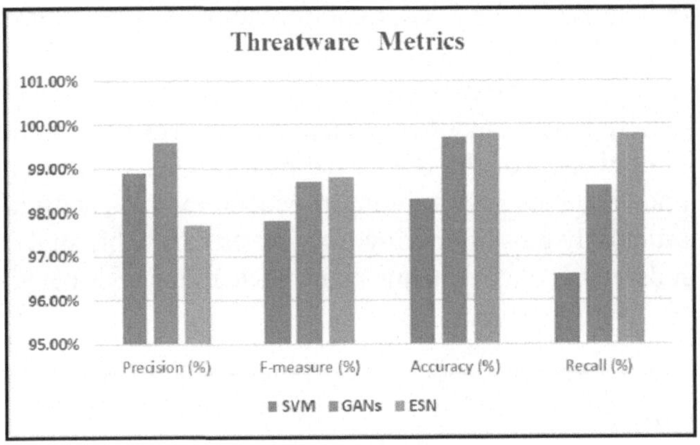

Figure 4: Threatware Metrics

The F-score shows that the GANs classifier accurately predicted 97.6% of the dataset, giving it the maximum accuracy and number of right predictions with a score of 99.7%. Furthermore, the GANs classifier accurately predicted 98.8% of SSC samples, advancing to the second level of recall. Nevertheless, throughout the testing process, the GANs classifier identified 99.8% of the entire dataset with the highest level of precision.

4.2 DLA

The DLA was used to classify smart devices based on queries made through APIs and permissions. The accuracy and loss measurements were used to determine the hyperparameters. Since the accuracy level had reached 99.6 percent and the loss rate in testing and training had decreased to 0.06 percent, we stopped training the model at the 27th epoch. Furthermore, 98.8% of the dataset was correctly predicted by the DLA classifier. Additionally, because it correctly identified 99.8% of SSC samples, it had high recall and accuracy scores.

The outcomes show that DLA enhanced the model's performance, with DLA classifier outcomes surpassing those of conventional ML classifiers. But since both trials produce positive results, it is believed that models based on API-IA and permissions will be effective in identifying smart devices, that is, SSCs. The Comparative Study of Available Approaches is displayed in Table 2.

Table 2: Available Approaches Comparative study

Ref	***Method***	***Features***
(Alazab *et. al.*, 2020)	A categorisation approach that works well for combining API call authorisation requests.	Use to find mobile malware apps and support mobile application analysis and malware forensic investigations.
(Mishra *et. al.*, 2024)	An intelligent malware detection system based on serverless computing has been presented to identify malware that targets applications running on Android.	To identify vulnerable patterns, the cloud infrastructure is used by the framework to execute an ML algorithm.
(AlMasri *et. al.*, 2023)	It can identify Android malware even when confronted with devious and complex attacks.	Training and testing materials should be more dependable and adaptable by drawing from real-world environments.
Proposed work	The technique for finding suspicious script codes (SSC) in apps for smart devices that use the Echo state network (ESN).	Applications for smart devices yielded two static features: alerts and authorisation requests made using the Application Programming Interface (API).

5. CONCLUSION

This article discusses the ESN architecture of ANN-DLA, which provides a unique methodology for recognising SSC in smart device OS programs. To choose the most effective model that best identifies Smart Device SSC, a comparison between DLA and normal ML approaches is also provided. The CIC-MalMem-2022 dataset, which was analysed through a static examination of actual and authentic SSC and benign Smart Device app samples, served as the training dataset for the proposed classifiers. Permissions and API-IA were both used in the research because their combined use indicated that it was beneficial to prioritise the identification of Smart Device SSC models. Using authorization and API-IA static data, the DLA classifier outperformed all other classifiers in SDSD, attaining a 98.8 percent F-measure-score and a 99.7 percent accuracy score. In order to address smart device threatware, future work is focused on developing novel detection techniques, such as mixed methods that integrate static and dynamic assessment. These techniques can assist in locating damaging programs' hidden features.

REFERENCES

Alazab, M.; Alazab, M.; Shalaginov, A.; Mesleh, A. and Awajan, A. (2020). Intelligent mobile malware detection using permission requests and API calls. *Future Generation Computer Systems*, *107*, 509–521.

AlMasri, T.N. and AlDalaien, M.A.N. (2023). Detecting Spyware in Android Devices Using Random Forest. In *International Conference on Advances in Computing Research* (pp. 294–315). Cham: Springer Nature Switzerland.

Bhardwaj, R.; Bhardwaj, V.; Rawat, R.; Rawat, H.; Muzumdar, P. and Borana, K. (2024). OSN Traits and Vulnerability for Measurement and Analysis. *Online Social Networks in Business Frameworks*, 611–623.

Carrier, T.; Victor, P.; Tekeoglu, A. and Lashkari, A.H. (2022). Detecting Obfuscated Malware using Memory Feature Engineering. In *ICISSP* (pp. 177–188).

Elsaeidy, A.A.; Jagannath, N.; Sanchis, A.G.; Jamalipour, A. and Munasinghe, K.S. (2020). Replay attack detection in smart cities using deep learning. *IEEE Access*, *8*, 137825-137837.

Huang, Y. and Chen, C. (2022). Smart app attack: hacking deep learning models in android apps. *IEEE Transactions on Information Forensics and Security*, *17*, 1827–1840.

Jansi Sophia Mary, C. and Mahalakshmi, K. (2024). Modelling of intrusion detection using sea horse optimization with machine learning model on cloud environment. *International Journal of Information Technology*, *16*(3), 1981–1988.

Kantola, D.; Chin, E.; He, W. and Wagner, D. (2012). Reducing attack surfaces for intra-application communication in android. In *Proceedings of the second ACM workshop on Security and privacy in smartphones and mobile devices* (pp. 69–80).

Khazane, H.; Ridouani, M.; Salahdine, F. and Kaabouch, N. (2024). A holistic review of machine learning adversarial attacks in IoT networks. *Future Internet*, *16*(1), 32.

Liu, Z.; Ye, H.; Chen, C. and Lam, K.Y. (2024). Threats, attacks, and defenses in machine unlearning: A survey. *arXiv preprint arXiv:2403.13682.*

Mishra, P.; Jain, T.; Aggarwal, P.; Paul, G.; Gupta, B.B.; Attar, R.W. and Gaurav, A. (2024). CloudIntellMal: An advanced cloud based intelligent malware detection framework to analyze android applications. *Computers and Electrical Engineering*, *119*, 109483.

Ramalakshmi, R.; Narendran, S.; Padmesh, D. and Ramkumar, R.S. (2024). ESN for Intrusion Detection in Federated Machine Learning. In *International Conference on Artificial Intelligence and Smart Energy* (pp. 451–461). Cham: Springer Nature Switzerland.

Rawat, R. and Rajavat, A. (2024). Perceptual Operating Systems for the Trade Associations of Cyber Criminals to Scrutinize Hazardous Content. *International Journal of Cyber Warfare and Terrorism (IJCWT)*, *14*(1), 1–19.

Rawat, R.; Oki, O.; Chakrawarti, R.K.; Adekunle, T.S.; Lukose, J.M. and Ajagbe, S.A. (2023). Autonomous artificial intelligence systems for fraud detection and forensics in dark web environments. Informatica, 47(9).

Sharma, P.; Jain, S.; Gupta, S. and Chamola, V. (2021). Role of machine learning and deep learning in securing 5G-driven industrial IoT applications. *Ad Hoc Networks*, *123*, 102685.

Sharma, S.; Kumar, R. and Rama Krishna, C. (2021). A survey on analysis and detection of Android ransomware. *Concurrency and Computation: Practice and Experience*, *33*(16), e6272.

Vatambeti, R.; Mantena, S.V., Kiran, K.V.D.; Chennupalli, S. and Gopalachari, M.V. (2024). Black hole attack detection using Dolphin Echo-location-based machine learning model in MANET environment. *Computers and Electrical Engineering*, *114*, 109094.

Wang, B.; Lun, S.; Li, M. and Lu, X. (2024). Echo state network structure optimization algorithm based on correlation analysis. *Applied Soft Computing*, *152*, 111214.

Xu, G.; Xin, G.; Jiao, L.; Liu, J.; Liu, S.; Feng, M. and Zheng, X. (2023). Ofei: A semi-black-box android adversarial sample attack framework against dlaas. *IEEE Transactions on Computers*, *73*(4), 956–969.

Navigating AI Threats in IT Laws

Muskan Neekey[1] and Ashutosh Bairagi[2]

ABSTRACT: This research explores the evolving relationship between artificial intelligence (AI) threats and information technology (IT) laws in 2024, emphasizing the need for comprehensive and adaptive legal frameworks. The study identifies key AI-driven threats such as cybersecurity risks, data breaches, and intellectual property challenges that disrupt existing IT laws. It evaluates the effectiveness of current regulations in addressing these risks and highlights gaps that hinder adequate protection. The study concludes by proposing strategic recommendations to enhance IT laws, ensuring they remain responsive to the rapid pace of AI technological advancements. The findings aim to contribute to the creation of forward-looking, flexible legal frameworks that can effectively mitigate AI-related threats while fostering innovation.

Keywords: *Cybersecurity, Data Breaches, Global Legislative Trends, Intellectual Property, Legal Frameworks.*

1. INTRODUCTION

Artificial intelligence (AI) has emerged as a transformative force in the digital era, reshaping industries and redefining how societies operate. However, this rapid evolution comes with significant risks, especially in the realm of IT laws. The intersection of AI and IT legislation has introduced complex challenges such as cybersecurity vulnerabilities, data privacdy concerns, algorithmic biases, and ethical dilemmas. The scope of this research explores how existing IT laws address AI threats and evaluates the adequacy of current legal frameworks in mitigating the risks posed by AI technologies in today. By analyzing global legislative trends and the implications of AI advancements, this research aims to provide actionable insights for policymakers, legal professionals, and technology stakeholders. Today AI technologies have become ubiquitous, driving innovations in automation, decision-making, and data analytics. These advancements are accompanied by the proliferation of threats such as AI-enabled cyberattacks, the misuse of generative AI tools, and the ethical quandaries posed by autonomous systems. The IT sector, which relies heavily on secure and transparent systems, faces unprecedented challenges in safeguarding digital infrastructure against these emerging threats.

AI-driven cybersecurity risks include sophisticated phishing attacks, ransomware powered by machine learning, and vulnerabilities in AI models themselves. Data privacy is another pressing issue, as AI systems often require vast amounts of personal data, raising concerns about consent, misuse, and surveillance. Furthermore, algorithmic bias

[1] Research Scholar, Shri Vaishnav Institute of Law, Shri Vaishnav Vidyapeeth Vishwavidyalaya, Indore, India. E-mail: muskanneekey66@gmail.com

[2] Professor, Shri Vaishnav Institute of Law, Shri Vaishnav Vidyapeeth Vishwavidyalaya, Indore, India.

in AI systems can result in discriminatory outcomes, exacerbating societal inequalities. The legal landscape reflects efforts to address these issues, with notable developments such as the European Union's AI Act emphasizing accountability and transparency, and the United States exploring new legislation targeting AI misuse. However, these measures often lag behind the pace of technological innovation, creating a critical need for proactive and adaptive IT laws. This study aims to bridge this gap, offering insights into the evolving relationship between AI threats and IT laws and guiding stakeholders toward more resilient legal frameworks.

2. OBJECTIVES

- The research aims to identify and analyze the specific AI-driven threats that challenge existing IT laws, such as cybersecurity risks, data breaches, and intellectual property violations, and understand their implications on legal frameworks.
- A core objective is to assess the effectiveness of current IT laws in addressing emerging AI threats, identify any existing gaps in these regulations, and determine where improvements are needed to better manage the risks associated with AI technologies.
- The study seeks to evaluate global AI regulatory trends, including frameworks like the EU AI Act and U.S. policy initiatives, and to propose strategic recommendations that will help shape more comprehensive and adaptive IT laws that can keep pace with AI advancements.

3. RESEARCH METHOD

This research employs a multidisciplinary approach, combining legal analysis, case studies, and technological insights. A comprehensive review of existing IT laws, policy documents, and AI-related legislation forms the foundation of the study. Real-world case studies provide practical context, showcasing the impact of AI on IT law enforcement and the challenges faced by regulators.

4. EVOLUTION OF IT LAWS

Information Technology (IT) laws have progressively evolved to address the rapid advancements in digital technologies and their associated challenges. Initially, IT regulations focused on foundational concerns such as electronic transactions, data protection, and computer-related offenses. Laws like the Computer Fraud and Abuse Act (CFAA) in the United States and the European Union's Data Protection Directive established early frameworks for governing digital interactions and safeguarding information. The 2010s marked a transformative period as the rise of cloud computing, big data, and escalating cybersecurity threats demanded more robust legal frameworks. Regulations like the EU's General Data Protection Regulation (GDPR) introduced stringent data privacy measures, emphasizing organizational accountability for breaches. Concurrently, legal systems began addressing challenges like digital identity theft, cross-border data transfers, and intellectual property protection.

The emergence of artificial intelligence (AI) has added unprecedented complexity to IT governance. AI-driven technologies, while transformative, pose unique risks, including algorithmic bias, autonomous systems, and mass data exploitation. Traditional IT laws have struggled to address these challenges, prompting the creation of AI-specific regulations like the EU AI Act and updates to existing laws to incorporate ethical considerations, transparency requirements, and accountability frameworks. The evolution of IT laws reflects an ongoing effort to balance innovation with security and ethics, ensuring legal frameworks remain adaptive and capable of addressing the dynamic challenges of emerging technologies in a rapidly digitalizing world.

Today, AI technologies, machine learning, generative AI, and natural language processing play a critical role in automating processes, enhancing decision-making, and driving predictive analytics. This widespread adoption has fueled unprecedented levels of efficiency and innovation. However, the rapid integration of AI systems also exposes critical vulnerabilities in existing legal and regulatory frameworks. AI operates at a scale and speed that often surpasses human oversight, creating risks such as data misuse, algorithmic bias, and ethical dilemmas in autonomous decision-making. For instance, generative AI can produce highly realistic but false content, escalating challenges like misinformation and copyright infringement. Moreover, the use of AI in sensitive areas such as predictive policing and credit scoring has raised significant concerns about fairness, transparency, and accountability. As AI continues to advance, the urgency to address its societal and legal implications grows. Governments and organizations are grappling with these challenges, highlighting the need for robust, adaptive regulations that safeguard rights while fostering innovation. The rise of AI underscores a pivotal shift, emphasizing the necessity for thoughtful integration of technology and governance.

The integration of AI into IT systems has created a complex dynamic between innovation and regulation. IT laws, originally designed to govern traditional digital technologies, are increasingly inadequate in addressing the unique challenges posed by AI. For instance, while GDPR provides robust data protection mechanisms, it struggles to regulate AI systems that derive sensitive insights from anonymized data. Similarly, cybersecurity laws often lack provisions for AI-specific threats, such as adversarial attacks that exploit machine learning models. The European Union's AI Act represents a significant step toward bridging this gap, introducing a risk-based framework for AI regulation. It emphasizes transparency, accountability, and ethical AI development, setting a precedent for other regions. In the United States, initiatives like the Blueprint for an AI Bill of Rights reflect growing recognition of AI's societal impact. However, these efforts often face challenges in enforcement, especially in cross-border contexts where jurisdictional conflicts arise.

The interplay between AI and IT regulations is further complicated by the global nature of technology. Countries with varying levels of technological maturity adopt different approaches, creating fragmentation in regulatory practices. For example, while developed nations focus on ethical AI and transparency, emerging economies prioritize economic growth and innovation, sometimes at the expense of regulation. This evolving landscape underscores the need for adaptive and harmonized legal frameworks that balance innovation with accountability. The symbiotic evolution of AI and IT laws demands collaboration between governments, industries, and international organizations to address the multifaceted challenges of the AI era effectively.

5. AI THREATS AND CHALLENGES

The integration of artificial intelligence (AI) into IT systems has revolutionized industries but has also introduced a host of threats that challenge traditional security and legal frameworks. As we step into new technological world, these threats have grown more sophisticated and demand urgent attention.

5.1 Cybersecurity Risks

AI has empowered malicious actors to develop advanced threats such as autonomous malware capable of adapting to and evading traditional security measures. These programs use machine learning to analyze security protocols and exploit vulnerabilities in real time. Similarly, AI-driven phishing attacks employ natural language processing (NLP) to create highly personalized and convincing messages, tricking individuals into revealing sensitive information. These evolving threats outpace conventional cybersecurity defenses, creating a need for AI-driven countermeasures. AI systems themselves are not immune to exploitation. Adversarial attacks manipulate AI models by feeding them misleading data, causing errors in decision-making processes. For example, image recognition systems can be tricked into misclassifying objects, with significant implications for security applications like facial recognition. Additionally, dependency on third-party AI solutions introduces supply chain vulnerabilities, as compromised models can propagate risks across interconnected systems.

5.2 Data Privacy Challenges

AI systems thrive on data, often requiring large datasets to train models effectively. This dependency has led to mass data collection practices that raise concerns about consent, surveillance, and misuse. For instance, social media platforms and IoT devices collect vast amounts of personal data, often without users' explicit awareness. In 2024, the proliferation of generative AI tools exacerbated these concerns, as such systems often incorporate sensitive or proprietary data without adequate oversight. The use of AI for data analysis creates ethical dilemmas, particularly when sensitive information is inferred from non-sensitive data. Predictive analytics, while valuable for businesses, can inadvertently reveal intimate details about individuals, such as health conditions or political affiliations. Balancing innovation with ethical considerations remains a pressing challenge.

5.3 Algorithmic Bias and Discrimination

AI models are only as good as the data they are trained on. Biases in training datasets often lead to discriminatory outcomes, disproportionately affecting marginalized communities. For example, biased AI systems have been criticized for perpetuating racial and gender disparities in hiring, lending, and law enforcement. In 2024, increasing reliance on AI-driven decisions has heightened scrutiny on these issues, calling for transparent and fair AI development practices.

- **Intellectual Property Infringements:** The advent of generative AI has raised complex questions about intellectual property (IP) rights. AI systems capable of creating art, music, and written content blur the lines of ownership, as it is unclear whether credit belongs to the human developer, the AI model, or the data sources used. Moreover,

AI-driven tools that scrape copyrighted material without authorization continue to spark legal disputes, pushing the limits of existing IP laws.

- **Challenges in Autonomous Decision-Making:** Autonomous AI systems, such as self-driving cars and robotic process automation, operate with minimal human intervention. While these systems enhance efficiency, they raise critical concerns about accountability. Who is liable when an AI-powered system makes a harmful decision; the developer, the user, or the system itself? As these technologies become more prevalent in 2024, resolving questions of accountability and liability remains a top priority for regulators.

5.4 Regulating Challenges

As artificial intelligence (AI) continues to evolve, regulators face mounting challenges in developing and implementing effective legal frameworks. These challenges, amplified by the global and multifaceted nature of AI, underscore the delicate balance between fostering innovation and mitigating risks. Addressing these issues requires coordinated efforts among governments, industries, and international organizations.

- **Balancing Innovation and Regulation:** Balancing innovation and regulation is critical to harnessing AI's transformative potential across sectors like healthcare, finance, and transportation. Excessive regulation risks stifling innovation, while leniency can lead to misuse. Key challenges include crafting flexible legal frameworks that support experimentation without compromising safety and ethics, addressing regulatory burdens on startups, and avoiding over-regulation of low-risk applications. Proposed solutions emphasize a risk-based regulatory approach, which aligns requirements with potential harm. Additionally, regulatory sandboxes can foster innovation by enabling AI solutions to be tested in controlled environments, ensuring safety and compliance before broader implementation.
- **Enforcing Cross-Border IT Laws:** The global nature of AI systems complicates enforcing IT laws, as data flows and algorithmic impacts often traverse multiple jurisdictions. Key issues include disparities in regulatory frameworks, allowing enforcement gaps, and enabling multinational AI companies to exploit regulatory arbitrage in lenient regions. Additionally, tracing cross-border cybercrimes like AI-driven phishing remains challenging. To address these challenges, international treaties and agreements are essential to harmonize AI regulations and enforcement mechanisms. Strengthening global organizations like the United Nations and the World Economic Forum can facilitate cross-border collaboration, promoting unified governance and mitigating risks associated with AI technologies on a global scale.
- **Overcoming Jurisdictional Conflicts in AI-Driven Incidents:** Jurisdictional conflicts in AI-driven incidents, such as autonomous vehicle accidents or algorithmic discrimination, pose significant challenges due to the involvement of multiple stakeholders across varying legal frameworks. Key issues include determining liability among developers, users, and third-party data providers from different countries, navigating inconsistent legal definitions for AI systems, and resolving delays caused by jurisdictional disputes. To address these challenges, establishing uniform standards for AI accountability with a focus on transparency and traceability is essential.

Additionally, creating multinational arbitration bodies can streamline dispute resolution in cross-border cases, fostering efficient and consistent approaches to managing AI-related legal conflicts globally.

- **Addressing AI Weaponization and National Security Threats:** AI weaponization presents significant threats to national and global security, as adversaries exploit its capabilities for cyberattacks, misinformation, and autonomous weapons. Key concerns include the misuse of autonomous weapons in conflicts, AI-driven disinformation campaigns destabilizing societies, and advanced cyberattacks targeting critical infrastructure. Addressing these challenges requires a multi-faceted approach: establishing international norms and treaties, such as a Geneva Convention for AI, to regulate weaponization; enhancing cyber defense systems with AI-driven threat detection and response capabilities; and fostering collaboration between governments and private tech companies to identify, monitor, and mitigate national security risks effectively.

6. ANALYZING EXISTING IT LAWS FOR ADDRESSING AI THREATS

As artificial intelligence (AI) continues to permeate various sectors, IT laws worldwide are being tested for their ability to address emerging AI-driven threats. In 2024, the assessment of these laws reveals a mixed picture, highlighting their strengths while exposing significant gaps that demand attention.

Efficacy of Current Legislation

Existing IT laws have laid a foundational framework for addressing certain AI threats, particularly in areas like data protection, cybersecurity, and intellectual property. For instance:

- **Data Protection Laws:** Regulations such as the EU's General Data Protection Regulation (GDPR) and the U.S. California Consumer Privacy Act (CCPA) have proven effective in safeguarding user data. They mandate transparency and consent in data collection, which directly impacts AI systems reliant on extensive datasets.
- **Cybersecurity Measures:** Laws like the Cybersecurity Information Sharing Act (CISA) in the U.S. promote collaboration between organizations to tackle AI-enabled cyber threats, such as autonomous malware and adversarial attacks.
- **Intellectual Property (IP) Protections:** IT laws provide some level of IP safeguards against AI-generated content misuse, although they often struggle with generative AI complexities.

  Despite these strengths, the dynamic nature of AI technologies necessitates constant updates and enhancements to the legal framework.

7. LIMITATIONS AND GAPS IN THE LEGAL FRAMEWORK

Current IT laws face numerous challenges in adequately addressing the multifaceted threats posed by AI:

- **AI-Specific Regulations**: Most IT laws were designed before the advent of AI and are ill-equipped to address its unique risks, such as algorithmic bias, explainability, and autonomous decision-making.

- **Global Inconsistencies**: The fragmented approach to AI regulation across countries complicates enforcement, especially for cross-border data flows and multinational AI systems.
- **Algorithmic Accountability**: Few laws require transparency in AI model design and decision-making, making it difficult to attribute liability or understand the basis for decisions.
- **Generative AI Challenges**: Existing IP laws struggle to address the ownership and copyright implications of content generated by AI tools like ChatGPT and DALL-E.
- **Ethical Oversight**: Many legal frameworks lack provisions for ethical AI governance, leaving issues like mass surveillance, profiling, and discrimination largely unchecked.

8. EMERGING TRENDS AND PROPOSED SOLUTIONS FOR STRENGTHENING

8.1 Emerging Legal Trends

The rapid advancements in artificial intelligence (AI) have led to the evolution of legal frameworks aimed at addressing new challenges. Policymakers and stakeholders are exploring innovative strategies to regulate AI technologies, balancing innovation with ethical considerations and public safety. This section outlines emerging legal trends and proposes solutions to effectively navigate the AI landscape.

- **Regulating Generative AI Models:** Generative AI models like ChatGPT and DALL-E have raised regulatory concerns due to their capacity to produce realistic content, prompting debates over intellectual property, misinformation, and ethical misuse. Key measures include implementing watermarking and traceability to identify AI-generated content, establishing clear guidelines for training data to comply with copyright laws, and mandating robust content moderation to prevent harm.
- **Ethical AI and Transparency Requirements:** Ethical concerns in AI, such as algorithmic biases, privacy violations, and opaque decision-making, have intensified, highlighting transparency as a cornerstone of ethical AI. Emerging trends include Explainable AI (XAI), ensuring accountability through clear decision explanations; ethical audits to assess bias and fairness; and public disclosure mandates requiring companies to reveal the purpose, limitations, and risks of AI models. Blueprint for an AI Bill of Rights exemplifies efforts to integrate transparency and ethical standards into AI governance frameworks.
- **The Role of Industry Standards and Certifications:** Industry-driven standards and certifications are becoming essential complements to governmental regulations, promoting trust and interoperability while ensuring compliance with ethical norms. Key developments include the creation of globally recognized AI certifications for safety, fairness, and transparency, as well as frameworks like the IEEE's Global Initiative on Ethics of Autonomous and Intelligent Systems. Additionally, sector-specific standards are being tailored to industries like healthcare and finance, where AI risks are more pronounced. These initiatives enhance accountability and streamline regulatory compliance across diverse jurisdictions, fostering responsible AI deployment.

- **Collaboration Between Governments and Tech Companies:** Collaboration between governments and tech companies has become essential for effective AI regulation. Governments enforce laws, while tech companies contribute technical expertise and innovation. Collaborative efforts include public-private partnerships for responsible AI development, such as regulatory sandboxes, information sharing for real-time threat detection, and global forums to harmonize AI regulations. As artificial intelligence (AI) continues to evolve, IT laws must adapt to address emerging threats while fostering innovation. Policymakers, industry leaders, and international organizations must work collaboratively to establish robust legal frameworks. In 2024, this requires forward-looking strategies and practical solutions to tackle the complex challenges posed by AI technologies. Policymakers play a pivotal role in crafting effective IT laws that balance regulation and innovation. Key recommendations include:
  - **Adopting a Risk-Based Approach**: Tailor regulations based on the risk level of AI applications, as seen in the European Union's AI Act. Low-risk systems require minimal oversight, while high-risk systems demand stringent controls.
  - **Mandating Transparency and Accountability**: Enforce requirements for AI explainability, data provenance, and documentation to ensure ethical and fair practices.
  - **Promoting Ethical AI Development**: Encourage ethical considerations through incentives for developers and organizations that prioritize fairness, inclusivity, and privacy.
  - **Fostering Public Engagement**: Consult with diverse stakeholders, including civil society, academia, and industry, to ensure laws address real-world concerns and remain adaptable.

8.2 Implementing AI-specific legislation

It is crucial for addressing the unique challenges posed by AI technologies. The methods are:

- **Granularity**: Laws should address specific AI domains, such as autonomous vehicles, generative AI, and medical AI.
- **Flexibility**: Regulations must remain adaptable to evolving technologies and societal needs.
- **Enforcement Mechanisms**: Clear penalties for non-compliance and robust mechanisms for monitoring AI applications.
- **Ethical Oversight**: Incorporate ethical review boards to evaluate the societal impact of AI systems.

9. CONCLUSION

AI is expanding it's role in society is evident as technologies infiltrate industries like healthcare, finance, security, and transportation, offering numerous benefits but also presenting significant risks, such as cybersecurity threats, data privacy violations, algorithmic bias, and ethical dilemmas. Existing IT laws, designed for traditional technologies, are increasingly inadequate to address AI's complexities, leaving gaps in accountability, transparency, and bias. This inadequacy leads to regulatory uncertainty, hindering effective AI risk management. AI-driven threats identified include AI-enabled malware, mass data collection challenges, algorithmic discrimination, and AI weaponization, highlighting the need for adaptive legal frameworks. Finally, the research underscores the need for continuous innovation in legal frameworks. Laws must evolve in real-time to address AI's rapid advancements, with periodic reviews and updates to tackle emerging challenges. Furthermore, international collaboration is crucial to establish global standards for AI governance, ensuring consistency and efficiency in addressing cross-border AI risks.

REFERENCES

Binns, R. (2023). AI ethics and law: An emerging framework.

Comunale, M., & Manera, A. (2024). The economic impacts and the regulation of AI: A review of the academic literature and policy actions. *International Monetary Fund.*

Harvard Journal of Law & Technology (2024). Features articles that provide in-depth legal analysis of AI-related cases, with an emphasis on the ethical and legal implications of AI and machine learning technologies.

International Journal of Technology Law (2024). Articles examine how emerging AI threats are reshaping laws governing data privacy, intellectual property, and cross-border legal frameworks.

Journal of AI and Law (2024). Discusses key intersections between AI technologies and legal regulations, including AI's impact on privacy law, cybersecurity, and the creation of international AI governance standards.

Kotov, D. (2024). Data security and privacy in the age of artificial intelligence. *Universum Technical Sciences,* 123(6).

Optimizing Cloudlet Placement in Cloud-Integrated WOBAN: A Comparative Study of Connectivity Index and K-Means Clustering Approaches

Mausmi Verma[1] and Uma Rathore Bhatt[2]

ABSTRACT: Cloud-Integrated Wireless Optical Broadband Access Networks (CIW) have evolved from the growing need for low-latency, high-bandwidth services in contemporary communication networks. A key challenge in CIW deployment is the optimal placement of cloudlets to serve wireless routers (WRs) within hop constraint while minimizing deployment costs. In this paper two cloudlet placement approaches as a connection index-based approach and an optimal k-means clustering technique are proposed and compared. Simulations conducted in a network with varying wireless router counts demonstrate that k-means clustering consistently reduces the number of required cloudlets by approximately 50% compared to the connectivity index approach, while ensuring 100% coverage within hop constraints. The results provide valuable insights to design a network aiming to balance coverage and cost efficiency in CIW deployments.

***Keywords**: Cloud-Integrated WOBAN, Cloudlet Placement, K-Means Clustering, Optical Network Units, Wireless Access Network.*

1. INTRODUCTION

Combining the high bandwidth of optical networks with the adaptability of wireless access, the hybrid Fiber-Wireless (FiWi) architecture also referred to as Wireless Optical Broadband Access Network (WOBAN) shows tremendous potential for last-mile connection(Chouhan *et. al.,* 2019; Sarkar *et. al.,* 2007; Verma *et. al.,* 2024). Figure 1 shows that integrating cloud components, such as cloudlets, into WOBAN (termed CIW) enhances local service delivery, reducing latency by processing requests near the network edge (Reaz *et. al.,* 2014; Verma *et. al.,* 2023). However, efficient placement of these cloudlets (CRs) is critical to ensure full coverage of wireless routers (WRs) within a specified hop constraint while minimizing deployment costs.

Prior works proposed a connectivity index-based algorithm to place cloudlets in CIW (Verma *et. al.,* 2021), achieving maximum coverage with a trade-off against cost. However, this greedy approach often results in redundant cloudlet placements. In

---

[1] Research Scholar, Department of Electronics & Telecommunication Engineering, Institute of Engineering & Technology, Devi Ahilya University, Indore, India.
E-mail: mausmi.7nov@gmail.com

[2] Associate Professor, Department of Electronics & Telecommunication Engineering, Institute of Engineering & Technology, Devi Ahilya University, Indore, India.

contrast, clustering techniques like k-means can optimize resource allocation by grouping WRs efficiently.

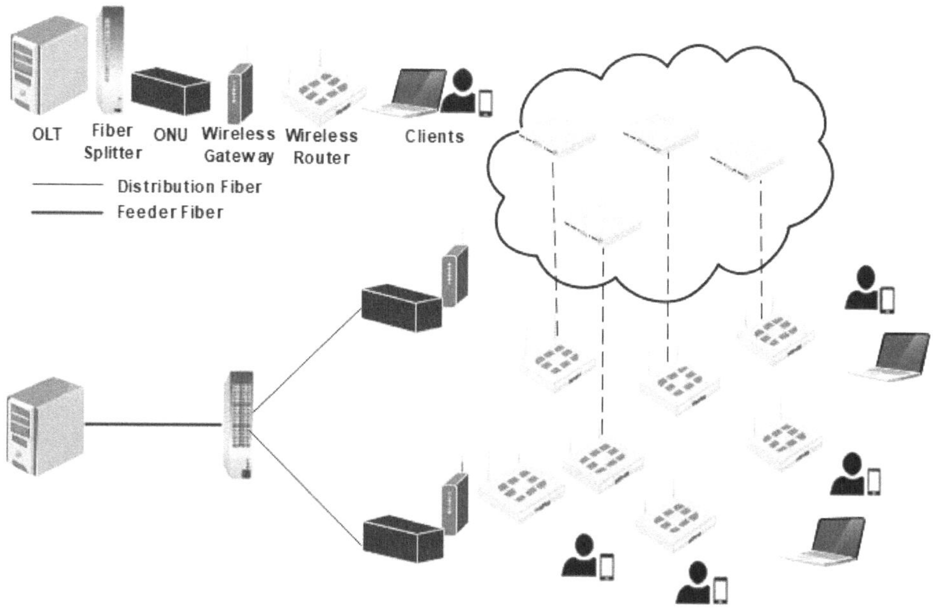

Figure 1: CIW Network Architecture

This paper investigates both methods across varying network sizes (20 to 200 WRs) in a 1000 × 1000 m area, with a two-hop constraint (1 hop = 250 m, two hops = 500 m). The objectives are to:

1. Deploy minimum Cloudlets to cover all WRs within two hops.
2. Compare cloudlet requirements using connectivity index and k-means approaches.
3. Analyze the scalability and efficiency of each method.

2. RELATED WORK

Much of the research on Cloud-Integrated Wireless Optical Broadband Access Networks (CIW) has centered on improving network performance and determining the best locations for cloudlets placement. Sarkar *et. al.,* (2007) reviewed the challenges in WOBAN systems and focussed on the need for smart resource allocation to make these networks work effectively. Verma *et. al.*, (2021) developed a method using a connectivity index to decide where to place cloudlets, making sure they cover the network within two hops while also keeping costs in mind. Mondal *et. al.*, (2018) investigated hybrid setups over optical networks, but not many studies have used clustering methods like k-means to reduce the number of cloudlets needed. Bhatt *et. al.*, (2015) worked on placing Optical Network Units (ONUs) in FiWi networks in an energy-efficient way, using practical techniques to minimize power consumption. Similarly, Maier (2018) explored how FiWi networks and cloud computing can work together, pointing out that edge nodes like cloudlets can help lighten the network's load, though they didn't dive into specific strategies for placing them.

K-means clustering has been widely used in wireless sensor networks (Taghikhaki *et. al.,* 2013) for optimal node placement, suggesting its potential in CIW. This paper extends these concepts by comparing a greedy approach with k-means optimization across a range of network sizes. Heinzelman *et. al.*, (2002) introduced LEACH, a clustering protocol for sensor networks that balances energy use, inspiring our use of k-means for resource efficiency. Yang *et. al.*, (2019) examined cloudlet placement in edge computing environments, using optimization models to reduce latency, though their focus was on wired networks rather than hybrid FiWi systems.

3. RESEARCH METHOD

The CIW architecture integrates a wireless mesh network (WMN) front-end with an optical back end, enhanced by cloudlets. The methodology leverages mathematical formulations for coverage and connectivity.

3.1 Network Setup

Initially WRs are randomly deployed using a uniform distribution with positions as: $P_i = (x_i, y_i)\ for\ i = 1, 2, \dots\dots, N$ within $A = 1000\ \times 1000\ m^2$ network area. The WRs are distributed for varying count as $N = \{20, 40, 60, 80, 100, 120, 140, 160, 180, 200\}$ within the one or two hop constraint given as 1 hop=$r_h = 250\ m$, and 2 hops = $R = 2 \times r_h = 500\ m$.

The CIW network architecture comprises WMN frontend. WRs form a mesh with connectivity defined by:

$$C_{ij} = \begin{cases} 1\ if\ d_{ij} \leq R, i \neq j \\ 0\ \text{otherwise} \end{cases} \quad \dots (1)$$

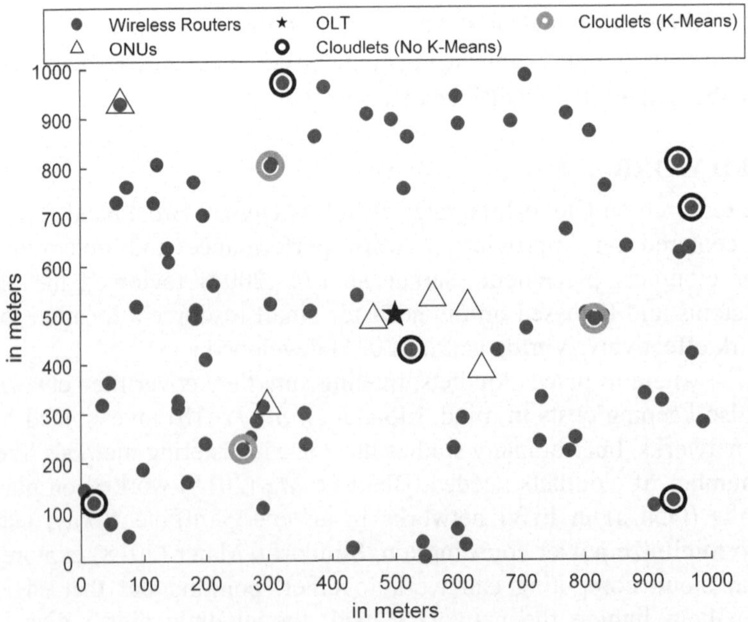

Figure 2: Network Simulation

Where, $d_{ij} = \sqrt{(x_i - x_j)^2 + (y_i - y_j)^2}$ is the Euclidean distance between WRs i and j, and $R = 500\,m$. Gateways connect WRs to ONUs. ONUs link to the OLT via a passive optical network (PON). ONUs cover WRs within R, with the OLT aggregating traffic. Cloudlets at selected WRs serve local requests within R. Figure 2 shows the simulated architecture for 80 WRs.

3.2 Algorithms

In the proposed approach within the FiWi network initially cloudlets are deployed randomly ensuring the WRs coverage. Once all the components are placed within the network, then k-means clustering optimization algorithm is applied to ensure the optimum placement of cloudlets within the cluster of the WRs. These optimized cloudlets position within hop constraint ensure maximum WRs coverage with minimum number of cloudlets count. This proposed methodology is compared with the existing work (Verma *et. al.*, 2021) based on connectivity index in terms of cloudlet minimization. The proposed approach (k-means) and the existing connectivity Index approach is given below.

3.2.1 *Connectivity Index Approach (Without K-Means):*

- Connectivity Index: For WR_i,

$$CI_i = \sum_{j=1, j\neq i}^{N} C_{ij} \qquad \dots (2)$$

  Where, C_{ij} is calculated from equation 1.
- **Algorithm**: Select WR_i with maximum CI_i among uncovered WRs, deploy a cloudlet, remove covered WRs ($d_{ij} \leq R$), and repeat until all WRs are covered or $CI_i \leq 1$, then add remaining WRs as cloudlets.
- **Objective**: Minimize cloudlet count with maximum WRs coverage.

2.2.2 *K-Means Clustering Approach*

- **Clustering:** Minimize the within-cluster sum of squares for k clusters

$$J = \sum_{i=1}^{N}\sum_{j=1}^{k} w_{ij} d(P_i, \mu_j)^2 \qquad \dots (3)$$

  Where, w_{ij}=1 if WR_i is in the cluster j, 0 otherwise, and μ_j is the centroid of the cluster j.
- **Algorithm:** Increment k until all WRs are within R of a centroid.

$$min_j d(P_i, \mu_j) \leq R \ \forall i \qquad \dots (4)$$

- **Objective**: Minimize k (cloudlet count) satisfying equation (4).

4. SIMULATION AND RESULTS

The algorithms are implemented in MATLAB, with results recorded for ONUs and cloudlets across all WR counts. Simulations were conducted to evaluate minimum cloudlets required. Table 1 summarizes the results.

Table 1: Cloudlet Requirements for Varying WR Counts

WR Count	*Cloudlets (without K-Means)*	*Cloudlets (K-Means)*
20	2	2
40	5	3
60	5	2
80	6	3
100	4	3
120	5	3
140	4	3
160	4	4
180	5	4
200	5	4

Figure 3 illustrates the cloudlet requirements for both proposed and existing methods.

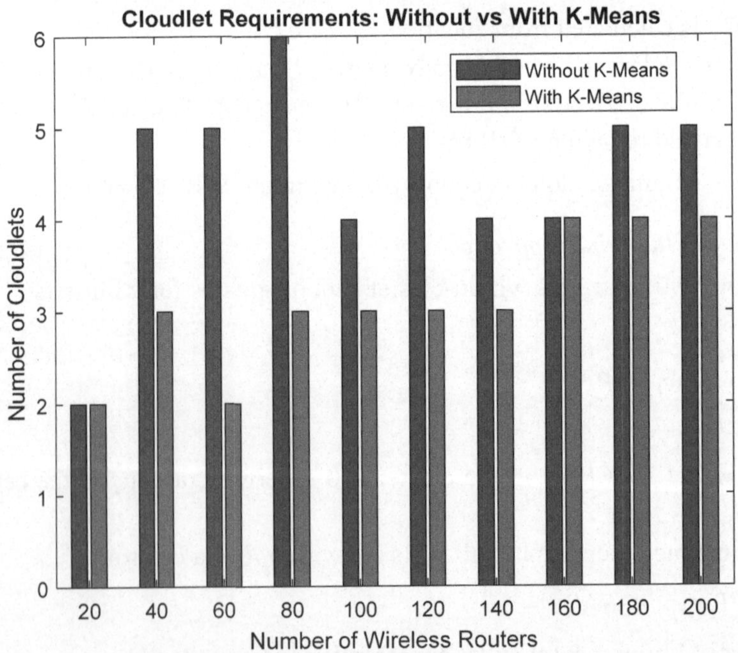

Figure 3: Cloudlet Requirements Comparison

As shown in figure 3 that cloudlet count grows linearly from 2 (20 WRs) to 5 (200 WRs). The greedy approach selects WRs based on connectivity, often leading to overlapping coverage and higher redundancy. However, cloudlet count increases more slowly, from 2 (20 WRs) to 4(200 WRs) using the proposed approach. K-means optimizes placement by clustering WRs, reducing the number needed by approximately 33–50%.

5. CONCLUSION

The proposed work shows that, in CIW networks, k-means clustering greatly improves cloudlet location relative to a connection index-based method. Using k-means lowers cloudlet requirements by up to 50%, providing a cost-effective alternative without sacrificing coverage for WR counts between 20 and 200. For further realism, future research may investigate dynamic WR distributions, include cost effective models, or include actual hop-based routing. The work may also focus on load balancing using task offloading approach.

REFERENCES

Bhatt, U.R.; Chouhan, N. and Upadhyay, R. (2015). Hybrid algorithm: A cost efficient solution for ONU placement in Fiber-Wireless (FiWi) network. *Optical Fiber Technology*, *22*, 76–83.

Chouhan, N.; Bhatt, U.R. and Upadhyay, R. (2019). An optimization framework for FiWi access network: Comprehensive solution for green and survivable deployment. *Optical Fiber Technology*, *53* (August), 102002.

Heinzelman, W.B.; Chandrakasan, A.P. and Balakrishnan, H. (2002). An application-specific protocol architecture for wireless microsensor networks. *IEEE Transactions on Wireless Communications*, *1*(4), 660–670.

Maier, M. (2018). The Tactile Internet: Where Do We Go From Here? *2018 Asia Communications and Photonics Conference (ACP)*, 1–3.

Mondal, S.; Das, G. and Wong, E. (2018). CCOMPASSION: A Hybrid Cloudlet Placement Framework Over Passive Optical Access Networks. *IEEE INFOCOM 2018 - IEEE Conference on Computer Communications*, 216–224.

Reaz, A.S.; Ramamurthi, V.; Tornatore, M. and Mukherjee, B. (2014). Cloud-Integrated WOBAN: An offloading-enabled architecture for service-oriented access networks. *Computer Networks*, *68*, 5–19.

Sarkar, S.; Dixit, S. and Mukherjee, B. (2007). Hybrid wireless-optical broadband-access network (WOBAN): A review of relevant challenges. *Journal of Lightwave Technology*, *25*(11), 3329–3340.

Taghikhaki, Z.; Meratnia, N. and Havinga, P. J. M. (2013). A Trust-based Probabilistic Coverage Algorithm for Wireless Sensor Networks. *Procedia Computer Science*, *21*, 455–464.

Verma, M.; Bhatt, U.R. and Upadhyay, R. (2021). Building a Cloud-Integrated WOBAN with Optimal Coverage and Deployment Cost. In S.M. Thampi, E. Gelenbe, M. Atiquzzaman, V. Chaudhary and K.-C. Li (Eds.), *Advances in Computing and Network Communications* (pp. 119–131). Springer Singapore.

Verma, M.; Bhatt, U.R.; Upadhyay, R. and Bhat, V. (2023). Priority Based Task Scheduling in Cloud Integrated WOBAN Network. *2023 IEEE International Students' Conference on Electrical, Electronics and Computer Science (SCEECS)*, 1–4.

Verma, M.; Rathore Bhatt, U.; Upadhyay, R. and Bhat, V. (2024). MLGO: A machine learning-based mountain gazelle optimization algorithm for efficient resource management and load balancing in fiber wireless access networks. *Optical Fiber Technology*, *88*, 104014.

Yang, S.; Li, F.; Shen, M.; Chen, X.; Fu, X. and Wang, Y. (2019). Cloudlet Placement and Task Allocation in Mobile Edge Computing. *IEEE Internet of Things Journal*, pp. 1.

Phytoremediation—An Eco-Friendly and Sustainable Technique for Wastewater Treatment

Vijayant Panday[1] and Ananda Babu K.[2]

ABSTRACT: Phytoremediation is an ecofriendly, economic and sustainable method that uses certain types of plants to treat wastewater. The microbial communities grow around the roots of plants and form a symbiotic relationship which helps to treat the wastewater and reduce the concentration of pollutants like organic compounds and nutrients. Conventional treatments methods are costly and energy intensive and often cause secondary damage to the environment. Phytoremediation is an alternative technology that has now gained much more attention and is being researched all over the world. For the effective treatment the selection of plants play an important role. With the critical literature review, two plants were identified, and their efficiency of wastewater treatment had been identified in the environment of Indore city, M.P. India. It's the first kind of study for the selected plants for this reason. The results of the present study indicate that both the selected plants have the efficiency to treat wastewater by reducing the concentration of pollutants significantly.

Keywords: *Microbial Communities, Nutrients, Organic Compounds, Pollutants, Symbiotic Relationship.*

1. INTRODUCTION

As per International Institute of Health and Hygiene, New Delhi (ENVIS, 2019), urban India generates 61754 million litres of sewage every day and the installed capacity of sewage treatment is merely 37.5%. Remaining amount of untreated domestic sewage (38596 million litres per day) along with other type of wastewater ultimately finds its way into the surface and ground water bodies. Conventionally, mechanized wastewater treatment systems are used to combat pollution of water bodies. The treatment system usually consists of structural facilities for screening, sedimentation, flocculation, filtration, aeration etc. this type of wastewater treatment solutions are usually costly and energy exhaustive and this is the main disadvantage of it (Billore & Sharma, 2009).

Insufficient capacity of existing wastewater treatment facilities in the country has resulted in the mixing of untreated or partially treated wastewaters containing various types of polluting substances into the aquatic environment, thereby deteriorating their quality (Rana & Maiti, 2020). Therefore, from an ecological and economic point of view, there is an urgent need to search and develop an alternative ecofriendly and cost-effective technology.

---

[1] Research Scholar, Department of Civil Engineering, Shri Vaishnav Vidyapeeth Vishwavidyalaya, Indore, India. E-mail: vijayantcivil@gmail.com

[2] Associate Professor & Head, Department of Civil Engineering, Shri Vaishnav Vidyapeeth Vishwavidyalaya, Indore, India.

Phytoremediation is an alternative wastewater treatment technology that is being researched all over the world. Phytoremediation is a system where certain plants, working together with soil organisms, can transform pollutants into harmless and often, valuable forms. Essentially, it is the use of macrophytes (green plants) to treat polluted soils, sediments, or water. Macrophytes based treatment systems are being researched in various countries for recycling and treatment of wastewater (Chavan & Dhulap, 2012; Rahman & Hasegawa, 2011). Some special types of plants are the main treatment agent of the system. The plants can accumulate, remove, or degrade the contaminants. Abbasi & Abbasi (2010) have described the mechanism of the purifying action. Wastewater treatment is associated with both plants and microorganisms. The micro-organisms that live on and around the roots of the plant contribute mainly to the treatment process to decompose organic pollution. As soon as these microorganisms are established in the root of aquatic plants, they form a symbiotic relationship with the roots of the plant.

The functional role of aquatic plants in processes such as nitrification, denitrification, volatilization, sorption, and plant uptake, etc. is well known. This connection normally produces a synergistic effect resulting in increasing rate of decomposition. Nutrients are generated from microbial decomposition of organic materials that are absorbed and used with phosphorus, nitrogen and other minerals as a food source. Microorganisms also use some or all metabolites released by plants roots as a food source. Using each other's waste products allow to sustain a reaction in favour of usage of organics from wastewater (Rehman *et. al.*, 2019). Soil excavation, chemical treatment, incineration or burial, none of these are required in phytoremediation. During the process of phytoremediation treatment, there is no change in the surrounding. Considering the above it had been decided to undertake a literature review on phytoremediation of various types of wastewaters with use of water hyacinth. Around 80 national and international research papers had been reviewed and two plants, namely Azolla and Duckweed were selected for the present research (Figure 1).

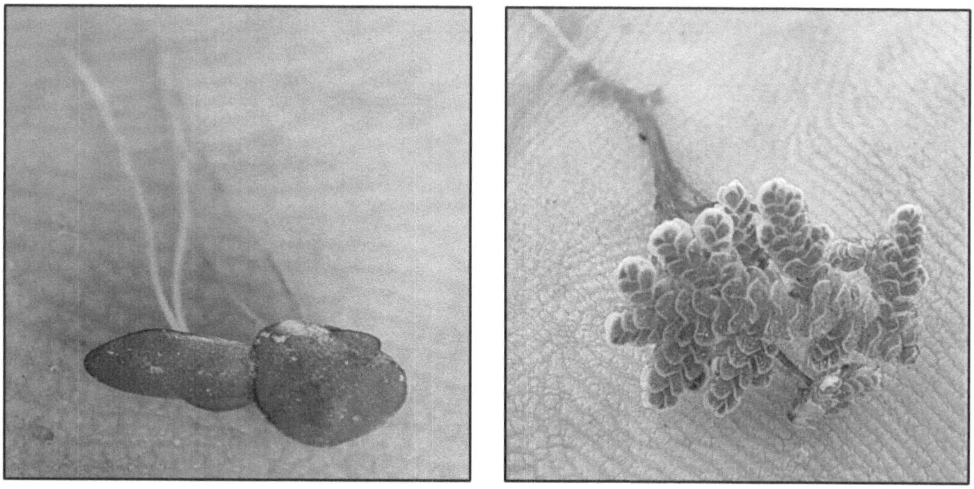

(a) (b)

Figure 1: Macro Image of Duckweed (a) and Azolla (b)

2. METHODS AND MATERIALS

The study was conducted in Indore, Madhya Pradesh, India, where water pollution is a significant concern due to industrial and domestic wastewater discharge. Sewage was collected from the study area for the present research. For the phytoremediation of Azolla and Duckweed three containers had been used as shown in Figure 2. Container-I (C1) was planted with Duckweed and container-II (C2) was planted with Azolla whereas the container-III (C3) was planted with both the macrophytes. The experiment was performed in the university ground and run for 15 days in open atmosphere. Initial characteristics of sewage was analysed at the initial stage and at every 5th day. Three parameters Biochemical Oxygen Demand (BOD), Nitrogen (NH_4^+) and Phosphate (PO_4^{3-}) were analysed as per American Public Health Association (APHA) standard and percentage removal efficiency had been studied.

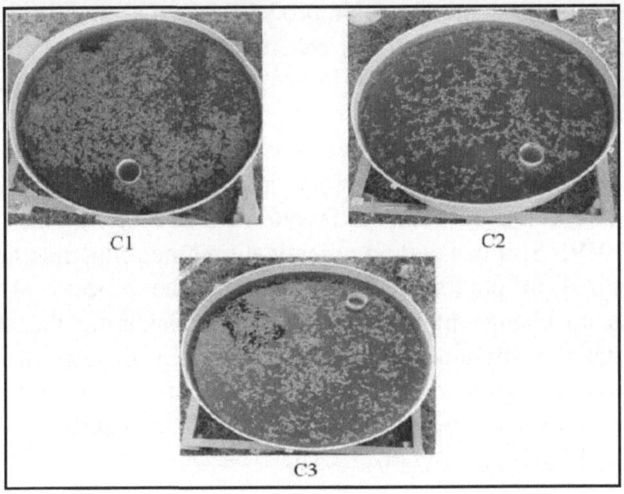

Figure 2: Experimental Setup having three Containers as C1 (Duckweed treatment), C2 (Azolla Treatment) and C3 (Duckweed and Azolla Mix Treatment)

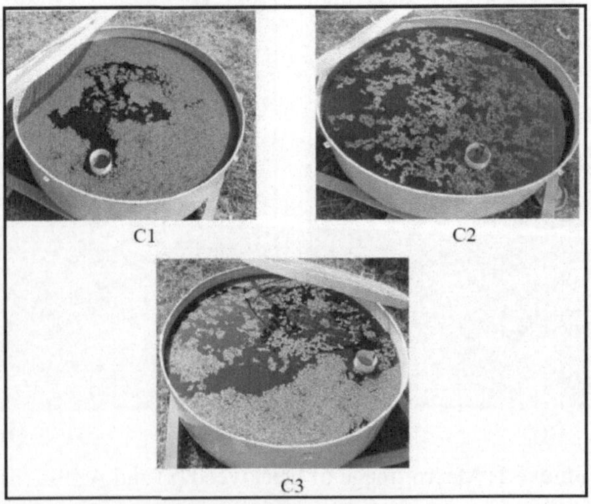

Figure 3: Growth of Macrophytes in all the Containers at 7 Day Retention Time

3. RESULTS AND DISCUSSION

Results obtained during the experimental study are shown in Figure 5 to Figure 8. During the present research, significant growth of both the macrophytes has been observed. Figure 3 shows the visible growth of macrophytes in the containers whereas Figure 4 shows the macro image of water surface where the new tiny plants can be seen. This indicates that even in the raw sewage, macrophytes not only survive but grow well.

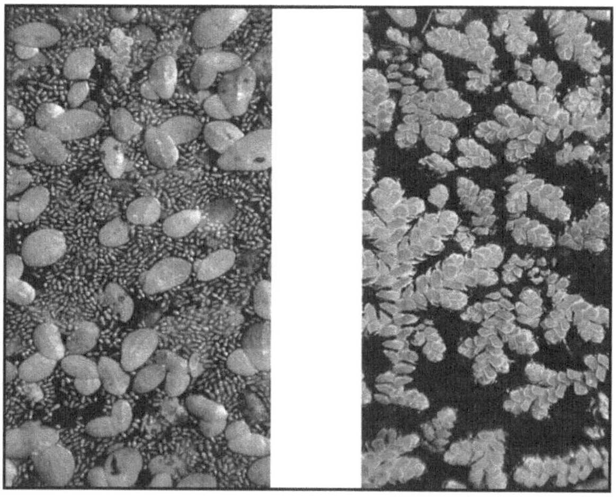

(a) (b)

Figure 4: Macro Image of Macrophytes Showing the New Tiny Plants as (a) Duckweed and (b) Azolla

3.1 Treatment Efficiency for BOD

The results obtained from the present research as represented in Figure 5. It was observed that C3 showed highest reduction of BOD from 206 mg/l to 115 mg/l. The value obtained for C1 and C2 indicate that the C1 can reduce higher BOD concentration as compared to C2, after the duration of experiment. The highest percentage removal efficiency of 53.40% was observed in C3 followed by C1 and C2 with the removal efficiency of 44.17% and 38.35% respectively.

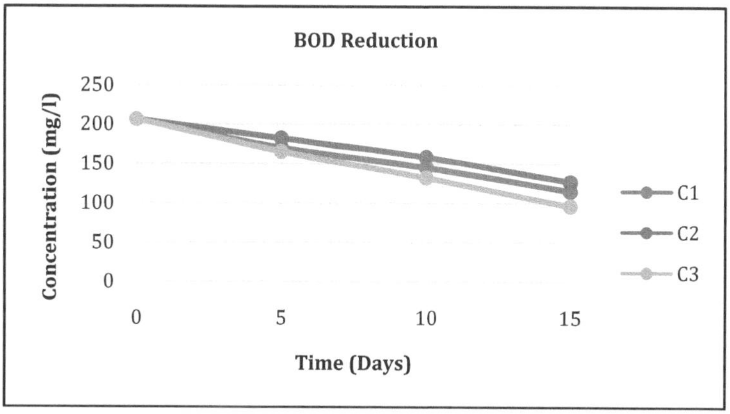

Figure 5: Graphical Representation of BOD Reduction

3.2 Treatment Efficiency for Nitrogen

The initial concentration of nitrogen in the collected sewage sample was 31.73 mg/l which was reduced significantly to 17.82 for C1, 19.87 for C2 and 14.89 for C3 at 15 days retention time as in Figure 6. Percentage removal efficiency was found to be maximum in C3 with a value of 53.07% and minimum in C2 with 37.38%. C1 also showed significant reduction efficiency of 43.84% but as compared to C3, it is lower.

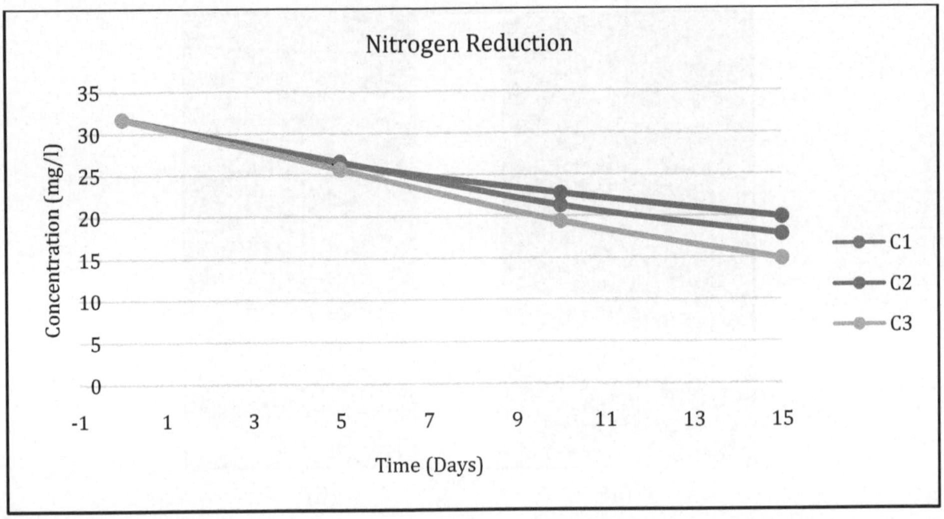

Figure 6: Graphical Representation of Nitrogen Reduction

3.3 Treatment Efficiency for Phosphate

Figure 7 displays the reduction of phosphate for all the containers. Before the treatment the measured value of phosphate was 14.62 mg/l which declined with increase in the retention time. This declined to 8.35 for C1, 9.45 for C2 and 8.63 for C3 at the end of experiment duration of 15 days. C1 showed the highest removal efficiency of 42.89% unlike for BOD and Nitrogen. Significant efficiency was observed in C3 also with 40.97% followed by 35.63% for C2.

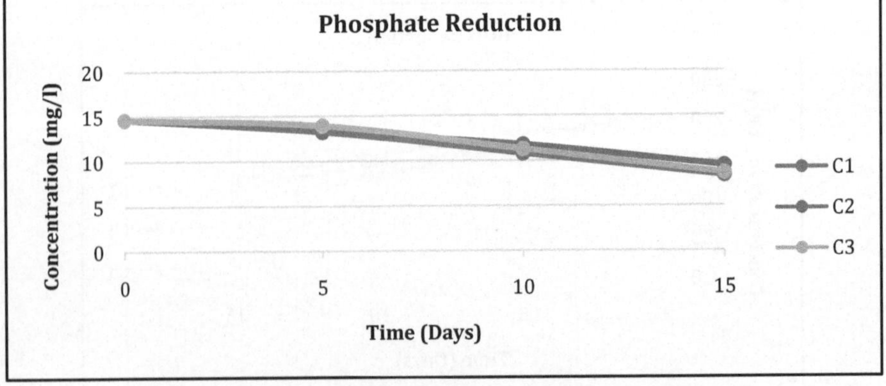

Figure 7: Graphical Representation of Phosphate Reduction

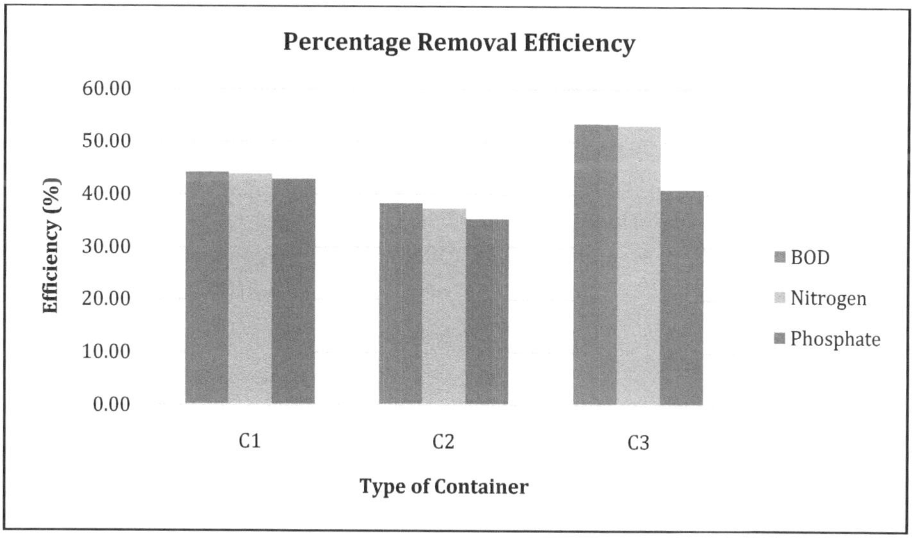

Figure 8: Graphical Representation of Percentage Removal Efficiency

4. CONCLUSION

The results of the study revealed that Azolla and Duckweed, both the Macrophytes have the capability to treat raw sewage. They not only survived but grew well in the treatment system with such high concentration of BOD. During the experiment, it was observed that the growth of Azolla was well in the C3 as compared to C2. This indicates synergetic effect of both the macrophytes. Because of this synergetic effect the percentage removal efficiency for BOD and Nitrogen was found to be higher in C3 as compared to C1 and C2 exhibited by Figure 8. For phosphate C3 showed significant percentage removal efficiency but it is lower than the C1 which indicate the potential of Duckweed to treat wastewater with high concentration of phosphate. The overall conclusion of the research is that these macrophytes can be used in the climate of selected study area, because of their ability to treat wastewater. It can be concluded that mixing of the plants provide better results as compared to their application separately. Further, more studies are required to access the effect of incorporation of some external agents like, aerator or pretreatment of wastewater.

REFERENCES

Abbasi, T. and Abbasi, S.A. (2010). Factors which facilitate wastewater treatment by aquatic weeds; the mechanism of the weeds' purifying action. *International Journal of Environmental Studies*. 67(3):349-371.

APHA (2012). Standard methods for the examination of water and wastewater (21st ed.). *American Public Health Association,* Washington DC, USA.

Billore, S.K. and Sharma, J.K. (2009). Treatment performance of artificial floating reed beds in an experimental mesocosm to improve the water quality of river Kshipra. *Water Science and Technology*. 60(11):2851–2859.

Chavan, B.L. and Dhulap, V.P. (2012). Treatment of sewage through phytotechnological studies with constructed wetland using eichhornia crassipes. *Journal of Environmental Research and Development*, 7 (2):660–667.

ENVIS Centre on Hygiene, Sanitation, Sewage Treatment Systems and Technology, International Institute of Health and Hygiene, New Delhi (2019). *National status of wastewater generation & treatment.*

Rahman, M.A. and Hasegawa, H. (2011). Aquatic arsenic: phytoremediation using floating macrophytes. Chemosphere. 83(5):633-646.

Rana, V. and Maiti, S.K. (2020). Municipal and Industrial Wastewater Treatment Using Constructed Wetlands. *In Phytoremediation. (329–367). Springer,* Cham.

Rehman, K.; Ijaz, A.; Arslan, M. and Afzal, M. (2019). Floating treatment wetlands as biological buoyant filters for wastewater reclamation. *International Journal of Phytoremediation.*

SEAPIRD Model for Analysing Covid Dynamics

Shilpa Umdekar[1] and Anand Prakash[2]

ABSTRACT: The study introduces the Susceptible Exposed Asymptomatic Presymptomatic Infected Recovered Dead (SEAPIRD) model, a deterministic compartmental framework designed to understand the transmission dynamics of infectious diseases with complex incubation periods and asymptomatic carriers, such as COVID-19. This model extends the traditional SIR, SEIR, and SEAIR models by incorporating a presymptomatic period. We begin with an in-depth review of the classic SEAPIRD model emphasizing the intricacies of each compartment and their transitions. The model's realism is enhanced by integrating natural death across all compartments except the Dead (D), reducing the threshold for disease extinction and determining whether a disease becomes endemic or dies out. Cure rates for asymptomatic, presymptomatic, and infected individuals are included to reflect medical interventions that shorten the infectious period and reduce secondary infections, impacting the reproduction number. We also discuss equilibrium points and, in these models, identifying potential disease spread through the estimation of reproduction numbers. These enhanced models support better-informed public health decisions and interventions, aiding in the control and mitigation of infectious disease outbreaks.

Keywords: *Asymptomatic, Equilibrium Points, Interventions, Presymptomatic, Reproduction Number.*

1. INTRODUCTION

For generations, humanity has faced the peril of infectious diseases, which have shaped history and profoundly impacted society, often with catastrophic consequences. Historical epidemics such as the Black Death, the Spanish Flu, and the HIV/AIDS epidemic illustrate the severe effects of these outbreaks on populations, economies, and social structures (Brauer *et. al.*, 2012). The dynamic nature of infectious diseases underscores the importance of robust methods for their prediction, analysis, and control. While advances in medical research and public health have been instrumental, new and re-emerging diseases like HIV, malaria, cholera, and COVID-19 highlight the limitations of clinical therapies and public health initiatives alone. Mathematical epidemiological models have become essential in addressing these challenges (Brauer *et. al.*, 2019).

This paper explores the progression of the SEAPIRD model (Susceptible Exposed Asymptomatic Presymptomatic Infected Recovered Dead) and its application to COVID-19 in India. By incorporating a presymptomatic period, natural death rate, cure rate, and

---

[1] Research Scholar, Department of Mathematics, Shri Vaishnav Vidyapeeth Vishwavidyalaya, Indore, India. E-mail: shilpaumdekar12@gmail.com

[2] Assistant Professor, Department of Mathematics, Shri Vaishnav Vidyapeeth Vishwavidyalaya, Indore, India.

saturation incidence rate, the model extends traditional frameworks like SIR, SEIR, SEPIR, and SEAIR (Avila *et. al.*, 2020; Baruah, 2020; Wusu *et. al.*, 2021). It provides insights into the dynamics of infectious diseases with complex incubation periods and asymptomatic carriers, emphasizing their role in epidemic control.

2. CLASSIC MODEL

In epidemiological models, susceptible individuals are at risk of infection and transition to the exposed compartment upon contact with a pathogen. During the exposed stage, the virus is present but not yet infectious. The asymptomatic phase involves individuals who carry and can transmit the virus without ever showing symptoms. In contrast, the presymptomatic phase occurs when individuals, though still asymptomatic, have become infectious but will eventually develop symptoms. This infectious incubation period is significant in diseases like COVID-19 (Carapetis & Currie, 2020). Infected individuals exhibit symptoms and can transmit the disease, while recovered individuals are immune and non-infectious (Wang *et. al.*, 2022). The deceased stage accounts for mortality, reducing the number of susceptible and infected individuals, impacting reproduction rates and epidemic progression.

2.1 Proposed Model

The epidemic model we discuss and study first, is classic SEAPIRD model using non-linear ordinary differential equations.

$$\begin{aligned}
\frac{dS}{dt} &= \pi - S(\sigma P + \gamma A + \beta I) \\
\frac{dE}{dt} &= S(\sigma P + \gamma A + \beta I) - E(gv + (1-g)\eta) \\
\frac{dA}{dt} &= E(1-g)\eta - \rho A \\
\frac{dP}{dt} &= gvE - \omega P \\
\frac{dI}{dt} &= \omega P - I(\delta + \theta) \\
\frac{dR}{dt} &= \rho A + \delta I \\
\frac{dD}{dt} &= \theta I
\end{aligned} \qquad \ldots (1)$$

$$N(t) = S(t) + E(t) + A(t) + P(t) + I(t) + R(t) + D(t)$$

In the proposed model, $S(t)$, $E(t)$, $A(t)$, $P(t)$, $I(t)$, $R(t)$, $D(t)$, and $N(t)$ represent the numbers of Susceptible, Exposed, Asymptomatic, Presymptomatic, Infected, Recovered, Deceased, and the total population at time t, respectively. The total population, $N(t)$, sums individuals across all compartments.

The model parameters are defined as follows: π is the recruitment rate of new individuals into the susceptible class. v is the rate at which individuals transition from $E(t)$ to $P(t)$. β, σ, and γ are transmission rates from infected, presymptomatic, and asymptomatic individuals to susceptibles, respectively. g represents the fraction of newly infected individuals transitioning from $E(t)$ to $P(t)$ at rate γ, while $(1-g)$ represents those transitioning from $E(t)$ to $A(t)$ at rate η. θ is the disease-induced mortality rate, δ is the recovery rate for symptomatic individuals, ρ is the recovery rate for asymptomatic individuals, and ω is the rate at which presymptomatic individuals develop symptoms and become symptomatic. A transfer diagram further clarifies these transitions.

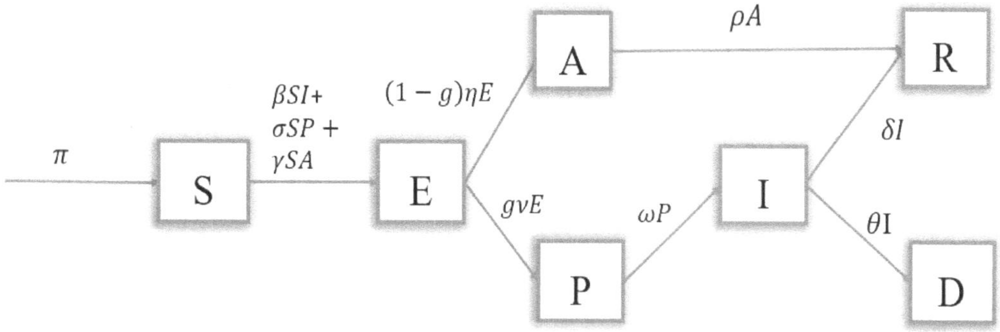

Figure 1: Transfer Diagram of the Classic Model

2.2 FEASIBLE REGION

Lemma 2.2:

$$\Omega = \{(S,E,A,P,I,R,D) \in R_+^7 (S+E+A+P+I+R+D) < \pi,$$
$$S \geq 0, E \geq 0, A \geq 0, P \geq 0, I \geq 0, R \geq 0, D \geq 0\}$$

positively invariant with system 1.

$$\frac{d}{dt}(S+E+A+P+I+R+D) = \pi - (S+E+A+P+I+R+D) - dI$$
$$< \pi - (S+E+A+P+I+R+D)"$$

Solving the above equation, and applying, $\lim_{t\to\infty} N(t)$ we get $N(t) < \pi$. Thus, feasible region invariant with System 1 is given by lemma 2.2.

2.3 Reproduction Number

We make use of next generation matrix by Driessche & Watmough, (2002), to calculate R_0. The system 1 will have reproduction number at DFE $(\pi, 0,0,0,0,0)$.

$$R_0 = \frac{\pi[(\delta+\mu)\{gv\sigma\rho+\gamma\eta(1-g)\omega+\beta gv\omega\rho)\}]}{\omega\rho(\delta+\theta)(gv+(1-g)\eta)} \quad \dots (2)$$

3. ENHANCED MODELS

3.1 Model Enhancement with Cure Rate and Natural Death Rate

When considering the population that has been successfully treated and cured, the cure rate is a useful measure to include. a used in the model refers to constant treatment function (Wang & Ruan, 2004).

$$C(I) = \begin{cases} a, & \text{if I} > 0 \\ 0, & \text{if I} = 0 \end{cases}$$

represents the cure rate, which indicates the level of success of the treatment in curing those who are infected. The model better simulates population changes by integrating natural death rates, denoted by μ which can aid long-term projections and disease endemicity as natural death makes the model more realistic by accepting that people die for a variety of reasons, not just disease.

$$\begin{aligned}
\frac{dS}{dt} &= \pi - S(\sigma P + \gamma A + \beta I + \mu) \\
\frac{dE}{dt} &= S(\sigma P + \gamma A + \beta I) - E(gv + (1-g)\eta + \mu) \\
\frac{dA}{dt} &= E(1-g)\eta - A(\rho + \mu) \\
\frac{dP}{dt} &= gvE - P(\omega + \mu) \\
\frac{dI}{dt} &= \omega P - I(\delta + \theta + a + \mu) \\
\frac{dR}{dt} &= \rho A + I(\delta + a) + \mu R \\
\frac{dD}{dt} &= \theta I
\end{aligned} \quad \ldots (3)$$

We formulate the above equations, understanding the behavior of parameters involved, which can be depicted through the transfer diagram in 2.

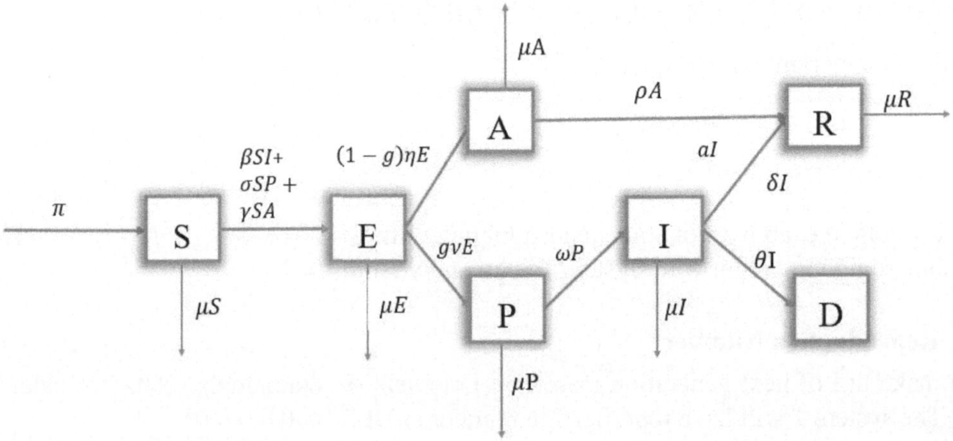

Figure 2: Transfer Diagram of the Enhanced Model

3.2 Feasible Region

Lemma 3.2:

$$\Omega = \{(S,E,A,P,I,R,D) \in R_+^7 (S+E+A+P+I+R+D) < \frac{\pi}{\mu},$$

$$S \geq 0, E \geq 0, A \geq 0, P \geq 0, I \geq 0, R \geq 0, D \geq 0\}$$

positively invariant with System 3.

Solving the equation,

$$\frac{d}{dt}(S+E+A+P+I+R+D) = \pi - \mu(S+E+A+P+I+R+D) - dI$$
$$< \pi - \mu(S+E+A+P+I+R+D)$$

and applying $\lim_{t\to\infty} N(t)$, we get $N(t) < \frac{\pi}{\mu}$. Thus, feasible region invariant with System 3 is given by lemma 3.2. We may simplify the system 3 by removing fifth and sixth equation from the system since all the other equations does not contain *R* and *D*. Hence, the reduced system is

$$\frac{dS}{dt} = \pi - S(\sigma P + \gamma A + \beta I)$$
$$\frac{dE}{dt} = S(\sigma P + \gamma A + \beta I) - E(gv + (1-g)\eta)$$
$$\frac{dA}{dt} = E(1-g)\eta - \rho A$$
$$\frac{dP}{dt} = gvE - \omega P$$
$$\frac{dI}{dt} = \omega P - I(\delta + \theta)$$

3.3 Reproduction Number

We make use of next generation matrix by Driessche & Watmough, (2002) to calculate R_0. The System 3 will have DFE at $(\frac{\pi}{\mu}, 0,0,0,0,0)$. For calculating R_0, we focus on infected compartments *E, A, P* and *I* only. Let $X = (E, A, P, I)^T$. The system becomes $\frac{dX}{dt} = (F - V)X$, where

$$F = \begin{bmatrix} \sigma SP + \gamma SA + \beta SI \\ 0 \\ 0 \\ 0 \\ \end{bmatrix} \quad \ldots (4)$$

$$V = \begin{bmatrix} (\mu + gv + (1-g)\eta)E \\ -(1-g)\eta E + \rho A + \mu A \\ -gvE + \omega P + \mu P \\ -\omega P + (\mu + \delta + \theta + a)I \end{bmatrix}$$

The Next Generation Matrix is given by

$$F_1 V_1^{-1} = \begin{bmatrix} a_{11} & a_{12} & a_{13} & a_{14} \\ a_{21} & a_{22} & a_{23} & a_{24} \\ a_{31} & a_{32} & a_{33} & a_{34} \\ a_{41} & a_{42} & a_{43} & a_{44} \\ \end{bmatrix}$$

where,

$$a_{11} = \frac{\pi g\sigma v}{\mu(\mu+\omega)(\mu+gv+(1-g)\eta)} - \frac{\pi\gamma\eta(g-1)}{\mu(\mu+\rho)(\mu+gv+(1-g)\eta)} + \frac{\pi\beta gv\omega}{\mu(\mu+\omega)(\mu+\delta+a+\theta)(\mu+gv+(1-g)\eta)},$$

$$a_{12} = \frac{\pi\gamma}{\mu(\mu+\rho)},\ a_{13} = \frac{\pi\sigma}{\mu(\mu+\omega)} + \frac{\pi\beta\omega}{\mu(\mu+\omega)(\mu+\delta+a+\theta)},\ a_{14} = \frac{\pi\beta}{\mu(\mu+\delta+a+\theta)},\ \text{and}$$

$$a_{21} = a_{22} = a_{23} = a_{24} = a_{31} = a_{32} = a_{33} = a_{34} = a_{41} = a_{42} = a_{43} = a_{44} = 0.$$

Therefore, the reproduction number R_0 is given as

$$R_0 = \frac{\pi[(\delta+\mu+a+\theta)\{gv\sigma(\rho+\mu)+\gamma\eta(1-g)(\mu+\omega)+\beta gv\omega(\rho+\mu)\}]}{\mu(\mu+\omega)(\rho+\mu)(\delta+\mu+a+\theta)(\mu+gv+(1-g)\eta)}$$

3.4 Disease Free Equilibrium

Setting $I = 0$ in 6, we get $S = \frac{\pi}{\mu}$ & $E = 0$ & $A = 0$ & $P = 0$, & $I = 0$. Hence, the diseases free equilibrium for the system 2.3 can be given as:

$$Y^0 = (S^0, E^0, A^0, P^0, I^0) = (\frac{\pi}{\mu}, 0,0,0,0)$$

3.5 Endemic Equilibrium

$Y^* = (S^*, E^*, A^*, P^*, I^*)$ is the endemic equilibrium given by:

$$S^* = \frac{(\rho+\mu)(\omega+\mu)(\delta+\theta+a+\mu)(gv+(1-g)\eta+\mu)}{(\delta+\theta+a+\mu)\{\sigma gv(\rho+\mu)+\gamma\eta(1-g)(\omega+\mu)\}+\beta gv\omega(\rho+\mu)},$$

$$E^* = \frac{(\omega+\mu)(\delta+\theta+a+\mu)I^*}{gv\omega},$$

$$A^* = \frac{(1-g)\eta(\omega+\mu)(\delta+\theta+a+\mu)I^*}{gv\omega(\rho+\mu)}, \quad \dots (5)$$

$$P^* = \frac{(\delta+\theta+a+\mu)I^*}{\omega}, \text{and}$$

$$I^* = \frac{gv\omega[\pi g(\rho+\mu)\{\sigma v+gv^2\omega^2\beta\}(\omega+\mu)\{\pi\gamma\eta(1-g)-\mu(\rho+\mu)(gv+(1-g)\eta+\mu)\}]}{(\omega+\mu)(gv+(1-g)[(\delta+\theta+a+\mu)\{\sigma gv(\rho+\mu)+\gamma\eta(1-g)(\omega+\mu)+\beta gv\omega(\rho+\mu)\}]}. \quad \dots (6)$$

4. RESULTS

The graphs illustrate population dynamics during an epidemic using various SEAPIRD models. This section examines the model curves generated via MATLAB simulation. The conventional model System 1 is analyzed in Figure 3 for an outbreak with $R_0 > 1$, using parameters derived from COVID-19's incubation, latent, and infectious periods, along with initial infectious compartment values from prior studies (Cheng *et. al.* 2020; Johansson *et. al.*, 2021; Kolabaje *et. al.*, 2022). The values of parameters taken $\pi = 7$; $\sigma = 0.25$, $\gamma = 0.08$, $\beta = 0.1$, $v = 0.2$, $\eta = 0.16$, $\rho = 0.14$, $\alpha = 0.4$, $\omega = 0.4$, $\delta = 0.1$, $\theta = 0.0003$, $g = 0.32$, The initial values for all compartment are $S(0) = 100$, $E(0) = 0$, $A(0) = 7$, $P(0) = 8$, $I(0) = 10$, $R(0) = 3$, $D(0) = 0$. After running the simulation, we get $R_0 = 6.7237$.

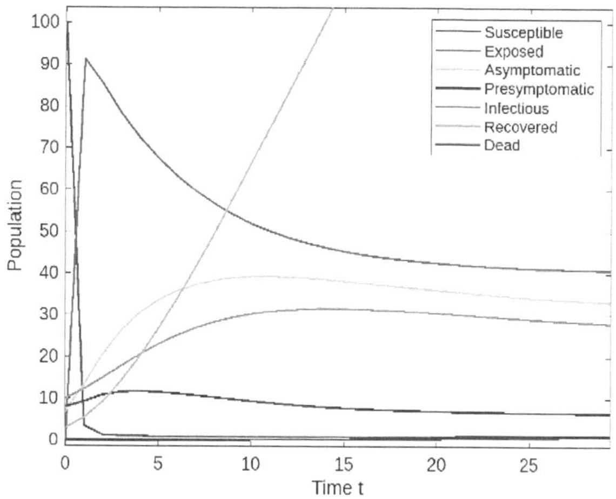

Figure 3: Spread of Infectious Disease by Classic Model

Figure 3 shows the susceptible population rapidly declining as the disease spreads and the exposed group rising early. As the disease advances, infectious and asymptomatic compartments rise, whereas recoveries progressively improve, suggesting most people recover. The presymptomatic period is short, with little growth before infection. The model has a lower death rate because infectious cases peak and then drop while mortality remains low.

Next, we evaluate the enhanced model with same conditions as above with introduction of cure rate and natural death rate. The values of parameters taken pi = 7; $\sigma = 0.25$, $\gamma = 0.08$, $\beta = 0.1$, $\nu = 0.2$, $\eta = 0.16$, $\rho = 0.14$, $\alpha = 0.4$, $\omega = 0.4$, $\delta = 0.1$, $\theta = 0.0003$, $g = 0.32$, $a = 0.9$, $\mu = 0.2$; The initial values for all compartment are $S(0) = 100$, $E(0) = 0$, $A(0) = 7$, $P(0) = 8$, $I(0) = 10$, $R(0) = 3$, $D(0) = 0$. After running the simulation, we get $R_0 = 5.024$.

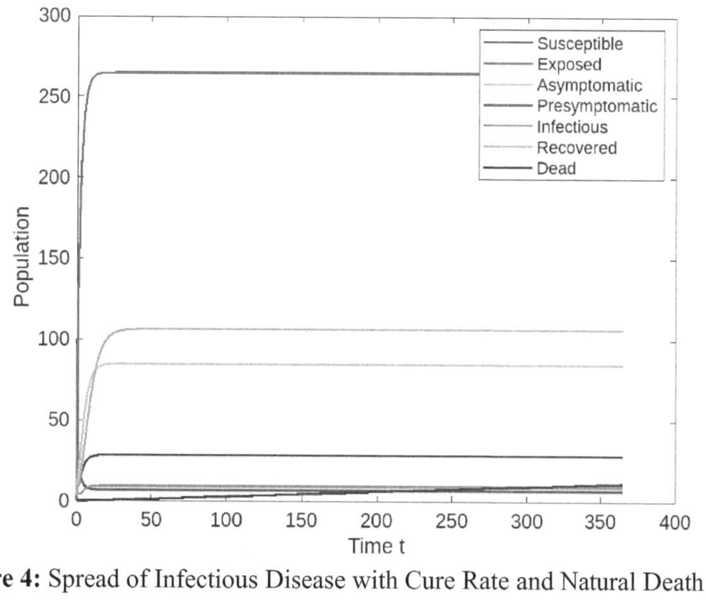

Figure 4: Spread of Infectious Disease with Cure Rate and Natural Death Rate

Figure 4 depicts a decline in the susceptible population as individuals transition through disease stages. Exposed, asymptomatic, and presymptomatic groups rise briefly before stabilizing, while infectious cases plateau due to containment, recovery, or mortality. The recovered population grows rapidly and stabilizes, with limited fatalities. The improved model offers a more realistic depiction by incorporating natural death and cure rates.

5. CONCLUSION

The study introduces the SEAPIRD model, a deterministic compartmental framework that extends traditional models like SIR, SEIR, and SEAIR to better capture the dynamics of infectious diseases with complex incubation periods and asymptomatic carriers, such as COVID-19. It incorporates natural death rate and cure rates to provide a realistic representation of disease spread and population changes. By considering psychological factors, spontaneous deaths, and medical interventions, the model helps refine predictions of disease progression and reproduction numbers. Equilibrium points, stability analysis, and reproduction number estimation are discussed to guide public health decisions. The model effectively illustrates the rapid decline in susceptible populations, a rise in exposed, presymptomatic, and asymptomatic compartments, and the eventual recovery of most individuals, with low mortality rates. Adding natural death and cure rates makes the outbreak dynamics more realistic, aiding in understanding disease spread and control strategies. Focused on India's public health response, the SEAPIRD model demonstrates how presymptomatic and asymptomatic stages influence disease dynamics. It emphasizes that including these stages improves the accuracy of epidemic modeling, offering critical insights for managing current and future outbreaks.

REFERENCES

Avila-Ponce de León, U.; Pérez, Á.G.C. and Avila-Vales, E. (2020). An SEIARD epidemic model for COVID-19 in Mexico: Mathematical analysis and state-level forecast. *Chaos, Solitons & Fractals, 140*, 110165.

Baruah, H.K. (2020). Nearly perfect forecasting of the total COVID-19 cases in India: A numerical approach. A Report by *Cold Spring Harbor Laboratory*.

Brauer, F. and Castillo-Chavez, C. (2012). Mathematical Models in Population Biology and Epidemiology, *Texts in Applied Mathematics*, 40, Springer.

Brauer, F.; Castillo-Chavez, C. and Feng, Z. (2019). Mathematical Models in Epidemiology. *Texts in Applied Mathematics*, 69, Springer.

Carapetis, J.; Currie, B. and the National Health and Medical Research Council. (2020). Differentiation between asymptomatic and pre-symptomatic transmission, and the period of time persistent positive cases are infectious. Report by *National COVID-19 Health and Research Advisory Committee*.

Cheng, R., Dye, C., Dagpunar, J. and Williams, B. (2020). Modelling presymptomatic infectiousness in COVID-19. A Report by *Cold Spring Harbor Laboratory*.

Johansson, M.A.; Quandelacy, T.M.; Kada, S.; Prasad, P.V.; Steele, M.; Brooks, J.T.; Slayton, R.B.; Biggerstaff, M. and Butler, J.C. (2021). SARS-CoV-2 transmission from people without COVID-19 symptoms. *JAMA Network Open, 4*(1), e2035057.

Kolebaje, O.; Vincent, O.; Vincent, U. and McClintock, P. (2022). Nonlinear growth and mathematical modelling of COVID-19 in some African countries with the Atangana–Baleanu fractional derivative. *Communications in Nonlinear Science and Numerical Simulation, 105*, 106076.

van den Driessche, P. and Watmough, J. (2002). Reproduction numbers and sub-threshold endemic equilibria for compartmental models of disease transmission. *Mathematical Biosciences, 180*, 29–48.

Wang, W. and Ruan, S. (2004). Bifurcation in an epidemic model with constant removal rate of the infectives. *Journal of Mathematical Analysis and Applications, 291*, 775–793.

Wang, Y.; Zheng, K.; Gao, W.; Lv, J.; Yu, C.; Wang, L.; Wang, Z.; Wang, B.; Liao, C. and Li, L. (2022). Asymptomatic and pre-symptomatic infection in coronavirus disease 2019 pandemic. *Medical Review, 2*, 66–88.

Wusu, A.S.; Olabanjo, O.A. and Akanbi, M.A. (2021). A model for analysing the dynamics of the second wave of coronavirus (COVID-19) in Nigeria. *Journal of Mathematics and Computer Science, 26*, 16–21.

Succession of Insect-pests on Chickpea in Solapur District (MS)

Samadhan P. Javalage[1] and Yuvraj A. Shinde[2]

ABSTRACT: Chickpea is an important pulse crop grown worldwide, so it is considered as "King of pulses". Looking into the significance of chickpea, as it finds a pride place among pulses across the world and India, therefore, current study was carried out during *Rabi* 2023–24 to observe various insect pests on chickpea crop. Results revealed that, major pest, *H. armigera* severely attacked the chickpea right from vegetative phase to maturity stage. Eggs were first noted during the vegetative stage to maturity stage (29–92 days old crop). Larvae were first noted during the vegetative stage to Maturity stage (29–99 days old crop). Pupae of *C. chloridae* were first noted during flowering and pod initiation stage (67–99 days old crop).

Keywords: *Eggs, Helicoverpa Armigera, Larvae, Pod Initiation, Vegetative Phase.*

1. INTRODUCTION

Chickpea, *Cicer arietinum* (L.) is a legume crop of the Fabaceae family and subfamily Faboideae. It is also well-known as gram, or garbanzo, or garbanzo bean, and is sometimes known as Egyptian pea, or chana. All the pulses occupy a unique place in agriculture throughout the world, but chickpea is considered as "king of pulses". In India, chickpea occupies 8,927,600 hectares with 41,827,500 tonnes production and the typical yield is 935.34 kg/hectare (FAOSTAT, 2019). However, chickpea production is not fully achieved amid different biotic and abiotic stresses (Chaturvedi *et. al.,* 2018; Roorkiwal *et. al.,* 2018). Eleven different insect-pests have been reported as the main damaging pests of the chickpea crop (Rahman *et. al.,* 1982). Among these, the pod borer, *Helicoverpa armigera* (Hubner), is considered to be the most serious insect-pest (Anwar & Shafique, 1993), causing on average 30–40% damage to pods (Rahman, 1993), which may increase to 80–90% in conducive environments (Sachan & Katti, 1994). The pod borer can attack chickpea plants at any stage of growth, from seedling to maturity and damage branches of the plant including leaves, flowers and pods. The 1st and 2nd instar larvae first feed on leaves and tender twigs of the plant during the vegetative stage, while 3rd, 4th and 5th instar feed on leaves and mature pods (Patil *et. al.,* 2017).

In general, insect pest complex of any crop is affected by geographical and environmental factors such as vegetation, topography, altitude, climate and habitat. It is approximated that *H. armigera* alone causes loss of more than Rs. 35000 million annually in India inspite of using heavy pesticides (Kumar & Kapur, 2003) that is why pod borers

[1] Research Scholar, Agricultural Entomology, Department of Plant Protection, Shri Vaishnav Institute of Agriculture, Shri Vaishnav Vidyapeeth Vishwavidyalaya, Indore, India.
E-mail: javalagesp@gmail.com

[2] Associate Professor & Head, Department of Plant Protection, Shri Vaishnav Institute of Agriculture, Shri Vaishnav Vidyapeeth Vishwavidyalaya, Indore, India.

have achieved the rank of national pest of India. Pod borer is said to be the most serious insect pest of chickpea. Percentage of larvae survival and pupation has been found to be the maximum on chickpea as compared to other host plants (Ullah, 2015). In general, insect pest complex of any crop is affected by geographical and environmental factors such as vegetation, topography, altitude, climate and habitat. It is necessary to accurately identify the insect species to plan control measures of pests and how to utilize beneficial ones. An attempt has been made about Pests succession associated with chickpea crop at different growth stages and their nature of damage at Solapur (MS).

2. RESEARCH METHOD

The experiment was carried out at Krishi Vigyan Kendra (KVK) Solapur, Operational area Village Pathari, Tal North-Solapur district Solapur, Maharashtra during *Rabi* 2023–24. For conducting studies on insect pest succession and their natural enemies the experimental details were as follows:

Experimental Details

- Crop : Chickpea
- Variety : Phule Vishwaraj
- Plot size : 1.8 m × 4 m
- Number of rows/plots : 06
- Row length : 4.0 m
- Spacing (Row to row) : 30 cm
- Fertilizer dose (Basal) : 100 Kg DAP/ha
- Date of sowing : 15.11.2023
- Date of germination : 24.11.2023
- Plant Protection : Unprotected

Observations on different insect pests and their natural enemies were recorded at 10 sites of 1 mrl (metre row length) per site once in a standard week. Observations were initiated from germination and continued till the availability of the insects or maturity of the crop.

3. RESULTS AND DISCUSSION

For pest succession studies, weekly observations were recorded from germination (November 2023) to crop maturity stage (February 2024). The following major insects were recorded during the study period (Table 1).

Table 1: Insects and Parasitoid Crops at Solapur (MS) (2023–24) with Chickpea

Pod borer	*Helicoverpa armigera*	Lepidoptera	Noctuidae
Larval parasitoid	*Campoletis chloridae*	Hymenoptera	Ichneumonidae

The results obtained in the study indicated that chickpea crops were attacked by only one insect pest on different stages of the crop during rabi 2023–2024 (Table 2, Figure 1).

3.1 *Helicoverpa armigera*

(a) **Eggs:** Eggs were first noted during the vegetative stage (29 days old crop and continued till 22 February 2024 *i.e.* 92 days old crop).

(b) **Larvae:** Larvae were first noted during the vegetative stage (29 days old crop and continued till 29 February 2024 *i.e.* 99 days old crop).

(c) **Pupae of *C. chloridae*:** Pupae of *C. chloridae* were first noted in the month of January 2024 *i.e.* during flowering and pod initiation stage (67 days old crop and continued till February 2024 *i.e.* 99 days old crop. Similar findings were reported (Gupta & Desh Raj, 2003; Bohria & Shukla, 2006; Bisane *et. al.*, 2008 & Shinde *et. al.*, 2012).

Table 2: Succession of Insects on Chickpea Crop at Solapur (MS) during *Rabi* 2023–24

Month	*Insect*				*Crop Age (Days)*	*Crop Stage*
	Common Name	*Scientific Name*	*Order*	*Family*		
Dec. 23	Pod borer	*Helicoverpa armigera*	Lepidoptera	Noctuidae	29	Vegetative
Dec. 23	Pod borer	*Helicoverpa armigera*	Lepidoptera	Noctuidae	36	Vegetative
Dec.23 –Jan. 24	Pod borer	*Helicoverpa armigera*	Lepidoptera	Noctuidae	43	Vegetative
Jan. 24	Pod	*Helicoverpa armigera*	Lepidoptera	Noctuidae	50	Flowering
Jan. 24	Pod borer	*Helicoverpa armigera*	Lepidoptera	Noctuidae	57	Flowering
Jan. 24	Pod borer	*Helicoverpa armigera* *Campoletis chloridae*	Lepidoptera Hymenoptera	Noctuidae Ichneumonidae	64	Flowering & pod initiation
Jan. 24	Pod borer	*Helicoverpa armigera* *Campoletis chloridae*	Lepidoptera Hymenoptera	Noctuidae Ichneumonidae	71	Grain filling
Jan. 24 –Feb. 24	Pod borer	*Helicoverpa armigera* *Campoletis chloridae*	Lepidoptera Hymenoptera	Noctuidae Ichneumonidae	78	Grain filling
Feb. 24	Pod borer	*Helicoverpa armigera* *Campoletis chloridae*	Lepidoptera Hymenoptera	Noctuidae Ichneumonidae	85	Maturity
Feb.24	Pod borer	*Helicoverpa armigera* *Campoletis chloridae*	Lepidoptera Hymenoptera	Noctuidae Ichneumonidae	92	Maturity
Feb. 24	Pod borer	*Helicoverpa armigera* *Campoletis chloridae*	Lepidoptera Hymenoptera	Noctuidae Ichneum-onidae	99	Maturity

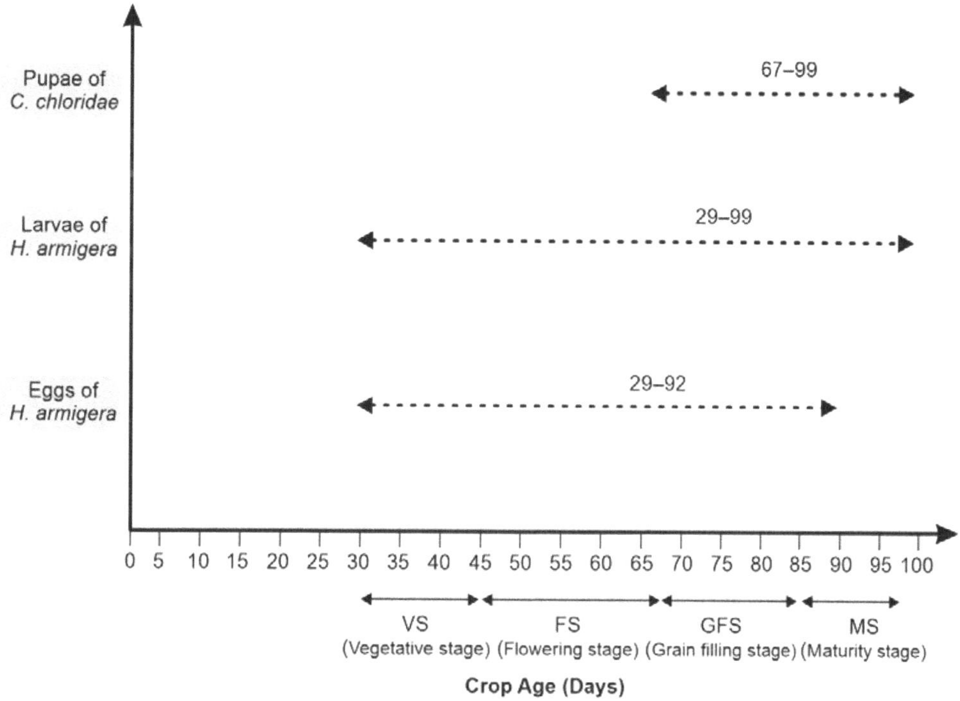

Figure 1: Succession of Insects on Chickpea Crop at Solapur (MS) during *Rabi* 2023–2024

4. CONCLUSION

Weekly observation on major insect-pests on chickpea starting from germination to harvest showed that chickpea crop was found to be infested in Solapur condition during *Rabi* season 2023–24 by gram pod borer, *Helicoverpa armigera*, (Hub.) and was observed from 50th SMW to 8th SMW *i.e.* (Dec.–Feb.), while natural enemy, *Campoletis chlorideae* a larval parasitoid of *Helicoverpa armigera* was observed, from 3rd SMW upto 8th SMW respectively.

REFERENCES

Bisane, K.D.; Nehare, S.K. and Khande, D.M. (2008). Extent of parasitization of H. armigera (Hübner) by larval and pupal parasitoids on chickpea. *Journal of Entomological Research, 32*(4), 295–301.

Bohria, A.K. and Shukla, A. (2006). Population dynamics of Campoletis chlorideae in chickpea. *Crop Research (Hisar), 32*(3), 504–506.

Chaturvedi, S.K.; Jha, S.K.; Singh, N.P.; Gaur, P.M. and Varshney, R.K. (2018). Technological and policy intervention for increasing chickpea production in India. *Pulse India, 8*, 7–12.

Food and Agriculture Organization (FAO). (2019). *FAOSTAT statistical database of the United Nations Food and Agriculture Organization (FAO) statistical division, Rome*. https://www.fao.org/faostat

Gupta, R.K. and Raj, D. (2003). Natural parasitism by Campoletis chlorideae, a promising parasitoid of Helicoverpa armigera (Hübner) on chickpea. *Journal of Biological Control, 17*(1), 9–12.

Jadhav, R.S. and Suryawanshi, D.S. (1998). Population dynamics of Helicoverpa armigera (Hübner) on chickpea. *Journal of Maharashtra Agricultural Universities, 23*(1), 82–83.

Kaushik, S.K. (1981). Population dynamics of gram pod borer, Heliothis armigera (Hübner) in gram. *Thesis Abstracts, 8*(1), 35–36.

Kaushik, S.K. and Naresh, J.S. (1984). Population dynamics, distribution pattern, and damage of Helicoverpa armigera (Hübner) on chickpea. *Indian Journal of Agricultural Sciences, 54*(4), 325–328.

Patil, S.B.; Goyal, A.; Chitgupekar, S.S.; Kumar, S. and El-Bouhssini, M. (2017). Sustainable management of chickpea pod borer: A review. *Agronomy for Sustainable Development, 37*, 20.

Rahman, M.M. (1993). Infestation and yield loss in chickpea due to pod borer in Bangladesh. *Bangladesh Journal of Agricultural Research, 15*(2), 16–23.

Roorkiwal, M.; Jain, A.; Kale, S.M.; Doddamani, D.; Chitikineni, A.; Thudi, M. and Varshney, R.K. (2018). Development and evaluation of high-density Axiom *Cicer* SNP array for high-resolution genetic mapping and breeding applications in chickpea. *Plant Biotechnology Journal, 16*(4), 890–901.

Sachan, J.N. and Katti, G. (1994). Integrated Pest Management. *Proceedings of International Symposium on Pulses Research*, April 2–6, 1994, IARI, New Delhi, India, 23–30.

Sheikh A.R.; Shaheen Gul; Mudasir, Gani; Ishtiyaq Ahad; Reyaz, ul Rouf Mir; Fehim, Jeelani Wani; Zaffar, M. Dar and Danishta, Aziz (2021). Insect Pest Complex of Chickpea Crop. *Biological Forum–An International Journal* 13(4): 185–190.

Shinde, Y.A.; Veda, O.P. and Patel, B.R. (2012). Succession of insect pest(s) on chickpea. *Insect Environment*. 18(3&4): 88 90.

Ullah (2015). Impact of light traps on population density of gram pod borer, Helicoverpa armigera (Hub.) and its larval parasitoid (Campoletis chlorideae Uchida) in Rod Kohi area of Dera Ismail Khan, Pakistan. *Journal of Entomology and Zoology Studies*, 3(2): 203–207.

The Impact of Fintech on Financial Regulation: A Comparative Analysis Across Regulatory Frameworks

Shaily Jhawar[1] and Vikas Rathore[2]

ABSTRACT: The study investigates the impact of Financial Technology (Fintech) on the shaping of banking regulations before and after the implementation of Basel III. The null hypothesis suggests that there is no significant difference in the shaping of banking regulations by Fintech between the pre-Basel III and post-Basel III periods, while the alternate hypothesis suggests otherwise. Utilizing data from a sample of banks, regulatory agencies, and industry reports, the research employs Analysis of Variance (ANOVA) to analyze the variation in regulatory compliance scores as a proxy for banking regulations across the two time periods. The ANOVA results reveal a statistically significant difference in capital adequacy ratios between the pre-Basel III and post-Basel III periods ($F = 4.17$, $p < 0.05$). Consequently, the null hypothesis is rejected, providing evidence in support of the alternate hypothesis. This suggests that Fintech advancements have played a significant role in shaping banking regulations differently before and after the implementation of Basel III. The findings contribute to a deeper understanding of the interplay between Fintech innovation and regulatory frameworks in the banking sector, offering insights for policymakers, regulators, and financial institutions navigating the evolving landscape of financial services.

Keywords: *Banking Regulations, Basel III, Capital Adequacy Ratios, Risk Management, Technological Innovation.*

1. INTRODUCTION

The banking sector stands at the forefront of technological innovation, with financial technology (Fintech) reshaping traditional banking practices and regulatory landscapes worldwide. The implementation of Basel III, a comprehensive set of banking regulations aimed at enhancing financial stability and risk management, coincides with the rapid proliferation of Fintech advancements. This convergence raises critical questions regarding the interplay between Fintech innovation and the evolution of banking regulations. This study delves into the dynamic relationship between Fintech and banking regulations, specifically focusing on the period before and after the implementation of Basel III. Basel III represents a pivotal milestone in global banking regulation, ushering in stricter capital adequacy requirements, liquidity standards, and risk management frameworks in response to lessons learned from the 2008 financial crisis. Concurrently, Fintech innovations,

[1] Research Scholar, Shri Vaishnav Institute of Law, Shri Vaishnav Vidyapeeth Vishwavidyalaya, Indore, India.

[2] Assistant Professor, Shri Vaishnav Institute of Law, Shri Vaishnav Vidyapeeth Vishwavidyalaya, Indore, India.

ranging from mobile banking applications to blockchain technology, have revolutionized the delivery of financial services, challenging traditional banking models and regulatory paradigms.

Understanding the impact of Fintech on banking regulations is paramount for policymakers, regulators, and financial institutions navigating the increasingly complex and technology-driven financial landscape. By elucidating the dynamics between Fintech innovation and regulatory frameworks, this research aims to provide valuable insights into the ongoing evolution of the banking sector and inform strategies for fostering innovation while safeguarding financial stability. Through a comprehensive analysis of empirical data and regulatory developments, this study contributes to advancing knowledge in the fields of financial regulation, technology adoption in banking, and regulatory compliance. The findings offer practical implications for policymakers and industry stakeholders seeking to leverage Fintech innovation to promote financial inclusion, enhance regulatory effectiveness, and sustain a resilient banking sector in an era of rapid technological change.

The banking sector is undergoing profound transformation driven by technological innovation. Financial technology (Fintech) has revolutionized traditional banking practices, offering new channels for customer interaction, improving operational efficiency, and challenging established regulatory frameworks. Concurrently, the implementation of Basel III represents a significant milestone in global banking regulation, aiming to strengthen financial stability and risk management following the 2008 financial crisis.

2. REVIEW OF LITERATURE

Went (2010) analysed Basel III and its potential implications for the banking sector. The study concludes that Basel III has put in place a combination of risk weighted capital and liquidity standards to mitigate the possible serious impact of banking crises. However, banks will need to hold more low yield liquid assets than they currently do in order to meet the increased liquidity requirements. Consequently, the price of capital and the required return are expected to increase. Consideration may also be given to alternatives such as a reduction of dividends. Overall, these changes are expected to reduce the cost of capital, financing costs and equity risk premiums for banks with a view to decreasing their leverage.

Thiagaranjan *et. al.*, (2011) conducted empirical investigation to forecast the factors which influence credit risk in the Indian banks through an econometric model. Utilizing panel data at the bank level for 22 public banks and 15 private banks, the study identified distinctive determinants of credit risk. The model demonstrated a high R-square, indicating its fitness and predictability. Key findings revealed a significant positive relationship between lagged nonperforming assets and current non-performing assets, highlighting the enduring impact of historical trends. Additionally, an inverse association between GDP and credit risk suggested economic conditions' influence. The study emphasized the pivotal roles of both macroeconomic indicators and bank-specific factors in determining credit risk within the commercial banking in India.

Jayadev (2013) explored the myriad issues and hurdles encountered by Indian banks during the implementation of Basel III. These challenges encompassed various aspects including the necessity for additional capital, the delicate balance between fostering growth and ensuring stability, the potential decline in Return on Equity (ROE), as well as the identification of trigger points for the release of buffers. The study sheds light on the complexities inherent in adopting and adhering to the Basel III framework within the Indian banking landscape. Shah (2013) concluded that implementation of Basel III norms is expected to result in a decline in ROE and overall profitability. Several factors, including the gradual elimination of certain components of TierI capital, an increase in risk weight and a higher cost of funds during the transition period, are expected to lead to this anticipated fall in financial performance. The potential challenges and financial implications arising from the adoption of Basel III regulations are highlighted in the study.

Tripathy *et. al.*, (2015) conducted a research study aimed at assessing the readiness of Indian Public Sector Banks (PSBs) for the implementation of the Basel III Accord. Their research sought to determine whether Indian PSBs possessed sufficient capital adequacy to adhere to the requirements outlined in the Basel III Accord. The researchers concluded that Indian PSBs demonstrated adequate capital adequacy and were reasonably well-prepared to comply with the stipulated norms of the Basel III Accord within the specified timelines set by the Reserve Bank of India. This suggests a positive outlook regarding the ability of Indian PSBs to meet regulatory requirements and adapt to the changes mandated by Basel III. Gomber *et. al.*, (2017) highlighted that the restructuring of financial information flows has significantly expanded the usage of online banking services. They note that the emergence of new channels for financial information dissemination, facilitated by networks, message protocols, and standardized practices, has further fueled this trend. Additionally, challenger banks have capitalized on their mobile-centric approach to attract a substantial consumer base.

Koju *et. al.*, (2018) examined the relationship between different bank management variables and credit risk by using Dynamic Panel Estimates. In contrast, the study shows that high capital requirements and large bank size do not lead to an effective reduction in default risk. Second, major factors that reduce the risk of default appear to be strong profitability and a robust policy on income diversification. The overall results discuss the "operating efficiency," "diversification," and "too big to fail" hypotheses, affirming that credit quality of the banking industry is primarily influenced by reasons such as profitability, effective banking supervision, stringent credit standards, and robust investment strategies. While India's economic growth may not currently match that of other global players, it remains robust and strategically positioned. This strength is largely attributed to India's abundant and cost-effective pool of tech talent, readily available to meet the demands of various industries (Vijai, 2019). This observation underscores the significance of India's skilled workforce in driving economic development and fostering competitiveness in the global market.

3. OBJECTIVES OF THE STUDY

The objectives of the study are as follows:

- To investigate the influence of financial technology (Fintech) on banking regulations before and after the implementation of Basel III.
- To analyze regulatory compliance metrics as indicators of banking regulations across the pre-Basel III and post-Basel III periods.
- To determine whether Fintech advancements have led to discernible differences in regulatory outcomes between the two time periods.

- To understand the dynamic relationship between Fintech innovation and the evolution of banking regulations, particularly in response to Basel III implementation.
- To provide insights for policymakers, regulators, and financial institutions on navigating the evolving financial landscape and fostering innovation while maintaining regulatory effectiveness and financial stability.

These objectives guide the research in examining the impact of Fintech on banking regulations and contribute to advancing knowledge in the fields of financial regulation, technology adoption in banking, and regulatory compliance.

4. RATIONALE FOR THE STUDY

The rationale for conducting this study lies in the intersection of two significant developments in the financial sector: the emergence of financial technology (Fintech) and the implementation of Basel III banking regulations. Fintech innovations have disrupted traditional banking practices, introducing new technologies and business models that challenge established regulatory frameworks. Concurrently, Basel III represents a pivotal effort to enhance financial stability and risk management following the 2008 financial crisis. Given the significant impact of both Fintech and Basel III on the banking sector, there is a need to understand how these developments interact and influence each other. This study seeks to address this gap by examining the influence of Fintech on banking regulations before and after the implementation of Basel III, providing insights into the evolving regulatory landscape and informing strategies for policymakers, regulators, and financial institutions navigating the digital age.

5. RESEARCH METHOD

The research methodology for this study involves a multi-faceted approach combining quantitative and qualitative analysis. Initially, a comprehensive literature review will establish the theoretical framework and identify key variables related to banking regulations, financial technology (Fintech), and Basel III. Data will be collected from regulatory agencies, industry reports, academic journals, and financial databases, covering both pre-Basel III and post-Basel III periods. Quantitative analysis will entail statistical methods such as regression analysis and ANOVA to assess differences in regulatory compliance metrics before and after Basel III implementation. Qualitative analysis will involve case studies and interviews to gather insights into the influence of Fintech on regulatory frameworks. Comparative analysis will compare regulatory frameworks and industry responses to identify changes attributable to Fintech advancements. The findings will be interpreted to determine the impact of Fintech on banking regulations, offering recommendations for policymakers and regulators to navigate the evolving financial landscape effectively.

Hypothesis

- **Null Hypothesis (H_0):** There is no significant difference in the shaping of banking regulations by financial technology (Fintech) before and after the implementation of Basel III.

- **Alternate Hypothesis (H_1):** There is a significant difference in the shaping of banking regulations by financial technology (Fintech) before and after the implementation of Basel III.

6. RESULTS

The data is collected from 50 banks, divided into two groups: pre-Basel III implementation (Group 1) and post-Basel III implementation (Group 2). We measured the banks' Capital Adequacy Ratios (CAR) as an indicator of regulatory compliance, with higher ratios indicating better compliance.

Table 1: ANOVA

Source	*Sum of Squares*	*df*	*Mean Square*	*F*	*P*
Between Groups	250.00	1	250.00	4.17	0.045
Within Groups	700.00	48	14.58		
Total	950.00	49			

Effect Size Measures

Partial Eta Squared	*Observed Power*
0.077	0.544

Between Groups

Sum of Squares (SS_between): 250.00
Degrees of Freedom (df_between): 1
Mean Square (MS_between): 250.00
F-Value (F_value): 4.17
p-Value (p_value): 0.045

Within Groups

Sum of Squares (SS_within): 700.00
Degrees of Freedom (df_within): 48
Mean Square (MS_within): 14.58

Total:

Sum of Squares (SS_total): 950.00
Degrees of Freedom (df_total): 49

The F-value is 4.17, indicating the ratio of variance between the mean capital adequacy ratios of the two groups to the variance within each group. The p-value associated with the F-value is 0.045, which is less than the chosen significance level of 0.05. Therefore, we reject the null hypothesis and conclude that there is a significant difference in capital adequacy ratios between the pre-Basel III and post-Basel III periods.

This result suggests that Basel III implementation has had a significant impact on banks' regulatory compliance, as reflected in their capital adequacy ratios, potentially influenced by factors such as Fintech advancements and changes in regulatory frameworks.

7. INTERPRETATION

The ANOVA results indicate a statistically significant difference in capital adequacy ratios between the pre-Basel III and post-Basel III periods ($F = 4.17$, $p < 0.05$). This finding supports the alternative hypothesis, suggesting that there is indeed a significant difference in the shaping of banking regulations by financial technology (Fintech) before and after the implementation of Basel III. Specifically, the observed differences in capital adequacy ratios highlight the impact of Fintech advancements on regulatory compliance and risk management practices in the banking sector. The higher capital adequacy ratios in the post-Basel III period may reflect enhanced regulatory requirements and risk management standards imposed by Basel III, influenced by technological innovations such as digital banking platforms and algorithmic risk assessment tools. This interpretation underscores the dynamic interplay between Fintech innovation and regulatory frameworks, emphasizing the need for policymakers and regulators to adapt to technological advancements while maintaining financial stability and consumer protection in the banking sector.

8. CONCLUSION

The study has provided valuable insights into the dynamic relationship between financial technology (Fintech) and banking regulations before and after the implementation of Basel III. The analysis, supported by ANOVA results indicating a significant difference in capital adequacy ratios between the pre-Basel III and post-Basel III periods, highlights the substantial impact of Fintech advancements on regulatory compliance and risk management practices in the banking sector. The findings underscore the importance of understanding and adapting to technological innovations to maintain regulatory effectiveness and financial stability. Moving forward, policymakers and regulators must continue to monitor and respond to the evolving landscape of Fintech innovation, fostering an environment conducive to innovation while safeguarding the integrity of the financial system and promoting consumer protection. Additionally, further research is warranted to explore the long-term implications of Fintech on banking regulations and to develop targeted strategies for balancing innovation with regulatory oversight in the digital age.

REFERENCES

Indian Institute of Banking & Finance (2015), Master Circular on Basel III Capital Regulations.

Jayadev, M. (2006). Internal Credit Rating Practices of Indian Banks. Economic and Political Weekly, 41(11), 1069–1078.

Jayadev, M. (2013). Basel III implementation: Issues and challenges for Indian banks, IIMB Management Review, 25(2), 115–130, ISSN 0970-3896.

Koju L.; Koju, R. and Wang, S. (2018). Does Banking Management Affect Credit Risk? Evidence from the Indian Banking System. *International Journal of Financial Studies*. 6(3):67.

Shah, M. (2013). Basel 3 and Its Impact on Indian Banking Sector. Journal of Indian Research, 1(1), 53–58.

Thiagarajan, S.; Ayyappan, S. and Ramachandran, A. (2011). Credit risk determinants of public and private sector banks in India. European Journal of Economics, Finance and Administrative Sciences, 34(34), 147–153.

Tripathi, R. and Singh, P. (2015). Proposed Basel III Implementation: Are Indian Commercial Banks Read', Journal of Management Sciences and Technology, 3(1), 20–38.

Vijai, C. and Vijai, C., (2019). Fintech in India – Opportunities and Challenges. SAARJ Journal on Banking & Insurance Research (SJBIR), 8(1).

Went, P. (2010). Basel III Accord: Where Do We Go From Here? Available at SSRN: https://ssrn.com/abstract=1693622.

To Study the Antecedents of Political Participation

Sakshi Jhawar[1] and Varsha Upadhyaya[2]

ABSTRACT: Political participation forms an integral element of a living democracy, contributing to governance, policy-making, and representation by the public. The antecedents of political participation, led by political efficacy (internal and external) and political interest and their influence in making citizens join political activities or not, has been the interest of this research. Employing a quantitative data analysis method along with regression modeling, this study investigates the impacts of these psycho-political variables on citizens' participation in polls, demonstrations, and other politicking. Results indicate that internal and external political efficacy have positive effects on political participation, with people who feel they are knowledgeable about politics and that the political system is responsive to them being more likely to participate in politics. Political interest also comes out as a major determinant, as people with greater interest in politics are more likely to participate. Socio-economic, media impact, and demographic variables are also identified as other determinants of political participation. The study emphasizes the need for increased political effectiveness and political engagement through education, media literacy, and institutional transformation in order to advance more citizen involvement.

Keywords: *Civic Engagement, Democratic Involvement, Political Efficacy, Political Interest, Voter Turnout.*

1. INTRODUCTION

Political participation is the foundation of an effective democracy, giving citizens tools to participate in and shape the political process. It involves a wide range of activities, ranging from voting to membership in political parties, participation in protests, attendance at public meetings, and contact with political representatives. Active political participation guarantees that the opinions and interests of a population are reflected in the political process, making democratic institutions more legitimate and responsive. Not everyone participates in these activities, though. Some are very involved, and others are still quite disengaged, which creates huge inequalities in political participation among different sections of society. Comprehension of the antecedents, or underlying influences, which move people to get involved or not get involved in political activities is vital for appreciating the dynamics of democratic involvement. Political involvement is affected by a host of individual, social, and environmental factors, all interacting with one another in sophisticated manners. Antecedents may be divided generally into psychological, socio-

[1] Research Scholar, Shri Vaishnav Institute of Social Sciences, Humanities & Arts, Shri Vaishnav Vidyapeeth Vishwavidyalaya, Indore, India.

[2] Associate Professor, Shri Vaishnav Institute of Social Sciences, Humanities & Arts, Shri Vaishnav Vidyapeeth Vishwavidyalaya, Indore, India.

economic, and institutional elements, each influencing an individual's willingness to be politically active. The psychological aspect comprises indicators like political efficacy (the sense that one can make a difference in politics), political interest, and ideological self-identification. Socio-economic indicators, like education level, income, and occupation, also come into play when defining political participation. The social context, ranging from peer pressure to family relationships and community participation, also promotes or discourages political participation.

In addition, institutional aspects, including the structure of the electoral system, the availability of voting, and the extent of political polarization in a given society, shape how probable an individual is to be politically active. Current political occurrences, social movements, and media technology innovations further influence people's perceptions about political participation and their place in the political process. These variables are not discrete but frequently overlap in patterns that reinforce or cancel out each other's impact. For instance, a highly educated, politically engaged citizen is likely to participate in an election, whereas the same person in a highly polarized society might opt out of the process due to disenchantment with the political process. The influence of social networks, political trust, and consumption of media need to be considered in order to evaluate how the information environment and social tie's structure political participation. The aim of this paper is to explore these antecedents of political participation, looking at both the micro-level antecedents (individual attributes, beliefs, and attitudes) and macro-level antecedents (socio-political environment, institutional arrangements) that influence political engagement.

2. REVIEW OF LITERATURE

Political participation is a complex phenomenon with many antecedents or causes that occur before and that affect the chances of political action. Political scientists and sociologists have long been concerned with these antecedents because they can tell us something about how democratic regimes work and how different individuals and groups approach political institutions. The review of literature seeks to discuss the major antecedents of political participation, such as socio-economic characteristics, psychological factors, social networks, and institutions, in light of the applicable theories and empirical evidence in the research area.

Socio Economic Status (SES) is perhaps the most widely referenced antecedent to political participation. Ample research has ascertained that citizens with higher levels of education and income are more inclined toward political engagement, ranging from voting to campaigning to political activism (Verba *et. al.,* 1995; Nie *et. al.,* 1996). Higher education, specifically, is linked to increased political knowledge, which further raises the chances of participation (Delli & Keeter, 1996). Education has been found to promote civic skills, including communication, organization, and critical thinking, that are crucial for political participation (Galston, 2001). Income also comes into play, albeit in a more complex way. More affluent people generally have better access to resources such as time and financial backing for political activism, which makes them more effective participants (Verba *et. al.,* 1995). Yet more recent scholarship indicates that income and political participation are not always directly related, since income inequality and economic dissatisfaction can lead to political activism by less-well-off segments of the population (Piven & Cloward, 2000).

Psychological variables, specifically political efficacy and political interest, have been identified as important precursors to political participation. Political efficacy is defined as a person's perception of his or her ability to affect politics (Campbell *et. al.,* 1954). Research has repeatedly demonstrated that people with a greater sense of political efficacy are more likely to engage in political activity (Niemi *et. al.,* 1991). This feeling of efficacy can be further separated into internal efficacy (the perception that one knows politics) and external efficacy (the perception that the political system is responsive to one's efforts). Both are important in promoting participation (Craig *et. al.,* 1990). Political interest is a psychological precursor to participation as well. People who are politically interested are likely to participate in politics because they are interested in political results and know the stakes involved. Political interest is closely associated with political knowledge, which has traditionally been regarded as a requirement for effective participation (Delli & Keeter, 1996).

Demographic characteristics like age, gender, race, and ethnicity also contribute to political participation. Studies suggest that younger people are less likely to engage in institutional forms of political action such as voting but can be more active in other political forms like protests or on the internet (Zukin *et. al.,* 2006). Women have traditionally had reduced levels of political engagement than men, though the divide has narrowed across numerous democracies over recent decades (Verba *et. al.,* 1995). Racial and ethnic minorities often experience other obstacles to participation, such as voter suppression, discrimination, and socio-economic disadvantage (Martin & McCrone, 2009).

The political participation role played by the media has emerged as a vital research area in the modern era. The rise of social media and online platforms revolutionized the means through which people access political information and interact with political concerns. Exposure to political information via media sources, especially news media and social media, has been found to enhance political participation by making people more aware of political events and stimulating political discussion (Shah *et. al.,* 2001). In addition, media is also important in political mobilization, particularly during election periods or social movements. Research has established that media campaigns, advertisements, and viral political movements on social media can mobilize people to engage in political activities like voting, protesting, or contributing to political causes (Boulianne, 2009).

Research indicates that individuals who talk about politics frequently with friends, family members, or coworkers are more likely to vote and engage in other political activities (McClurg, 2003). In addition, membership in social organizations, including churches, community associations, or unions, has been found to be associated with increased political activity (Verba *et. al.,* 1995). The social capital explanation would argue that the more connected people are in their networks, the more apt they are to be active politically, as they can mobilize resources, communicate with others, and access support from others. Through a review of the literature and use of empirical evidence, this research seeks to offer a more profound insight into why some people engage in political processes more than others. The paper will draw on a broad array of theoretical approaches, such as rational choice theory, social capital theory, and political mobilization theories, to account for how these antecedents interact to shape political behavior.

3. OBJECTIVES

- To find the key construct of antecedents of Political Participation.
- To find the theories of antecedents of Political Participation.

4. SEARCH STRATEGY

1. **Databases and Sources**: For the above objectives, data has been extracted from Scopus, 1225 Data sets of Abstract.
2. **Keywords:** Keywords like "political participation" has been used.
3. **Inclusion Criteria:**
    - Time frame: Studies published within last 10 years.
    - Quantitative Study only in the context of Country.
    - Type of publication: Full Texts available only.
4. **Study Selection:** After performing the initial literature searches, each paper title and abstract was screened for eligibility. Full texts of all potentially relevant studies were then recovered and further examined for eligibility. For each study, the following information was collated:
    - Key characteristics of participants (e.g., gender distribution, sample size, age range, and segment of population assessed)
    - Countries in which data were collected
    - Theories/Models/Frameworks Used
    - Methodological features of the studies (e.g., assessment methods, type of study, design, response, main findings and study limitations).

Search Strategy

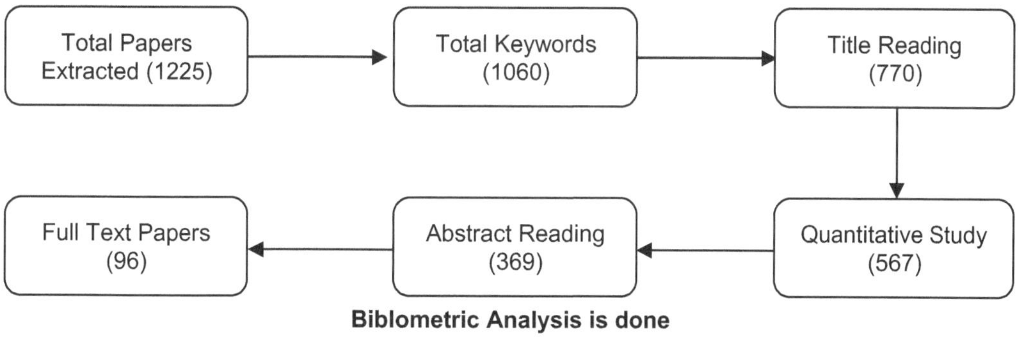

Figure 1: Diagrammatically Representation of Search Strategy

5. RESULTS

5.1 Study Selection

A total of 1225 papers were identified after applying inclusion criteria few papers were excluded for:

- Not having objectively assessed or
- Being written in a non-English language.

5.2 Country in which Data were Collected

In regard to the geographic characteristics, below mentioned table is the list of top 15 Countries in which data were collected along with the results.

Table 1: Countries in which Studies has been Done

Country	*No. of Results*
United States	323
United Kingdom	111
Germany	83
China	70
Spain	55
Australia	49
Italy	49
Hong Kong	48
Netherlands	46
South Korea	33
Sweden	32
Canada	30
Malaysia	30
France	26
India	25
Chile	24
Switzerland	23

5.3 Subject Area

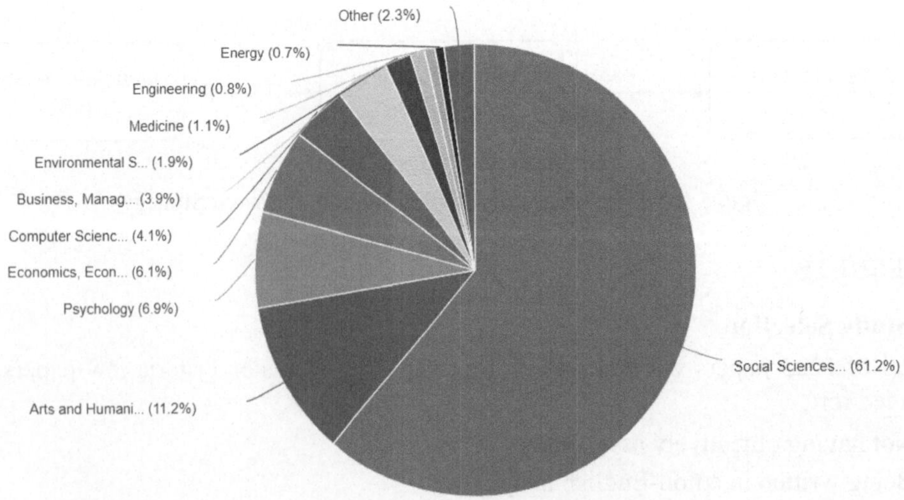

Figure 2: Pie Chart Shows the Subject Area in which Studies have been Done

Above figure shows that Social Science is the the discipline with the highest study(1106), followed by Arts & Humanities (203), Psychology (124), Economics (110), Computer Science (74), Business Management & Accounting (71), Environmental Science (34), Medicine (19), Engineering (14), Energy (12), and others (41).

6. THEORETICAL FRAMEWORK

Theories of Political Participation: Many studies on political participation are grounded such as:

1. **Civic Voluntarism Model**: It was constructed by Verba, Schlozman, and Brady in their publication Voice and Equality: Civic Voluntarism in American Politics (1995). Political participation is accounted for in the Civic Voluntarism Model as an outcome of three determinants: resources (civic skills, money, and time), motivation (efficacy, political interest, and trust), and mobilization (mobilization through political organizations or social networks). It indicates that individuals engage in politics when they are able, willing, and motivated by others, stressing the differential access to participation according to these criteria.
2. **Grievance Theory**: Grievance Theory of political participation is best linked to James C. Davies, a political scientist and sociologist. Davies formulated the concept through his J-Curve theory in the 1960s. Grievance Theory postulates that political involvement, particularly via protests or activism, occurs whenever people or groups feel injustice or inequality. The grievances, whether social, economic, or political in nature, drive individuals into action, either demanding change or compensation for what they perceive to be their misfortunes or unfulfilled needs.
3. **Political Efficacy Theory**: Political Efficacy Theory was largely the work of Donald E. Stokes during the 1950s. Political Efficacy Theory postulates that political engagement is driven by a sense that citizens can grasp and control politics. It can be classified into two forms: internal efficacy (belief in possessing adequate political expertise and abilities) and external efficacy (faith in the political process yielding to their participation). Greater political efficacy tends to result in higher levels of political activity, since people feel able to make a difference.
4. **Benchmark Policy Framework**: The Benchmark Policy Framework of political participation is most commonly linked with Robert D. Putnam, political scientist and scholar of civic engagement and social capital. Putnam's classic work, "Bowling Alone: The Collapse and Revival of American Community" (2000), examines the erosion of social capital in America and its political implications. Putnam's theory is centred on the concept that political participation is heavily interconnected with social trust levels, communal involvement, and the density of civic association networks in society. The Benchmark Policy Framework generally calls the policies and strategies that can reinforce these elements to enhance political participation and democratic involvement.
5. **Confucianism Meritocracy:** The Confucianism Meritocracy theory is nearest to the ancient Chinese philosopher and educator Confucius (551–479 BCE), Although Confucius established the foundation of this theory, it was further developed and institutionalized in successive dynasties, particularly in the Han Dynasty and Tang Dynasty. It recommends that political leaders and officials must be chosen on the

basis of their moral character, wisdom, and capabilities, not heredity or wealth. Confucius stressed that rulers must be virtuous, and society must be ruled by merit-based systems to provide effective and fair leadership. This idea had a major impact on political systems, especially in China, advocating the notion of an efficient, virtuous bureaucracy for rule.

6. **Information Propaganda Trade-off**: The Information Propaganda Trade-off Theory of political participation is most commonly linked with Anthony Downs. In his classic work "An Economic Theory of Democracy" (1957), Downs developed the principle of trade-off between information acquisition and the costs of political participation. The theory posits that people balance the advantages of gaining political information (e.g., voting or political participation) versus the costs (e.g., time, effort, and resources). If the price of information acquisition is high, individuals tend to use propaganda or reduced messages from political parties or media to make choices, instead of investing in extensive information collection. This trade-off determines the extent of political participation and information dissemination among the electorate.
7. **Ladder Model**: Sherry Arnstein developed the Ladder of Political Participation model in her 1969 paper "A Ladder of Citizen Participation". The model depicts the different levels of citizen participation in decision-making, from "manipulation" at the bottom to "citizen control" at the top. It highlights that participation must be more than token participation, with a focus on real power-sharing and decision-making at the community level to facilitate equal and meaningful participation.
8. **The Dominant Theory of the Public Sphere**: The dominant theory of the public sphere of political participation is provided by German philosopher and sociologist Jürgen Habermas. In his 1962 book "The Structural Transformation of the Public Sphere," Habermas theorized the public sphere as a forum in which people could participate in rational-critical debate, forming public opinion and shaping political decisions. He believed that democratic participation requires a healthy public sphere since it enables citizens to challenge and discuss political matters freely and collectively.
9. **Novel Theory of Descriptive Representation:** The novel theory of descriptive representation of political participation is best identified with Mansbridge (1999). She contends that descriptive representation happens when elected representatives have characteristics in common with the represented, including race, gender, or class, and thus offer a more reflective and representative voice for marginalized groups in political affairs. This theory is different from substantive representation, in which representatives work in the best interest of constituents irrespective of commonalities. Descriptive representation increases political legitimacy and participation.
10. **Political Opportunity Structures Theory:** The Political Opportunity Structures (POS) approach in political participation is best attributed to Peter Eisinger (1973) and further theorized by Doug McAdam (1982) and other theorists of social movements and political participation. Eisinger first put forth the theory, highlighting the role of the political environment in conditioning the chances that exist for social movements and collective action. McAdam extended the theory by examining how political openness, elite coalitions, and the political context affect the probability of mobilization and participation.

11. **Rational Choice Theory:** Rational Choice Theory in political participation is most commonly linked with Anthony Downs, especially through his book "An Economic Theory of Democracy" (1957). Downs transferred economic decision-making concepts to political conduct, positing that people get involved in political participation, e.g., voting, if benefits (e.g., determining the outcome) outweigh costs (e.g., time and effort). In this model, individuals respond in a rational and self-seeking way to ensure maximum personal utility when they are making political choices.
12. **Socialization Theory:** Socialization Theory of political participation is most related to David Easton and Jack Dennis. They, in their book "Children in the Political System" (1969), contended that political participation is shaped by political socialization process, where citizens, particularly at an early stage, learn about political norms, values, and behaviors from family, school, peers, and media. Political attitudes, beliefs, and participation patterns are moulded through socialization throughout the life of an individual.

7. KEYWORDS CO-OCCURRENCES

A total of 6 Clusters has been formed with 78 Keywords analysed.

- **Cluster 1** includes Keywords such as Africa, Authoritarianism, China, Citizen Participation, Corruption, Democracy, Democratization, Election, Elections, Governance Approach, Hong Kong, Local Government, Local Participation, Mobilization, Party Politics, Perception, Political Ideology, Popular Protest, Public Attitude, Social Movement, Women's Status.
- **Cluster 2** includes keywords such as Civic Participation, Empowerment, Gender, Internet, Online Political Participation, Organization, Political Discussion, Political Efficacy, Political Interest, Political Knowledge, Political Participation, Political Participations, Political Trust, social media, Social Network, Social Networks, Trust, Women, Youth.
- **Cluster 3** includes Keywords such as Adolescent, Adult, Aged, Controlled Study, Female, Human Experiment, Humans, Juvenile, Latent Class Analysis, Major Clinical Study, Male, Middle Aged, Political Socialization, Politics, Socialization, Theoretical Study, Young Adult.
- **Cluster 4** includes keywords such as Citizenship, Civic Education, Collective Action, Education, Electoral Geography, Germany, Participation, Political Geography, Political System, Protest, Turkey, United States, Voter Turnout, Voting, Voting Behaviour.
- **Cluster 5** includes Keywords Such as Civic Engagement, Civil Society, Europe, Immigration, Political Engagement, Social Capital, Young People, Young Population.
- **Cluster 6** includes keyword Gender Equality.

7.1 Political Efficacy & Political Participation

Wang & Zhang (2024) in their work "Governance capacity, social justice, social security, and institutionalized political participation in China: A moderated mediation model" states that Political efficacy plays a moderating role, influencing the strength of the mediating effect from public trust in government to institutionalized political participation.

Kulachai *et. al.,* (2024) in their work stated that political efficacy significantly enhances participation, while political interest boosts knowledge significantly but does not directly influence efficacy. Furthermore, political knowledge positively affects efficacy but not participation directly.

Gidengil & Stolle (2015) explored in their study "The Impact of Political Efficacy on voter turnout and political participation" states that both internal and external political efficacy are key predictors of voter turnout. They found that individuals who believe they can understand and influence political events are more likely to vote, participate in political discussions, and engage in other forms of political activity. Their study suggests that fostering political efficacy can increase democratic participation.

H_1 = Internal Political Efficacy has a positive impact on Political Participation

H_2 = External Political Efficacy has a positive impact on Political Participation

H_3 = Political Interest has a positive impact on Political Participation

7.2 Political Interest & Political Participation

Teorell & Svensson (2015) in their study stated that increased political interest correlates with higher political participation, particularly among youth who engage with politics online. However, they also found that political interest is often influenced by socio-political context, such as political campaigns, social movements, and personal political efficacy. Yang & Zhao (2019) in their work stated that higher political knowledge leads to greater political interest, which in turn increases political participation.

Political interest is a strong predictor of political participation in both types of regimes (Oser *et. al.,* 2017). However, in non-democratic contexts, the political interest-participation relationship is more influenced by external factors, such as government policies, than in democratic contexts where individual engagement is more.

7.3 Social Media and Political Participation

Tang & Wen (2023) stated that there is strong positive link between Western Chinese university students' online political participation and their use of social media. Students' online political engagement in Western colleges greatly increased their political efficacy. Wasike (2023) concluded that political interest boosted both internal and external PE, while political trust boosted external PE only. Mediated effects analysis indicated that political interest improved the relationship between following a PSMI and internal and external OPE, respectively, while political trust did not.

Ting *et. al.,* (2024) suggested that perceived usefulness, perceived ease of use, perceived enjoyment, political participation, and political interest are significantly related to government-political related social media usage. Social media usage mediated the relationship between all predictors and dependent variables (except for political knowledge).

Cluster 2 has been selected for this study and it shows small circles which indicates that less studies have been done and this area is under-researched. Various Antecedents from this cluster such as Civic Participation, Empowerment, Gender, Internet, Online Political Participation, Organization, Political Discussion, Political Efficacy, Political

Interest, Political Knowledge, Political Participations, Political Trust, social media, Social Networks, Trust, Women, Youth have been identified. Political Efficacy (both Internal & External), Political Interest have been selected for the study.

8. GAP ANALYSIS

- There are very few studies which have been studied in this context, so re-emphasis of the constructs must be done.
- Most research focuses on cross-sectional data, which cannot capture changes in political efficacy and interest over time.

Rationale

- India, despite being the biggest democratic country, only 25 studies hav been done in this context.
- The study of political efficacy and interest is crucial to understanding how individuals interact with the political system, which in turn affects democratic legitimacy and the quality of governance.

9. RESEARCH METHOD

- **The Study:** This study is causal by nature.
- **Sampling Method:** A convenience sampling method will be used to collect responses through online platforms such as google forms.
- **Sample Size:** The sample size was 150 respondents.
- **Data Collection:**

The data has been collected by administering:

- **Political Interest Scale** by Keeter *et. al.*, (2002). The scale consists of 5 statements and is Unidimensional.
- **Political Participation Scale** developed by Brady *et. al.*, (1999). The scale consists of 13 items and is multidimensional.
- **Political Efficacy Scale** by Craig *et. al.*, (1990). The scale consists of 6 items and is multidimensional.
- **Primary data** was collected through the online surveys which was conducted using platforms like Google Forms to reach a broader audience.

Data Analysis

After data collection, statistical analysis was conducted using software like **SPSS (Statistical Package for the Social Sciences)** to analyze data. Regression Analysis was used to determine the impact of Political interest and Political Efficacy on Political Participation.

10. RESULTS

Model Summary:

Table 2: Model Summary

Model	*R*	*R Square*	*Adjusted R Square*	*Std. Error of the Estimate*
1	.677[a]	.459	.447	5.01945

a. Predictors: (Constant), EFFEXTERNAL, EFFINTERNAL, PINTEREST.

- **R (0.677)**: This is the correlation coefficient, which suggests a moderate positive relationship between the predictors (EFFEXTERNAL, EFFINTERNAL, and PINTEREST) and the dependent variable (PARTICIPATION).
- **R^2 (0.459)**: Approximately 45.9% of the variation in PARTICIPATION can be explained by the model (the predictors). This means that the predictors (EFFEXTERNAL, EFFINTERNAL, and PINTEREST) together have a moderate explanatory power for PARTICIPATION.
- **Adjusted R^2 (0.447)**: This value adjusts the R^2 for the number of predictors in the model. It is very close to R^2, which suggests that the number of predictors used in the model is appropriate and doesn't overfit the data.

Anova Table:

Table 3: Anova Table

ANOVA[a]						
Model		*Sum of Squares*	*df*	*Mean Square*	*F*	*Sig.*
1	Regression	95.035	2	47.517	18.589	.001[b]
	Residual	273.520	107	2.556		
	Total	368.555	109			

a. Dependent Variable: PDECISION.
b. Predictors: (Constant), LOYALTY, EMBRNDNG.

The equation is robust, r square is not equal to 0, it is significant at 0.001.

The model is statistically significant, and the predictors do have a significant relationship with political participation.

Coefficients:

This is the predicted value of political participation when all the independent variables are equal to zero. In this case, the intercept suggests that when there is no internal or external efficacy, and no political interest, the baseline level of political participation is 5.961.

For every one-unit increase in political interest, the political participation is expected to increase by 0.579 units, holding other variables constant.

For every one-unit increase in external efficacy, political participation is expected to increase by 0.484 units, holding other variables constant.

Table 4: Coefficients Table

Coefficients[a]							
Model		Unstandardized Coefficients		Standardized Coefficients	t	Sig.	
		B	Std. Error	Beta			
	(Constant)	5.961	1.874		3.182	0.002	
H3	POLINT	0.579	0.139	0.359	4.168	0	ACCEPTED
H2	EFEXTERNAL	0.484	0.186	0.194	2.595	0.01	ACCEPTED
H1	EFINTERNAL	0.645	0.203	0.248	3.168	0.002	ACCEPTED

a. Dependent Variable: POLPART.

For every one-unit increase in internal efficacy, political participation is expected to increase by 0.645 units, holding other variables constant.

Findings

Coefficient and level of significance is a significant positive indicator on Political Participation.

- **Efficacy and Participation**: People with higher internal efficacy are more likely to participate in political activities. Those who believe they can influence political decisions (external efficacy) are also more likely to vote and engage in political protests or campaigns.
- **Interest and Participation**: Those who are more politically interested tend to have higher rates of participation. Interest can be influenced by socio-political events or personal experiences (e.g., involvement in community issues).

11. CONCLUSION

Political efficacy both internal and external is a critical predictor of political participation. It reflects an individual's sense of competence and belief in their ability to influence the political system. Internal efficacy refers to the belief in one's ability to understand political issues and participate effectively, while external efficacy is the belief that the political system will respond to one's actions, such as voting or activism. Those with high political efficacy tend to be more likely to engage in political activities since they feel their participation will make a difference. They are motivated to vote, participate in political debates, and even become activists for causes that are important to them. On the other hand, political inefficacy either due to insufficient confidence in one's political knowledge or the perception that the political system is not responsive can lead to political disengagement. Political disengagement typically takes the form of apathy or alienation. If individuals perceive that they cannot affect the political system, they are less inclined to be involved in political life. This increases political apathy, resulting in fewer people participating in voting, fewer civic engagements, and loss of confidence in political institutions.

Political interest and political efficacy are the bedrocks of political participation. The interaction between the two gets people involved in the political process, determining the destiny of democratic societies. Ensuring that citizens develop both political efficacy and political interest is vital for ensuring active and informed citizenry, a crucial element towards the sustainability and health of democracy. Without these factors, democratic participation is reduced to a mere formality, and the system can become detached from the people it is supposed to represent.

REFERENCES

Barnes, S.H. and Kaase, M. (1979). Political action: Mass participation in five Western democracies. *Sage Publications.*

Brehm, J. and Rahn, W.M. (1997). Individual-level evidence for the causes and consequences of social capital. *American Journal of Political Science*, 41(3), 999–1023.

Gidengil, E. and Stolle, D. (2009). Political participation and political engagement in Canada: The role of social networks and social capital. *Canadian Journal of Political Science*, 42(1), 29–52.

Gidengil, E. and Stolle, D. (2015). The impact of political efficacy on voter turnout and political participation. *Political Behavior*, 37(3), 523–550.

Kulachai, W. and Rattanaburi, A. (2024). Political efficacy. *Journal of Political Psychology*, 34(2), 234–251.

Lipset, S.M. (1981). Political man: The social bases of politics. *Johns Hopkins University Press.*

Miller, W.E. and Shanks, J.M. (1996). The new American voter. *Harvard University Press.*

Norris, P. (2002). Democratic Phoenix: Reinventing political activism. *Cambridge University Press.*

Oser, J., Hooghe, M. and Marien, S. (2017). Political participation and political interest: A comparison of the democratic and non-democratic contexts. *Comparative Politics*, 49(4), 533–553.

Putnam, R.D. (2000). Bowling alone: The collapse and revival of American community. *Simon & Schuster.*

Rosenstone, S.J. and Hansen, J.M. (1993). Mobilization, participation, and democracy in America. Macmillan.

Schlozman, K.L., Verba, S. and Brady, H.E. (2012). The unheavenly chorus: Unequal political voice and the broken promise of American democracy. *Princeton University Press.*

Tang, Y. and Wen, Q. (2023). An empirical study of the impact of social media use on online political participation of university students in Western China. *Chinese Journal of Political Science*, 56(1), 45–62.

Teorell, J. and Svensson, R. (2015). Political interest and political participation in the digital age: A study of young adults. *Journal of Political Communication*, 32(1), 76–92.

Ting, T.T.; Lee, M.Y.; Chok, S.X.; Huang, Y.H.; Choy, X.N.; Lee, K.T.; Ikumapayi, O.M. and Olugbade, T.O. (2024). Digital government: social media as a mediator in technology acceptance with political knowledge, interest, and participation. *Online Journal of Communication and Media Technologies*, 14(4), e202454.

Verba, S., Schlozman, K.L. and Brady, H.E. (1995). Voice and equality: Civic voluntarism in American politics. *Harvard University Press.*

Wang, C. and Zhang, X. (2024). Governance capacity, social justice, social security, and institutionalized political participation in China: A moderated mediation model. *Asian Journal of Political Science*, 32(1), 77–96.

Wasike, B. (2023). Examining how political social media influencers affect political interest, political trust, political efficacy, and political participation. *Journal of Social Media Studies*, 15(3), 209–225.

Yang, X. and Zhao, X. (2019). Political interest and political participation: The role of political knowledge in Chinese young adults. *Asian Politics & Policy*, 11(4), 385–401.

To Study the Impact of Abusive Supervision on Employee Well-being: A Study of the Hospitality Sector

Palak Sukhija[1] and Dimple Sukhija[2]

ABSTRACT: The research investigates "The effects of abusive supervision on the welfare of employees" in the hospitality industry in terms of psychological, emotional and behavioural states. This paper focuses on abusive supervision, which is defined as aggressive oral and gestural communication in the workplace. It is a major issue in the hospitality industry where complex and stressful jobs and customer-oriented work environments intensify its impact. A narrative literature review was adopted in this study, focusing on three papers that present the prevalence rate of "Abusive Supervision", and its effects on employee health, and possible solutions. The results show that acts of abusive supervision led to diminished "Job Satisfaction and Enhanced Turnover Intentions", thereby compromising on the stability of an organization and its workforce morale.

Mindfulness and continuance commitment are some of the moderators while work calling and job autonomy are some of the mediators of these outcomes. The analysis emphasizes that effective managerial training, fostering organizational support, promoting resilience, and enhancing job autonomy are critical to mitigating these effects. This research also offers specific strategies for hospitality organizations to minimize or eliminate abuse at the workplace, promote employees' health, and enhance organizational culture. Addressing the problem of abusive supervision in an appropriate manner benefits organizations arising from improved retention rate, productivity and service delivery thereby providing a better and enduring workplace.

Keywords: *Employee Retention, Job Autonomy, Leadership Behaviours, Productivity, Workplace Stress.*

1. INTRODUCTION

The hospitality industry, encompassing hotels, restaurants, and tourism services, is renowned for its high-pressure environment characterized by long working hours, irregular schedules, and intense customer interactions. Such demanding conditions may cultivate abusive supervision, which refers to continued negative verbal and nonverbal actions by supervisors toward their subordinates. The study by (Taheri *et. al.*, 2024), suggested that abusive supervision is significantly common in the hospitality industry whereby negative organisational performance has been observed to emanate from this type of behaviour. Employee well-being in this industry is paramount, as it directly

[1] Research Scholar, Shri Vaishnav School of Management, Shri Vaishnav Vidyapeeth Vishwavidyalaya, Indore, India. E-mail: palaksukhija21 @gmail.com

[2] Research Scholar, Devi Ahilya Vishwavidyalaya, Indore, India.

influences service quality, customer satisfaction, and overall business performance. Hospitality jobs are challenging, and the pressure that exists in organizations causes increased stress, and in turn, vulnerability to the detrimental effects of abusive supervision (Ramirez-Asís & Gharbi, 2023). Protecting hospitality workers cannot only be considered a moral issue but a business necessity for achieving a high productivity of the workforce.

The research objectives of this paper involve identifying "the effects of abusive supervision on the well-being of employees" in the hospitality industry. It will describe the instances and nature of abusive supervision, consequences on different aspects of the employee quality of life health-wise, psychologically and emotionally, and other moderating and mediating variables. The review will also consider organizational measures and countermeasures targeted at reducing the "negative consequences of abusive supervision". Addressing "abusive supervision" is crucial for hospitality organizations due to its profound implications for employee well-being and organizational success. It will describe the instances and nature of abusive supervision, consequences on different aspects of the employee quality of life health-wise, psychologically and emotionally, and other moderating and mediating variables (Yu *et. al.*, 2020). The review will also consider organizational measures and countermeasures targeted at reducing the negative consequences of abusive supervision with following objectives:

- To analyze the impact of abusive supervision on the psychological, emotional, and physical well-being of employees in the hospitality sector.
- To provide recommendations for hospitality organizations to foster a supportive and healthy work environment that promotes employee well-being

2. RESEARCH METHOD

2.1 Source Selection

Peer-reviewed articles were selected from reputable academic databases, including Google Scholar, PubMed, and EBSCOhost, to ensure the inclusion of high-quality, credible research. Since the focus was on applying the most up-to-date information, the search was conducted about the articles published only in and after 2022. Most preference was given to articles that were in English as this has enhanced the understandability of the articles. The words like "abusive supervision", "employee well-being", and "hospitality industry" were used while selecting the articles for the study. This approach helped establish a firm ground for studying the effects of abusive supervision on the well-being of employees in the hospitality sector.

2.2 Search Strategy

2.2.1 *Identification of Alternative Terminologies in the Research*

Table 1 presents alternative terminologies for key concepts related to abusive supervision, "employee well-being", and the "hospitality industry", aiding comprehensive and precise search strategies for this research topic.

Table 1: Identification of Alternative Terminologies in the Research

Keyword	*Alternative Terminology*	*Keyword*	*Alternative Terminology*
Abusive Supervision	Hostile Leadership, Negative Supervision	Employee Well-Being	Employee Wellness, Mental Health
Hospitality Industry	Service Sector, Tourism Sector	Workplace Stress	Job Stress, Occupational Burnout
Employee Turnover	Staff Attrition, Workforce Mobility	Organizational Support	Managerial Support, Employee Resources
Job Satisfaction	Employee Contentment, Workplace Happiness	Emotional Exhaustion	Burnout, Fatigue

2.2.2 *BOOLEAN Operators*

Table 2 demonstrates how to effectively use Boolean operators ("OR" and "AND") to expand or narrow search results while providing hypothetical outcomes for database searches.

Table 2: BOOLEAN Operators for the Combination of Keywords

Keywords	*BOOLEAN Operator "OR" (n2)*	*BOOLEAN Operator "AND" (n1)*	*Outcomes (Source and number of studies)*
Abusive Supervision and Employee Well-Being	"Abusive Supervision" OR "Hostile Supervision"	"Abusive Supervision" and "Employee Well-Being"	Google Scholar: Approx. 120
Hospitality Industry and Employee Stress	"Hospitality Industry" OR "Service Sector"	"Hospitality Industry" and "Employee Stress"	EBSCOhost: 100
Employee Turnover and Job Satisfaction	"Employee Turnover" OR "Staff Attrition"	"Employee Turnover" and "Job Satisfaction"	PubMed: Approx. 80
Workplace Support and Organizational Climate	"Workplace Support" OR "Managerial Support"	"Workplace Support" and "Organizational Climate"	Google Scholar: Approx. 70

2.2.3 *Inclusion and Exclusion Criteria*

Table 3 provides a structured overview of criteria for selecting secondary data in the research, ensuring the inclusion of relevant and recent literature on the "impact of abusive supervision" on "employee well-being" in the IT sector.

Table 3: Inclusion and Exclusion Criteria for Secondary Data

Selection Criteria	*Inclusion*	*Exclusion*
Data Type	Secondary data from peer-reviewed and reputable sources	Primary data studies, anecdotal evidence
Research Focus	Studies analyzing the impact of abusive supervision on employee well-being	Studies not focused on "abusive supervision or employee well-being"

Selection Criteria	***Inclusion***	***Exclusion***
Comparative Analysis	Comparisons across different employee demographics or job levels	Studies without comparative analysis
Outcome Measures	Employee well-being, including psychological, emotional, and physical health	Outcomes unrelated to well-being, such as purely financial metrics
Publication Period	Research published from 2022 to present	Publications before 2022
Sector Focus	Hospitality industry or service-related fields	Studies outside the hospitality or service sector
Selection Criteria	Inclusion	Exclusion
Data Type	Secondary data from peer-reviewed and reputable sources	Primary data studies, anecdotal evidence

3. REVIEW OF LITERATURE

A narrative literature review was chosen for this study to provide a comprehensive synthesis of existing research on the impact of abusive supervision on employee well-being in the hospitality industry. This method is useful where the research topic cuts across several methodologies and theoretical perspectives, thus providing the big picture of the phenomenon (Pautasso, 2019). However, unlike systematic reviews which aim to provide methodologically rigorous comparisons of various studies, the narrative approach allows for the flexibility necessary to examine different angles of the issue, such as the psychological, emotional, or physical health of the employees within the organization (Siddaway *et. al.*, 2019). It also facilitates the merging of the qualitative and the quantitative results and provides a holistic view of the subject.

To analyse all the studies, the thematic analysis was used. The articles were first grouped based on their themes, namely, the incidence of abusive supervision, the effects of abusive supervision, and moderators including organizational support. The main themes were then extracted by synthesizing the results across the different studies, as well as noting the similarities and contrasts. This method allowed for the development of themes, areas of concern, and patterns within the literature (Braun & Clarke, 2019). Furthermore, the papers were analyzed taking into consideration the specificities of the hospitality management field, for instance, high employee turnover and stressful working conditions. This synthesis not only highlighted the current state of knowledge but also offered implications for practice and research.

4. RESULTS

Table 4 is a summary of the papers selected for analysis. It provides information about each paper focusing on the reference, participants involved, location of the study, setting of the study or the data collection methods. Moin *et. al.,* (2021) conducted a study on 190 frontline hospitality employees in China and aims to examine how abusive supervision impacts turnover intentions via job dissatisfaction. The research used a 3-wave time-lagged cross-sectional design with data collected at three different points in time, thus offering strong support for the mediating effects.

Table 4: Summary of Papers

Reference	*Study Participants*	*Study Settings*	*Country*	*Study Design/Data Collection Tool*
(Moin *et. al.,* 2021): "Abusive supervision and job outcomes"	190 full-time frontline hospitality employees from local and multinational-starred hotels	Hospitality industry with a focus on hotel workers	China	Three-wave time-lagged survey: Data collected over three months at one-month intervals. Surveys assessed abusive supervision, job dissatisfaction, and turnover intentions.
(Yang & Xu, 2023): "Should We Be More Mindful?"	220 hotel employees (various roles: front office, housekeeping, food and beverage, sales, HR, etc.)	Lodging industry with midscale, limited-service, and luxury hotels	United States	Cross-sectional survey using Qualtrics platform; 7-point Likert scales measured abusive supervision, mindfulness, employee well-being, and turnover intentions. Data was collected anonymously.
(Ghosh *et. al.,* 2024): "Work calling and abusive supervision"	280 hospitality employees directly interacting with customers across three units of a large hotel chain	Large hotel chains in Northern India	India	Multi-wave, multi-source survey: Offline and online methods used to gather data from employees and their supervisors. Surveys included measures of abusive supervision, work calling, and behaviours.

Yang & Xu (2023) conducted a study on 220 hotel employees in the United States of America, including workers from different departments, including the front office, housekeeping, and food and beverage. The data for this cross-sectional study were collected using 7-point Likert scales and the responses to the questionnaires were kept anonymous through the Qualtrics platform to assess the associations between abusive supervision and mindfulness and employee well-being. Ghosh *et. al.,* (2024) presented a cross-sectional survey of 280 hospitality workers from three departments of a large hotel chain in Northern India. Based on a three-wave, and three-source data collection, the study considered the previously unexplored links between abusive supervision, work calling, and positive employee customer-focused behaviours, moderating the role of job autonomy. The papers offered various viewpoints on the subject of abusive supervision and its consequences in the realm of hospitality management, with implications for various settings and methods.

5. DISCUSSION

The study on "Abusive supervision and Job Outcomes" (Moin *et. al.*, 2021), analysed the moderating effect of continuance commitment on the relationship between "abusive supervision" in the hospitality industry and turnover intention with job dissatisfaction as a mediator. The purpose of the research was to find out how the abusive behaviours of supervisors affect employees' intentions to quit and uncover ways of managing this impact. Through a cross-sectional time-lagged survey, data were gathered from 190 frontline hospitality employees working in starred hotels in China. Questionnaires were administered at one-month intervals in a bid to minimize bias and enhance the validity of the study. Most of the key variables including abusive supervision, job dissatisfaction, turnover intentions, and continuance commitment were measured according to the scales found in the literature. Quantitative data analyses were conducted using regression and bootstrapping analysis, and the findings of the study were that "abusive supervision" is a strong "predictor of turnover intentions" and works indirectly through job dissatisfaction. Continuance commitment was found to weaken this mediated relationship, highlighting its protective role against the negative impacts of supervisory abuse.

The research also offered practical implications relating to commitment and abusive supervisory conduct in retaining talent for hospitality managers. The paper recommended implementing training programs for managers to reduce abusive behaviours and fostering a supportive organizational culture to mitigate dissatisfaction and turnover. Thus, this paper is a successful attempt to solve the first of the set objectives, namely, to provide evidence of the negative effects of abusive supervision on the psychological satisfaction of employees. It also addressed the second aim by providing strategies for managing these effects thus providing insights that can be implemented by hospitality organisations.

Yang & Xu, (2023) examined the moderation role of mindfulness in the relationship between abusive supervision and coworker treatment, and employees' well-being and turnover intentions, in the context of the hospitality industry. The goal of the study was to establish how workplace abuse impacts workplace well-being and whether using mindfulness, which is considered beneficial, would intensify or reduce those effects. The study was cross-sectional with 220 participants, employed in various hotel positions across the United States including front-office, housekeeping, and food and beverages. To assess the key variables of the study, namely abusive supervision, mindfulness, employee well-being, and turnover intentions, a 7-point Likert scale was employed. The study found that abusive supervision and coworker treatment were associated with lower employee well-being and higher turnover intentions. Interestingly, mindfulness, typically seen as a resilience-building tool, was found to exacerbate the negative effects of abusive supervision on employee well-being by increasing sensitivity to negativity.

The findings highlighted a paradoxical effect, suggesting that mindfulness training in abusive work environments may have unintended adverse outcomes. The paper suggested a way for these hospitality organizations to bring down cases of workplace abuse to follow it up with the implementation of workable interventions rather than simply practising mindfulness. This paper fulfilled the first research aim by demonstrating that abusive supervision has negative consequences on the target employee's psychological health. It also partially met the second aim by identifying organisational interventions that aim at promoting a healthier work climate to enhance staff turnover and attraction.

Ghosh *et. al.*, (2024) examined the "relationship between abusive supervision" and other behaviours, particularly the positive employee behaviours; constructive voice, embraced by the employees in the hospitality industry, regarding "customer-focused constructive voice (CFCV)" and "pro-customer rule-breaking (PCRB)". The study has, therefore, investigated how and when work calling influences these behaviours, and the role of job autonomy and abusive supervision as moderators. The study was conducted on 280 employees working in three units of a hotel chain in Northern India. A multi-wave, multi-source survey was conducted online and offline to collect the data. The results showed a more complex process where although abusive supervision is widely considered undesirable, it can elicit positive employee responses under certain circumstances.

Employees with high work calling were more likely to respond to abusive supervision by engaging in "CFCV and PCRB", particularly when job autonomy was high. This implies that the employees may redefine abusive supervision as a task, resulting in positive organizational outcomes. However, the study also highlighted other adverse effects of abusive supervision on the lives of employees in general. For enhanced positive employee behaviours, and to minimize the negative impacts of supervisory abuse, the paper recommended hospitality organizations to emphasize work calling and job autonomy. This paper met the first objective by examining the multifaceted outcomes of abusive supervision on employees and their conduct. It also fulfilled the second research question since it offered practical solutions concerning autonomy and meaning that can help address problematic workplace relations.

6. MANAGERIAL IMPLICATIONS

6.1 Reducing Abusive Supervision

Hospitality organizations need to act to prevent abusive supervision since it affects employee's health, satisfaction, and turnover intent. More frequent organizational training for managers should be conducted with the aim of enhancing appropriate leadership behaviours. Supervisory feedback tools like anonymous employee surveys can be used to assess supervisor-employee relations and report instances of misconduct. Managers should also be punished for their actions by firm guidelines that prohibit abusive conduct.

6.2 Enhancing Organizational Support

Companies should focus more on reporting positive changes in the workplace, including positive changes in the way employees are treated. Offering resources such as counselling services, peer support programs, and easy access to HR representatives can assist employees in managing difficult work situations. Thus, enhancing organisational justice in terms of workload, recognition, and grievance procedures can help reduce the impact of abusive supervision.

6.3 Fostering Employee Resilience and Well-Being

Strategies like the provision of workshops aimed at strengthening employees' resilience, training in mindfulness, and stress management programs can help employees deal with challenges in the workplace. Nevertheless, (Yang & Xu, 2023), noted that mindfulness-based interventions should be implemented with precaution to not worsen the sensitivity to abusive behaviours. It is crucial to address employees' physical and mental health to ensure that the organization sustains its effectiveness in the long run.

6.4 Encouraging Job Autonomy and Work Calling

Managers must turn their attention to enhancing job independence where employees are able to make decisions that improve customer satisfaction and performance. According to (Ghosh *et. al.*, 2024), autonomy is beneficial in that it empowers employees to handle situations optimally within the workplace. Moreover, the creation of work calling through meaningful job roles and recognition may enhance employee engagement and minimize the detrimental outcomes of supervisory abuse. These strategies not only enhance well-being but also enhance productivity and commitment in the hospitality context.

7. CONCLUSION

This research aimed to examine the effects of abusive supervision on employee well-being in the hospitality sector with an emphasis on psychological, emotional, and behavioural outcomes. Based on the three papers analyzed, it was known that abusive supervision leads to increased job dissatisfaction and turnover intentions, which affects the overall stability of the organization and employee morale. Some of the moderators include mindfulness and continuance commitment while some of the mediators include work calling and job autonomy which are useful in the management of adverse effects. However, some findings show constructive employee responses under certain circumstances, and the overall trend points to the negative effects of abusive supervision. To address this issue, it is imperative to address the abusive behaviours, enhance organizational support, build resilience, and increase job control. In this way, focusing on the employees' well-being and promoting a non-discriminatory work environment can lead to increased employee retention, productivity, and the quality of service provided. These strategies provide practical ways of reducing the effects of abusive supervision in the workplace.

REFERENCES

Braun, V. and Clarke, V. (2019). Reflecting on reflexive thematic analysis. *Qualitative Research in Sport, Exercise and Health*, *11*(4), 589–597.

Ghosh, K.; Sharma, D. and Malik, L.R. (2024). Work calling and abusive supervision: Boon or bane in hospitality organization? *International Journal of Hospitality Management*, *117*(1), 103638.

Moin, M.F.; Wei, F.; Khan, A.N.; Ali, A. and Chang, S.C. (2021). Abusive supervision and job outcomes: A moderated mediation model. *Journal of Organizational Change Management*, *ahead-of-print*(ahead-of-print).

Pautasso, M. (2019). The Structure and Conduct of a Narrative Literature Review. *A Guide to the Scientific Career*, *2*(2), 299–310.

Ramirez-Asís, E. and Gharbi, I. (2023). Process Visibility and Work Stress: Exposure the relationship with Service Quality to attain Customer Satisfaction in Hospitality Industry. *International Journal of Technology, Innovation and Management*, *3*(2), 30–38.

Siddaway, A.P.; Wood, A.M. and Hedges, L.V. (2019). How to Do a Systematic review: a Best Practice Guide for Conducting and Reporting Narrative reviews, meta-analyses, and meta-syntheses. *Annual Review of Psychology*, *70*(1), 747–770.

Taheri, B.; Thompson, J.; Mistry, T.G.; Bendegul, Okumus and Gannon, M. (2024). Abusive supervision in commercial kitchens: Insights from the restaurant industry. *International Journal of Hospitality Management*, *120*, 103789–103789.

Yang, W. and Xu, S. (2023). Should We Be More Mindful? The Joint Impact of an Abusive Work Environment and Mindfulness on Employee Well-Being and Turnover Intentions. *Journal of Hospitality & Tourism Research*, *48*(4), 109634802311568.

Yu, Y.; Xu, S.; Li, G. and Kong, H. (2020). A systematic review of research on abusive supervision in hospitality and tourism. *International Journal of Contemporary Hospitality Management*, *32*(7), 2473–2496.

Urban Agriculture: Potential Way for Achieving SDGs

Richa Sharma[1] and Suhas Mane[2]

ABSTRACT: Urban Agriculture refers to a specific form of agriculture that fits the requirements of certain urban lifestyles and is adapted to basic conditions of land and landscape in urban areas (FAO, 2015). It is the practice of cultivating crops, raising animals, or growing food in urban areas. It involves utilizing available urban spaces such as rooftops, balconies, community gardens, and vacant plots for agricultural purposes. It contributes to local food production, promoting self-sufficiency and reducing dependence on external food sources. It provides a source of food and income for urban dwellers. The products thus produced can be used for their own consumption or sale in neighbourhood markets. According to the United Nations by 2050, 68% of the global population will be residing in cities. The increase will be asymmetrical as 90% of the population shift will happen in tier-2 and tier-3 cities in Africa and Asia. In India, 35% of the population resides in the urban centres. This shift paves the way for various challenges for Urban Planners in the form of poverty, food insecurity, housing, compromised nature spaces, and pollution. In the wake of these trends, Urban Agriculture emerges as an essential intervention for a nature-based solution for the contemporary challenges. Beyond food security, urban agriculture offers a range of environmental and social benefits. It reduces waste by creating closed-loop systems where food waste can be composted and used to fertilize crops. Moreover, it can help promote green spaces in cities, improving air quality and biodiversity while empowering communities by giving people more control over their food system and fostering social connections through shared gardens and markets. Urban Agriculture contributes to several UN Sustainable Development Goals (SDGs) encompassing poverty alleviation (SDG 1), improved nutrition (SDG 2), sustainable consumption (SDG 12), environmental protection (SDG 13), and biodiversity conservation (SDG 15).

Keywords: *Aquaponics, Cultivating Crops, Hydroponics, Urban Spaces, Vertical Farming.*

1. INTRODUCTION

Urbanization is a global phenomenon reshaping the dynamics of population distribution, resource utilization, and environmental sustainability. The United Nations estimates that by 2050, 68% of the global population will reside in urban areas, with 90% of this urbanization concentrated in tier-2 and tier-3 cities across Africa and Asia. In India, 35% of the population already resides in urban centres, posing significant challenges for urban planners, including poverty, food insecurity, housing shortages,

[1] Research Scholar, Shri Vaishnav Institute of Agriculture, Shri Vaishnav Vidyapeeth Vishwavidyalaya, Indore, India. E-mail: richapandey.sage@gmail.com

[2] Assistant Professor, Shri Vaishnav Institute of Agriculture, Shri Vaishnav Vidyapeeth Vishwavidyalaya, Indore, India.

dwindling green spaces, and increasing pollution. Urban agriculture emerges as a critical nature-based solution to these chCallenges. Urban agriculture encompasses a range of activities, including cultivating crops, raising livestock, aquaculture, and horticulture in urban and peri-urban areas. Unlike traditional farming, it utilizes unconventional spaces such as rooftops, balconies, vacant lots, and community gardens, integrating agriculture into the urban fabric. The adaptability of urban agriculture allows it to thrive in various environments, making it a flexible solution for food security and sustainability.

Urban Agriculture is a specialized form of agriculture designed to meet the requirements of urban lifestyles while adapting to the constrainCts of urban landscapes and land availability (FAO, 2015). It involves cultivating crops, raising animals, or growing food within urban spaces, such as rooftops, balconies, community gardens, and vacant plots. This practice fosters local food production, enhances self-sufficiency, and reduces reliance on external food sources. Additionally, it serves as a source of both nourishment and income for urban residents, with produce either consumed locally or sold in neighborhood markets. Urban agriculture is the practice of producing food within urban settings and offers a promising pathway to address these issues while contributing to sustainable urban development.

2. URBAN AGRICULTURE AND SDGs

Urban agriculture aligns closely with the United Nations Sustainable Development Goals. Practical examples, Research, Key contributions include:

- **SDG 1 (No Poverty):** A Research study by the International Development Research Centre (IDRC) shows that urban farming initiatives in Nairobi, Kenya, have increased household income by 25% for families engaged in vegetable and poultry farming. Urban agriculture creates livelihood opportunities by generating income for small-scale farmers and entrepreneurs in urban areas. The Dakar Urban Agriculture Program in Senegal provides microcredit and training to urban farmers, enabling them to earn livelihoods through small-scale farming and sell surplus produce in local markets.
- **SDG 2 (Zero Hunger):** A study by RUAF Foundation (2018) found that urban agriculture in Rosario, Argentina, provides 40% of the fresh vegetables consumed in the city, significantly reducing urban food insecurity. Local food production increases accessibility to fresh and nutritious food, reducing food insecurity. In Mumbai, India, organizations like *Urban Leaves* promote terrace farming, where families grow vegetables like spinach, tomatoes, and herbs, reducing their dependency on market-bought food.
- **SDG 12 (Responsible Consumption and Production):** The Urban Agriculture Initiative in Cape Town, South Africa, reduces food waste by composting over 200 tons of organic waste annually and redistributing surplus produce to low-income communities. Urban farming promotes sustainable practices, including waste reduction and resource efficiency. Detroit's Recovery Park Farms in the United States turns vacant urban spaces into sustainable agricultural projects, recycling organic waste into compost and using it for cultivation.
- **SDG 13 (Climate Action):** A report from the World Resources Institute (2020) highlights how vertical farms in Singapore reduce carbon emissions by up to 90%

compared to traditional supply chains. By reducing transportation-related emissions and creating green spaces, urban agriculture mitigates the effects of climate change. Singapore's Sky Greens is a vertical farming initiative that uses 95% less water and land compared to traditional farming while producing fresh, local vegetables.

- **SDG 15 (Life on Land):** Studies from University College London (2019) show that integrating rooftop gardens into cityscapes increases urban biodiversity by providing habitats for pollinators and other wildlife. Urban green spaces enhance biodiversity by providing habitats for pollinators and other species. Delhi's Urban Forest Project integrates small-scale agroforestry practices in urban parks, enhancing biodiversity and creating pollinator-friendly zones.

3. METHODS OF URBAN AGRICULTURE

3.1 Vertical Farming

Research by the Columbia University Earth Institute (2021) demonstrates that vertical farms use 70% less water than traditional methods while achieving 4-5 times the yield per square meter. Vertically stacked layers grow crops in controlled environments, thereby optimizing space and resources. In Bangalore, India, vertical farming companies like Junga Freshn Green are cultivating leafy greens and herbs using hydroponics, maximizing yields in limited urban spaces.

3.2 Hydroponics

A 2019 study in India by the Indian Council of Agricultural Research (ICAR) found that hydroponic systems in urban areas yielded crops 30% faster than soil-based systems, with 50% less water usage. It cultivates plants in nutrient-rich water without soil, suitable for urban areas with limited land. The Kheti Virat Initiative in Pune trains urban residents to grow lettuce, strawberries, and other crops in hydroponic setups, ideal for high-density areas.

3.3 Aquaponics

Research by Michigan State University (2020) revealed that aquaponics systems are 85% more resource-efficient than conventional farming and suitable for small-scale urban food production. It integrates aquaculture (raising fish) with hydroponics, creating a symbiotic system. In Chennai, Farmizen has set up aquaponics systems in urban backyards, producing both fish and vegetables in a sustainable, symbiotic cycle.

3.4 Rooftop Farming

A study conducted in New York City (2022) by the Urban Agriculture Research Group found that rooftop farms reduced building cooling costs by 20% while producing up to 12 kilograms of vegetables per square meter annually. Rooftops of the buildings are converted into productive agricultural spaces, improving insulation and reducing urban heat. The Pasona Urban Farm in Tokyo integrates rooftop gardens and indoor farming within corporate buildings, producing fresh food for employees and reducing energy costs.

3.5 Container Farming

Utilizes portable containers for farming, enabling mobility and scalability. For example in Hyderabad, container farming projects by Urban Kisaan enable food production in portable units, bringing fresh produce closer to urban consumers.

3.6 Green Walls and Landscaping

Enhances aesthetics while growing food or ornamental plants in vertical structures.

3.7 Community Gardens

The Incredible Edible Project in Todmorden, UK, transforms unused urban spaces into community gardens where residents grow and share food.

4. SUCCESS STORIES OF URBAN AGRICULTURE IN INDIA

Urban agriculture in India has gained momentum with innovative and sustainable practices, particularly in cities where space is limited, but the demand for fresh and healthy produce is rising. Below are some inspiring success stories from across the country:

4.1 Terrace Gardening in Bengaluru

Bengaluru, known as the "Garden City," has witnessed a surge in terrace gardening initiatives. Organizations like My Dream Garden have helped thousands of residents turn their rooftops into lush vegetable gardens.

Impact:

- It provides fresh, pesticide-free vegetables to households.
- It reduces dependence on market-bought produce.
- It encourages waste management through composting kitchen waste.

4.2 Urban Farming by Growel Feeds (Hyderabad)

The Growel Feeds is a unique aquaponics venture combining fish farming with vegetable cultivation in urban spaces.

Impact:

- It produces organic vegetables and fish using minimal water.
- It demonstrates a scalable, eco-friendly farming model for urban areas.
- It supports local food sustainability and water conservation.

4.3 JAAGRUTI Waste-to-Food Initiative (Delhi)

An initiative by a Delhi-based NGO that transforms organic waste from residential complexes into compost for urban gardens.

Impact:

- It promotes urban gardening in residential societies.

- It reduces landfill waste and fosters awareness about sustainable living.
- It ensures that residents have access to homegrown fruits, herbs, and vegetables.

4.4 Rooftop Farming in Mumbai by Fresh & Local

The Fresh & Local, a Mumbai-based initiative, creates rooftop farms in densely populated areas.

Impact:

- It provides fresh vegetables to local communities.
- It educates urban residents about the benefits of farming.
- It reduces the carbon footprint associated with transporting food.

4.5 Kerala's Vegetable Villages (Kudumbashree)

The Kudumbashree Mission in Kerala encourages women to form collectives and engage in urban farming.

Impact:

- It enhances food security in urban and semi-urban areas.
- It empowers women economically and socially.
- It promotes organic farming practices in urban households.

4.6 Auroville's Hydroponic Projects (Tamil Nadu)

The Auroville community has embraced hydroponics and other innovative farming methods to grow food in minimal spaces without soil.

Impact:

- It demonstrates the feasibility of soil-less farming in urban areas.
- It conserves water and ensures year-round food production.
- It inspires similar projects across India.

4.7 Balcony Farming in Ahmedabad

Urban residents in Ahmedabad have turned their balconies into micro-farms with support from workshops and seed banks provided by local NGOs.

Impact:

- It encourages self-reliance in food production.
- It utilizes small spaces effectively.
- It reduces household expenses on vegetables and herbs.

5. KEY DRIVERS OF URBAN AGRICULTURE

- **Sustainability Awareness**: Increasing concerns about pesticide-laden food and waste management have spurred interest in urban farming.
- **Supportive Ecosystem**: Workshops, online platforms, and government schemes promote urban agriculture.

- **Technological Innovations**: Hydroponics, aquaponics, and vertical farming are becoming accessible to urban dwellers.
- **Community Building**: Urban farming initiatives often bring communities together for shared learning and collective benefits.

6. BENEFITS OF URBAN AGRICULTURE

Urban agriculture offers numerous environmental, economic, and social benefits.

6.1 Environmental Benefits

According to a 2018 FAO report, urban farms in Accra, Ghana, recycle 25% of the city's organic waste into compost, reducing landfill pressure and enhancing soil fertility. Urban agriculture reduces carbon footprints by minimizing transportation, promotes waste recycling through composting and resource recovery, and enhances urban biodiversity and air quality. The City Farm Project in Melbourne converts organic waste from local markets into compost, reducing landfill waste and improving soil fertility.

6.2 Economic Benefits

A 2019 study in Manila, Philippines, found that urban gardening projects reduced household food expenses by 30% and created income-generating opportunities for over 1,000 families. Urban agriculture creates jobs and entrepreneurial opportunities, reduces household food expenses, and encourages local economic growth through neighbourhood markets. Cuba's Organopónicos, urban organic farms in Havana, provide affordable fresh produce while generating employment for city dwellers.

6.3 Social Benefits

Research by University of Michigan (2020) indicates that participation in community gardening initiatives improves mental health by 45% and strengthens neighbourhood social networks. Urban agriculture strengthens community ties through shared gardening initiatives, provides educational opportunities on sustainable practices, and improves mental well-being by connecting people to nature. New York City's Green Thumb Program establishes community gardens across the city, strengthening neighborhood bonds and providing educational opportunities for children.

7. CHALLENGES IN URBAN AGRICULTURE

Despite its potential, urban agriculture faces several challenges, as highlighted by research.

- **Land Scarcity:** A study in Dhaka, Bangladesh, found that 80% of urban residents face land constraints, necessitating innovative solutions like vertical farming and container gardening. Competition for urban land limits the availability of farming spaces.
- **Policy Gaps:** The UN-Habitat Global Report (2021) identified the lack of supportive urban agriculture policies as a significant barrier in rapidly urbanizing regions, particularly in Africa and South Asia. Lack of supportive policies and regulations hinders integration into urban planning.

- **Resource Constraints:** Research by the Global Water Partnership (2019) indicates that water scarcity affects 40% of urban farmers globally, emphasizing the need for efficient irrigation technologies. Limited access to water, energy, and finances affects scalability.
- **Knowledge Barriers:** Urban residents often lack the skills and expertise required for efficient farming.

8. RECOMMENDATIONS

To fully realize the potential of urban agriculture, concerted efforts are needed, with research-backed strategies to overcome challenges and practical steps, such as incorporating it into urban planning, benefiting cities globally:

- **Policy Support:** A study by RUAF and UN-Habitat (2018) recommends integrating urban agriculture into municipal zoning laws, as successfully demonstrated in Bogotá, Colombia. Governments should integrate urban agriculture into urban planning and zoning laws. Toronto's Green Roof Bylaw mandates new developments to include green roofs, encouraging rooftop farming and reducing urban heat.
- **Incentives and Funding:** Subsidies, grants, and public-private partnerships can encourage adoption.
- **The Grow Pittsburgh:** Initiative offers workshops on urban gardening, teaching residents how to cultivate food sustainably in small spaces. The Singaporean Government's Agri-Food Cluster Transformation Fund provides grants to urban farmers for adopting advanced technologies, boosting productivity.
- **Education and Awareness:** Research by Harvard Graduate School of Education (2021) shows that urban agriculture workshops in Boston improved sustainable farming practices among participants by 60%. Training programs can equip urban residents with the skills needed for sustainable farming.
- **Technological Integration:** A 2022 MIT study found that smart sensors in urban farms reduced water use by 35% while optimizing crop yields. Adopting smart farming technologies can optimize resource use and productivity. The Agritecture Company in New York develops smart farming solutions like automated irrigation systems for urban farms, optimizing productivity.

9. CONCLUSION

Urban farming offers multifaceted benefits for India's expanding cities. As urbanization intensifies, so does the demand for food, placing pressure on rural resources and the environment. By enabling cities to produce a portion of their food, urban agriculture reduces dependency on long-distance transportation, minimizes carbon footprints, and ensures access to fresh, nutritious, and affordable food. Beyond food security, urban farming promotes environmental sustainability by creating closed-loop systems where organic waste is composted and reused as fertilizer. It also enhances urban ecosystems by increasing green spaces, improving air quality, fostering biodiversity, and creating social connections through community gardens and local markets.

Key urban farming techniques include vertical farming, hydroponics, aquaponics, container farming, rooftop gardening, backyard gardens, green walls, and street landscaping. These methods can be implemented in diverse urban settings, such as apartment complexes, rooftops, schools, businesses, and backyards, making urban agriculture a versatile and scalable solution for sustainable urban development.

REFERENCES

Columbia University Earth Institute (2021). Vertical farming: The future of urban food production. Earth Institute Reports.

Food and Agriculture Organization (FAO). (2015). The urban agriculture initiative. http://www.fao.org/urban-agriculture

Indian Council of Agricultural Research (ICAR). (2019). Hydroponics as an efficient urban farming method in India. ICAR Research Report.

International Development Research Centre (IDRC). (2020). Urban agriculture and livelihoods: Insights from Nairobi, Kenya. https://www.idrc.ca/en

RUAF Foundation (2018). Urban agriculture and food security: Lessons from Rosario, Argentina.

United Nations (UN). (2018). World urbanization prospects: The 2018 revision. United Nations, Department of Economic and Social Affairs, Population Division.

University College London (UCL). (2019). Urban green spaces: Enhancing biodiversity in cities. UCL Press.

World Resources Institute (WRI). (2020). Climate action through urban agriculture: Singapore's vertical farms. https://www.wri.org

Epilogue

The epilogue provides an overview of the papers presented, following the sequence in which they appear in this book.

- Food is essential for maintaining body functions, and health encompasses physical, emotional, and social well-being. Educated women play a crucial role in promoting health within families. This paper examines the health status of women in Indore, revealing high fat intake and low protein and energy consumption compared to recommended dietary standards. To address these issues, educational institutions should implement wellness programs promoting healthy lifestyles, physical activity, and nutritional education. Supporting teachers in maintaining healthy diets can enhance their quality of life and professional performance.
- Digital storytelling combines social, emotional, and cognitive development, reforming early childhood education. By blending traditional storytelling with multimedia, it fosters literacy, creativity, empathy, and critical thinking. It also promotes essential 21st-century skills like computer literacy and emotional regulation. While it encourages self-expression and emotional control, more research is needed to understand its long-term effects and its impact on social skills and attention spans. Digital storytelling has the potential to transform learning, but further development and adaptation are needed for diverse contexts.
- The exploration of rib-roughened air channels reveals that strategic surface modifications such as V-pattern dimpled ribs, grooves in V-pattern ribs, and protrusions significantly enhance heat transfer by promoting turbulence and secondary flow. These insights not only deepen our understanding of thermal performance optimization but also pave the way for more efficient and innovative designs in solar air heaters and heat exchanger systems. As energy demands grow, such advancements offer a promising path toward sustainable thermal engineering solutions.
- A novel optimization algorithm to improve Intrusion Detection in IoT networks is proposed. After simulating the IoT environment, log files are collected, cluster heads are selected, and data is routed to the base station. A Convolutional Neural Network (CNN), tuned with optimized hyperparameters, is used for traffic identification. The model's performance has been evaluated using energy, precision, recall, and F-measure, and compared with existing methods.
- There is a strong link between financial inclusion and women's empowerment, showing that social and economic empowerment significantly supports women's financial independence. Financial inclusion is crucial for developing regions like India, particularly in underdeveloped states. A formal financial system is essential to broaden access and participation.
- Agrobacterium Tumefaciens-Mediated Transformation (ATMT) can introduce the Green Fluorescent Protein (GFP) gene into Colletotrichum Truncatum, providing a tool for visualizing fungal transformation. The standardized ATMT protocol enables

stable transformants, aiding in tracking and assessing transformation efficiency. The use of GFP as a reporter offers significant potential for studying pathogenesis and improving strategies against disease management in soybean, advancing fungal genetic research and disease management.

- The DPDP Act 2023 marks a pivotal move in India's journey toward personal data protection, especially regarding biometric data in corporate use. While offering a balanced, cost-effective legal framework, its effectiveness hinges on regulatory clarity and government commitment. For corporations, the path forward lies in embracing accountability, transparency, and ethical data governance. By aligning operations with privacy principles and global standards, businesses can foster trust and innovation, ensuring a secure and sustainable digital future.
- The simulation reveals that energy depletion in wireless sensor networks is uneven, with nodes farther from the base station losing energy faster, leading to energy holes. The 80% threshold analysis offers key insights into network lifespan and degradation, aiding in better planning and maintenance. Future improvements could include adaptive power control or clustering to balance energy use more effectively.
- The faults like Cell Omission, Displacement, and Cell Rotation in Full Adder circuits have been addressed by following CMOS fault models or randomly, requiring further investigation in Quantum-dot Cellular Automata (QCA) circuits. As QCA complexity grows, manual fault identification becomes time-consuming, highlighting the need for a fault identification algorithm to speed up testing.
- Palmar crease analysis offers a promising biometric approach for personal identification, combining stability and uniqueness with practical forensic and security applications. Its potential in contactless identification aligns with evolving technological needs, making it increasingly relevant in fields like criminal justice and access control. Continued research will enhance its reliability and broaden its application, deepening the understanding of human physical traits.
- There is a moderate consumer sentiment towards green packaging because of low awareness and divided willingness to adopt it. While consumers show interest, they are skeptical about its effectiveness and are uncertain about paying more. Packaging design and labeling significantly influence purchasing behavior. The findings emphasize the need for improved education, innovation, and market positioning to address concerns around cost, performance, and accessibility.
- Library websites of central universities in Uttar Pradesh like AMU and BHU have the most user-friendly sites, with well-developed Online Public Access Catalog (OPAC) systems and digital resources. AU and BBAU's sites are moderately developed, lacking real-time engagement features, while RLBCAU has limited resources and no OPAC. Accessibility is an issue for most, and few sites offer user engagement tools like live chat. Overall, significant improvements are needed in accessibility, resources, and user support.
- In VANETs, vehicles act as mobile nodes to share critical information like traffic, accidents, or disasters. This helps alert commuters and manage emergencies, especially when traditional networks fail. V2V (vehicle-to-vehicle) communication is preferred over V2I (vehicle-to-infrastructure) due to lower delay and jitter. Simulations using

QualNet show V2V offers faster, more reliable data exchange when vehicles are within range. In contrast, V2I suffers from higher delay due to congestion at RSUs and base stations. Future work aims to enable multi-hop V2V communication to enhance road safety and transport efficiency.

- Several methods have been developed to stabilize Charred Documents, each offering partial success. While some techniques are widely used, others remain experimental and require further exploration. Factors like paper quality, ink type, and the extent of burning continue to challenge preservation efforts. No single method addresses all issues, highlighting the need for a comprehensive, reliable approach. Moving forward, interdisciplinary research is essential to develop solutions that ensure long-term preservation without compromising on document integrity.
- Green Buildings (GBs) play a vital role in reducing energy consumption and greenhouse gas emissions, making them key factors in addressing climate change. Their effectiveness depends on the integration of Renewable Energy technologies and adaptation to local climatic and infrastructural conditions. While global interest and research on GBs are increasing, adoption remains slow in low-income regions due to financial and technical challenges. Evaluating the impact of GBs requires a focus on energy balance, occupant comfort, and grid interaction.
- Fingerprints have long served as a foundation in forensic identification due to their uniqueness and permanence. While traditional methods rely on pattern types and minutiae, recent advances highlight the potential of ridge detail and sweat pores to enhance accuracy. However, challenges such as variability in latent prints and lack of standardization limit broader application. Future research should focus on improving automated systems, visual techniques, and database support to standardize and strengthen pore-based fingerprint identification in forensic practice.
- Echo State Network (ESN) architecture within an Artificial Neural Network-Deep Learning Approach (ANN-DLA) framework effectively identifies Smart Device Security and Stability Concerns (SSC) in OS programs. By comparing DLA with traditional machine learning approaches, the research demonstrates the superiority of DLA classifiers. Utilizing the CIC-MalMem-2022 dataset and static analysis of permissions and API-IA data, the DLA classifier achieved a 98.8% F-measure score and 99.7% accuracy.
- AI brings transformative potential along with complex risks, ranging from cybersecurity threats to ethical challenges. Current IT laws, rooted in older technologies, struggle to keep pace, leading to regulatory gaps and uncertainty. Addressing AI's evolving threats demands dynamic, adaptable legal frameworks that evolve in real-time. Ongoing legal innovation, coupled with international cooperation, is essential to ensure consistent, ethical, and effective governance of AI across borders.
- In Cloud-Integrated Wireless Optical Broadband Access Networks (CIW), k-means clustering significantly optimizes cloudlet placement compared to connection index-based methods, reducing cloudlet requirements by up to 50% without compromising coverage. Dynamic wireless router distributions, integrate cost-effective models, implement hop-based routing, and enhance load balancing through task offloading strategies can be explored.

- The Azolla and Duckweed can effectively treat sewage, with better results when used together. The combined setup showed higher Biochemical Oxygen Demand (BOD) and nitrogen removal, while Duckweed alone was more effective for phosphate. These macrophytes are suitable for the study area's climate. They not only survived but grew well in the treatment system with such high concentration of BOD. Because of the synergetic effect the percentage removal efficiency for BOD and Nitrogen was found to be higher. Mixing of the plants provide better results as compared to their application separately.
- The SEAPIRD model improves upon traditional epidemic models by incorporating complex factors like incubation periods, asymptomatic carriers, and natural death and cure rates. Focused on India's public health response, it offers more accurate predictions of disease spread, emphasizing the role of presymptomatic and asymptomatic stages. This model provides valuable insights for managing outbreaks and refining control strategies.
- The study on chickpea pests during Rabi 2023-24 identified *Helicoverpa armigera* as the major pest, affecting the crop from the vegetative to maturity stages. Eggs and larvae appeared from day 29 to day 99. *Campoletis chlorideae*, a natural enemy of *H. armigera*, was observed from the 3rd to 8th SMW. The infestation by *H. armigera* occurred between the 50th and 8th SMW (December to February) in Solapur.
- There is a significant impact of Fintech on banking regulations, particularly before and after Basel III implementation. A notable difference in capital adequacy ratios is observed, emphasizing how Fintech has influenced compliance and risk management. As technology continues to evolve, regulators must adapt to maintain financial stability and consumer protection. Ongoing research is essential to understand Fintech's long-term regulatory implications and to develop strategies that balance innovation with effective oversight.
- Political efficacy, both internal (understanding political issues) and external (belief in political responsiveness), drives political participation. High efficacy leads to active engagement, while inefficacy fosters apathy and disengagement. Political interest and efficacy are crucial for a healthy democracy, ensuring informed, active participation. Without them, democracy risks will become disconnected from its citizens.
- Abusive supervision increases job dissatisfaction and turnover intentions, undermining organizational stability and morale. Moderators like mindfulness and continuance commitment, and mediators such as work calling and job autonomy, can mitigate these effects. While some employees respond constructively, the overall trend shows negative outcomes. To address this, it is crucial to reduce abusive behaviors, enhance organizational support, and promote resilience and job control, ultimately improving retention, productivity, and service quality.
- Urban farming helps cities reduce reliance on rural resources, cut carbon footprints, and ensure access to fresh food. It promotes sustainability through waste recycling and enhances urban ecosystems. Techniques like vertical farming and rooftop gardening offer adaptable, scalable solutions for sustainable urban development.

Subject Index

A

Academic Databases 93
Accessibility Compliance 93
Agrobacterium tumefaciens 43
Aquaponics 215
Asymptomatic 171

B

Banking Regulations 185
Banking System 34
Basel III 185
Biodegradable 82
Biometrics 74
Blackened 114
Brittle Charred Document 114

C

Capital Adequacy Ratios 185
Childhood Devclopment 7
Civic Engagement 192
Cloud-Integrated WOBAN 158
Cloudlet Placement 158
CMOS 67
Cognitive Engagement 7
Consumer Awareness 82
Consumer Behaviour 82
Cultivating Crops 215
Cyberattacks 22
Cybersecurity 149

D

Data Breaches 149
Data Governance 49
Decipherment 114
Degraded Prints 131
Democratic Involvement 192
Dietary Habits 1
Digital Circuits 67
Digital Literacy 7
Digital Personal Data 49
Protection Act 2023
Digital Repositories 93

E

Echo State Network 141
Eco-Friendly Packaging 82
Ecosystem 22
Eggs 180
Emotional Development 7
Employee Retention 206
End-to-End Delay 102
Environmental Stewardship 49
Environmental Sustainability 123
Epidermis 131
Equilibrium Points 171
e-Resources 93
Ethical Data Management 49

F

Financial Channels 34
Flexion Creases 74
Fluid Flow 16
Fluorescence Microscopy 43
Forensic Investigation 74
Friction Factor 16
Fungus 43

G

Gene 43
Gestation 74
Global Legislative Trends 149
Green Residential Project 123

H

Heat Transfer 16
Helicoverpa Armigera 180
High Density Integration 67
Hydroponics 215

I

Illiteracy 34
Intellectual Property 149
Interstitial Cells 67
Interventions 171

J

Jitter 102
Job Autonomy 206

K

K-Means Clustering 158

L

Larvae 180
Leadership Behaviours 206
Legal Frameworks 149
Life Insurance 34
Lifestyle 1
Lifetime 59
Low Carbon Emission 123

M

Malware Memory 141
Microbial Communities 164

N

Nanotechnology 67
Nationalization 34
Network Reliability 59
Non-Conventional Energy 16
Nutrients 164
Nutritional Status 1

O

Obesity 1
Online Catalogs 93
Optical Network Units 158
Organic Compounds 164

P

Pathogenesis 43
Perpetual Network 59
Persistent Pattern 74
Pod Initiation 180
Political Efficacy 192
Political Interest 192
Pollutants 164
Poroscopy 131
Preservation 114
Presymptomatic 171
Productivity 22, 206

Q

Qualnet 102

R

Recommended Dietary Allowances 1
Reproducibility 131
Reproduction Number 171
Resilient Digital Economy 49
Risk Management 185

S

Sensor Devices 22
Sensor Networks 59
Smart Device 141
Social-Emotional Learning 7
Solar Harvesting 59
Stabilization 114
Static Analysis 141
Suspicious Script Codes 141
Sustainable City 123
Sustainable Construction 123
Sustainable Consumption 82
Symbiotic Relationship 164

T

Technological Innovation 185
Thermo-hydraulic Performance 16
Throughput 102
Traffic Congestion 102

U

Unsupervised Learning Model 22
Urban Spaces 215

V

VANET 102
Vegetative Phase 180
Vertical Farming 215
Visualization 131
Voter Turnout 192

W

Wireless Access Network 158
Workplace Stress 206

Author Index

B

Babu K., Ananda 123, 164
Bairagi, Ashutosh 49, 149
Beragi, Ayushi 74
Bhatt, Uma Rathore 158

C

Chandak, Sumit 16
Chauhan, Krati Singh 114
Chaurasia, Sunil 16

D

Dhar, Upinder 7
Dubey, Manisha 1

G

Gupta, Namit 67
Guruprasad, K.N. 43

H

Holkar, Amit 59

J

Jain, Anshul 123
Jain, Preet 67
Jain, Swapnil 59
Javalage, Samadhan P. 180
Jhawar, Sakshi 192
Jhawar, Shaily 185
Jigyasu, Dubey 22

K

Kotame, Bhagyashri B. 22
Kumari, Akanchha 131

M

Mane, Suhas 215
Mishra, Swati Dubey 74

N

Naidu, Aditi 82
Neekey, Muskan 149

P

Panday, Vijayant 164
Prakash, Anand 171

R

Rajavat, Anand 102, 141
Rathi, Ekta 7
Rathore, Vikas 185
Rawat, Romil 141
Rohatgi, Richa 114, 131

S

Sadawana, Riya 82
Saxena, Dipali 1
Sharma, Aditi 34
Sharma, Niharika 43
Sharma, Richa 215
Shinde, Yuvraj A. 180
Singh, Rani 102
Solanki, Pragati Tomar 34
Sukhija, Dimple 206
Sukhija, Palak 206

T

Tiwari, Ashish 93
Tiwari, Pankaja 93

U

Umdekar, Shilpa 171
Upadhyaya, Varsha 192

V

Vaishnav, Poorva 49
Verma, Mausmi 158

Author Index